STUDIES IN HISTORY, ECONOMICS AND
PUBLIC LAW

Edited by the
FACULTY OF POLITICAL SCIENCE
OF COLUMBIA UNIVERSITY

Number 348

*THE SUEZ CANAL*
Its History and Diplomatic Importance

BY

CHARLES W. HALLBERG

# THE SUEZ CANAL

## Its History and Diplomatic Importance

BY

### CHARLES W. HALLBERG

## OCTAGON BOOKS

A DIVISION OF FARRAR, STRAUS AND GIROUX

New York    1978

Copyright, 1931 by Columbia University Press

*Reprinted 1974*
*by special arrangement with Columbia University Press*

*Second Octagon printing 1978*

OCTAGON BOOKS
A DIVISION OF FARRAR, STRAUS & GIROUX, INC.
19 Union Square West
New York, N.Y. 10003

Library of Congress Cataloging in Publication Data

Hallberg, Charles William, 1899-
   The Suez Canal, its history and diplomatic importance.

   Reprint of the ed. published by Columbia University Press, New York, which was issued as no. 348 of Studies in history, economics and public law.

   Originally presented as the author's thesis, Columbia University.

   Bibliography: p.
   1. Suez Canal.   2. Egypt—Foreign relations.   3. Egypt—History—British occupation, 1882-1936.   I. Title.   II. Series: Columbia studies in the social sciences, no. 348.
TC791.H3   1974                    386'.43'09                    73-20042
ISBN 0-374-93381-2

Manufactured by Braun-Brumfield, Inc.
Ann Arbor, Michigan
Printed in the United States of America

To

# GEORGES EDGAR BONNET

IN HONOR AND APPRECIATION

# PREFACE

FROM the earliest times the highways of communication between Europe and Asia have been of the greatest importance. To a considerable degree they have influenced the course of history. They have occasioned bitter rivalries and long wars, have brought power and wealth to some nations and decadence and ruin to others.

The construction of the Suez Canal was a great landmark in the history of communications. By connecting the Mediterranean with the Red Sea, it cut off half the distance by water from Europe to the East. It brought back to the Mediterranean the traffic in oriental commodities which, ever since the epochal voyage of Vasco da Gama late in the fifteenth century, had followed the long route around the Cape of Good Hope. The revival of the Suez highway was a question of profound interest in France for several centuries and in the reign of Louis XIV was one of the principles of French diplomacy. In the eighteenth century Austria began to see its possibilities for her commerce but England was too firmly attached to the Cape route to desire any change. Napoleon's expedition of 1798 directed England's attention to Egypt and to the advantages of a shorter route to her Indian empire. When the question of a ship canal in Egypt came into prominence late in the administration of Mehemet Ali, Lord Palmerston denounced it in the strongest terms as a menace to the integrity of the Ottoman Empire. England's opposition was the most serious obstacle confronting the efforts of Ferdinand de Lesseps. For twelve years he struggled against it until she reluctantly accepted the canal as inevitable. But it was no sooner

7

opened to navigation than its importance to England became apparent. Three of every four vessels passing through the canal flew the British flag, and as it was the shortest route to India it naturally evoked a desire in England to participate in its management. In 1875 Disraeli purchased nearly half of the shares from the spendthrift Khedive, Ismail, thereby converting the canal from Franco-Egyptian to Franco-British ownership. When the nationalist movement under Arabi Pasha occurred a few years later, England showed how highly she prized the safety of the new highway. The installation of her troops in Egypt brought the canal completely under her military control, and to maintain that control has been ever since one of the cardinal principles of her foreign policy.

The purpose of this study is not only to present an historical survey of the Suez route from ancient times to the present but also to show its importance as a factor in European diplomacy. An attempt is also made to set forth the financial and commercial development of the canal, its strategic importance and the attempts to give it a secure juridical status. The author makes no pretense of giving anything but a general account of the ancient canals, for he realizes that the ancient period could be handled adequately only by an expert in archeology and Egyptology. Admirable work has been done on the period to about 1840 by J. C. T. Roux and his son, Francois Charles-Roux, upon whose scholarly volumes much reliance has been placed in the preparation of parts of the earlier chapters of this book. The wider range, however, of documents available to the present author has thrown new light on many aspects of the subject and particularly upon the negotiations since 1840.

A considerable amount of the material for this study was obtained in the Archives des Affaires Étrangères in Paris, the Public Record Office in London, and the Haus, Hof and

Staatsarchiv in Vienna. Many of the unpublished documents are presented for the first time. Most of the published material was secured at the New York Public Library, the Columbia University and Yale University libraries, the British Museum, the Bibliothèque Nationale, the British Library of Information in New York, and especially at the Suez Canal Library in Paris. The author gratefully acknowledges the kindness of the librarians and owes a special debt of gratitude to M. Georges Edgar Bonnet, Director of the Suez Canal Company, for his courtesy in placing at his service the facilities of the Company's library and for the interest he has shown in this work; and to Dr. Anton Bundsmann, Governor of the Austrian Tirol, for his assistance at the Haus, Hof und Staatsarchiv in Vienna. He also acknowledges his special indebtedness to Professor Charles Downer Hazen who has read the entire manuscript and offered many suggestions; and to Professors W. L. Westermann and C. C. Hyde for their careful examination of chapters I and XVII respectively. Finally, the author expresses his deep indebtedness and gratitude to Professor Parker T. Moon for his numerous suggestions, unfailing kindness, consideration and encouragement in the course of the preparation of this book.

# TABLE OF CONTENTS

## CHAPTER V

### Mehemet Ali, The Eastern Question and the Revival of English Interest

## CHAPTER VI

### The Saint-Simonian " Mission "

## CHAPTER VII

### Metternich Makes An Offer

## CHAPTER VIII

### Technical Studies: The Société d'Études

## CHAPTER XII

### France Intervenes

## CHAPTER XIII

### ENGLAND RELUCTANTLY AGREES

## CHAPTER XIV

### DIFFICULTIES

## CHAPTER XV

### DISRAELI'S MASTER STROKE—PURCHASE OF THE KHEDIVE'S SHARE'S

## CHAPTER XVI

### PROTECTION OF THE CANAL—ENGLAND OCCUPIES EGYPT

## CHAPTER XVII

### "Neutralization"

## APPENDICES

### A.

### B.

### C.

### D.

### E.

## ABBREVIATIONS

The following abbreviations are used in footnotes for the citation of archives:

Corr. Cons.—" Correspondance Consulaire ", unpublished documents in Archives Affaires Étrangères, Paris.

Égypte. — Unpublished documents filed under title " Égypte: Dépêches Politiques", in Archives Affaires Étrangères, Paris.

Turquie. — Unpublished documents filed under title " Correspondance Politique Turquie", in Archives Affaires Étrangères, Paris.

H H S A.— Unpublished documents in Haus, Hof und Staatsarchiv, Vienna.

22

# CHAPTER I

## An Ancient Highway

EGYPT owes much of her greatness, and conversely much of her misfortune, to her geographical position. Touching two seas, the Mediterranean to the north and the Red Sea to the southeast, and connected with the Arabian peninsula by the Isthmus of Suez, she has been since the early times a meeting place for merchants and traders from far and near, a link binding three continents, Europe, Asia and Africa. A location so strategic for trade made it inevitable that Egypt should become one of the world's highways, the Gate to the East. In the middle ages one of the three great trade routes to India, the southern, passed through Egypt on the way to the Red Sea, and the city of Alexandria on the Mediterranean was one of the largest commercial centers of the world. This unique position in eastern trade was changed with the discovery of the Cape route late in the fifteenth century, Levantine traffic was diverted from the old medieval channels and much of this commerce shifted from the Mediterranean to the Atlantic. Almost four hundred years passed before Egypt regained her commercial importance. The opening of the Suez Canal in 1869 brought back the eastern traffic and was the first step in the revival of the medieval highways. Today the Suez Canal is the principal gateway to the East. It is, moreover, the "spinal cord" of the British Empire, the link connecting India, Australia, New Zealand, Hongkong and the British settlements on the east coast of Africa with the mother country.

By virtue of its exceptional location between the Nile, the

Mediterranean and the Red Sea, the Isthmus of Suez has occupied a conspicuous place in the commercial history of ancient and modern times.   It is through this region that the present Suez Canal passes, and it was across this land that the ancient Egyptians carried on a part of their commerce with neighboring countries.   North and west of the Isthmus is Lake Manzala, a shallow basin separated from the Mediterranean by a narrow stretch of marshy land.   Only a few miles to the south is Lake Balla, cut off from Lake Manzala by a spur of the plateau of El Ferdan which in ancient times was known as the " Road of Horus ", employed by caravans entering Egypt from Syria.   The plateau of El Ferdan or El Guisr separates Lake Balla from Lake Timsah, while the latter is detached from the Great Bitter Lake by the plateau of Tussum.   Between the Red Sea and the Small Bitter Lake is the plateau of Chaluf.   The topography of the Isthmus has changed somewhat since ancient times.   For one thing, the Red Sea extended much farther to the north than it does today.[1]   In ancient times the Nile had seven branches, possibly eight, but today it has only two, the Damietta, and the Rosetta.   Such changes have influenced the history of communications through the Isthmus.

In addition to land routes which traversed the Isthmus in ancient times, the Egyptians constructed canals in order to

According to Edouard Naville, *The Store-City of Pithom and the Route of the Exodus* (London, 1888), p. 10, the Red Sea as late as the XIX Dynasty probably covered the region of the Bitter Lakes if not that of Lake Timsah; the retreat of the sea left salt marshes which became the Bitter Lakes.  On the other hand, Jean Clédat, *Bulletin de l'Institut français d'archéologie orientale*, " Notes sur l'Isthme de Suez (Cairo, 1920), vol. xxi, p. 84, states that in a remote period there was a branch of the Nile passing through the Wadi Tumilât to Lake Timsah, west of the modern town of Ismailia, which inclined southward and ended in the Red Sea.  He mentions alluvial deposits of the neolithic period between the Small Bitter Lake and the Gulf of Suez which prove the existence of such a branch.

facilitate communications between the Nile and the Red Sea or the Nile and the eastern Mediterranean. The origin of these early canals has been the subject of considerable discussion among writers both ancient and modern, and their conflicting views as well as (in many cases) their inaccurate deductions, have given rise to much confusion. It is necessary to distinguish at least three canals in the ancient period.[1]

The most famous is the Canal of the Pharaohs. Concerning its origin, the course which it followed, the extent to which it was employed and how long it remained navigable, various opinions have been given. Recent studies, notably by Clédat, Bourdon and Blanchère,[2] have done much to clear up the confusing accounts in Herodotus, Aristotle, Diodorus, Strabo and Pliny.

Arabian tradition ascribes the origin of this canal to the Pharaoh Tarsis-ben Malia.[3] The name Tarsis seems to be a corruption for Sesostris, the Greek for Senusret, a king of the XII dynasty.[4] Clédat affirms that it is highly probable that the canal was started during the XII dynasty.[5]

The accounts given by the classic writers upon this point are quite contradictory. According to Herodotus the first canal was commenced by Necho (c. 609-593 B. C.), a king of the XXVI dynasty and the son of Psammitichus (663-

---

[1] Clédat, *Bulletin de l'Institut français d'archéologie orientale*, vol. xxiii, p. 54 *et seq.*

[2] Clédat, cited above; C. Bourdon, *Anciens canaux, anciens sites et ports de Suez* (Cairo, 1925); article "fossa" by de la Blanchère, *Daremberg-Saglio, Dict. des ant.*, p. 1331 *et seq.*

[3] Bourdon, *op. cit.*, p. 7; Clédat, *Bulletin de l'Institut français d'archéologie orientale, loc. cit.*, p. 63.

[4] Clédat, *loc. cit.*, p. 63. Senusret is a name given to three kings of the XII dynasty. Their dates according to J. H. Breasted, *A History of Egypt* (N. Y., 1916), are: Senusret I (1980-1935 B. C.); Senusret II (1906-1887 B. C.); Senusret III (c 1887-1849 B. C.).

[5] Clédat, *loc. cit.*, vol. xxiii, p. 63.

609 B. C.).[1]    This is also the version of Diodorus of Sicily, while Strabo relates that according to certain authors the canal was begun by Psammitichus.[2]    However, Strabo as well as Pliny and Aristotle trace it back to Sesostris and the Arabian tradition is in agreement with them.[3]    The classic writers do not say that the canal was completed by any of these rulers.    Herodotus tells us that Necho attempted to connect the Red Sea and the Bitter Lakes but desisted after 120,000 Egyptians had perished in the undertaking and after the king had been warned " that he was laboring for the barbarian." [4]    According to his version, the canal was completed by Darius Hystapsis (521-486 B. C.), the Persian king.    Strabo and Diodorus, on the other hand, maintain that Darius discontinued the work when it was nearly completed, being influenced by the opinion that the level of the Red Sea was higher than Egypt and that as a consequence the cutting of the canal would flood the country.[5]

In spite of this conflicting testimony, it is certain that the connection between the Nile and the Red Sea had been established long before the Persian conquest.[6]    However, epigraphic evidence shows that Darius reexcavated the canal.

[1] C. Hude (editor), *History of Herodotus* (2nd ed., Oxford, 1913-1914), bk. ii, ch. 158.

[2] Diodorus Siculus, i, 33; *Strabo's Geography*, trans. by H. C. Hamilton and W. Falconer (London, 1854-1857), bk. xvii, ch. 2.

[3] *Strabo's Geography, op. cit.*, bk. i, ch. 2; *The Natural History of Pliny*, trans. by J. Bostock and H. T. Riley (London, 1855), vol. ii, bk. vi, ch. 3; Aristotle, *Meteorologica*, Eng. trans. by E. W. Webster (Oxford, 1925), bk. i, ch. 14.

[4] *History of Herodotus, op. cit.*, bk. ii, ch. 159.

[5] *Strabo's Geography, op. cit.*, bk. xvii, ch. i; Diodorus, bk. i, ch. 1.

[6] Clédat believes that the canal was navigable as far as the Red Sea in the reign of Necho (*Bulletin de l'Institut français d'archéologie orientale*, vol. xvi, p. 225). J. H. Breasted in *The Cambridge Ancient History*, vol. ii, p. 62, mentions the canal in the reign of Queen Hatshepsut (1501-1479 B. C.) as connecting with the Red Sea.

Fragments of a monument of that ruler bearing cuneiform and hieroglyphic inscriptions have been found in the vicinity of Kabret to the north of Suez.[1] On one of these fragments the texts are in three languages: Persian, Medo-Scythian and Assyrian. Only the Persian is sufficiently preserved and it consists of twelve lines. Darius is represented as saying: " I am a Persian: with [the power of] Persia I conquered Egypt [Mudrâya]. I ordered this canal to be dug from the river called Pîrava [the Nile] which flows in Egypt, to the sea which comes out of Persia [Erythraean or Red Sea]. This canal was afterwards dug as I had commanded. . . ."[2] It would appear from these lines that Darius reestablished the communication as far as the Red Sea. But as Bourdon points out, the text adds: "Then I said: go from Bira to the littoral and destroy this half of the canal as it is my wish."[3] Xerxes, reexcavated the part which had been destroyed and conducted the canal to the Red Sea.[4]

As finally completed, the Canal of the Pharaohs connected the Nile with the Red Sea and may have been chiefly intended to facilitate the transport of supplies from Punt to Egypt.[5] Commencing, so Clédat holds, at the Pelusiac branch of the Nile a little above the ancient city of Bubastis, the canal went

---

[1] For an account of these tablets see Bourdon, *op. cit.*, pp. 11-13.

[2] Quoted in Heinrich Brugsch-Bey, *Egypt under the Pharaohs* (new ed., London, 1891), p. 433. *Cf.* Bourdon, *op. cit.*, p. 54.

[3] Bourdon, *op. cit.*, p. 56. The part destroyed is thought to have been from Kabret to the Red Sea.

[4] A tablet found at Kabri only six kilometers north of Suez bears out this fact. See Bourdon, *op. cit.*, p. 57. *Cf.* Clédat, *Bulletin de l'Institut français d'archéologie orientale*, vol. xvi, p. 224.

[5] Punt [Puenet], was probably modern Somaliland. (*The Cambridge Ancient History*, i, p. 289). On the early trade relations of Egypt see August Köster, *Schiffahrt und Handelsverkehr des alten Orient* (Leipzig, 1924), and his *Das antike Seewesen* (Berlin, 1923).

in a general west-east direction into the Wadi Tumilāt, a long
narrow valley extending from east of the Nile to Lake Timsah.  Here nature assisted the builders, for at one time a
branch of the Nile had passed through this valley to the west
of Ismailia, and turning southward crossed the Bitter Lakes
into the Red Sea.[1]  The canal utilized this ancient bed of the
river, traversed the Bitter Lakes and entered the Red Sea at
Clysma north of modern Suez.

To what extent this canal was used for navigation is not
known though commercial relations with the Punt had been
established very early.  As far back as the II dynasty the
Egyptians constructed great ships for the Nile and in the
V dynasty we hear of a naval expedition on the Red Sea.[2]
A text of the XI dynasty mentions an Egyptian port on the
Red Sea called Taoou, probably situated in a direct line
from Coptos on the Nile.[3]  Egyptian vessels navigated the
Red Sea and frequented ports of southern Arabia and
Ethiopia, receiving ivory, spices, aromatics, precious woods,
wild beasts and even dwarfs who were employed for certain
dances in the temples.[4]  " The popular idea of the Egyptians
as no sailors and as afraid of the Red Sea is entirely erroneous. . . . Egyptian trading and revictualling settlements
existed all along the Red Sea coast and ships were always
coasting from one to the other on the way to or from
Puenet [Punt]." [5]  Such expeditions were difficult and required much preparation.  The rocky coasts, the innumer-
able coral reefs and the presence of pirates exposed the
Egyptian mariners to constant danger.

[1] Clédat, *Bulletin de l'Institut français d'archéologie orientale*, vol.
xxi, p. 84.

[2] *The Cambridge Ancient History*, vol. i, p. 289.

[3] Clédat, *Bulletin de l'Institut français d'archéologie orientale*, vol.
xxi, p. 169.

[4] *Ibid.*, p. 171.  *Cf. The Cambridge Ancient History*, vol. i, p. 289.

[5] *The Cambridge Ancient History*, vol. i, p. 320.

A second canal, the Canal of Djifar or Zarou [Tharu], began at the Nile and proceeded in a northward direction to Lake Balla.[1] Its construction may go back to the XI or XII dynasty. It is said to have been navigable as far as the town of Zarou and was used by the kings in sending expeditions to Sinai and Syria.[2] A bas-relief on one of the walls of the great temple at Karnak, from the time of Seti I (XIX dynasty), shows the triumphant entry of this ruler into Zarou after his first campaign in Syria and the canal is represented as passing through the town.[3] In the Roman period the channel was extended as far as Ostracine, a port on the Mediterranean.

A third canal cut by Ptolemy II, Philadelphus (285-246 B. C.) began at the Pelusiac branch of the Nile near the town of Daphnae, crossed the plateau of El Ferdan and Lake Timsah and joined the Canal of the Pharaohs near Bir Abou-Balla or Sabah-Abiar.[4] From this point the old canal was reexcavated and Strabo tells us that Ptolemy constructed a lock with a double gate at its entrance in order to prevent the water of the sea from contaminating the fresh water of the Nile.[5] At the point where the canal entered the sea the king built the port of Arsinoë.[6] According to Diod-

[1] Lake of Zarou in ancient times.

[2] Clédat, *Bulletin de l'Institut français d'archéologie orientale, loc. cit.*, vol. xxiii, p. 55.

[3] *Ibid.*, p. 54.

[4] *Ibid.*, vol. xxi, p. 95; vol. xxii, p. 54.

[5] *Strabo's Geography, op. cit.*, bk. xvii, 12. The opinion of Clédat is that Ptolemy constructed the lock not at the entrance to the canal but at the point where it joined the Canal of the Pharaohs. (*Bulletin de l'Institut français d'archéologie orientale*, vol. xxiii, p. 79). *Cf.* de la Blanchère, article " fossa ", *Daremberg-Saglio, Dict. des ant.*, p. 1331.

[6] According to Clédat the site of Arsinoë has not yet been determined but he thinks it was near Suez, probably to the left of the Gulf, with Clysma on the right (*op. cit.*, vol. xxiii, p. 71). Naville places Clysma or Clisma at a distance nine miles south of Pithom, called by the Greeks

orus, Ptolemy II also contemplated the construction of a direct canal across the Isthmus but abandoned the project because the level of the Red Sea was supposed to be higher than the Delta.[1]   Clédat agrees that the idea of a direct canal came from the Greeks, who were very active in Egypt and who clearly recognized the commercial importance of the Isthmus.[2]   The Canal of Ptolemy was a most important undertaking from the commercial viewpoint, for it greatly facilitated the transportation of merchandise and the traffic in the Red Sea became very extensive.   It avoided the difficulties of the land route, the dangers from wild nomads and the tedious delays.

How long the canal remained navigable is not known, though some writers believe it was neglected under the later Ptolemies.   The Emperor Trajan in 98 A. D. cleaned out the Canal of the Pharaohs but instead of having it leave the Pelusiac branch of the Nile, he carried its source to the main stream at Babylon near modern Cairo.[3]   From this time until about a century after the Arab contest the new channel was called the " River of Trajan."   Starting from Babylon, it proceeded in a westward direction until it joined the an-

Heroopolis and by the Romans, Ero (the Patumos of Herodotus), which was located near the Bitter Lakes (Naville, *op. cit.*, p. 24).  He adds that Clysma "is a common name which means a place beaten by the waves or the surf, the shore, the edge of the wave, or the tide."

[1] Clédat, *Bulletin de l'Institut français d'archéologie orientale*, vol. xxi, p. 95.

[2] *Ibid.*, p. 75.   See on the Greek period the article by W. L. Westermann, "The Greek exploitation of Egypt," *Pol. Science Quarterly*, vol. xl, no. 4, pp. 517-539, Dec. 1925.

[3] The change in course was probably due to the gradual silting up of the Pelusiac branch (J. W. Grover, "Suez Canals from the most ancient times to the present," *Journal Brit. Archeol. Assoc.*, vol. xxxiii, p. 451). Clédat, however, states that the Pelusiac branch of the Nile was the most important during the Roman period (*Bull. de l'Institut français d'archéologie orientale*, vol. xvii, p. 106).

cient canal near Belbeis. Clédat believes that it remained navigable for about a century but was altogether abandoned in the reign of Constantine.[1]

Meanwhile trade between Egypt and the East had developed rapidly.[2] Merchandise was brought to one of the ports on the Red Sea and transported overland or by canal to the Nile and then up to Alexandria where it was reshipped to European markets. Under the Romans, the port of Pelusium on the Mediterranean (near modern Port Said) was, next to Alexandria, the greatest emporium of Egypt.[3] Before the first century the trade between Egypt and India was carried on by Arab merchants and it was not until the discovery of the monsoons by Hippalos about 100 B. C. that direct trade took place.[4] By the time of Domitian (81-96 A. D.) this direct trade was fully established and in the following century had reached all the way to China.[5]

[1] Clédat, loc. cit., vol. xxiii, p. 66.

[2] See M. P. Charlesworth, Trade-Routes and Commerce of the Roman Empire (Cambridge, 1924). Cf. E. H. Warmington, Commerce between the Roman Empire and India (Cambridge, 1928).

[3] Clédat, Bulletin de l'Institut français d'archéologie orientale, vol. xxiii, p. 58.

[4] See Walter Otto Pauly-Wissowa, Realenzyklopdie, viii, p. 1660. The date of Hippalos is given as 47 A. D. by Jean Raimondi, Le désert oriental Egyptien—Du Nil à la Mer Rouge (mémoires de la société royale de géographie d'Égypte, tome iv, Cairo, 1923), p. 23; and as 40-70 A. D. by M. P. Charlesworth in Class. Quarterly, vol. xxii (1928), p. 93. However, this evidence is purely negative and about 100 B. C. seems to be nearer to the truth.

[5] M. Rostovtzeff, The Social and Economic History of the Roman Empire (Oxford, 1926), pp. 91, 146. It is probable that direct trade between Egypt and India began before the first century, as early as the visit of Strabo to Egypt (26 B.C.), for the latter mentions that 120 vessels were sailing to India that season from the port of Myos Hormos on the Red Sea (Strabo's Geograhy, op. cit., bk. ii, ch. 118). Cf. The Cambridge History of India (6 vols., Cambridge, 1922), vol. i: Ancient India, p. 425.

Rome maintained command of the Mediterranean and the route through Egypt until the fifth century, when the western part of the Empire fell before the barbarians. The East, more favorably located, was able to defend itself for another two hundred years, until the Arabs sweeping westward in their might between 620 and 690 took Syria, Mesopotamia, Egypt and the whole of north Africa. Commerce with the East then became a Mohammedan monopoly.

The new rulers restored prosperity and order to Egypt and reopened the Canal of the Pharaohs. This work was undertaken by Amr, the governor of Egypt, who received permission from the Caliph Omar.[1] It was ready for navigation in the winter of 641-642 and was named the Canal of the Prince of the Faithful.[2] Amr is also said to have contemplated the construction of a branch canal from Lake Timsah north to join the Mediterranean but was forbidden by the Caliph Omar, who thought it would open the country to Christian vessels.[3] The Canal of the Prince of the Faithful remained navigable until 776, when it was closed by order of the second Abbasid Caliph, Aben-Jafar-Al Mansour, who wished to prevent supplies from reaching the rebellious cities of Mecca and Medina.

The closing of the canal did not put an end to the traffic with India through Egypt. The Venetians and Genoese employed the southern route extensively in the later middle ages. It was only after the establishment of the Cape route at the beginning of the modern era that the Italians and Arabs lost their supremacy. The Cape route, though longer, offered better facilities. Merchandise was loaded and unloaded only once and there were no customs duties or land transportation charges to pay.

[1] Bourdon, *op. cit.*, p. 7.

[2] A. J. Butler, *The Arab Conquest of Egypt and the Last Thirty Years of the Roman Dominion* (Oxford, 1902), footnote, p. 345.

[3] *Ibid.*, p. 346.

Rather than surrender their oriental trade to Portugal, the Venetians thought of cutting a canal across the Isthmus of Suez. In 1504, the Council of Ten while discussing the instructions to be given to the new Ambassador to Cairo, considered the advisability of proposing the scheme to the Egyptian Sultan.[1] But on second consideration the Council concluded that there were too many obstacles in the way. Consequently the project was dropped, and the old trade route *via* the Mediterranean, Egypt and the Red Sea was virtually abandoned.

From the sixteenth century until the third quarter of the nineteenth century, the oriental trade deserted Egypt, and the Suez Canal was but a memory. But during this long period there was, especially in France, a good deal of agitation for the revival of the ancient highway.

[1] F. Charles-Roux, "L'Isthme de Suez et les rivalités Européens au XVI siècle," *Revue de l'histoire des colonies françaises,* 1924, trim. xi, vol. xvii, p. 159. Charles-Roux says that this was "the first manifestation of the idea of opening a maritime communication between the Mediterranean and the Red Sea." As we have seen, however, the idea was entertained by Ptolemy II and perhaps even by Necho.

## CHAPTER II

THE crusades gave a powerful stimulus to eastern trade and were especially important for France. The feudal kingdoms and principalities set up in Palestine were French as were the Latin Emperors at Constantinople, and the French language was extensively used throughout the Levant. Moreover it was the Seventh Crusade which awakened French interest in Egypt and the efforts of St. Louis to conquer the country were never forgotten. After his death in 1270 crusades were no longer fashionable and French interest in the East was temporarily diverted by the Hundred Years' War.

During the reign of Francis I (1515-1547) attention was again directed eastward. Unable to get support from other European Powers against the Emperor Charles V, with whom he was continually quarreling, Francis sought an alliance with the Sultan, Suleiman. A political and commercial treaty was concluded in 1536 by which the Sultan agreed to send a fleet to the western Mediterranean to cooperate with the French in return for a large payment.[1] This alliance, however, was far from popular with the Catholic sentiment of France though the commercial provisions gave her a privileged position in the Levant. Trade was carried only in French vessels until the wily Turk gave similar privileges shortly after to the Venetians, English and Dutch. Of more lasting significance were the concessions which France

[1] Great Britain, Foreign Office, Historical Section, *Peace Handbook*, vol. xi, no. 66, *France and the Levant*, p. 4.

secured by the capitulations of 1536 and which were confirmed many times thereafter.[1]  By these she acquired " a
position of uncontested influence throughout the Turkish
Empire," with the right of appointing her own consuls who
were to judge cases involving her subjects, as well as the
right of free Catholic worship.[2]  For half a century she had
the exclusive enjoyment of these privileges.  Christians of
all nationalities came under her protection, and though this
was not specifically provided for in any treaty, " it came to
be accepted not only in Turkey but by all the Christian
Powers, including the Papacy." [3]

Simultaneously with her waxing influence in the Levant,
France developed an interest in the old route by way of
Egypt and the Red Sea.  Proposals for the revival of this
route began to appear in the last two decades of the sixteenth
century.  In April 1584, a project was presented to Henry
III by Du Plessis-Mornay setting forth " methods of dimin-
ishing Spain." [4]  France at this time was fighting Spain and
Philip II by his naval victory of the Azores, July 26, 1583,
had shattered the hopes which Catherine de Medici and her
son had nourished for the acquisition of the Portuguese
possessions of the East Indies.  The author of the project
proposed the revival of the ancient route as a means of dis-
puting Spanish control of the oriental trade.  But his plan
was " too grandiose " for such a weak king as Henry III
and it was not considered.[5]  Two years later (July 25, 1586)

---

[1] Text given in Baron I. de Testa, *Recueil des Traités de la Porte
Ottomane avec les Puissances étrangères depuis le premier traité conclu
en 1536* (6 vols., Paris, 1864), vol. i.

[2] *France and the Levant*, p. 6.

[3] *Ibid.*, p. 7.

[4] F. Charles-Roux, " L'Isthme de Suez et les rivalités européennes au
XVIe siècle," *Revue de l'histoire des colonies françaises*, 1924, trim. xi,
vol. xvii, p. 170.

[5] *Ibid.*

the French Ambassador at Constantinople, Savary de Lancosne, informed Henry III that the Pasha, El-Eudj-Ali, had proposed to the Turkish Sultan the construction of a canal from the Nile to the Red Sea.[1] The new waterway would enable warships to sail from the Mediterranean to the Red Sea, where a Turkish fleet had for some time been stationed in order to suppress revolts in Arabia and Persia and to oppose the Spanish and Portuguese. The Pasha called attention to the difficulties of transporting materials from the Nile to Suez and asserted that a canal would result in a great economy of time and money. " This wonderful scheme," wrote de Lancosne, "has so greatly inflated their [the Turks] usual vanity and has so stirred their ambition and avarice that they already believe they have the treasures and gems of India, and that they have ensnared the Persian, but they have not reckoned with Spain. . . ." Some weeks later the Ambassador reported that the project would not be executed because the Sultan recoiled before the great expense it would involve.[2]

In the next century the question of reviving the old route became one of the principal objects of French diplomacy. The development of industry and trade under Henry IV and Sully, under Louis XIII and Richelieu, awakened a desire to share in the great traffic with the Orient which was bringing untold wealth to Holland and England. As these countries were struggling for the control of the Cape route, France turned her attention to the Suez route as the one which would give her the best chance of competing with her rivals.

During the administration of Richelieu, an anonymous writer proposed the colonization of India and Australia and

---

[1] E. Charrière, *Négociations de la France dans le Levant* (4 vols., Paris, 1860), vol. iv, pp. 527-539.

[2] *Ibid.*, pp. 540-542. Date of letters : Aug. 6 and 20, 1586.

the opening of a canal connecting the Mediterranean with the Red Sea. " A canal could be cut from Suez to Cairo," said this writer, " as was done under the ancient kings of Egypt and perhaps under Solomon. The Turk will hope to enrich his country; Venice will recover; the ancient commerce with Abyssinia will pick up again. By this junction of the seas, the Spaniards shall be weakened in the Mediterranean and all other princes strengthened." [1]

Numerous projects advocating the Suez route for French trade appeared in the reigns of Louis XIV and his successors. They were the work of ministers, economists and merchants. Some advocated a land route across the Isthmus, others the construction of a canal; some believed that France should take possession of Egypt, while others merely advised the conclusion of a treaty. But " underneath all these various propositions, the primary object remains the same, namely, the opening of a shorter route to India. The question of the passage by the Isthmus of Suez and the Red Sea is not considered as an Egyptian question: the invariable object of those who studied it is India, the Far East." [2]

In the reign of Louis XIV attempts were made to secure the shorter route to India by negotiating with the Porte in order to permit French vessels to frequent Suez and the Red Sea. To Colbert the trade with India represented the commerce *par excellence,* " the great commerce." [3] He attached much importance to the privilege of trading in the Rea Sea, which, because of its proximity to the holy cities, was pro-

---

[1] Quoted in Le Vicomte G. d'Avenel, *Richelieu et la monarchie absolue* (2nd ed., 4 vols., Paris, 1895), vol. iii, pp. 218-219.

[2] J. C. T. Roux, *L'Isthme et le Canal de Suez: Historique—état actuel* (2 vols., Paris, 1901), vol. i, p. 56.

[3] F. Charles-Roux, " Le projet français de commerce avec l'Inde par Suez sous le règne de Louis XVI," *Revue de l'histoire des colonies françaises,* t. xvii, trim. iii, p. xiv of introduction.

hibited to Christian vessels. Egypt was given an important place in his program for reviving French commerce. In 1664 he presented a memoir to the Council of Trade in which he urged the reopening of the route across Egypt as the one most advantageous for French commerce.[1] His policy concerning Egypt was twofold: first to secure a privileged position for French nationals along the Nile; second, to establish a system of rapid communication between the Indian Ocean and the Mediterranean by the Red Sea, Suez and Alexandria.

The memoir impressed Louis and in the same year he organized the *Compagnie des Indes,* giving it the exclusive monopoly of commerce with the East Indies, the Ile de France and Madagascar. It was stipulated, however, that the return to France must be to the port of Lorient. As this was an Atlantic port on the west coast of France, it was better situated for the eastern trade by way of the Cape than by the Mediterranean and the Red Sea. Hence, the Company opposed every attempt to reopen the Suez route. To solve this difficulty, Colbert organized the Company of the Levant and opened negotiations with the Sultan to give French merchants protection and a monopoly of transport as well as the right to navigate the Red Sea. Having obtained these concessions, Colbert authorized the new Company to transport merchandise from Alexandria to Marseilles and other ports.[2] However, the Company of the Indies was to serve as intermediary from India to Suez.

For a time French merchants profited by this activity on the part of their government. Their ships were allowed in

---

[1] *Lettres, introductions et mémoires de Colbert,* publiés d'après les ordres de l'Empereur par Pierre Clément (9 vols. in 7, Paris, 1861-1870), vol. ii (Paris, 1863), annex ii: *mémoire sur le commerce,* Aug. 3, 1864, pp. cclxiii-cclxxii.

[2] J. C. T. Roux, *op. cit.,* p. 60.

the Red Sea subject to a small tax paid to the Sultan, and as they enjoyed a monopoly, other nations were compelled to trade under the French flag.

The revival of French commerce with the East by way of Egypt was cut short, however, when the Sultan renewed the prohibition against Christian vessels in the Red Sea. But Colbert continued his search for a shorter route and in 1665 instructed La Haye Vantalet, the new Ambassador at Constantinople, to demonstrate to the Porte the community of interest which would come to the two countries from the opening of the Suez route, and to emphasize the injury which frequent use of the Cape route had upon both French commerce with India and the treasury of the Sultan.[1] More specifically, La Haye Vantalet was to obtain permission for Frenchmen to establish stations at Suez, and to assure them protection in transporting their merchandise from the Red Sea to the Mediterranean. He failed to win the consent of the Porte to these demands and four years later the Marquis de Nointel was directed to resume negotiations. According to his instructions, he was to obtain authorization to establish communications between the Red Sea and the Mediterranean by way of Suez.[2] But though de Nointel pushed these negotiations actively for a number of years his efforts were unavailing.

Among those who recognized the importance of reviving the ancient route to the East was Leibnitz, the German phil-

---

[1] A. Vandal, "Louis XIV et l'Égypte," *Académie des sciences morales et politiques* (Paris, 1888), vol. 130, p. 674. *Cf.* Arch. Aff. Étr. Const., vol. vii, f. 202, Aug. 22, 1665, Second mémoire du Roy pour servir d'instruction au sieur de la Haye-Vantalet s'en allant à Constantinople, en qualité d'ambassadeur de Sa Majesté vers le Grand Seigneur.

[2] *Ibid.*, vol. 131 (Paris, 1889), pp. 292-294. *Cf.* Archives de la Marine, vol. B. 7, 51, Instruction pour le sieur de Nointel envoyé par le roi en qualité de son ambassadeur vers le Grand Seigneur concernant les affaires du commerce.

osopher. In 1671 he composed a memoir entitled *Fabula Ludovisia* in which he urged the conquest of Egypt.[1] Hoping for an introduction to the French king, Leibnitz sent his memoir to the Elector of Mainz, who forwarded an account of it to Louis XIV.[2] The latter was sufficiently interested to express a desire for further details and in February 1672 Leibnitz set out for the French court, only to arrive as France and England declared war on Holland. From army headquarters, Arnaud de Pomponne, French minister of Foreign Affairs, sent the Elector the discouraging message that holy wars had ceased to be the fashion since St. Louis. In the following June, however, relations between France and Turkey became so strained that war was expected momentarily. Seizing the opportunity, Leibnitz, who had remained in Paris awaiting the king's return, enlarged upon his plan and composed his *Concilium Aegyptiacum*.[3]

In this memoir Leibnitz refers to the expedition to Egypt as the most important France could undertake, for it would assure her military preponderance over all European Powers, supremacy in eastern trade and the position of protector over the Christian Church.[4] Egypt, he said, was the Holland of the East, the great commercial entrepôt of the trade with India.

[1] *Oeuvres de Leibniz publiées pour la première fois d'après les manuscrits originaux . . . avec notes et introduction . . . par* A. Foucher de Careil (Paris, 1864), vol. v: *Projet d'expédition d'Égypte—présenté à Louis XIV*, pp. 268 *et seq.*

[2] The Elector was the friend and patron of Leibnitz, who had won his goodwill through Baron de Boinebourg, Minister of the Elector and pensioner of Louis XIV. The French Minister at Mainz, the Marquis de Feuquières, was favorable to the project of Leibnitz. *Ibid.,* p. xxvi, introduction. Why Leibnitz proposed his plan to Louis XIV is not clear though he may have wished to divert the attention of the French monarch from the Germanies to more distant conquests.

[3] *Ibid.*

[4] *Ibid.,* p. 5.

Who, indeed, can expect to compete by the Cape of Good Hope when everything will arrive cheaper and more rapidly by way of Egypt? Before the discovery of the new world, it was the great route for vessels, it is by this route that Venice, Genoa and . . . the free cities of Germany had acquired their prosperity. The tyranny of the Turks forced the search for other routes . . . If France, whose manufactures are already where they will soon be first of Europe, joins to that monopoly the spices of the Orient, what nation will dispute with her the supremacy in the markets of the world? . . . The conquest of Egypt is easier than the conquest of Holland, that of the entire Orient easier than that of Germany alone.[1]

He asserted that 30,000 men would suffice for the expedition and that there were no real difficulties. Moreover, the possession of Egypt was the only means of dethroning the commerce of Holland. He advised that the expedition be carried out secretly and rapidly. If France did not take advantage of this opportunity to possess Egypt, Holland would get a monopoly of all the trade with the Orient.

The Dutch will possess the wealth of the Orient, the commerce of Egypt, in a word all the advantages that I have promised to the French. They will occupy the East Indies where they will become the sovereigns and eternal possessors to the exclusion of all other peoples.[2]

Not only would the conquest of Egypt threaten Dutch supremacy in eastern trade, but it would inflict a mortal blow upon the Turks and win the applause of all Christendom.

Sovereign of the Mediterranean, France will revive the empire of the East. From Egypt she will extend the limits of her

[1] *Ibid.,* p. 7.
[2] *Ibid.,* p. 216.

power, she will reign supreme in the Red Sea, will possess the neighboring islands of Madagascar . . . she will also have under her control the Ethiopian Sea, the Gulf of Arabia, and the island of Ormuz, which dominates the Persian Gulf.[1]

It belongs to France to become the arbiter of trade with the Levant. Egypt is the center of this trade. Once masters of Egypt, you would obtain more in one year than by all your recent enterprises at Madagascar. France wishes to ruin Holland, but Holland will be conquered in Egypt where she cannot defend herself.

France aspires to be the first of Powers, oh well! she will acquire the title of Queen of the Orient. . . . Not content with being called the eldest daughter of the Church, France wishes still a title which is the appanage of the Emperor. . . . Here is the occasion for acquiring both of these titles and of meriting the applause and approbation of the entire world, in waging a war a hundred times more useful than all other military enterprises in a sacred or profane purpose, a war such as Machiavelli would have approved.[2]

This memoir was never presented to Louis, who was too busy with his continental wars to give much heed to more distant ventures. After the defeat of the Turks by Sobieski, France made another attempt to secure the Suez route for her commerce. In 1685, the Marquis de Seignelay, Secretary of State for Marine and son of Colbert, directed the French Ambassador at Constantinople, M. Girardin, to renew the negotiations relative to the Red Sea.[3] M. Girardin submitted a memoir to the Grand Vizir which pointed out

[1] *Ibid.*, pp. 55-56.

[2] *Ibid.*, p. 253.

[3] A. Vandal, " Louis XIV et l'Égypte," *Académie des sciences morales et politiques* (Paris, 1889), vol. 131, pp. 282-283. *Cf.* Bibliothèque Nationale, *Mémoires manuscrits de l'ambassade de M. Girardin*, fonds français, nos. 7162 et suiv.

the possibility of constructing a canal connecting the two seas and requested a reduction in the tax on merchandise transported from Suez to the Mediterranean.[1]  Though the memoir was approved by the Grand Vizir, nothing came of it since the authority of the Porte in Egypt was at this time overthrown by military chiefs who temporarily secured control of the Red Sea.

Having failed to open a passage to the Red Sea through the Isthmus of Suez, the French Government decided to seek an alternative.  Thus, in 1697, Benoist de Maillet, French agent at Cairo, was instructed to study the possibilities of reaching the Red Sea by way of Abyssinia.[2]  The following year he sent a lengthy report to the French Ambassador at Constantinople concerning this plan.  " But such was . . . the force of tradition supported by evidence . . . that . . . de Maillet himself recalled the attention of his government to the only practical route of placing the Red Sea in communication with the Mediterranean . . . and renewed the project of connecting the two seas by a canal." [3]

This report did not, however, divert the French Government from its search for an alternative and in 1704 Le Noir de Roule was charged with making a survey of the route by way of Abyssinia.  Leaving Cairo in July, he was assassinated the following year and his mission perished with him.[4]  A few years later, Jean Baptiste Fabre was sent to Persia to study the possibility of securing the route through that country for French commerce.  Upon his arrival at Erivan he died, but some time later a treaty was concluded per-

[1] *Ibid., cf.* J. C. T. Roux, *op. cit.*, vol. i, p. 71.

[2] F. Charles-Roux, *Les origines de l'expédition d'Égypte* (2nd ed., Paris, 1910), p. 21.

[3] *Ibid.*

[4] J. C. T. Roux, *op. cit.*, vol. i, p. 86.

mitting French traders to enter Persian territory.[1]  This, however, was nullified shortly afterwards by anarchic conditions in Persia.

The activity displayed by the Government of Louis XIV concerning a shorter route to India was abandoned, temporarily, during the reign of his successor.  Not until the close of the Seven Years' War did the French Government evince any interest in the question, and then its attention was directed not to Egypt and the Red Sea but to Asiatic Turkey and Persia.  In the meantime, writings of private individuals kept alive the interest in the Suez route.  As far back as 1679, in the reign of Louis XIV, there appeared a second edition of Jacques Savary's *Le Parfait Négociant*.[2]  Written from the standpoint of a business man, the book sets forth the advantages of the Suez route for France.  Savary declared that " all that would be necessary to establish this communication of the two seas, was to construct a canal from Suez to Damietta or . . . from the Red Sea to the nearest approach of the Nile." [3]  In 1735 the Abbé Le Mascrier published the notes and memoirs of Benoist de Maillet, French agent at Cairo during the latter part of the seventeenth and beginning of the eighteenth century.[4]  The services rendered by the ancient canals were recalled and an intelligent discussion was given to the possibilities of conducting trade between Europe and India by the Red Sea.

[1] A. Vandal, *Une ambassade française en Orient sous Louis XV*, cited by J. C. T. Roux, *op. cit.*, vol. i, p. 83.

[2] Jacques Savary, *Le parfait négociant* (2nd ed., Paris, 1679).  *Cf.* F. Charles-Roux, *Les origines etc.*, p. 20.

[3] Cited by F. Charles-Roux, *Les origines etc.*, p. 20.

[4] *Déscription de l'Égypte.  Contenant plusieurs rémarques curieuses sur la géographie ancienne et moderne de ce Païs, sur les monumens anciens, sur les moeurs, les coutumes, et la religion des habitans, sur le gouvernement, et le commerce, etc., etc.*  Composé sur les mémoires de M. de Maillet, ancien Consul de France au Caire.  Par M. l'Abbé le Mascrier (Paris, 1735).

In England no attention was paid to this agitation for a shorter route and the Government was seemingly unaware of the French negotiations. There is no mention of them in the correspondence of the English ambassadors.[1] As compared with France, England was slow to interest herself in Egypt. She maintained no regular agent there and was seldom in a position to dispute French commercial supremacy in the Levant. Indeed, for a brief period (1683-1686), the English were compelled to carry on their trade in Egypt under the names of French merchants. Ten years later, however, England began an agitation at Constantinople for the reestablishment of her consulate at Cairo (suppressed 1679) and for a reduction of the customs duties equal to that enjoyed by the French. In 1696 an English Consul was appointed, but for two years the French Ambassador at Constantinople succeeded in persuading the Porte to withhold official recognition.[2] English competition in the Levant during this period was not threatening.

The reentry of her merchants at Cairo, the introduction of her flag in the Red Sea, her entrance into the Arabian ports, are not followed by any attempts on the part of England to establish direct commercial communications between Suez and India, to lead toward Egypt the channel of commerce which had been diverted since the discovery of the Cape route. . . . This is an object which to the end of the seventeenth and during three-quarters of the eighteenth century still seems foreign to the thoughts of the British Government and traders, and which is excluded from their aims. The economic and political activity of the English East India Company, the rapid development of its business, the founding of its principal stations, provoked no interest in England for the Suez route.[3]

[1] F. Charles-Roux, *L'Angleterre, l'Isthme de Suez et l'Égypte au XVIII siècle . . . Autour d'une route* (Paris, 1922), p. 10.

[2] *Ibid.*, p. 3.

[3] *Ibid.*, p. 9.

But while England was not herself interested in the Suez route, she was determined to prevent its use by other Powers. This was seen when Austria attempted to reopen the route. During the middle of the eighteenth century there appeared in Austria three books by the Chevalier Dominique Jauna. In one of these, *État Présent d'Égypte,* he examined the question of trade by the Red Sea and Egypt, recalled the negotiations carried on under Colbert and de Seignelay, and compared the various projects which had been proposed concerning the Suez route.[1] He also advocated a crusade by Christian princes for the conquest of Egypt and Cyprus, and urged his government to revive Colbert's projects for its own advantage. This last suggestion was adopted and the Austrian Government despatched a commissioner, an Englishman by name of Lander, to Egypt. Upon hearing of this, the English Ambassador at Constantinople instructed the Consul at Cairo to spend 600 sequins in order to drive out Lander.[2]

This negative attitude displayed by England with regard to the Suez route is not difficult to understand. France was then a great Mediterranean Power, strongly established in the Levant and in Egypt, and was thus in a position to dispute the control of that route. Moreover, the English East India Company was invested with a monopoly of trade with India by the Cape route and was forbidden to operate in the Mediterranean.

[1] *Ibid.,* p. 13.
[2] *Ibid.,* p. 19.

# CHAPTER III

## Beginnings of European Rivalry in Egypt

Except for the writings of private individuals and the lone attempt of Austria, there was no very great agitation for the Suez route during the first half of the eighteenth century. France was much less active than at the time of Colbert though she was committed to a policy of securing a shorter route for her trade, while England was not interested except to prevent other Powers from getting a foothold in Egypt or on the Red Sea.

In the second half of the century, however, three events occurred which had far-reaching consequences. The first was the abandonment by France in the Treaty of Paris (1763) of her dreams of an Indian Empire. Second, in 1766, one of the Mameluke beys of Egypt, Ali, succeeded in raising himself above the others and revolted against the authority of the Porte. Egypt thus became virtually independent. Finally, there broke out the Russo-Turkish War (1768-1774).

As a result of the first of these events England gained a dominance in India which tended to awaken, on the part of individual Englishmen, a new interest in the Suez route. The second event made Cairo the center of negotiations in the attempts to establish commercial relations between Europe and India across Egypt. French diplomacy under Louis XIV had quite appropriately addressed itself to the Porte. But now that Egypt was practically independent, the

French and English who were interested in the question of
a shorter route, carried on their negotiations at Cairo rather
than Constantinople. The effect of the Russo-Turkish War
was twofold.[1] First, the war seemed to herald the dismemberment of the Ottoman Empire and thus aroused the ambitions of France, Austria and Russia to share in the spoils,
the interest of France being centered on Egypt. Second, it
resulted in a more determined policy on the part of Turkey
to close the Suez route to all European commerce.

European vessels had long appeared at Suez despite the
tradition which closed the Red Sea to Christians because of
the proximity of Mecca and Medina. In 1774 the Sultan
addressed a Firman to the Pasha at Cairo prohibiting all
traffic by Suez route.[2] But the ineffectiveness of Ottoman
authority in Egypt made it virtually impossible to enforce
the injunction and as a consequence many Englishmen were
inspired to send their vessels to Suez. They were encouraged by a treaty which Warren Hastings, Governor of
Bengal, concluded with Mohamed Abou-Dahab, Bey of
Cairo, on March 7, 1775. This provided for the freedom
of navigation and trade for the subjects of the two countries between Egypt and India, and for certain reductions in
the customs duties. It was also stipulated that English merchandise would be transported from Tor or Suez to Cairo
at the risk of the Bey or his successors.[3] Though the Bey
died in the following year, English vessels continued to appear at Suez for some time thereafter.

These violations of the Firman did not escape the notice
of the Porte and in 1776 it made a formal protest to the

---

[1] F. Charles-Roux, *Autour d'une route*, p. 21.

[2] Text is given in George Baldwin, *Political Recollections Relative to
Egypt etc.* (London, 1801), p. 8. For a general discussion of the subject, see F. Charles-Roux, *Autour d'une route,* pp. 42-47.

[3] Provisions of this treaty given in F. Charles-Roux, *op. cit.,* p. 48.

British Chargé d'Affaires at Constantinople.[1] In the follow-ing year Ainslie, the British Ambassador, forwarded to London a categorical statement from the Porte that no Christian vessel had ever been authorized to navigate as far as Suez.[2] To this the British Government replied on July 11, 1777 that positive orders had been given to the East India Directors prohibiting " all Persons in India employed in their Service, or remaining there under Their License, from trading to any Port in the Red Sea but Judda and Mocha. . . ."[3]

The French watched the activities of English traders in Egypt with a good deal of suspicion. The Vice-Consul at Cairo reported that England "aims at a superiority more effective than mercantile superiority by attempting to dis-cover means of possessing herself of a country which, by its location and fertility, will be more advantageous for her than anyone else. She knows how important it will be to possess a country which, making her mistress of the Red Sea, will gave her a monopoly of the commerce with India."[4] Mure, the French Consul-General, also believed that England had designs on Egypt and reported that private Englishmen

[1] State Papers, Turkey, vol. 52, Hayes to Weymouth, no. 15, Const., Jan. 3, 1776. The reason given by the Porte was that the Sultan was deprived of revenues, since the vessels which touched at Suez paid customs duties to the authorities in Egypt, who were not always under his control.

[2] *Ibid.*, vol. 53, Ainslie to Weymouth, May 17, 1777, enclosure: Trans-lation of a representation from the Ottoman Porte to his Britanick Majesty's Ambassador, dated May 5, 1777.

[3] *Ibid.*, no. 5, Weymouth to Sir Robert Ainslie, July 11, 1777. Ainslie was instructed to request of the Porte the privilege for the East India Company to send dispatches by way of Suez "provided they have no Goods or Merchandise on board for carrying on any kind of Traffick."

[4] Arch. Aff. Étr. Corr. Cons., vol. 24, Cairo, June 8, 1777. Vice-Consul to Minister.

had boasted that they would become masters of the country.[1]
He added that England would find in Egypt an ample reward
for her loss of the American colonies. Such suspicions were
unwarranted, for there is no mention in the correspondence
between Ainslie and his government of any designs on
Egypt.[2] Ainslie himself was opposed to the employment of
the Suez route for commerce partly because he feared that
France would obtain the advantage.

The most persistent advocate of the Suez route for British
trade was George Baldwin, who in 1779 became the English
agent at Cairo, though without official rank. He was a
member of the Levant Company and for several years had
been engaged in mercantile operations in the East and was
well acquainted with Egypt. Convinced that the Suez route
could be made profitable for commerce, he tried to win over
Ainslie but without success. Ainslie, however, in accordance with the instructions of his government made several
attempts to secure from the Porte the right of transporting
dispatches by way of the Red Sea and Egypt. His demands
were finally acceded to and it was agreed that no harm would
come to certain English vessels arriving at Suez with dispatches.[3] Baldwin was instructed to see that no commerce
was transacted.

As the Ministers of the Sublime Porte have made frequent
complaints to me, of an illicit Trade carried on between the
British Settlements in the East Indies, and the Port of Suez in
the Red Sea, and have lately notified their determination not
only of confiscating their Cargoes, which may in future arrive
at Suez, but even of condemning the Captain and crews of all
frank ships trading thither to perpetual slavery, I must recom-

---

[1] *Ibid.*, vol. 24, no. 64, Mure to Minister, Cairo, June 17, 1777.

[2] F. Charles-Roux, *Autour d'une route*, p. 89, makes this statement after
a careful study of the documents.

[3] *Ibid.*, p. 118.

mend in the strongest manner, that you use your utmost endeavours, to suppress all such Trade to the Port of Suez, and to conform to the inclosed Copy of the Orders, sent out by the East India Company to all their different Presidencies in India, which have been transmitted to me by His Majesty's Ministers, as well as by the Levant Company: but in case these orders are violated or eluded, and that this Trade, equally repugnant to the Interests of Great Britain, and to the East India and the Levant Companies, should be continued, I must recommend it to you, and I have no doubt of your ready compliance, as a Member of the Levant Company, that you will do everything in your Power, to enforce the Laws and regulations of the said Levant Company, in order to obstruct this trade. . . . [1]

A few months after Baldwin took up his new post at Cairo, an incident occurred which put an end for the time being to further agitation on the part of the English for the Suez route.[2] There arrived at Suez in May 1779 two Danish vessels commanded by an Englishman, George Moore. Permission was obtained from the Bey to unload the merchandise and transport it overland to the Nile. When the caravan reached the desert it was set upon and pillaged by Arabs. This was a sufficient warning to traders and for the next few years no English vessel appeared at Suez.

The withdrawal of the English left the way clear for another Austrian attempt to reopen the route through Egypt. Baron Herbert, the Internuncio at Constantinople, engaged as Austrian Consul the Chief Customs Officer at Cairo. Upon hearing of this, Ainslie wrote to his government: " It is certain that a Project exists for opening the Navigation between Egypt and India under the Imperial Flag." [3]   But

---

[1] *State Papers*, vol. 55, Ainslie to Baldwin, Pera, Feb. 26, 1779.

[2] See F. Charles-Roux, *Autour d'une route*, pp. 136-137.

[3] FO Turkey, vol. iii, no. 22, Sir Robert Ainslie to Lord Grantham, Const., Aug. 26, 1782. Sir Robert said that the new Consul was a Greek subject who had placed himself under Austrian protection. The Internuncio was personally interested in the scheme and stood to benefit to the extent of £5000 annually if it succeeded.

this Austrian attempt, like the earlier one, came to nothing, for the newly appointed Consul fled on a supposed visit to the Holy Land.[1]

In the meantime, French interest in the Suez route had grown considerably and in the last quarter of the century many projects appeared advocating the construction of a canal or the conquest of Egypt. One of these projects was submitted to the French Government by Louis de Langier in December 1774. " A most important subject occupies my attention," he wrote; " it is the canal of communication between the Mediterranean and the Red Sea. This canal, so important for Egypt, so essential to our direct trade with the East, which in a few years would place us in a position to lay down the law there to competitor nations, this canal is not a dream." [2] About the same time Baron de Tott, French military instructor in Turkey, proposed to the Sultan the reopening of the Canal of the Caliphs between the Nile and the Red Sea.[3] Though the Sultan was much impressed, he died before the project could be carried out. Baron de Tott returned to France and presented a memoir to the French Government describing the political situation in Turkey and advising the conquest of Egypt. " It is only necessary to glance at the map of Egypt," he said, " in order to perceive in its position—relative to Europe, Asia, Africa and the Indies—the entrepôt of a universal commerce." [4] To facilitate communications with India, he again proposed

[1] F. Charles-Roux, *Autour d'une route*, p. 158.

[2] *Ibid.*, " Le projet français de commerce avec l'Inde par Suez sous le règne de Louis XVI," *Revue de l'histoire des colonies françaises* (trim. iii, Paris, 1925), vol. xvii, p. 7.

[3] *Mémoires du Baron de Tott sur les Turcs et les Tartares* (4 vols., Amsterdam, 1784), vol. iv, p. 74.

[4] Arch. Aff. Étr. Turquie, Mémoires et Documents, vol. viii, Baron de Tott, July, 1776. Examen de l'état physique et politique de l'Empire Ottoman et des vues qu'il détermine relativement à la France.

a canal between the Nile and the Red Sea. In 1777 he was sent on a mission by the French Government to inspect the Levantine ports but was secretly instructed to secure information concerning the possibilities of conquering Egypt.[1] During his sojourn in France in 1777-1778, Saint Priest, French Ambassador at Constantinople, presented to the government a memoir urging the conquest of Egypt and maintained that it would be comparatively easy, and that Egypt was the only region France should consider in the event of a dismemberment of the Ottoman Empire.[2]

During the ministry of Vergennes, the government was literally flooded with proposals concerning Egypt or the Suez route. Baron de Waldner advocated a direct canal across the Isthmus of Suez and set forth in minute detail the dimensions, cost, and length of time required for its construction.[3] Moreover, he declared that the legend regarding the difference in the levels of the two seas was a " phantom of ignorance," a " vulgar fear." Volney, who had traveled in Egypt and Syria, considered that a direct canal was impossible because of the sandy nature of the soil and the lack of ports and fresh water; he preferred the indirect route from the Nile to the Red Sea.[4] He also proposed that France should take Egypt in case the Turkish Empire was dismembered. " By Egypt we shall touch India, we shall secure all the trade in the Red Sea, we shall reestablish the ancient traffic by Suez and we shall cause the route by the Cape of Good Hope to be deserted."[5] Mure, the French Consul-

---

[1] F. Charles-Roux, *Les origines, etc.*, p. 68.

[2] Arch. Aff. Étr., Mémoires et Documents, Turquie, vol. viii. Mémoire présenté par Monsieur le Comte de St. Priest pendant son séjour en France, 1777-1778.

[3] F. Charles-Roux, *Les origines etc.*, pp. 106-107.

[4] C. F. Volney, *Voyage en Syrie et en Égypte ... pendant les années 1783, 1784 et 1785* (2 vols., Paris, 1787), vol. i, p. 193.

[5] *Ibid., Considérations sur la guerre actuelle des Turcs* (London, 1788), p. 123.

General in Egypt, repeatedly urged the conquest of the country by France.

The proximity of India, the activity that would result from the communication of this part of the world [with the East] by the Red Sea, the facilities for transporting merchandise from Suez to the Nile by a canal which needs only to be recut in part, . . . will infinitely lessen the time, expense and loss of seamen which voyages by the Cape of Good Hope occasion, and will assure preference to merchandise employing the ancient route.[1]

These projects awakened no response on the part of the government, for France was then in no position to consider them. Wars on the Continent, in America and in India had left her too weak for other undertakings. But after the restoration of peace in 1783 the French Government again took up the question of a shorter route to India. The instructions given to Choiseul-Gouffier, the new Ambassador to Constantinople, showed clearly " the intention of retaking simultaneously in Egypt, in the Persian Gulf, in the Black Sea, the action so long suspended, and of renewing on all these points . . . a vigorous attempt to open the routes to India to French commerce." [2]

This time the French efforts were attended with a certain measure of success. Late in 1784 Choiseul-Gouffier sent M. de Truguet, laden with gifts, to negotiate a treaty with the Beys. Upon his arrival at Cairo, de Truguet communicated with a French merchant, Charles Magallon, whose wife had acquired a certain standing in the harem of Murad-Bey.[3] This connection enabled him to conclude a treaty with Murad-Bey on January 10, 1785 which assured protection

[1] Quoted in F. Charles-Roux, *Les origines etc.*, p. 128.

[2] *Ibid.*, p. 145.

[3] Arch. Aff. Étr., Mémoires et Documents, Turquie, vol. 172, Choiseul-Gouffier to M. le Maal de Cestrie, Const., Feb. 26, 1785.

for French traders and granted the right of way through Egypt for goods from India.[1]

Unfortunately, the treaties did not give the French the advantages they expected to derive from them. This was due to several reasons.[2] In the first place, Catherine II, who had designs on Egypt and encouraged the Beys toward independence, sent her agents to Egypt in order to intrigue against French traders. Secondly, there was the opposition of the *Compagnie des Indes,* which ever since its organization had favored the Cape route to the exclusion of all others. Thirdly, the Porte was prevailed upon by Russians, English and Venetians to refuse official sanction of the treaties.[3] As a final blow to French trade by the Suez route, the Beys were deposed in 1789 and Ottoman authority was reinstated in Egypt.

With the outbreak of the Revolution in France less attention was paid to the problem of securing a shorter route to India. But even the stirring events of the next ten years did not check the agitation entirely. French interest in

[1] *Ibid.*, enclosure. *Cf.* de Truguet to Minister of Marine, Const., Feb. 24, 1785. In addition to the treaty with Murad-Bey, de Truguet concluded one with the Chief Customs Officer at Cairo, and another with a powerful Arab Sheik who controlled the passage across the desert. In general, these treaties provided for moderate customs duties and transportation charges, and promised to facilitate in every way the unloading, inspection, transport and security of the merchandise.

[2] J. C. T. Roux, *op. cit.*, vol. i, p. 111 *et seq.*

[3] Although Ottoman authority in Egypt was practically nil at this time, Choiseul-Gouffier, in order not to offend the Sultan, decided to submit the treaties for his approval. He expected the opposition of the English Ambassador, who had given "considerable sums" to the Turkish ministers in order to prevent the use of the Suez route to Christian vessels (Arch. Aff. Étr. Mémoires et Documents, vol. 172, Choiseul-Gouffier to M. le Maal de Cestrie, Const., Feb. 26, 1786). On the other hand, de Truguet reported that the English in Egypt had spent over a million francs in order to get concessions for their trade by the Suez route (*ibid.*, de Truguet to Minister of Marine, Const., Feb. 24, 1785).

Egypt had by this time become a tradition, too deeply rooted to be easily forgotten. In the first years of the Revolution, French merchants residing in Egypt petitioned for the return of the Consulate to Cairo. " The abandonment of Cairo," they said, " entails the loss of communications with India." [1] Charles Magallon, whose name has already been mentioned in connection with the treaties of 1785, and who had since been appointed Consul-General, was especially active in urging the conquest of Egypt. His dispatches had an important influence on the decision later taken by the Directory for the Egyptian expedition.

In acquiring preponderance in this country we would soon be masters of the Red Sea trade. . . . We would in a short time be the only nation to have a monopoly of commerce with India and would furnish coffee, muslins and spices to all Turkey, Syria and the Barbary States. . . . I repeat, Citizen, that of all the establishments the Republic has in view, there is none which can be as extended and as useful as Egypt. . . . I pray, Citizen, that you will not neglect the means of giving Egypt to France.[2]

Magallon was recalled to France in the summer of 1797 to explain his views to the Directory.

Meanwhile, the attitude of Englishmen towards the Suez route had become more favorable. Since 1779 " the conviction had been growing that the withdrawal from Egypt had been a mistake." [3] Maps of the Red Sea and the Gulf of Suez now appeared together with descriptions which directed attention to the Suez route. In 1785, Colonel James Capper, employed in the service of the British East India

---

[1] Corr. Cons., le Caire, vol. 25, Les Français résidents au Caire au Citoyen Ministre de la Marine, May 17, 1793.

[2] *Ibid.*, Copy of a letter from the Fr. Consul-General in Egypt (Charles Magallon), to Citizen R. Verninac, Envoyé Extraordinaire de la République près la Porte Ottoman, Alex., 27 Prairial, l'an III.

[3] H. L. Hoskins, *British Trade Routes to India* (N. Y., 1928), p. 32.

Company, published a book describing a voyage from Bombay to London.[1]  Concerning the Suez route, he wrote:

When the Venetians lost the India trade, no violence, no finesse was used to deprive them of it; the trade died away of itself, because the Portuguese and other European nations, passing round the Cape of Good Hope, could by means of the shortness and safety of the voyage, afford to undersell them in those articles of India commerce which they received only by the more tedious, dangerous, and expensive channel of the Red Sea.  But the probability of the danger of the trade by this route becoming prejudicial to ours by the Cape of Good Hope, being admitted in its fullest extent; are we to suppose that other European nations are so blind to their own interest, so strangely ignorant, or so absurdly indolent, as not to discover it, and immediately avail themselves of their knowledge?  If goods can really be brought cheaper from India to Europe that way, in vain shall we attempt to oppose the general interests of Europe and Asia; the Indian trade must in the course of a few years unavoidably find its way to the easiest and most profitable channel.  He who thinks otherwise, knows but little of human nature, and still less of the principles of politics and trade.[2]

But the most ardent advocate of the Suez route was George Baldwin, who had returned to England in 1781. When the French treaties of 1785 became known, he was requested by the India Board to present his views on Egypt. Accordingly, he wrote a memoir discussing the geographic position of the country, its commerce, resources, means of defense, strategic importance and the French designs.[3]

[1] James Capper, *Observations on the Passage to India Through Egypt. Also Vienna through Constantinople to Aleppo, and from thence by Bagdad and directly across the Great Desert to Bassora* (London, 1785).

[2] *Ibid.*, introduction, p. xxxiii.

[3] George Baldwin, *Political Recollections Relative to Egypt; Containing observations on its Government under the Mamelukes; its Geographic Position; its intrinsic and extrinsic Resources:—its relative Importance*

France in possession of Egypt, would possess the master-key to all the trading stations of the earth.   Enlightened, as the times are, in the general arts of navigation and commerce, she might make it the emporium of the world: she might make it the *awe* of the Eastern world, by the facility she would command of transporting her forces thither, by surprise, in any number, and at any time; and England would hold her possessions in India at the mercy of France.[1]

This memoir made a strong impression in England, and in 1786 the government decided to reestablish the Consulate (suppressed in 1756) with Baldwin as Consul-General.   He was instructed to watch the French activities in Egypt; to conclude a treaty with Murad Bey or " whoever is at the head of the Government of Cairo "; to emphasize that England had " prior claim over every other Nation and a positive right by our subsisting Capitulations [2] with the Porte " of trading in the Red Sea; to secure for English merchants the same privileges accorded to the French by treaties of 1785; and to do everything " consistent with the great object of opening the Communication to India." [3]

Hardly had Baldwin entered upon his new duties when the Revolution in France caused England to lose all interest in Egypt and the Suez route.   A dispatch of February 8,

*to England and France; also its Dangers to England in the Possession of France* . . . (London, 1801).

[1] *Ibid.*, p. 79.

[2] Capitulations of 1675.  See Hertslet's *Commercial Treaties*, vol. ii, p. 346.

[3] FO Egypt, vol. i, Heads of Instructions for Mr. Baldwin, May 19, 1786.  The instructions further provided that if Baldwin succeeded in negotiating a treaty giving English merchants the privilege of trading by the Suez route, it would be left to the discretion of the East India Company to determine whether it desired to avail itself of this privilege or not.  On the other hand, the English Government intended to make immediate use of the Suez route for receiving and forwarding public dispatches.

1793 suppressed the Consulate, but for some reason it did not reach Baldwin, and in May 1794 he concluded a treaty with the Beys, Murad and Ibrahim. This was similar to the French treaties of 1785 and conceded the right of navigation in the Red Sea, freedom of passage through Egypt, and entrance into the port of Suez.[1] Baldwin's efforts were unrewarded. The treaty was received in London " with absolute indifference " and became a dead letter.[2]

[1] Provisions are given in F. Charles-Roux, *Autour d'une route*, p. 320.
[2] *Ibid.*, p. 328.

## CHAPTER IV

### NAPOLEON AND THE SUEZ CANAL

BEGINNING with St. Louis' ill-fated venture in the thirteenth century, French interest in Egypt, occasionally promoted by the activity of the government and continually nourished in the writings of merchants, economists and philosophers, had developed to a considerable extent. Many of the writers, as we have seen, advocated the conquest of Egypt; but long and costly wars in all parts of the world during the seventeenth and eighteenth centuries prevented France from making any move in this direction, even if she had so desired. The right moment for such an undertaking was now at hand. Victories over Austria and Italy made Revolutionary France supreme on the Continent, but England, the paymistress of her enemies, remained undefeated. To invade that "nation of shopkeepers" was a most difficult task with British warships patrolling the Channel, but perhaps England could be defeated in another way. If France were to seize Egypt and secure the Suez route for her commerce, drive out the British from India and cut off their communications with the East, would not England, whose very existence depended upon her commerce, be compelled to sue for peace? Just as Leibnitz a century before had urged the Great Monarch to destroy Dutch power by taking Egypt, so now the French Government determined to employ this means of crushing England. The command of the Egyptian expedition fell to Napoleon, the most popular man in France since his victories in the Italian Campaign.

60

From his youth Napoleon had turned his thoughts to the mysterious East—the place where all great reputations had been made. Notes written in the period from 1786 to 1793 reveal that he clearly understood the importance of Egypt and the Suez route.[1] He was acquainted with the works of the Abbé Raynal, Baron de Tott and others. Sometimes in reading such books he would take notes or make comments concerning certain passages. Thus, under a passage copied from Diodorus, he wrote: " This monument has been found near Suez at the entrance of the canal which still exists and which only a little work will render navigable." [2]

Returning to Paris after the Treaty of Campo Formio (October 17, 1797), Napoleon was given command of the Army of England. A brief inspection of the northern coast of France convinced him that an invasion of England would be impracticable. It has been said that this inspection " was probably a blind to hide from the world his real intent," namely, an expedition to Egypt.[3] Only a few months before he had written to Talleyrand: " The time is not far distant when we shall feel that in order really to destroy England, it is necessary for us to possess Egypt." [4]

[1] *Napoléon Inconnu . . . Papiers inédits* (1786-1793), edited by Frederic Masson and Guido Biagi (2 vols., Paris, 1895), vol. ii.

[2] *Ibid.,* vol. ii, p. 507.

[3] *Cambridge Modern History,* vol. viii, ch. xix, p. 594. This is denied by F. Charles-Roux, *Les Origines etc.,* p. 309.

[4] F. Charles-Roux, *Les origines etc.,* p. 298. The letter is dated Aug. 16, 1797. The distinguished British military historian, Fortescue, maintains that Ireland, not Egypt, would have been the logical objective for an attack against England. " To affirm that an unwieldy raid of this kind upon British commerce in the East was at that moment the most effective means of injuring England is, looking at the state of Ireland, ridiculous. . . . A really patriotic Frenchman would never for a moment have lifted his eye from Ireland, where even five thousand men, landed at the right moment, would have been more dangerous to England, than thirty thousand in Egypt." J. W. Fortescue, *A History of the British*

Napoleon was not the author of the Egyptian expedition. If any one should be given the credit, it is Charles Magallon who had urged it continuously in his dispatches. Summoned by the Directory to explain his views, he arrived in Paris late in 1797 and submitted a memoir to Talleyrand setting forth in detail the possibilities of taking Egypt.[1] He believed that a force of 25,000 troops, four or five vessels of the line and six transports would suffice; while an expedition should be sent against India to cooperate with Tippoo-Sahib, Sultan of Mysore, who had declared his independence of British rule. Some days later Talleyrand read a memoir to the Directory which was based on Magallon's and was really a paraphrase of it. " Not only the general inspiration, the plan, the argumentation," says Charles-Roux, " but entire phrases have passed from the memoir of Magallon to that of Talleyrand." [2] His own contribution was limited to a few additional touches designed to impress the Directory. He called particular attention to the advantages of Egypt for French trade.

That event of establishing the French in Egypt will bring about a revolution in European commerce which will strike particularly at England. It will destroy her power in India, the only basis for her grandeur in Europe. The revival of the Suez route will have an effect upon her . . . as fatal as the discovery of the Cape of Good Hope was to the Genoese and Venetians in the sixteenth century. The result of this revolution will be wholly to the advantage of the Republic because it is by its geographical position, population, genius and activity . . . the

*Army* (London, 1906), vol. iv (1789-1801), pt. i, p. 584. The Egyptian expedition was at the least a very hazardous undertaking so long as England controlled the seas. The entrance of the British fleet into the Mediterranean would cut off communications between Egypt and France.

[1] Charles Magallon, " Mémoire sur l'Égypte, 9, fev., 1798 ", *Revue d'Égypte* (Cairo, 1896), pp. 205-224.

[2] F. Charles-Roux, *Les origines etc.,* p. 327.

one of all Powers which can derive most from it. Let us never forget that the ancient and modern nations which have controlled the trade with India have always reached a high degree of wealth. When the French Republic becomes master of Cairo and consequently of Suez, it will make little difference in whose hands the Cape of Good Hope happens to be . . .[1]

Napoleon in the meantime was considering the means for carrying out such a vast undertaking. Already he had acquired for France the Ionian Islands and had informed the Directory that Corfu and Malta should also be taken. These posts would give France control of the Mediterranean and would make the conquest of Egypt comparatively easy. At Passeriano, in September 1797, he had discussed with Desaix the plans for an expedition to Egypt.[2] He had also directed Monge to secure documents concerning Egypt, the navigation of the Red Sea, and the commerce of India.[3] With Talleyrand and other advocates of the expedition he was in direct communication. By March 1798 he had worked out the details of the plan, which was accepted by the Directory.

The aims of the expedition were set forth in secret decrees drawn up by Napoleon and signed by the Directory on April 12th.[4]

The Army of the East shall take possession of Egypt. The Commander-in-Chief shall chase the English from all their possessions in the East which he can reach, and in particular he shall destroy all their *comptoirs* in the Red Sea. He shall have the Isthmus of Suez cut through, and he shall take the necessary steps to assure the free and exclusive possession of the

[1] *Ibid.*

[2] *Ibid.*, p. 355.

[3] *Ibid.*

[4] *France and the Levant, op. cit.,* p. 12. *Cf. Cambridge Modern History,* vol. viii, p. 597.

Red Sea to the French Republic. He shall ameliorate the lot of the natives of Egypt and shall maintain a good understanding with the Sultan and his subjects.

In addition to these aims, Napoleon was to seize Malta. Preparations were hastened at Toulon, and on May 19th the expedition set sail. It was the beginning, said one writer, of " The Egyptian Question." [1]

The preparations at Toulon had been carried on with the utmost secrecy although the concentration of troops there did not escape the observation of other countries. The Tsar Paul thought the expedition would be directed against the Balkan Peninsula, while Austria suspected that Napoleon would strike at Italy.[2] As for England, she was no better informed and had no idea that Egypt would be the objective. However, she decided to take steps to check Napoleon.

In the latter part of April 1798, the Admiralty directed Earl St. Vincent, then engaged in blockading Cadiz, to dispatch a squadron to the Mediterranean under the command of Nelson.[3] The instructions which Nelson received from his commander-in-chief on May 21st show clearly enough that there was no realization that the expedition was headed for Egypt.[4] Nelson was ordered " to proceed in quest of the armament preparing by the enemy at Toulon and Genoa : the object whereof appears to be either an attack upon Naples or Sicily, the conveyance of an army to some part of the coast of Spain for the purpose of marching towards Portugal, or to pass through the Straits, with a view of proceeding to Ireland." Additional instructions suggested that

---

[1] C. de Freycinet, La question d'Égypte (2nd ed., Paris, 1905), p. 4.

[2] J. W. Fortescue, op. cit., vol. iv, pt. i, p. 582.

[3] William James, The Naval History of Great Britain (6 vols., London, 1902), vol. ii, p. 66. Cf. F. Charles-Roux, L'Angleterre et l'expédition française en Égypte (2 vols., Cairo, 1925), vol. i, p. 7.

[4] Ibid., p. 171. Cf. F. Charles-Roux, op. cit., vol. i, p. 7.

he should pursue the French to "any part of the Mediterranean, Adriatic, Morea, Archipelago, or even into the Black Sea." [1]

With such vague instructions to go on, Nelson could only guess at the destination of Napoleon. He set sail for Alexandria. Arriving there on June 28th, he saw no sign of the enemy and turned back only a few days before the French vessels made their appearance. Thus Napoleon was able to disembark his troops and proceed to the conquest of Egypt.

One of the aims of the expedition, it will be remembered, was to cut a canal. The task of making a survey of the Isthmus of Suez was assigned to J. M. Le Père, a famous engineer, who was a member of the group of distinguished scholars and scientists who had accompanied the expedition and who had been enrolled in the Institute of Egypt, established at Cairo in August 1798.

Napoleon himself made plans to visit Suez but events delayed his departure from Cairo for several weeks. He had two objects in view: to open up commercial relations with Arabia; and to join forces with the French fleet which had been ordered to Suez from the Ile de France and Réunion.[2] On November 30th, Beauharnais and Bon were sent to drive the turbulent Arabs to cover and to occupy Suez by force. When this had been done, Napoleon left Cairo, December 24th, accompanied by several generals and members of the Institute of Egypt. Arriving at Suez, he set out to find the ruins of the ancient canal. He himself discovered the first traces and with his party followed it for several leagues.[3] In the preface to the *Description de l'Égypte,* Fourier gives the following account:

[1] *Ibid.,* p. 172.

[2] De La Jonquière, *L'Expédition d'Égypte, 1798-1801* (5 vols., Paris, 1899-1907), vol. iii, bk. vii, p. 445.

[3] *Ibid.,* vol. iii, p. 488.

He [Napoleon] went to the port of Suez . . . and advancing north, discovered and pointed out to those who accompanied him, the vestiges of the canal constructed by the ancient kings in the design of joining the Nile to the Red Sea. He followed its lines for a long time and a few days later, again drawing near to the lands made fertile by its waters, he recognized the opposite extremity of the canal, to the east of ancient Bubastis. He ordered all necessary measures to prepare the execution of the great work he meditated. The annals of men offer no more heroic scene than that which took place at the Gates of Asia. The Liberator of Egypt himself had come to decide a famous question, which belonged at once to history, to politics, to the exact sciences and to the civil arts. He stamped a new route on the commerce of the East.[1]

From Suez Napoleon journeyed to Belbeis, where he continued his survey. "The Commander-in-Chief," wrote Reynier, "spent two days here; yesterday he went into the desert toward the remains of the ancient Suez Canal, in the direction of Abou-el-Cheib and Sab-Biar."[2] Leaving Belbeis, January 3, 1799, he rode through the region from Tel-el-Kebir to Ismailia and completed his inspection tour. He ordered Le Père to proceed to Suez and survey the entire region of the canal and to report on the possibilities of re-establishing it.

The surveying party, with General Junot in command, left for Suez on January 16th. The work was carried on under immense difficulties.

At any moment lack of water would force the expedition back to Suez or Cairo and leave the work unfinished; the Syrian campaign interrupted them for six months; the defective materials and means of transport caused loss of time; attacks by

[1] Quoted in F. Charles-Roux, *L'Angleterre et l'expédition etc.*, vol. i, p. 253.

[2] Reynier to Grange, cited by De La Jonquière, vol. iii, p. 497.

the enemy, treason of a guide, placed the engineers in danger, isolated as they were from the rest of the French troops; the rising of the Nile prevented them from following the direction of the ancient canal; all these causes, natural and human, seemed as if fate had decided to increase the journal of the trip at the expense of the surveying tables.[1]

Le Père set forth the results of his survey in a report addressed to Napoleon.[2] He had found that the level of the Red Sea was over thirty feet higher than that of the Mediterranean and because of this he recommended an indirect canal from the Nile to the Red Sea, which he estimated would cost twenty-five or thirty million francs. Though his conclusion as to the difference in the levels of the two seas was combated at the time by Laplace and Fourier, it was not definitely disproved until 1847.

The French expedition did not realize the aims which had called it forth. Kléber, who took command after Napoleon's departure for France, was assassinated; and Menou, his successor, proved incompetent and was forced to surrender to the British in August 1801. But Napoleon never lost interest in Egypt. No sooner had he returned to France than he opened negotiations with Russia in the hope of retaining his African possession. " Peace with the Emperor," he wrote to Talleyrand on January 20, 1801, " is nothing in comparison with an alliance which makes us masters of England and preserves to us Egypt." [3] To Joseph he wrote: " The interest of all Mediterranean Powers, as those of the

---

[1] J. C. T. Roux, *op. cit.*, vol. i, p. 142.

[2] *Description de l'Égypte, ou recueil des observations et des récherches qui ont été faites en Égypte, pendant l'expédition de l'armée française,* publié par les ordres de Napoléon le Grand (10 vols., Paris, 1809-1822), vol. i, *État moderne*, pp. 57-58.

[3] Albert Sorel, *L'Europe et la Révolution française* (Paris, 1903), vol. vi, p. 104.

Black Sea, is that Egypt remains with France.  The Suez
Canal which joined the waters of India to the Mediterranean
is already traced, it is an easy task and will take little
time. . . ." [1]   The news that England was preparing an expedition against Egypt made him anxious to come to an
understanding with the Tsar Paul.  Egypt was his first
consideration.  To Kolytcheff, the Russian Ambassador, he
declared that he would never voluntarily cede Egypt.  "That
colony is the price of the purest blood of France.  It is the
only possession by means of which France can some day
balance the enormous maritime power of the English in
India." [2]   Indeed, the thought of Egypt never ceased to
haunt his mind.  At St. Helena he said: " The English
trembled to see us occupy Egypt.  We would show Europe
the true way to deprive them of India." [3]

[1] *Ibid.,* p. 105.

[2] *Ibid.,* p. 116, March 28, 1801.

[3] Marcel Dubois and Auguste Terrier, *Un siècle d'expansion coloniale,
1800-1900* (Paris, 1902), p. 65.

# CHAPTER V

## MEHEMET ALI, THE EASTERN QUESTION, AND THE REVIVAL OF ENGLISH INTEREST

THE failure of the French expedition left Egypt once more under the Sultan's authority. English troops remained, however, despite the Peace of Amiens, March 20, 1802, which provided that both France and England should renounce claims to Egypt. As that Peace proved little more than a truce, and as Napoleon realized that England had no intention of withdrawing her troops, he thought seriously of resuming the struggle in the Orient. In 1802 he sent Colonel Sebastiani on a mission to Egypt, instructing him to study the situation, particularly the strength of the British force. Sebastiani reported that the English were strongly installed in Alexandria and had apparently no intention of leaving; that the Mamelukes desired the return of the French, and that 6000 soldiers would suffice to regain possession of the country.[1] His report, published in the *Moniteur*, January 30, 1802, created a considerable stir in England and war broke out again in May. Though France was compelled to abandon her designs on Egypt, it was not destined to remain in English hands. The stage was set for the appearance of a new conqueror who was to influence in no small degree the course of Near Eastern history.

Mehemet Ali was a native of Kavala on the Ægean. He had for several years been a simple tobacco merchant but during the French occupation of Egypt had served in the

[1] Georges Péméant, *L'Égypte et la politique française* (Paris, 1909), p. 77.

Turkish army and had taken part in the Battle of Aboukir
(1799). The unpopularity of Turkish rule in Egypt impressed him, and he threw in his lot with the Mamelukes.
In 1805 he succeeded in driving out the Turkish Governor,
Khowret-Pasha, and in the following year he overthrew
Ibrahim-Bey, whose affiliation with the Turks had caused
him considerable loss of prestige. Mehemet Ali then proclaimed himself Viceroy and through French influence obtained the sanction of the Porte. In 1807 he defeated the
English before Alexandria, and was thereafter the real power
in Egypt, though he still had to cope with disaffected elements among the Mamelukes until 1811, when he had them
all massacred.

The Near Eastern question did not take definite form
until after 1830. Before that time the probability of Turkey's dismemberment had often been considered, but it was
not until after the Greek War of Independence that European statesmen were brought face to face with it.

The views of the four Great Powers, Austria, Russia,
England and France, varied somewhat in regard to that
problem. Under the reactionary Metternich, Austria abandoned her former policy of aggression and took her stand
with the *status quo*. Russia considered the Dying Turk as
her natural victim in the policy of expansion she had been
pursuing since the time of Peter the Great. Both France
and England were for the maintenance of the Ottoman Empire, but were willing to see particular provinces detached
and made independent. This policy, as stated by Guizot,
was:

to maintain the Ottoman Empire in order to maintain the European equilibrium and when by the force of circumstances, by
the natural course of events, some dismemberment takes place,
when some province detaches itself from that decadent empire,
the right policy is to favour the transformation of that province

into a new and independent sovereignty, which shall become a member of the family of states, and serve one day in the new European equilibrium—the equilibrium destined to take the place of the ancient elements when these are no longer in existence.[1]

Palmerston, however, was inclined to lean more strongly toward the maintenance of the Turkish Empire. There were two reasons for his attitude. In the first place, he looked upon that Empire as the natural guardian of the road to India. Secondly, he was sanguine enough to believe that Turkey might regenerate herself and become respectable. When in 1832 Mehemet Ali, dissatisfied with his share in the Greek War, sent his son Ibrahim to Syria and there defeated the Turks, the Near Eastern Question came to the fore. But it was only when the Sultan, unable to cope with the Egyptian forces, and unsuccessful in his appeals to France and England, as a last resort turned to Russia and concluded the Treaty of Unkiar Skelessi (1833), that Palmerston roused himself. He had before him three principal objects: to prevent Mehemet Ali from further disrupting the Ottoman Empire, to secure the suppression of the Treaty of Unkiar Skelessi, and to prevent France and Russia from coming to an understanding.[2]

Russia was willing to abandon the Treaty and to come to terms with England. The Tsar Nicholas was aware " that to invoke the Treaty would mean war with England, while not to invoke it, but instead, to join with England in driving Mehemet Ali out of Syria, meant the rupture of the Anglo-French Alliance—a prospect not at all unpleasing to Russia." [3] On the proposal of Baron Brunnow, the Russian

[1] Ward and Gooch, *Cambridge History of British Foreign Policy, 1783-1919*, vol. ii, 1815-1866, p. 161.

[2] *Ibid.*, p. 170.

[3] *Ibid.*, p. 173.

diplomat, the Treaty was allowed to lapse in return for an Anglo-Russian understanding in the Near East.[1] France had cast in her lot with Mehemet Ali and was counting on the supposition that Russia and England could not agree. When the news of the agreement reached Paris, Soult, the Prime Minister, recalled Sebastiani, the Ambassador at London, and appointed Guizot in his place (February 1840). By this move he hoped to maintain the Anglo-French Alliance. But Soult fell from power shortly thereafter and was replaced by Thiers, who hoped that the question would be settled through the mediation of France. The French Ambassador at Constantinople, Pontois, was endeavoring to bring about an understanding between the Porte and his vassal. Thiers was, however, too optimistic. On July 15, 1840, representatives of England, Austria, Prussia and Russia signed a treaty which called for a settlement of the dispute on the basis of giving Mehemet Ali the hereditary pashalik of Egypt, and Acre and southern Syria for life. This treaty was also signed by the Turkish Ambassador. But Mehemet Ali's refusal to accede to the wishes of the Powers, followed by his deposition, September 14, 1840, and then the withdrawal of the act of deposition by the Sultan, February 12, 1841, while denying Syria and Crete to the Viceroy, called for a final settlement of the question. This took place at the Conference of London, July 1841, at which France joined with the other Powers in signing two treaties, one of which confirmed Mehemet Ali in the hereditary pashalik of Egypt, while the other settled the Straits Question.[2]

The new status of Egypt was a simple one. She was autonomous and yet limited by the sovereignty of the Sultan.

[1] A. Cecil, *British Foreign Secretaries, 1807-1916* (London, 1927), p. 152.

[2] Ward and Gooch, *op. cit.,* vol. ii, p. 180.

She could conclude no political engagements nor participate in any war without permission from the suzerain. As a province of the Ottoman Empire she was protected to a certain extent from the ambitions of the Western Powers. Her integrity, as that of the whole empire, was guaranteed by the Concert of Europe. All this had an important bearing on the Suez Question, for without the autonomy of Egypt and the investiture of the hereditary pashalik, de Lesseps would probably have failed to secure his concession for a maritime canal. Negotiations would have been confined to Constantinople, where English influence was predominant.

During the period covered by the rule of Mehemet Ali, from about 1811 to his death in 1849, there were several attempts to revive the route through Egypt to the East. It is in this period, moreover, that England displayed an increasing interest in Egyptian affairs and a strong realization of the importance of safeguarding all approaches to her great Indian Empire.

The French expedition not only directed the attention of British statesmen to the Near East, but it revealed the need of a shorter route to India. The Cape route was no longer regarded as entirely adequate.[1] Though still the main channel for commerce, it was too long for the transmission of business and official correspondence which required greater speed as British industry and trade developed. Hence, Great Britain in the nineteenth century evinced an ever-growing interest in the possibility of developing a shorter route to her Asiatic possessions whether by the Red Sea and Egypt or the Persian Gulf and the Euphrates Valley.

During the period of occupation in Egypt following the surrender of the French force, the English, according to the reports of the French agent, intrigued actively with the Beys and encouraged a state of anarchy in order to further their

[1] H. L. Hoskins, *op. cit.,* p. 79.

own interest.[1] These intrigues continued after their occupation had come to an end in 1807. The return of the English Consul to Alexandria in 1810 was the signal for "cabals and intrigues of all sorts."[2] By supporting the Mamelukes, the English hoped to establish a preponderant position in the country. As they watched the rising power of Mehemet Ali they sought to win him over to their scheme, advising him to renounce the authority of the Sultan.[3] Mehemet Ali, however, "refused every condition which seemed to place him under the protection of the English."[4] Nevertheless, he was willing to accept English aid in order to secure his independence of the Porte. While protesting that he was the friend of all Europeans, he leaned more and more (at this time) toward the English "because they flattered his ambition and satiated his avarice."[5] The French Consul reported that there existed a "liaison between the English and Mehemet Ali."[6] However, it was not long before the events in the Near East induced the Pasha to throw in his lot with France.

One factor which accelerated British interest in the Suez route was the development of steam navigation. Beginning in the 'twenties, definite attempts were made to show the advantages of the "overland" route for travelers and dispatches.[7] As early as 1822 an effort was made to organize

[1] Corr. Cons., le Caire, vol. 26, dispatches from Fr. Consul in Egypt, no. 20, 10 frimaire, an XII; no. 23, 30 nivôse, an XII.

[2] *Ibid.*, Drovetti to Minister of Exterior Relations of the Empire, March 10, 1810.

[3] *Ibid.*

[4] *Ibid.*, disp. of April 28, 1810.

[5] Corr. Cons., Alexandrie, Carton, 1812-1817, no. 53, Alexandria, Nov. 28, 1812.

[6] Ibid., no. 104, Alexandria, Dec. 12, 1812.

[7] The term "overland" was applied to the route by way of Egypt. For a discussion of the development of steam navigation on the Suez route, see H. L. Hoskins, *op. cit.*, chs. iv, v.

a company for the maintenance of steamship service between Calcutta and Suez. This led, in 1825, to the formation of a *Society for the Encouragement of Steam Navigation between Great Britain and India* by residents of Calcutta.[1] During the 'thirties the agitation for the employment of the Suez route for steam vessels gained considerable momentum and was carried on by British residents of India, by representatives of the East India Company and by private Englishmen at home.

Especially active in this agitation was Lieutenant Thomas Waghorn, who " became distinguished as the projector of communication with India by almost all the known routes, and particularly that through Egypt." [2]   He saw in Egypt a natural ally for England and repeatedly urged his government to support her move for independence. "The cooperation of Egypt," he said, " situated as she is, half way between us and India, is only wanting to fix our eastern empire firmer than it ever can be by any other means." [3] He was aware that his optimistic picture of Egypt's future might provoke some criticism.

I doubt not that, by some, my opinions may be called enthusiastic; and, as such, subject me to attack; however, they led me to Egypt eight years ago.   I felt convinced that that country ought to be the road to India; and I maintained my principle in three quarters of the globe.   I have travelled, since then, some hundreds of thousands of miles to disseminate my opinions, and I will never content myself till I *find it* the high road to India.[4]

As Palmerston was throwing all England's weight towards

[1] *Ibid.,* p. 90.

[2] *Ibid.,* p. 99.

[3] Lieut. Thomas Waghorn, *Egypt as it is in 1837* (London, 1837), p. 22.

[4] *Ibid.,* p. 26.

the maintenance of the Ottoman Empire, Waghorn's efforts were to no avail. Too persistent to give up, he addressed public meetings, put his views in print, harassed the authorities with his incessant appeals, and sought by example to prove the advantage of the Suez route. In October 1829 he was permitted to carry some dispatches from London to Bombay and was able to cover the distance of 2700 miles to Suez in 40½ traveling days.[1] After various adventures he finally reached Bombay in March 1830. Though he had demonstrated the rapidity of the Suez route in the first part of his journey, his exertions awakened no response in England at this time. Still he did not abandon hope.

Some years later he set himself up in the business of transporting mails, passengers and goods from Suez to Alexandria but soon encountered competition from other Englishmen engaged in the same enterprise.[2] In 1841 he joined forces with one of those competitors, J. R. Hill, and for a time the new concern enjoyed a monopoly of the transportation service through Egypt. Two years later, however, it was bought out by the Egyptian Transit Company which had received a new monopoly from Mehemet Ali.[3] Waghorn, who died in 1850, contributed in a large measure toward keeping the importance of the Suez route before the English public. His persistent efforts aroused the admiration of de Lesseps, who wrote that " it was the courage he exhibited that left a deep impression on my mind, and served as an example." [4]

----

[1] From London to Calcutta by sail took 5 to 8 months; from Suez to Calcutta about 6 weeks.

[2] H. L. Hoskins, *op. cit.,* p. 227.

[3] *Ibid.,* p. 230.

[4] F. de Lesseps, *Entretiens,* 1864, p. 11. Quoted in Percy Fitzgerald, *The Great Canal at Suez* (2 vols., London, 1876), vol. i, p. 6. Waghorn was opposed to a maritime canal. " The Suez Desert ", he wrote to

Another individual who played an important rôle in the search for a shorter route to India was Lieutenant-Colonel F. R. Chesney. In 1830 he was commissioned to make a survey in Egypt to determine its advantages for communication. While there he studied the possibilities of cutting a canal and discovered that there existed no difference in the levels of the two seas. After completing his survey, however, he embarked for Jaffa and studied the Euphrates route, which he reported more suitable for British commerce.[1]

Meanwhile interest in the Suez route continued to grow. Surveys were made of the Red Sea and by 1838 steam navigation between India and Suez had become quite regular.[2] The acquisition of Aden (1839) and Perim (1847) increased English influence in the Red Sea. In 1840 there was organized the Peninsular and Oriental Company which operated a fleet of steam vessels between Suez, the Indian ports and the Far East.

In 1841, Mr. Arthur Anderson, a director and one of the founders of the Peninsular and Oriental Company, visited Egypt with the object of studying means for improving transit through this country. His attention was directed to the possibility of reopening the ancient canal.[3] He became

Stephenson on March 13, 1847, " will not do for a ship canal and if it did, a ship canal at this particular place is one of the most uncalled for schemes I ever yet have heard broached. . . . I only consider it emanating from the brain of an old man who being a semi-barbarian fancies that he is greater than the Pharaohs of old or Alexander the Great and the like. So fallen is he [Mehemet Ali] from the sound sense he used to exercise that I have no other feeling for him than Pity!!" Fo 78/411, Suez Canal 1833-1851, vol. i.

[1] Lieut.-Col. F. R. Chesney, *Narrative of the Euphrates Expedition* (London, 1868). *Cf. The Expedition for the Survey of the Rivers Euphrates and Tigris—carried on by order of the British Government in the years 1835, 1836 and 1837* (4 vols., London, 1852).

[2] H. L. Hoskins, *op. cit.,* p. 193.

[3] See Arthur Anderson, *Communications with India, China, etc. Obser-*

acquainted with Adolphe Linant who, as engineer in the
service of the Viceroy, had devoted much time to the study
of the subject. Anderson was soon converted to the idea
of a canal. In a letter to Lord Palmerston he declared that
no physical difficulties existed to obstruct the execution of
such an undertaking.[1]

Your Lordship is, no doubt, aware that the matter has been
discussed, and its practicability asserted, by various individuals
who have visited and written on Egypt, and that the great im-
pediments which have hitherto prevented the attention of
British capitalists from being turned to the subject have been
of political nature.

Anderson believed that the time had come " when these
obstacles may be removed, and an object of almost universal
utility, whether viewed in commercial, or political light, be
accomplished as a natural consequence of your Lordship's
policy." [2]

In 1842 Mehemet Ali directed M. Linant to study the
possibility of constructing a canal. Upon completing this
study, Linant presented a memoir to the Viceroy setting forth
his findings.[3] He accepted Le Père's theory concerning the
difference in the levels of the two seas, and recommended
an indirect canal connecting with the Nile. The cost he
estimated at 3,750,000 francs.

Linant's report made a deep impression upon Anderson,
who proposed that the canal should be constructed with the
cooperation or approval of the Viceroy. " I consider it

*vations on the Practicability and Utility of opening a Communication
Between the Red Sea and the Mediterranean by a Ship Canal Through
the Isthmus of Suez* (London, 1843).

[1] FO 97/411 Suez Canal 1833-1851, vol. i, Letter from Arthur Anderson
to Lord Palmerston, Feb. 20, 1841.

[2] *Ibid.*

[3] Arthur Anderson, *op. cit.,* pp. 9-15.

doubtful," he said, "whether Mehemet Ali will be induced
to enter upon such a speculation as the opening of the contemplated canal, except through the intervention of one or
more of the European powers, who may have the greatest
interest in such an improved means of communication with
the East." [1]    Great Britain would gain most from such a
canal, which would enable her to send troops to India in a
comparatively short time. "The opening of the canal route
would tend to facilitate our intercourse with the five hundred
million people who inhabit India and China, and hence its
commercial importance must be sufficiently obvious." [2]

Anderson also saw certain moral advantages in the construction of the canal.

Five hundred millions of human beings inhabiting Hindostan
and China remain to this day enslaved by debasing superstitions,
and sunk in mental darkness and delusion. What a field is here
opening to the Christian philanthropist! To aid in the removal of ignorance and superstition by the diffusion of useful
knowledge, and an enlightened religion, to plant industry and
the arts where indolence and barbarism have hitherto prevailed,
are noble efforts, tending no less to elevate those who engage in
them, than the objects of their exertions. The opening of the
proposed communication would obviously subserve the promotion of such objects, and therefore can scarcely fail to excite
an interest in the mind of every well-wisher to his fellow
creatures. [3]

Anderson's eloquence won him little support in England,
where the construction of a railroad across Egypt was, as
we shall see later, considered much more advantageous for
British trade than a canal. [4]

[1] *Ibid.*, p. 18.
[2] *Ibid.*, p. 42.
[3] *Ibid.*, p. 43.
[4] See ch. ix.

# CHAPTER VI

## The Saint-Simonian Mission

During the same period which witnessed the growth of English interest in a shorter route to India, the project of constructing a canal across the Isthmus of Suez was revived in France among the followers of Saint-Simon. When Count Henry de Saint-Simon died in 1825 he left to his disciples a program for the social regeneration of the world which included the construction of a canal across the Isthmus of Suez. Under the leadership of Prosper Enfantin the Saint-Simonians embarked for Egypt in 1833. They planned not only to cut a canal but to regulate the flow of the Nile, establish schools, and carry out other reforms, social and economic.[1] " It is for us," declared Enfantin, " to establish between ancient Egypt and old India one of the new routes from Europe to India and China; later we can also cut the other at Panama. We shall then have one foot on the Nile, the other on Jerusalem, our right hand extended toward Mecca. Our left arm shall cover Rome and yet rest on Paris. Suez is the center of our *vie de travail*." [2]

From the Viceroy no opposition was expected. " The Suez Canal will certainly be built," said Enfantin, " as soon as Mehemet Ali gives less thought to his army. . . . It is a work . . . which should be executed by the Saint-Simonians.

[1] J. C. T. Roux, *op. cit.*, vol. i, p. 196.
[2] *Oeuvres de Saint-Simon et d'Enfantin . . . Notices Historiques,* vol. ix, pp. 55 *et seq.*

. . . Engineers will be sent over. . . . Money will be easy to procure when we have the concession signed by Mehemet Ali." [1] England's attitude would be the only obstacle, but this, thought Enfantin, " will give way before the recognized interest of all other peoples. . . ." [2]

There was indeed some reason to expect that Mehemet Ali would be favorably disposed. The profound admiration which he had for Napoleon, he quite naturally extended to all Frenchmen. In his efforts to westernize Egypt, he turned to France for military and naval experts, engineers, chemists, astronomers, savants, physicians, professors and architects. The army was reorganized, and the navy rebuilt after Navarino; schools were founded, industries established, and the resources of the country developed. So great was French influence, that an English writer declared: " There is no nation which has contributed so much to the civilization and to the development of Egypt as France." [3] Moreover, the Viceroy was interested in the problem of communications, as the rebuilding of the ancient canal between the Nile and Alexandria in 1818 shows.

But if Enfantin counted on the good will of the Viceroy for France in order to secure a concession for the canal, he was far too optimistic. Mehemet Ali had no desire to displease England and refused to permit the construction of a canal.[4] This refusal together with the death and desertion of some of his disciples, caused Enfantin to return to France in 1837.

The failure of the Saint-Simonians to win the approval of Mehemet Ali to their project, did not discourage En-

[1] *Ibid.*, p. 40.

[2] *Ibid.*, p. 83.

[3] Bowring, *Report on Egypt, 1840*, cited by Dubois and Terrier, *Un siècle d'expansion coloniale française, 1800-1900* (Paris, 1902), p. 165.

[4] C. de Freycinet, *op. cit.*, p. 107.

fantin. For some years after his return to France, he continued his agitation for a canal. Assisted by some of his disciples, he sought to interest the French people in his project. "Little by little," he said some years later, "the French press began to concern itself with the communication of the two seas as one of the highest questions of international politics. . . . Journals, books propagated, popularized that great idea of the union of the two worlds, of the Orient and the Occident, of Musselmen and Christians." [1] Saint-Simonians prepared statistics of the trade of England and France with the East, and studied the possibilities of getting financial assistance in Germany for the moment when they could realize their project.[2] One of them, Michel Chevalier, advocated a " System of the Mediterranean," whose object was to conciliate the interests of the East with those of the West as a step toward universal peace and association.[3] This association, thought Chevalier, could be brought about by improving the means of communication.

Let us conceive that, advancing civilization before it, Europe extends itself little by little upon Asia, by the Russians to the north, by the English to the center, by Turkey to the west; let us suppose that, from their side, the Americans expand it to the East; let us imagine that, in order to put in action the double current which from America and from Europe comes to visit old Asia, the two Isthmuses of Suez and Panama are cut, and let us represent, if it is still possible, the delightful picture which the ancient continent will soon present.[4]

---

[1] Dr. Georgi and Albert Dufour-Feronce, *Urkunden zur Geschichte des Suezkanals* (Leipzig, 1913), p. 11.

[2] *Ibid.*

[3] M. Chevalier, " Système de la Méditerranée ", *Religion Saint-Simonienne, politique industrielle* (Paris, 1832), pp. 101-127. *Cf.* J. C. T. Roux, *op. cit.*, vol. i, p. 198.

[4] *Ibid.*, p. 102.

Chevalier was a firm believer in the possibility of constructing a canal connecting the Mediterranean with the Red Sea. Though he accepted the legend of the difference of levels of the two seas, he considered it of no great consequence and held that a direct canal would still be possible. " It does not appear to me that there is any other way of cutting the Isthmus of Suez, in the general interests of commerce, than of projecting a direct canal from Suez to the Mediterranean." [1]

While the Saint-Simonians were busily propagating the idea of a canal across the Isthmus of Suez, Lamartine tried to warn his countrymen against nourishing any design on Egypt. His warning was directed against the policy which Thiers was pursuing and which, he thought, would lead to war with England. A visit to the Near East had convinced him that the Ottoman Empire must soon fall. This would bring Russia to Constantinople and England to Cairo.[2] In order to secure some compensation for France, he proposed a novel scheme. Troops should be sent to Syria which should be proclaimed under the sovereignty of Turkey and the guarantee of France. This accomplished, a congress should be called at Vienna where France and Austria would force a settlement on the basis of a general protectorate over the Ottoman Empire. Each of the four Powers would then be given a special protectorate: the Black Sea and its mouth to Russia; the shores of the Adriatic to Austria; Syria, the Euphrates Valley, Rhodes and Cyprus to France; Egypt and the Suez passage to England.[3]

That Egypt and the route to India should fall to England, seemed to Lamartine a legitimate aim. He treated with

[1] Cited in J. C. T. Roux, *op. cit.*, vol. i, p. 207.
[2] *Ibid.*, p. 178.
[3] *Ibid.*, p. 179.

scorn the interest of France in Egypt and warned her against trying to prevent England from establishing herself there.

England will accept a century of war on the Mediterranean with us and the whole world rather than concede the keys of Suez to a legitimate sovereign supported by the hostile influence of France in Egypt. Why? Because England being mistress of 75 million subjects in India, and Suez being today and in the future, the gate to her immense Indian Empire, she could not allow that gate to be closed to her power, policy, and commerce, without defending it to the bitter end. You have at Algiers only 3000 colonists and an eternal battlefield; but if a power tried to set up a barrier between Algiers and yourselves, you would fight to the end. What then would not England do for the richest and vastest empire that a state has ever conquered? [1]

Referring to the regions which might fall to France with the dismemberment of the Ottoman Empire, he asked:

Egypt? It is still more impossible. I have said and you must yourselves be convinced that England will fight to the last ditch before permitting French power to close Suez, directly or indirectly. Do you want proof? You need only mention the name of a Syrian-Egyptian Empire protected by France, and immediately the English alliance will be torn; coalitions will form again, the world will be upset and France compelled to take arms.[2]

[1] *Ibid.*, p. 179. Lamartine in *Journal de Saône-et-Loire,* Aug. 29, 1840.
[2] *Ibid.*, p. 180. *Journal de Saône-et-Loire,* Aug. 30, 1840.

## CHAPTER VII

### METTERNICH MAKES AN OFFER

WHILE France and England were seeking to advance their influence in Egypt at the expense of the Viceroy, the Austrian Government became interested in the question of a canal. As far back as 1818 Austria had sought to induce Mehemet Ali to favor her commerce with India through Egypt.[1]

In 1842 a copy of M. Linant's report on the canal was given by the Viceroy to Laurin, the Austrian Consul-General, who in turn submitted it to Metternich.[2] Mehemet Ali, for his part, had no intention of undertaking the work immediately, since he believed that the prior construction of a Nile dam would be more advantageous to Egypt. With this view Laurin did not agree. He pointed out to the Viceroy that his "interest and his glory lies with accomplishing the connection of the two seas," while the dam could be built later from the revenues of the canal.[3] The agents of France and Russia took the same stand and warned Mehemet Ali that the canal could be executed without his cooperation. He feared, however, that once the canal were constructed, England would get possession of it. "I did not fail to

---

[1] Arch. Aff. Étr., Corr. Cons., Alexandrie, 1818-1820, no. 48, Fr. Consul, Alexandria, June 9, 1818. For the earlier projects of Austria see ch. ii, pp. 46; ch. iii, pp. 51-52.

[2] HHSA, Enclosure in Ad. Reg. Fach 13, Suez Canal, 1842-1869, Laurin to Metternich, Cairo, Dec. 24, 1842.

[3] *Ibid.*, Laurin to Metternich, Cairo, Feb. 1, 1843.

assure Mehemet Ali," wrote Laurin, " that the canal would be a guarantee for the permanent possession of Egypt by his family, for as all Europe has an interest that this great commercial highway should not fall to some one power . . . the canal would be of no less importance than the Bosphorus." The Viceroy thereupon demanded guarantees which would assure to him and his successors the possession of the canal, and would give him the right to levy tolls for defraying the cost of construction and upkeep, as well as providing a reasonable income. He suggested that Austria should intervene with the other Powers to secure these guarantees.[1]

Metternich was much interested in the project. " I consider the canal," he said, " as a world event of the first importance . . . and place it among the occurrences which mark epochs of great development. I am convinced that it will open a future for Austria . . . and the more I recognize the importance of the subject . . . the more I feel called upon to devote to it my earnest attention." [2] While not prepared to assume the initiative in regard to the guarantees, he was willing to support them.[3]

These views were shared by other members of the government who were convinced that a canal would direct a large part of the eastern trade to Austrian harbors. Studies were made of the home products which could be exchanged for those of the East. Metternich was told that the Viceroy recognized the importance of Austria's participation in this trade, and would promote it as much as possible. " From my standpoint," he said, " I shall do everything to induce the Pasha to occupy himself with the construction of the

[1] *Ibid.*, May 19, 1844.

[2] *Ibid.*, Metternich to Kübeck, Hofkammer Präsident, Vienna, April 28, 1843.

[3] *Ibid.*, Metternich to Laurin, April 25, 1843. By way of Constantinople.

Suez Canal, and with the elimination of everything which stands in the way of that enterprise." [1]

A memoir presented to Metternich by Count Fiquelmont in March 1843 discussed the political difficulties confronting the realization of the project.[2] Chief among these was the attitude of England.

The establishment of the canal . . . projected by Mehemet Ali would . . . increase the greed of England; the interests are too gigantic for her to resist; the Government, moreover, will be constantly pressed by the India Company, by the City of London, and by merchants of Calcutta; these three centers of action, of which one alone has sufficed in the past to stir up all Asia from Afghanistan to China, to combine in the same interest, will necessarily conduct England, sooner or later, . . . to an enterprise in which she will allow herself to be easily led.

That event cannot fail to occur some day, but meanwhile it will bring England, in order to be prepared out of the policy of preservation which she has adopted relative to the Ottoman Empire; for it is only by disturbing that empire that she will arrive at the possession of Egypt.

If it were only a question of commerce, she would be satisfied to see a canal open to navigation which, although placed at the disposal of the entire world, would yet assure greater advantages to her than to others because her commerce is the most considerable and because it is a matter of connecting the metropolis with her vast possessions in Asia; but England will be led to desire more: she will wish to make Egypt a vast armed camp, in order to protect and defend an empire which . . . without this establishment is rendered more difficult if not . . . impossible to conceive.

In the meantime Laurin was bending every effort to persuade the Viceroy to undertake the construction of a canal.

[1] *Ibid.*, Metternich to Kübeck, Vienna, April 28, 1843.

[2] *Ibid.*, Considérations sur l'établissement d'une canal de navigation qui réunirait la Mer Rouge à la Méditerranée, Vienna, Mar. 2, 1843.

Although the Austrian agent was able to win the support of the Egyptian ministers,[1] the Viceroy still held back, declaring that he would give his consent only when an acceptable offer was made concerning the guarantees.[2] Without them he would do nothing, for he was alive to the dangers which might arise from the Anglo-French rivalry, both for his own power and for the welfare of his country. That rivalry was now becoming more pronounced than ever. French merchants were planning to establish a direct steamship line from Marseilles to Alexandria to compete with the English line from London by way of Malta. To this the Viceroy was not opposed, for he considered that it might make him less dependent on the Peninsular and Oriental Company. When the news reached England, however, an agent was sent in all haste to oppose the French scheme and to offer the Viceroy funds to construct a railway from Alexandria to Suez. This, in turn, caused the French to defend the canal project more vigorously than ever, and they prevailed upon Mehemet Ali to reject the English offer.[3]

The old Pasha was frankly alarmed by this rivalry and concluded that any transit through Egypt would in the end become a source of annoyance to him. Thus, if a canal were to be built, he preferred that it should be on the outskirts of the country.[4] Meanwhile, he had been told that the English intended to secure a right-of-way from Alexandria to Suez free from " any encroachment by Mehemet Ali and his successors." [5] Since this could only mean that Alexandria and Suez would become " English ports," he

---

[1] *Ibid.*, Telegram from Laurin, April 25, 1843.

[2] *Ibid.*, Laurin to Metternich, Jan. 10, 1843.

[3] *Ibid.*

[4] *Ibid.*, Laurin to Metternich, May 16, 1844.

[5] *Ibid.*, May 19, 1844.

was prepared to offset this danger by constructing a canal if the necessary guarantees could be secured.[1]

It appeared to Metternich that the time had come to make definite proposals concerning the guarantees in question. He communicated these to Laurin with the request that the Viceroy be confidentially informed.[2] What he suggested was a general European agreement which would guarantee reimbursement for the cost of construction, and the upkeep and protection of the canal. A part of the revenues should be turned over to Turkey in order " to give her an immediate interest in the enterprise." To assure the possession of the canal to Mehemet Ali and his heirs, it would be necessary for the Powers and the Porte, whose sovereignty must be acknowledged, to settle this question. The intervention of the Porte, in Metternich's opinion, was absolutely necessary, for only in this way could " the Powers create a lasting work."

In communicating these proposals Laurin thought it best to omit those parts concerning the intervention of the Porte. The Viceroy was highly pleased and declared that he had only two desires to realize during his lifetime: the canal and the Nile dam.[3] He intimated, however, " that he would extremely dislike any intervention of the Porte." As Laurin realized, this attitude of the Viceroy's was enough to wreck the scheme.

Though the Austrian negotiations had apparently failed, interest in the subject continued as lively as before. On August 25, 1845, the Leipzig Society, a group organized for the express purpose of propagating the idea of a canal,

---

[1] Ibid.

[2] Ibid., Metternich to Laurin, Ischl, Aug. 6, 1844.

[3] Ibid., Laurin to Metternich, ZL. 21918, Alexandria, Sept. 19, 1844.

submitted a memorial to Metternich.[1] For several years the Society had gathered information concerning the probable influence of a canal on European, but especially German, commerce. They believed that with the canal established, Germany could import her products directly from the Orient instead of depending on the English as it was now necessary to do. This, in turn, would enable German manufacturers to compete with the English on more favorable terms. " Although the English would also enjoy the advantages of the canal, it cannot escape their acuteness that relatively more advantages would result from such an establishment for the Continent, and it is because of this that the enterprise is never seriously promoted in England."

The Society enclosed a letter from one of its agents in Egypt who had made a careful study of the possibilities of constructing a canal, and of the political difficulties confronting its realization. In an interview with Mehemet Ali on January 30, 1845, he discussed the geographical and political importance of Egypt, the interest displayed by the European Cabinets in the Egyptian question, and the "glory" which this canal would give to the reign of Mehemet Ali.

Egypt is the principal link in the chain which should bind the Occident and the ancient Orient—the rendezvous of the Indian, Chinese and European races which would gather there some day to cement the act of their union. The policy of His Highness and that of his dynasty can retard or accelerate the consummation of this union, which alone can give to his kingdom wealth, power, the political preponderance that its geographic position assigns to it; what I say of the possible destinies of Egypt is not a dream. With a territory less considerable than that possessed by His Highness, the Pharaohs were masters of the world. . . . The great traffic by the Cape has caused

[1] *Ibid.*, Leipziger Gesellschaft, Anträge behufs der Anlegung eines Kanals auf der Landenge von Suez, April 25, 1845.

Egypt to lose all its advantages, and it is for her to recover
them, and this is possible. . . .

The agent went on to show the advantages of the canal
for Egypt.  It would be a source of revenue which would
enable Mehemet Ali to promote the commerce, industry and
agriculture of the country.  The canal, he stated, " is not
only capable of being realized, but it is easy, its execution
will make the Pasha of Egypt the object of universal glory.
All Europe would become interested in maintaining his
powerful dynasty. . . . The Suez Canal would have the
immense advantage of being at once an Egyptian and a
European work. . . ."

The Viceroy listened attentively to this discourse and then
replied: " Yes, Austria and France may desire the canal,
but England, but Russia !"  The agent recognized this difficulty, but countered

that the position of the English Government in this question
was delicate, that it was possible it did not desire the execution
of this project, but that it was impossible that it would oppose
it.  The interests of the India Company are too powerful in
England and weigh too heavily in the counsels of her Britannic
Majesty, for her to dare to make a serious opposition.  The
Government can refuse its intervention, but it will not dare
to stand against it.  Thus its part would be limited to neutrality.
. . . As to Russia, she is only too desirous of intervening in
Mediterranean affairs in order that her vessels can be called
there. . . . .

The Viceroy seemed convinced and replied: " Well then, let
the Great Powers come to an understanding and demand it
of me and I am prepared to execute it.  Egypt does not lack
men; I can employ my whole army."

It was, as the agent perceived, the fear of England which
disturbed the Viceroy most of all.  It would therefore be

necessary to submit the question to the European Governments.

The first court to which it should be addressed, is Austria, whose sympathies have already been shown; the second, is that of the English Company; the third, Prussia; the fourth, Russia. The intervention of the secondary states can be utilized in order to engage that of the Powers of the first order. The support of France is assured when it will be necessary. The India Company will neutralize the British Cabinet. . . . The time for this work has arrived, and it is even urgent to take it up. The death of Mehemet Ali can occasion disorders, civil war, a new anarchy which will retard the execution a long time; it is necessary to profit from the last years which Providence has reserved to him in order to begin. . . .

# CHAPTER VIII

### Technical Studies: The Société d'Études

HARDLY had the Austrian negotiations come to an end, before an unofficial international financial and Saint-Simonian group undertook the project for the canal. This group, the *Société d'Études du canal de Suez,* was organized by Enfantin on November 27, 1846.[1] Among its members were former Saint-Simonians, engineers, representatives of banking and commercial houses, and some of the leading personages of France: Louis Philippe, Guizot, the Duke of Joinville and the Marquis de La Valette, who had served in Egypt for several years as the French Consul-General.[2] All countries were invited to join, but in recognition of the importance of the question to England, France and Austria, groups representing these powers were given charge of the work. The aim of the Société was to study the possibilities of constructing a canal across the Isthmus, to determine the main difficulties, and to estimate the cost. It would then construct the canal through the assistance of European capitalists and without the interference or the aid of the Powers. Paris was made the headquarters, and the capital was fixed at 150,000 francs, divided into three parts of 50,000 francs each.[3]

[1] Details concerning the formation of the Société will be found in Dr. Georgi and Albert Dufour-Feronce, *Urkunden zur Geschichte des Suez-kanals* (Leipzig, 1913), and in J. C. T. Roux, *op. cit.,* vol. i, p. 207 and annex 9.

[2] HHSA, Fach 13, Suez Canal 1842-69, ad. $\frac{2\ 415}{CP}$, **Paris, Nov. 30, 1846,** Negrelli to Kübeck, submitted to Metternich.

[3] Georgi and Dufour-Feronce, *op. cit.,* p. 29.

At the first meeting of the Société on November 27, 1846 the work of each group was decided upon. Austrian engineers under Negrelli, an employee of the General Office of the Austrian State Railway, were to find a suitable port on the Mediterranean coast. The English group, headed by Robert Stephenson, was commissioned to study the port of Suez. Practically everything else in connection with the project was left to the French group under Paulin Talabot. It was decided that the three groups should carry on their studies in Egypt. The Société received financial assistance from the Chambers of Commerce of Lyons, Marseilles, Trieste, Venice and Prague.

While permitting Negrelli to participate as a private engineer without any official character, Metternich was doubtful of success. He recognized that the canal would facilitate communication with the Orient and would be of the greatest advantage to Austria.

But [he said] it is just this circumstance—the facility of communication, which will in my opinion render the success of the plan doubtful. The English Government not only will not permit it, but, on account of British commercial interests as well as military-political considerations, will prevent it with all the means it commands. . . . A private company will not be allowed to bring the project into life without the assistance of the governments whose harmony is indispensable for its promotion. . . . [1]

In the meantime the Austrian Government would await results but its attitude would be "entirely passive." [2]

The success of the new group would, of course, depend to a large extent upon the willingness of the Viceroy to grant a concession. Having already refused the offers of the Saint-

[1] HHSA, Fach 13, Metternich to Kübeck, Schloss-Königswart, Aug. 4, 1846.
[2] *Ibid.*

Simonians and the Austrian Government, it was hardly to be expected that he would now adopt a different attitude. Yet, when he first heard of the Société, Mehemet Ali seemed to be favorably disposed and quite willing to facilitate its work, but he foresaw three main obstacles to its success.[1] First of all would be the "hidden or expressed opposition" of England. He believed that England stood to lose by the construction of a canal which would be open to the commerce of the Mediterranean countries. Moreover, England had a political interest in the question: to keep her possessions in India as far as possible from European contact. The French Consul-General to whom the Viceroy expressed this opinion, agreed that England would oppose the canal but declared that she would construct it herself if she were in possession of Egypt. Then she would be in a position to regulate navigation to suit herself. "It is for this reason," continued the Consul General, "that she presses the Viceroy to construct a railway between Cairo and Suez, which, while contributing to make the canal appear useless, will be exclusively advantageous for English travelers and will moreover serve . . . her future designs on this country."

The second difficulty envisaged by the Viceroy was that he himself would never entrust to a private company the construction, still less the exploitation, of the canal. He had the means for construction "without the help of foreign capital."

Finally, there was the attitude of the Austrian Government "which does not seem to be animated by very benevolent intentions for the government of His Highness." Metternich, as we have seen, considered that the intervention of the Porte would be necessary. In the opinion of the French Consul-General this would be sufficient "to destroy the project" and would, moreover, be contrary to the ideas of

---

[1] Égypte, vol. 19, no. 75, Barrot to Guizot, Cairo, Feb. 6, 1847.

law and justice. The Viceroy would never consent to this intervention. It was rumored that the Société would address itself directly to the Porte for authorization to make the preparatory studies and later to execute the project.[1] " The Viceroy of Egypt will . . . merely be considered as an ordinary governor of a province, charged with executing the orders transmitted to him from Constantinople." Mehemet Ali suspected that Austria was back of this scheme. The French Consul-General tells us that Laurin, " of whose bad disposition for the Viceroy there can be no doubt," was displaying " a very lively interest " in the affair.[2] However, while Laurin was instructed to facilitate the work of the Austrian engineers in every way, he was warned to act with the " utmost caution and reserve," and to " *abstain vigorously from any interference and expression which might have the character of publicity or of a direct participation of the government.*" [3]

The Austrian engineers were the first to reach Egypt. When informed of their arrival the Viceroy seemed none too pleased. " This affair of the Suez Canal," he said, " can give way to one of those complications . . . that I have sought more than anyone to avoid. It seems evident to me that there is some plot against me in this affair." [4] He was convinced that the Austrian Government had " taken it very much to heart," and he was distrustful of anything which came from that quarter.

> I declare to you [he said to the French Consul-General] that not only will I never lend my approval to an enterprise thus formed and conducted, but more . . . I will oppose to it the liveliest resistance. I am so much decided upon this, that if

[1] *Ibid.*, no. 80, Barrot to Guizot, Cairo, Mar. 26, 1847.

[2] *Ibid.*

[3] HHSA, Fach 13, Metternich to Laurin, Mar. 27, 1847.

[4] Égypte, vol. 19, no. 82, Barrot to Guizot, April 16, 1847.

today the great European Powers declared to me that it would be necessary to accept this humiliation or to abdicate the government of Egypt, I would not hesitate to take the last step.

The French Consul-General was alarmed lest this attitude should prompt the Viceroy to abandon altogether his interest in the canal. He thus tried to reassure him by declaring that the importance of the affair had been exaggerated, that it would take the engineers at least two years to complete their studies, and that the enterprise might then be shown to be impossible of execution. In the meantime, Mehemet Ali could count on the sympathies of the French Government, which recognized the importance of having the canal remain Egyptian. Yet the Consul-General himself believed that because of political difficulties, it would be necessary to submit the question to the Powers, including Turkey. In this case, however, France would warmly support the interest of the Viceroy. The latter's doubts were not so easily allayed and he demanded that once the political affairs were regulated, the canal should be turned over to Egypt. He was still of the opinion that the Austrian Government nourished " malevolent sentiments " against him.

Austria [he said] wishes me ill, she can do nothing by herself but in every circumstance her Consul-General threatens me with the intervention of the Porte; it is by the Porte that she seeks to harm me, when the occasion will present itself to her. She believes that she has found it in the project of the Isthmus of Suez. She will find, I know, a powerful auxiliary in her hatred for me in Reshid Pasha, who esteems himself happy every time he can manifest the aversion he has for Mehemet Ali.

In the meantime, he would have nothing to do with the Société; would neither oppose its work nor give it any manner of support.

The suspicion which Mehemet Ali entertained of the Austrian Government caused no little anxiety in France, and

Guizot instructed the Chargé d'Affaires at Vienna to sound out the Imperial Cabinet on the subject.[1] The Chargé was informed by Metternich that the Viceroy had no reason to be alarmed since the Austrian Government was not opposed to his determination to execute the canal himself. Thus reassured, Mehemet Ali declared: " I will cut the Isthmus as soon as the Powers come to an understanding on the subject." [2]

The Viceroy did not, as he had threatened, refuse assistance to the engineers. Indeed, he facilitated their work in every way and even defrayed their expenses, a matter of 100,000 francs. The Austrian group, having completed its study, submitted a report which concluded that the construction of a canal would be practical, that however great the technical difficulties, they could be overcome, and that the probable cost would be from sixty to one hundred million francs.[3] The Viceroy was satisfied. If the Powers agreed, if only Russia would come out strongly for the project, he would go ahead with it.[4] England would then remain isolated and could do no harm.

The report of the French engineers was also encouraging and more important for the future. They had studied the problem of whether the level of the Red Sea was actually higher than that of the Mediterranean, as Le Père and Linant had supposed. Their study, carried on in 1846-1847, revealed that there existed practically no difference in the levels.[5] This, of course, made possible a sea-level canal

[1] *Ibid.*, no. 27, Guizot to Benedetti, Paris, June 9, 1847.

[2] *Ibid.*, no. 7, Benedetti to Guizot, Alexandria, July 9, 1847.

[3] *Ibid.*

[4] HHSA, Fach 13, Laurin to Metternich, Alexandria, July 7, 1847.

[5] See article by Paulin Talabot, "Canal de Suez," *Revue des deux mondes*, May 1, 1855, pp. 31 *et seq*. *Cf*. Égypte, vol. 25, no. 29, Sabatier to Drouyn de Lhuys, Cairo, May 15, 1853, enclosure of report of Linant de Bellefonds.

across the Isthmus and removed the fear of inundating the country.

The three groups were not agreed as to how the canal should be constructed. Negrelli favored a direct sea-level canal, while Paulin Talabot believed this impracticable since it would be difficult to maintain the proper depth. He therefore advocated an indirect canal from Suez to Alexandria derived from the Nile and employing twelve locks. The proposed channel would be 392 kilometers long, 100 meters wide at water-level and 8 meters deep. The majority of the members favored this scheme. On the other hand, Stephenson believed that a canal would be impracticable and preferred a railway instead. More will be said about his attitude later.

Having thus completed its study, the Société could make no further progress. Mehemet Ali adhered to his policy of refusing to permit a foreign company to execute the work. Moreover, the revolutions of 1848 had set all Europe in turmoil and it was obvious that nothing could be done until a more favorable moment arose. In the meantime, the Société was forced to admit that only with the support of the Powers could the project succeed.[1]

Let us [said Enfantin] offer to the Diplomats the results of our labors and the support of the three engineers whose great idea can lead Europe to the pacific conquest of the Orient; let us see that our three Powers develop the germ we have hatched, let us request them to charge us officially in the interest of all, to realize the beautiful dream we have conceived; let us yield our studies to the Powers and obtain from them the means for their realization.[2]

The unsuccessful attempt of the Société to realize the

[1] HHSA, Fach 13, Negrelli to Metternich, Verona, Oct. 3, 1848.
[2] *Ibid.*, enclosure, letter from Enfantin to Negrelli, Paris, Aug. 23, 1848.

project for a canal independently of the Powers made it more apparent than ever that after all it was a matter for diplomacy. The Viceroy's insistence on the approval of the Powers, his objections to the intervention of the Porte, his suspicions of Austria and his fear of displeasing England, all contributed to block the enterprise. The opposition of England was in part due to the predominantly French character of the Société, but more especially to the English belief that a railway was more satisfactory than a canal. To this subject we shall turn in the next chapter.

# CHAPTER IX

## THE ENGLISH RAILWAY OR THE FRENCH CANAL

THE railway project made a strong bid for the Viceroy's favor and it became a powerful factor in the Anglo-French struggle for influence in Egypt. In 1834 Mehemet Ali commissioned an English engineer, Galloway-Bey, to make a survey for the route from Alexandria to Suez.[1] Upon completing his task, Galloway was sent to England in order to secure the approval of the British Cabinet for the proposed tariff on merchandise conveyed over the line. Anticipating no difficulties from this quarter, Galloway ordered the iron rails, ties and other equipment. But when the matter was presented to the Cabinet, it was rejected, largely because of the strained relations then existing between the Porte and the Viceroy.[2] Moreover, the scheme had aroused the opposition of France. When Galloway died in 1835, it was allowed to drop. The rails which had arrived in Egypt " were left to rust, the wooden ties were piled up and left to rot, while the railway became for the time being only a subject for speculation." [3]

A few years later the project was again brought up and the Viceroy was ready to execute it provided the British Government would consent to have its mails conveyed over

[1] FO 97/411, Suez Canal 1833-51, vol. i, Pamphlet by John Alexander Galloway, *Observations on the proposed improvements in the Overland Route via Egypt with remarks on the Ship Canal, the Boulac Canal, and the Suez Railroad* (London, 1844).

[2] H. L. Hoskins, *op. cit.,* 232.

[3] *Ibid.*

the railroad for a certain payment.  Once more the Cabinet refused, considering that the situation in the Near East was too unsettled to warrant the construction of a railway in Egypt.[1]

In France the project was suspiciously regarded as a maneuver designed to bolster English influence in Egypt. It was also looked upon as a threat to the canal because the usefulness of the latter would be lessened by the competition of a railroad.  Though England had twice rejected the proposals of the Viceroy, it was not long before she came out openly in support of the railway.  The result was that the two projects became opposing pawns, with France pushing the one and England the other.

Mehemet Ali was now the target for the intrigues of French and English agents.  He found his position somewhat embarrassing.  He was vexed by the French opposition to the railway which he considered as responsible for his present difficulty.[2]  But the French Consul-General reassured him that France desired only his best interests, and that in opposing the railway she was merely seeking to prevent English domination of Egypt.[3]  Pressed continually by the agents of the two Powers, the Viceroy announced that he would not consent to either project until after the construction of the Nile Barrage, which would take at least two years.[4]

Early in 1847 Lord Palmerston directed Mr. Murray, the Consul-General in Egypt, to point out to Mehemet Ali the advantages of the railway.[5]  As to the canal, however, he

[1] *Ibid.,* p. 239, Hoskins says that the Cabinet was unwilling " to endanger the recent arrangement concerning Egypt."

[2] Égypte, vol. 18, no. 38, Barrot to Guizot, Cairo, Mar. 23, 1846.

[3] *Ibid.*

[4] *Ibid.,* no. 40, Alexandria, Sept. 8, 1846.

[5] FO 97/411, no. 4, Palmerston to Murray, Feb. 8, 1847.

was to " lose no opportunity of enforcing on the Pasha and
his ministers the costliness, if not the impracticability of
such a project," and he was to make it clear " that the persons who press upon the Pasha such a chimerical scheme do
so evidently for the purpose of diverting him from the railway which would be perfectly practicable and comparatively
cheap." Murray was personally hostile to the canal and
when he received information (in this case erroneous) that
the Austrian engineers were unfavorable to the scheme, he
exultantly concluded " that we may safely number the Suez
Ship Canal among the most visionary projects of the day." [1]

At Constantinople Lord Cowley, the British Ambassador,
secured the promise of Reshid Pasha, the Grand Vizir, that
the Porte would express to Mehemet Ali its preference for
the railway.[2] A Turkish official, Cheoket Bey, was sent to
Egypt as the bearer of this message. But the Viceroy rejected the overture and informed Cheoket Bey that he would
sanction neither of the projects.[3] He made a similar statement to the French Consul-General.

I had known it for a long time [wrote the Consul-General]
and this declaration did not surprise me; the facilities which
His Highness has given the engineers charged with making the
preparatory studies for cutting the Isthmus, are only to satisfy
public opinion in France and Austria; he is happy to be able
to count upon the support of England to refuse the canal and
on France and Austria to oppose the railway.[4]

The Viceroy said, however, that he would undertake which-
ever project was accepted by the Powers.

I was content to say to him that if Egypt should one day

[1] *Ibid.,* no. 44, Murray to Palmerston, Alexandria, July 9, 1847.

[2] *Ibid.,* no. 215, Cowley to Palmerston, Therapia, July 3, 1847.

[3] *Ibid.,* October 17, 1847.

[4] Égypte, vol. 19, Barrot to Guizot, Cairo, Dec. 6, 1847.

become a great route toward Europe and India, it would be better that it should be open by means of a canal to the passage of all European nations who would naturally control it, than the construction of a railway which would make the passage through Egypt the monopoly of England, that is to say, the nation which most ardently covets the possession of this country, and which would not be slow to make of this concession . . . a pretext and a means of arriving at her ends.[1]

This suspicion of English designs on Egypt is repeatedly mentioned in the French dispatches. It is well brought out in the following of March 18, 1848.[2]

Egypt is, without contradiction, by its geographic position, one of the most important points of the globe, . . . the direct route to India. It is not, therefore, astonishing that England has always had her eyes fixed on this country, that for some years especially it has been the object of her liveliest ambitions. The peace which Europe has enjoyed for thirty-three years has not furnished her the occasion to realize the projects which she, without doubt, has concerning Egypt. But it is certain that she will profit from the first occasion which presents itself in order to possess it. When the pretext offers itself, the motives will not be lacking. These motives are evident.

When the Cape of Good Hope was made the route to India, England's first preoccupation was to control it and she occupied Ascension, St. Helena, the Cape. Now that the passage is open by the Isthmus of Suez and the Red Sea, she lacks only Egypt in order to be completely mistress of this route so direct and so rapid from her Western to her Eastern Empire. She has Gibraltar, Malta, and still other possessions in the Mediterranean; on the other side of the Isthmus, she has established herself at Aden and other places. . . . From the entrance of the Red Sea she has exclusive control of the sea as far as India. Egypt alone blocks the way from either coast; it is natural that she is irritated at this obstacle, that she is impatient to open this

[1] *Ibid.*

[2] *Ibid.*, vol. 20, no. 1, Barrot to Guizot, Alexandria, Mar. 18, 1848.

route. I would say furthermore . . . that the possession of Egypt is a necessity for the existence of England: for it would be the most severe check to her power, if this country falls into the hands of another great European Power, especially France, who would then find herself situated between the needs and the resources of England, able to attack how and when she wished the vital elements of her commercial prosperity. India would no longer be secure if the passage were open through Egypt to powerful enemies of England; it would be more dangerous to her than if France occupied a province of Great Britain. This is clearly understood by the British Government. . . . The events of 1840 are enough to show the disposition of England towards Egypt. It is true that she has given proof of her moderation and wisdom during the peace . . . but we may be certain . . . that if England finds herself engaged in war . . . her first endeavor will be to occupy Egypt. She is, no doubt, prepared for it today.

Even more conclusive was the report of Laurin in March 1849 to that effect that the French, regarding the railway as "a means of bringing Egypt into the hands of the English," had won from the Viceroy a pledge never to undertake the project.[1]

Not for long, however, did the French opposition remain so firmly intrenched. The aged Viceroy, now in his eighty-first year, was unsound in mind, unable to conduct the government; his reign was obviously drawing to a close. Even before the end came, the British were sufficiently forehanded to enter into negotiations with his nephew and prospective successor, Abbas Pasha. In March 1849 Sir John Pirie, former Lord Mayor of London, accompanied by Murray and several directors of the Peninsular and Oriental Company, arrived in Egypt with instructions to propose a railway from Alexandria to Suez.[2] He was prepared to offer

[1] HHSA, Fach 13, no. 308, Laurin to Schwarzenberg, Alexandria, Mar. 17, 1849.
[2] *Ibid.*

financial assistance if the Egyptian Government would undertake to construct the line. So confident was Sir John of his success, that he spoke of the railway as if it were a settled matter; all that remained was to demand the concession which would immediately be granted.[1] But Abbas, not wishing to be hurried into so important an undertaking, refused to consider the employment of foreign capital and dismissed the delegation "without a friendly smile."[2] "Egypt," he said, "is not today rich enough to construct the railway . . . as to permitting foreigners to build it, in what country of Europe has a concession of this kind been made to foreigners? Egypt will not build the railway and will not allow others to do so."[3]

Although Abbas rejected Sir John's offer, he gradually became more and more amenable to British influence. Succeeding his uncle as Viceroy on August 21, 1849, he soon showed his Anglophile tendency by discharging many Frenchmen and by cancelling French projects.[4] So friendly an ear did he lend to the persuasion of the British agents, who became daily more insistent in their demands for the railway, that by October 1850 he was ready to discuss the subject with the engineer Stephenson. He agreed to the construction of the railway on condition that he should supply the labor and capital himself, and that in order to lessen the French opposition, the line should be constructed in two sections, the first running from Alexandria to Cairo, the second from Cairo to Suez.[5] Meanwhile, the French

[1] Égypte, vol. 21, no. 56, Barrot to Minister, Cairo, Mar. 17, 1849.

[2] HHSA, Fach 13, no. 308, Laurin to Schwarzenberg, Mar. 17, 1849.

[3] Égypte, vol. 21, no. 56, Barrot to Minister, Cairo, Mar. 17, 1849.

[4] HHSA, Fach 13, Huber to FO, Alexandria, May 23 and Sept. 24, 1850.

[5] Par. Paper, 1851, no. 605, pp. 223-224. Examination of Robert Stephenson by Select Committee of House of Commons. Cited by Hoskins, op. cit., p. 302.

looked on with bitterness and suspicion. The French Consul-General, LeMoyne, described the new Viceroy as a man of " fantastic " character, habituated to " easy despotism," intolerant to contradiction, and susceptible to flattery.[1] Egypt, LeMoyne declared, was in danger of becoming a British protectorate.

Not only France, but also Austria was becoming alarmed at the waxing influence of England in Egypt. The Austrian agent at Cairo believed that Abbas was himself suspicious and desired the support of the other Powers against English pressure. " Since he distrusts France," he wrote, " it is natural that he places his hopes in the remaining Continental Powers. . . ."[2] He proposed that Austria should seize the opportunity for resuming negotiations relative to the canal. " These negotiations would be a splendid defense against any selfish designs of England on Egypt. The Porte will not seriously resist the Great Powers and Abbas Pasha, I am firmly convinced, . . . will, upon the request of the collective Powers, offer himself for the work and bear the cost." But he urged haste or France would step in and " carry off the prize." The Austrian Consul-General was also active in promoting the canal project. " A gigantic task," he said to Abbas, " which would open up the shortest route to India and the hinterland and would bring to its projector a fame exceeding that of the pyramid builders.[3] Abbas replied that he had the necessary means to execute the work but it was impossible so long as the Powers were not agreed. " It is not in Egypt but in Constantinople that the question must be decided. I need only a decided order from my master, the Sultan, and I shall

[1] Égypte, vol. 23, LeMoyne to Minister, Cairo, Dec. 29, 1851.

[2] HHSA, Fach 13, Becke to Schwarzenberg, Cairo, Jan. 5, 1850.

[3] *Ibid.*, Huber to Schwarzenberg, Alexandria, July 7, 1850.

vouch for the execution of the work." [1]  To the French Consul-General he declared it to be one of his ambitions to build a canal; he would do so if France, Russia and Austria would support him.[2]  He desired that these Powers should present their demands simultaneously at the Porte in order to neutralize British opposition to the canal.

While, on the one hand the French agents promoted the canal project, on the other they made every effort to prevent the realization of the railway.  LeMoyne, who kept close watch over the activities of his British colleague, was convinced that the latter was having secret interviews with the Viceroy and was attempting to establish an exclusive influence in Egypt.[3]  At the same time the Marquis de La Valette, Ambassador at Constantinople, endeavored to arouse the anxieties of the Porte by pointing to the complications which the construction of the railway would be almost certain to produce.  The Grand Vizir admitted that the project involved " the greatest inconveniences," and that it could under no circumstances be undertaken without the authorization of the Sultan, nor could it be conceded to a foreign company or financed by means of a foreign loan.[4]  The construction of the railway, declared the Ambassador, could never be justified.  It would have no utility for the inhabitants of Egypt or for the shipment of merchandise, and there would be no returns on the capital invested, or sufficient receipts to cover the cost of operation.  Moreover, there were political factors to consider.  " It is not necessary," he pointed out, " to be endowed with great perspicacity to be assured in advance that the railroad imposes a partial

---

[1] *Ibid.*

[2] Égypte, vol. 21, no. 3, LeMoyne to Minister, Cairo, Feb. 1, 1850.

[3] *Ibid.,* vol. 23, March 26, 1851.

[4] Turquie, vol. 305, no. 9, La Valette to Minister, Therapia, June 4, 1851.

alienation of the liberty of action and independence of the Egyptian Government; that it will consequently be the source of political difficulties which we have every interest to prevent." [1]

Abbas would not admit that the railway was anything more than a domestic enterprise similar to many others undertaken by his uncle, the late Viceroy. Hence there was no need to demand authorization of the Sultan—a viewpoint which was supported by the English Government. [2] Indeed, Sir Stratford Canning informed Reshid Pasha that once the Viceroy had paid his tribute to the Sultan he was free to employ his revenues as he pleased. [3] But so bitter was the French opposition that Canning thought it best to bring about an agreement between the Porte and the Viceroy. He therefore instructed Murray to make every effort to persuade Abbas to defer to the orders of the Porte. [4]

By this time English influence had gained the upper hand in Egypt and Abbas, convinced of Murray's support, paid little heed to Canning's suggestion. On July 18, 1851, without waiting for the Sultan's authorization, and " under pressure of British gold," he signed a contract for the line between Alexandria and Cairo. [5] An English group headed by Mr. Stephenson, was given charge of the construction. The rails, cars, locomotives and other equipment were to be purchased in England.

The announcement of the contract brought forth a storm of protests from the French agents. LeMoyne was con-

[1] *Ibid.*, June 23, 1851.

[2] FO 97/411, no. 195, FO to Sir Stratford Canning, July 24, 1851.

[3] Turquie, vol. 305, no. 9, La Valette to Minister, Therapia, June 4, 1851. Canning maintained that the Sultan's sanction was not necessary for the railway, FO 97/411, no. 195, Canning to FO, July 24, 1851.

[4] *Ibid.*, vol. 306, no. 29, La Valette to Minister, Therapia, June 25, 1851.

[5] Égypte, vol. 23, LeMoyne to Minister, Cairo, Aug. 6, 1851.

vinced that in defying the Sultan, Abbas must have been promised English support. Since he " has thrown himself completely into the arms of England," he declared, France, whose interests and influence were thus compromised, should seize the opportunity of persuading the Sultan to dethrone him on the ground of being " a fool or a rebel." If this were not done, he continued, " we must resign ourselves to see England almost absolute mistress of Egypt, and abandon to her at least the rôle that we ourselves play in Tunis." [1] He did not believe that Canning was sincere in his attempt to induce Abbas to defer to the orders of the Porte. Canning, he said, was " in perfect accord with Murray and far from trying to moderate the Britannic zeal of the latter had, on the contrary, pressed him to reach a conclusion for the railway." [2] As for Abbas, he " has blindly surrendered himself to English influence and has prepared for himself a heavy and dangerous yoke." [3] The Viceroy was completely surrounded by " British machiavellianism." [4]

The English were not slow in making the most of their opportunities. Large numbers of Britons, particularly Scots, " who are notorious for their greediness," flocked into Egypt to make their fortunes.[5] The Viceroy was congratulated by officials of the Peninsular and Oriental Company and by representatives of London merchants. In England, it was declared that the railway was the only means of transportation suitable for Egypt and the only one which would guarantee the interests of all nations. In the case

[1] *Ibid.*, no. 161, copy of a dispatch addressed by Le Moyne to Fr. Ambass. at Constantinople, annexed to no. 154 of July 18, 1851.

[2] *Ibid.*, Extract of a letter written by Le Moyne to Fr. Ambass. at Const., no. 174, July 31, 1851.

[3] *Ibid.*, Cairo, Dec. 29, 1851, Le Moyne to Minister.

[4] *Ibid.*, vol. 24, no. 189, Cairo, Feb. 16, 1852.

[5] HHSA, Huber to Schwarzenberg, Cairo, Dec. 17, 1851.

of a canal, " England would have been forced to take possession—at any cost, since it would be the key to the shortest
communication with India, and the Isthmus of Suez would
have been fortified as a second Gibraltar." This view was
vigorously combated by the Austrian Consul-General, who
believed that the manner in which England had set out to
secure the railway "at any cost," and with "so much national
spirit," threatened Egyptian neutrality. It would be necessary, he declared, for the remaining Powers " to check the
rapid growth of English influence in Egypt without loss of
time." [1]

Now that the Viceroy had granted the concession for the
railway, the French agents endeavored to prevent its execution on the ground that it had not received the Sultan's
sanction. The French Ambassador at London was " very
jealous " of the English success. " He said to me with an
air of satisfaction," wrote Count Buol, " that the conditions raised by the Porte were still far from being removed." [2] To Lord Palmerston, the French Ambassador
declared that while his government did not wish to erect any
obstacle to the construction of the line from Alexandria to
Cairo, it " would never consent to having this route prolonged to Suez under the auspices and control of England
or even of an English company." [3] At the same time, he
admitted that France encouraged the Porte to oppose the
scheme. " It is thus," continued Count Buol, " that a question of interest has completely reversed the rôles of the two
Powers. Great Britain, who until now has espoused the
cause of the Divan, is interested in the independence of
Egypt, while France, who would have gone to war with all

[1] *Ibid.*

[2] *Ibid.*, Affaires Politiques, no. 17 B, Count Buol to Schwarzenberg,
London, Oct. 2, 1851.

[3] *Ibid.*

Europe for the interest of the latter, intrigues to tighten the bonds of vassalage."

The Marquis de La Valette did not believe in merely opposing the railway. That would make the French attitude appear too narrow and exclusive. It was necessary to offer a substitute. Accordingly, he submitted a note to the Porte setting forth the manifold advantages which a canal would have for Turkey.[1]

It would assure to Turkey the possession of Egypt since it would create interests analogous to those which fix the attention of European diplomacy on the Bosphorus. The European Power in possession of the canal will be absolute mistress of the Indian Ocean. . . . All Europe would thus have an immense interest . . . in keeping the canal in the hands of a Power whose neutrality is certain; in no case could a European Power possess it to the exclusion of the others: it is a question of authority, of force, of commerce, of navigation, of life.

Moreover, " the canal would permit Turkey to get into direct, prompt and easy connection with Arabia; the communication would be extremely easy and this province would submit as all others to the authority of the Sultan." The problem of financing the enterprise could be solved by resorting to a loan, the interest on which could be paid out of the revenues of the canal.

This suggestion of the Marquis de La Valette was not seriously considered by the Porte. It was feared that Egypt would be separated from the other Turkish provinces if the canal were established. Later the Ambassador admitted he had made this proposal not so much in the hope that it would be accepted, as of offering a counterpoise to the railway.[2] So far as the latter project was concerned, he insisted that

[1] Turquie, vol. 306, no. 34, La Valette to Minister, Therapia, Aug. 4, 1851, enclosure.

[2] *Ibid.,* no. 46, Sept. 25, 1851.

the Sultan's sanction must be secured. This was necessary
not only for the general interest of Europe but to uphold
French prestige in the Near East. When Abbas finally submitted to the Porte and requested the sanction, the Ambassador withdrew his opposition. The construction of the line
from Alexandria to Cairo had proceeded in spite of French
protests and was completed in 1854, shortly before the death
of Abbas.

English influence remained supreme in Egypt during the
last years of Abbas. According to Sabatier, who succeeded
Le Moyne as French Consul-General, the conviction spread
that in the event of a dismemberment of the Ottoman Empire, England would get possession of Egypt, and even the
Viceroy came to believe this.[1] By playing on his fears, by
appealing to his sentiments of gratitude, the British Consul-
General brought Abbas completely under his influence.[2]

The relations between the agents of the two Powers became rather strained.

There is no real dissent between us [wrote Sabatier] for we
are never together, but I am convinced that when the day comes
when I would try to exercise an influence over the mind of the
Viceroy, Mr. Murray . . . would immediately do all in his
power to prevent me from arriving at my end. My English
colleague has made himself absolute master of His Highness
during the last years, by representing to him . . . that the English Government alone can and will protect him against his
enemies. . . . [3]

In this struggle for influence in Egypt, England had for
the moment won, leaving France completely overshadowed.
But Abbas was now succeeded by Mohammed Said Pasha,
whose sympathies were with the French and their projects.

[1] Égypte, vol. 25, no. 35, Sabatier to Minister, Alexandria, June 8,
1853.

[2] Ibid.            [3] Ibid., no. 21, Cairo, April 14, 1853.

## CHAPTER X

### Ferdinand de Lesseps Obtains the Concession

THE reign of Said Pasha marks an important step forward in the story of the Suez Canal. The failures of the past were almost forgotten in the glorious success which attended the efforts of Ferdinand de Lesseps. Yet the latter owed much to these failures, to the many precursors who had envisioned the connection of the two seas and the shortening of the route to the East. The earlier attempts influenced in a large measure the final realization of the project. They directed attention to the Suez route, to the difficulties— political, technical and financial — which opposed the construction of a canal across the Isthmus; and they made it clear that such a canal was no longer a mere subject for speculation. The expedition of Napoleon and the investigations of Le Père, the " mission " of the Saint-Simonians, the Austrian negotiations and the scientific studies of the Société d'Études — all prepared the way for the famous Frenchman. Yet, though he trod where others had gone before, his achievement remains one of the greatest of its kind. The obstacles were tremendous. For fifteen years he fought almost single-handed against odds which would have crushed a lesser man. He faced undaunted the wrath of mighty England whose opposition to his scheme grew in bitterness and obstinacy as she realized that its success was inevitable.

Ferdinand de Lesseps was singularly well equipped to carry through to successful completion the project which had resisted the efforts of so many other men. He was a man of exceptional courage and will power, not easily daunted by difficulties nor deterred from the achievement of his aim. Where his predecessors had failed because of their inability to cope with the opposition of the Powers, de Lesseps was a diplomat by instinct and training. Of capital importance to his success, moreover, was his friendship with Said Pasha which dated back to the latter's youth and which the passing years had failed to dim.

The de Lesseps family was well known in the annals of French diplomacy and several of its members had attained great distinction. Mathieu de Lesseps, the father of Ferdinand, had served as Commissioner-General under the Consulate and as Consul-General at Cadiz, in Egypt, Tuscany and Russia. He had been President of the Ionian Senate, Prefect and Count of the Empire, Consul-General in the United States, and Chargé d'Affaires at Tunis.[1]

Ferdinand de Lesseps was born at Versailles on November 19, 1805.[2] In recognition of his father's services, he was educated at the expense of the State in the Lycée Napoléon which, under the Restoration, was known as the Collège de Henri IV. For the first two years after leaving college he was employed in the Commissary Department of the French Army. In 1825, at the age of twenty, he was appointed Attaché to the French Consulate at Lisbon, where his uncle, Barthélemy de Lesseps, was in charge. This was the beginning of his long connection with the French diplomatic service.

It was in 1832 that Ferdinand de Lesseps made his first acquaintance with Egypt. In that year he was sent as Vice-Consul to Alexandria. Arriving there after a voyage of thirty-seven days from Tunis, he was compelled to remain for some time in quarantine and during this enforced sojourn on the ship the French Consul-General brought him

[1] Alphonse Bertrand and Émile Ferrier: *Ferdinand de Lesseps: Sa Vie, Son Oeuvre* (Paris, 1887), p. 11.

[2] He died at La Chênaie, December 7, 1894.

several books to help while away the time.  Among these
was Le Père's report on the canal, which fired his imagination and determined him to study the subject thoroughly.
It was in this way that he conceived the idea of joining the
two seas by a maritime canal.

His diplomatic career [1] was brought to a sudden end when,
in 1849, he was sent on a mission to Rome in order to negotiate a treaty with the revolutionary government which
would permit the reentrance of Pope Pius IX to the Vatican,
while preserving the independence of the Romans.  No
sooner had he entered upon these delicate negotiations than
the elections in France produced a change in foreign policy.
He was recalled from Rome, summoned before the Council
of State and criticized for his conduct, without an opportunity of defending himself.[2]  Incensed at this injustice, he
retired from the diplomatic service.  For the next five years
he lived on the estate of his mother-in-law at La Chênaie
and " studied everything connected with the relation of the
Occident and the Orient." [3]  In 1852 he prepared a memoir
on the subject of the canal which he sent to Ruyssenaers,
the Dutch Consul-General in Egypt, requesting him to give
his opinion as to the chance of having it accepted by Abbas
Pasha.[4]  Ruyssenaers replied that it was useless to expect
Abbas to entertain schemes of this nature.

[1] Ferdinand de Lesseps was attached to the French consular service
from 1825 to 1848.  He was assistant Vice-Consul at Lisbon from 1825
to 1827 and at Tunis from 1828 to 1832; Vice-Consul at Alexandria from
1832 to 1833; Consul at Cairo from 1833 to 1837, at Rotterdam from
1839 to 1840 and at Malaga from 1840 to 1842; Consul-General at
Barcelona from 1842 to 1848.  From 1848 to 1849 he was French
Minister at Madrid.

[2] Ferdinand de Lesseps, *Mémoire présenté au Conseil d'État—Exposé
des faits relatifs à la mission* (Paris, May, 1849).

[3] Bertrand and Ferrier, *op. cit.*, p. 23.

[4] Ferdinand de Lesseps, *Lettres, Journal et Documents pour servir à
l'histoire du Canal de Suez* (5 vols., Paris, 1875-1881), vol. i, p. 1-2,
1st ser.

It was while he was engaged in restoring an ancient castle once occupied by the famous Agnes Sorel, that he learned of the accession of Said Pasha. " While I was superintending all this," he says, " I learnt that Abbas Pasha, the Viceroy of Egypt, was dead. . . . His successor was the youngest son of Mehemet Ali, whom I had known as a child, and taught to ride. . . . I wrote to congratulate him, and he replied, begging me to come and see him at once." [1]

Upon receiving the Viceroy's invitation, de Lesseps set out from France, reaching Alexandria on November 7, 1854. The Viceroy urged him to join his party on a military tour to Cairo. Here was the opportunity he had waited for. One of the Egyptian ministers undertook to prepare the Viceroy for the reception of the project. The great moment arrived on the 15th, a day which began auspiciously. A rainbow of brilliant colors spread from east to west and de Lesseps believed he saw in this celestial manifestation that " sign of alliance spoken of in the Scriptures, the opportune moment for the true union of the Occident and the Orient . . . the day marked for the success of the project." [2] Some of his success, however, he later attributed to his clever horsemanship which won the approbation of the Viceroy and the generals of the party. Said Pasha listened attentively while de Lesseps unfolded his scheme without entering into details. He then asked a few questions and said: " I am convinced, I accept your plan; we shall concern ourselves with the means for its execution during the remainder of the journey; it is a settled matter; you can count on me." A few days later de Lesseps presented the Viceroy with the memoir he had prepared two years before. In this he recalled the previous attempts to connect the Mediterranean with the Red Sea by

[1] Ferdinand de Lesseps, *Recollections of forty years,* trans. by C. B. Pitman (2 vols. in 1, N. Y., 1898), vol. i, p. 139.

[2] Ferdinand de Lesseps, *Lettres etc.,* 1st ser., p. 17.

a canal, showed the advantages of such a canal, and declared that there were no serious obstacles to its realization. On November 30, 1854, he obtained the Concession for the canal.

The Concession was brief, containing only a preamble and twelve articles conceived in very general terms.[1] According to its provisions, de Lesseps was empowered to organize an international company under his own direction, to be known as *Compagnie Universelle du Canal Maritime de Suez.* The Director (presiding officer) of the Company was always to be named by the Egyptian Government, as far as possible from among the shareholders who were most interested in the enterprise. The Concession was to run for ninety-nine years from the date of the opening of the canal, and at the expiration of that period would revert to the Egyptian Government upon the indemnification of the Company. The latter would be given such lands as were necessary for the construction of the canal and would enjoy tax-free the privilege of working mines and quarries situated on these lands.[2]    It was stipulated that the Egyptian Government should receive 15% of the annual net profits of the Company in addition to dividends from whatever shares it might decide to purchase. The remaining profits would be distributed: 75% to the Company and 10% to the founders.[3] The tolls or charges would be the same for all nations. The Viceroy promised his loyal support in facilitating the exe-

[1] Compagnie Universelle du Canal Maritime de Suez, *Notice et Renseignements Généraux* (2ème partie, Paris, 1926), pp. 3-6. *Cf. British and Foreign State Papers*, vol. 55, pp. 970-973. This was replaced by a more detailed concession on Jan. 5, 1856, see chapter xi.

[2] The amount of such lands was not specified in the Concession.

[3] Article xi explains that the founders were those "whose works, studies, cares or capital," had contributed in the past to the promotion of the enterprise. A list of the founders was appended to the Company Statutes of January 5, 1856.

cution of the work. Finally, it was stipulated that the Concession must be ratified by the Sultan before work could be started.

In announcing the Concession to the Consular Corps, Said Pasha disclosed that he had not yielded to any external influence.[1] No objections were raised by the Consuls though it remained to be seen what attitude Great Britain would adopt.

At the Viceroy's suggestion de Lesseps called on Bruce, the British Consul-General. The latter announced that he would wait for instructions before expressing an official opinion.[2] Fearing, however that the announcement of the Concession would not be favorably received in England, he lost no time in going directly to the Viceroy with warnings against the canal and arguments for the British railway project. The canal, he told the Viceroy, was too great an undertaking for the resources of Egypt. Moreover, it " would give Egypt the go-bye, would have a constant tendency to escape from the jurisdiction of the Egyptian Government, and would in no way enrich it. . . ."[2] A few weeks later the French Consul-General learned that Bruce was strenuously opposing the Canal Concession, that he had pointed out to the Viceroy's entourage the dangers in the plan, declaring that it would be " nothing less than a question of life and death . . . besides England will never give her consent and Mr. Canning, the sovereign master at Constantinople, will compel the Porte to refuse its sanction." To Said Pasha himself he had stated that England would

[1] Égypte, vol. 25, no. 97, Sabatier to Minister, Cairo, Dec. 2, 1854.

[2] FO 78/1156, vol. 2, Bruce to Clarendon, no. 49, Dec. 3, 1854. *Cf.* Égypte, vol. 25, no. 97, Sabatier to Minister, Cairo, Dec. 2, 1854. The French Consul-General had the impression that Bruce was personally favorable to the scheme.

[3] *Ibid.*, Bruce to Clarendon, no. 49, Dec. 3, 1854.

never authorize an enterprise contrary to her own interests and one, moreover, which she had always rejected with all her power. He had also emphasized the difficulties of executing the work and the impossibility of securing European capital for it. The Viceroy, however, had replied that if European merchants refused their support, he would construct the canal at his own expense. " Take care, Highness," warned Bruce, " the alliance of France and England hangs by a thread; this thread you run the risk of breaking by persisting in your canal project. I still hope that you will draw back before so great a responsibility." [1] Later Bruce denied that he had held such language as reported by the French Consul-General, but admitted that he did endeavor " to throw cold water on the scheme." [2]

On January 9, 1855, Lord Clarendon informed Bruce that England continued to hold the same opinion of the canal as formerly, that it was inexpedient for Egyptian interests and impracticable of execution.

You will make it clear to the Pasha that the little favour with which the scheme is regarded by Her Majesty's Government does not originate in the circumstance that it had been submitted to His Highness by a native of France. If Her Majesty's Government saw any probability of advantage resulting from it to the Pasha, they would be as willing to recommend its adoption if proposed by a French as by a British subject. Whatever tends to facilitate intercourse between the British dominions in Europe and in Asia must necessarily be agreeable to Her Majesty's Government. It is only because they are convinced that no such advantage can result from the prosecution

[1] Égypte, vol. 25, no. 100, Sabatier to Minister, Cairo, Dec. 31, 1854. The French agent believed that Bruce's change in attitude was due to the influence of Murray, the former Consul-General in Egypt, who was then visiting at Alexandria. It was Murray, according to Sabatier, who inspired Bruce's interview with the Viceroy.

[2] FO 78/1156, vol. 2, private, Bruce to Clarendon, Cairo, Feb. 20, 1855.

of the scheme . . . that they instruct you to keep aloof from it, and frankly to state to the Pasha your reasons for so doing.[1]

The French Government naturally viewed the scheme with satisfaction but would give no official support to de Lesseps. Being allied to England in the Crimean War it was far less embarrassing for France to regard the scheme as a private affair than to recognize it officially in face of her ally's opposition. Hence she "denied most positively having any interests whatever in the plan. . . ."[2] On the other hand, Lord Cowley, the British Ambassador at Paris, informed Drouyn de Lhuys that England had no intention of pushing her opposition " beyond the bounds of courtesy " and that her attitude was in no way animated by a " spirit of rivalry to French interests."[3] To this Drouyn de Lhuys replied that France, considering the project as a private affair, had no other wish than that it should be left to the " unbiased consideration of the Egyptian Government." He instructed the French Consul-General in Egypt to abstain from acting officially in the matter.[4]

The Austrian Government was inclined to favor the de Lesseps' Concession, and would have given active support had the Minister of Commerce been able to prevail over Count Buol's diplomatic caution.[5] Although he favored the scheme and guessed that France would take no action without England's consent, Buol nevertheless hesitated to take sides with France against England. He therefore assumed

---

[1] *Ibid.,* no. 2, Clarendon to Bruce, Jan. 9, 1855.

[2] *Ibid.,* document 1573, Cowley to Clarendon, Paris, Dec. 26, 1854.

[3] *Ibid.,* no. 41, Cowley to Clarendon, Paris, Jan. 19, 1855.

[4] Égypte, vol. 26, Drouyn de Lhuys to Sabatier, no. 7, Paris, Jan. 2, 1855. The Minister held that the canal was a private affair since de Lesseps had negotiated with the Viceroy without the participation of the French Government.

[5] HHSA, fach. 13, Count Buol to Minister of Commerce, Jan. 5, 1855.

an attitude of benevolent neutrality, while instructing the Internuncio at Constantinople to report in detail any move made for or against the canal.[1]

Although he now had his Concession, de Lesseps could not begin work until he had secured authorization from the Sultan. This requirement was to raise again the old question of the latter's authority over Egypt and was to transfer the negotiations to Constantinople where English influence was supreme. While in the case of the railway England was quite ready to disregard the Sultan's authority, she now insisted that his sanction was absolutely necessary. Inconsistent though this attitude might appear, it was dictated by what Downing Street considered to be England's interests. Yet, for the next twelve years England was consistent upon one point, namely, her opposition (for imperial reasons) to the canal. At the moment she had command of the Cape route, her position in India was secure, and other Powers could offer no serious competition in the Eastern trade. With the construction of the canal, it was feared her supremacy would vanish, India might be threatened, and the Mediterranean countries would be more advantageously situated toward the Orient. London was determined that the route to India must never come under the control of another Power.

In February 1855 de Lesseps arrived at Constantinople to demand the authorization of the Sultan for the Concession. The Viceroy had prepared the way for him by informing Reshid Pasha, the Grand Vizir, of his mission. The situation at the Porte was decidedly unfavorable. Reshid Pasha was a pronounced Anglophile, completely dominated by Lord Stratford de Redcliffe, the British Ambassador. Since 1842

[1] *Ibid.*, Count Buol to Koller, Vienna, May 21, 1855. Count Buol's attitude was due not only to the Anglo-French rivalry in the question but also to the fact that the Crimean War was then in progress.

the latter had held a personal ascendancy over the Turks which is almost unparalleled in the annals of diplomacy. "From end to end of the Turkish dominions his power was felt." [1] Moreover, he had an exalted idea of what an ambassador should be.

A minister may be nothing more than a spokesman of his government, but an ambassador is the personal representative of his sovereign. . . . He felt that it belonged to him to sustain the dignity of his Queen by his every act, that he was the embodiment of the English Crown in the eyes of the Court to which he was accredited, that a slight offered to him was an insult to his sovereign.

So great was his personal magnetism that when he " penetrated the Sublime Porte, panic seized upon every official and the Grand Vizir himself would condescend to hasten in a tremor of anxiety to meet his inexorable visitor and learn his behests. . . ." [2] Lord Stratford had assumed an independence of action quite foreign to modern diplomacy. His one fixed policy was to maintain the Ottoman Empire. " He would save Turkey in spite of herself if she could be saved at all. . . . In spite of obstacles and with or without assistance, he would pursue the path he had marked out for himself and for the empire over which he dominated. To the Turks this immovable resolution carried with it something of the air of destiny." [3] Such was the man with whom de Lesseps crossed swords upon his arrival at the Porte.

There was still another obstacle to his success. France and England were at this time allied with Turkey in the

[1] Stanley Lane-Poole, *The Life of the Right Honourable Stratford Canning — Viscount Stratford de Redcliffe — From his Memoirs and Private and Official Papers* (2 vols., London, 1888), vol. ii, p. 58.

[2] A. L. Lee, *Lord Stratford de Redcliffe—A Sketch* (1897), p. 37.

[3] Stanley Lane-Poole, *op. cit.*, ii, p. 70.

Crimean War against Russia. While the war lasted there was little prospect of getting support from the Powers for the project, especially since England was so bitterly opposed to it. In spite of the unfavorable outlook, however, de Lesseps entered hopefully upon his mission.

Though Lord Stratford had received no instructions, he opposed the canal " with extreme vivacity." [1]  He persuaded Reshid Pasha to " discountenance the plan " and to recommend in its stead " the active prosecution of the railway." [2] A vizirial letter was dispatched to the Viceroy demanding further information concerning the canal and the railway and intimating that the Porte would much prefer the latter scheme.[3]

It was decided to submit the question to the Divan for consideration. The Turkish Ministers seemed disposed to approve the Concession as they had no desire to displease the Viceroy or the French Government by a refusal.[4]  On the other hand, they could not ignore Lord Stratford, for the fact that he had no instructions did not make him less formidable. Taking for his " leading star " the instructions which Lord Clarendon had sent to Bruce on January 9th, he called on Reshid Pasha and protested vigorously against " giving a rash assent to so expensive, ill-timed, and questionable an enterprise." [5]  The result was that the Divan, at its meeting on February 22nd, postponed giving a decision.

This was certainly a discouraging setback for de Lesseps,

[1] Turquie, vol. 319, no. 79, Benedetti to Minister, Pera, Jan. 18, 1855.

[2] FO 78/1156, vol. 2, no. 21, Stratford de Redcliffe to Clarendon, Const., Jan. 11, 1855.

[3] *Ibid.*, enclosure in no. 105, most confidential, Stratford to Clarendon, Const., Feb. 12, 1855.

[4] *Ibid.*, no. 136, most confidential, Stratford to Clarendon, Const., Feb. 22, 1855.

[5] *Ibid.*

but it revealed to him the source of the trouble. The Grand
Vizir was not himself opposed to the plan but was under the
thumb of Lord Stratford. De Lesseps felt certain that he
could count upon the support of the Austrian Internuncio
and the representatives of Spain and Holland.[1] Moreover,
Napoleon III showed the greatest interest in the scheme
and had repeatedly expressed himself in favor of it.[2] When
he learned what had taken place at the meeting of the Divan,
de Lesseps called on Reshid Pasha and protested against
the personal opposition of Lord Stratford who " by his
openly dominant conduct outraged the authority of the
Porte and the Sultan." The Grand Vizir promised to bring
the matter before the Divan a second time.[3]

An opportunity now presented itself which de Lesseps
seized eagerly. He was invited to dinner at the British
Embassy. The canal project came up for discussion and
Lord Stratford gave the impression of being open-minded
and desirous of knowing more about it.[4] He intimated,
however, that while the scheme might be sound, it would
" not be realized in a hundred years. The moment is inopportune." De Lesseps replied that he had perfect faith
in its execution in the near future and that it would, moreover, be futile to oppose a scheme at once so useful and so
powerfully supported.[5] " Not contented with an oral as-
sault," wrote Lord Stratford to Bruce, " he wrote to me on
the following day, and subsequently addressed me in a regular memorial. I fought my way through these embarrassments as well as I could, and felt a kind of relief when he

[1] Ferd. de Lesseps, *Lettres etc., op. cit.,* 1st ser., p. 117.

[2] HHSA, no. 830, Huber to F. O., Alexandria, May 17, 1855. The
Austrian Consul-General reports what de Lesseps had told him.

[3] Ferd. de Lesseps, *Lettres etc.,* 1st ser., p. 119.

[4] *Ibid.,* pp. 130-133 give an account of this conversation.

[5] FO 78/1156, no. 148, Stratford to Clarendon, Feb. 26, 1855.

went away, though, doubtless, he went with the intention of returning ere long to achieve his triumph." [1]

The situation was not altogether pleasing to Lord Stratford. " It is evident," he wrote to Lord Clarendon, " that the Porte is by no means inclined to assume the responsibility of a refusal or even of a suspension, such as I have recommended confidentially. It is expected of me that I should either declare my objections in an official form, or that I should leave the Porte to confirm the Viceroy's grant without further postponement." [2]

The Porte was indeed between the devil and the deep sea, for it wished neither to offend England by expressing its approval of the scheme, nor France by entering a positive refusal. Seeing the Concession in peril the French Government now temporarily abandoned its attitude of non-intervention and definitely took up cudgels for the " private " affair. Benedetti, the French Chargé d'Affaires, intimated to the Grand Vizir that the Emperor would be displeased if the project were rejected.[3]  But Lord Stratford did not propose to allow the Porte to give way before the threats of Benedetti. Before the second meeting of the Divan on March 1st, he again presented his objections to the Grand Vizir. The scheme, he said, involved financial contingencies which would probably be fatal to Egypt.

A time of war which fixes the attention and absorbs all the energies and resources of the Empire can hardly be deemed a propitious season for such an undertaking. Moreover, the success of the operation is thought by many to be visionary. At best its utility to Egypt is more than questionable. These objections derive additional strength from the progress of the railroad. That measure was deliberately selected as the prefer-

[1] *Ibid.*, private, Stratford to Bruce, Const., March 26, 1855.
[2] *Ibid.*, no. 148, Stratford to Clarendon, Const., Feb. 26, 1855.
[3] *Ibid.*

able mode of facilitating commerce with benefit to Egypt. It is, nevertheless, liable to a disastrous interruption from the depressed state of the Viceroy's revenue . . .[1]

For a second time Lord Stratford was successful and at his suggestion the Divan decided to submit the question to a special commission.[2] As that commission never met, the matter was indefinitely postponed.

Lord Stratford was finding it somewhat irksome to stand against the scheme on his own initiative and therefore requested instructions to enable him to act officially. He was told that " Her Majesty's Government were of the opinion that it would not be expedient to make any official protest. . . ."[3] To this he replied that it was only by means of an official interference that he had been able to obtain an indefinite postponement of the scheme.[4]

Realizing that he could make no headway at the Porte for the time being, de Lesseps decided to take his departure. Before leaving, he called on Reshid Pasha and accused the Porte of having temporized in the matter, declaring that after his return to Egypt, he would go to Paris and inform the Emperor of the situation.[5] Greatly embarrassed at this threat, Reshid begged Lord Stratford to secure definite instructions from his government and to urge Lord Clarendon to communicate with the French Government on the subject.

[1] *Ibid.*, Stratford to Stephen Pizani, Feb. 22, 1855, communicated to the Grand Vizir.

[2] Turquie, vol. 319, Benedetti to Minister, no. 90, Pera, March 1, 1855.

[3] FO 78/1489, vol. 5, " Memorandum of Correspondence respecting the Suez Canal projected by M. Lesseps. Confidential. Printed for the use of the Foreign Office. Dec. 28, 1859," F. O. to Stratford, no. 206, Const., Mar. 9, 1855.

[4] FO 78/1156, vol. 2, no. 217, Stratford to Clarendon, Const., Mar. 21, 1855.

[5] FO 78/1489, Mem. of Corr. etc., Lord Stratford, no. 173, Mar. 8, 1855; no. 197, Mar. 16, 1855.

De Lesseps arrived in Egypt somewhat disheartened by his failure but with a clear knowledge of the situation. Just as he was on the point of leaving again for Constantinople with new instructions from the Viceroy, the latter received two notes " evidently dictated by the same mind." [1] The first of these was from the Viceroy's brother-in-law, Kiamil Pasha, President of the Turkish Council. He was inspired, he said, by the deepest attachment for the Viceroy and devoted to the cause of Egypt but he felt it was his duty to warn him and to " open his eyes to the dangers of his situation." Finally, he expressed the hope that Said Pasha would not persist in a " fatal project which would embroil him in a certain struggle with England." The other letter was from Reshid Pasha. Admitting that the canal project was one of undoubted utility and that it commanded the sympathies of the Turkish Government, he nevertheless regretted that the Viceroy had " thrown himself into the arms of France." Mehemet Ali had made the same mistake. " France," declared the Grand Vizir, " can do nothing either for or against you, while England can cause you great harm if you lose her support." He intimated that the Sultan would be greatly displeased if Said Pasha continued to promote the scheme and warned him that he was running the risk of bringing warships to Alexandria.

These letters produced a veritable explosion in Egypt. The Viceroy was so excited that he summoned a council of war.[2] He was none the less determined, however, to support the scheme. " Reshid Pasha," he said to the French

---

[1] Égypte, vol. 26, no. 106, Sabatier to Minister, Alexandria, April 9, 1855. *Cf.* HHSA, no. 510, Huber to Buol, Cairo, Mar. 19, 1855. The Austrian dispatch states that de Lesseps carried with him the two letters from Constantinople. Moreover, it gives a different version of their contents than the French dispatch. Since M. Sabatier was personally informed concerning these letters, I have accepted his version.

[2] HHSA, no. 510, Huber to Buol, Cairo, Mar. 19, 1855.

Consul-General, " is only a comedian and a perfidious and corrupt intriguer. He is mistaken if he thinks he can exploit me as he exploited my father. I will not be his dupe." [1]

At the Porte the letters had a consequence quite unexpected. As soon as he was informed of Kiamil Pasha's letter, Benedetti called on Reshid Pasha and protested emphatically.[2] The Grand Vizir excused himself on the ground that he had not been made acquainted with the contents of that letter until after it had been dispatched. Benedetti was highly indignant at Reshid's apparent duplicity.[3] His protest resulted in the resignations of both Reshid and Kiamil. Lord Stratford was visiting in the Crimea when the change occurred. Upon his return he assured Reshid that the ministerial crisis would have been avoided had he been present. As it was, the resignation of Reshid was a severe blow to Lord Stratford. " English influence has lost an instrument at once docile and loyal," [4] wrote the Austrian Internuncio.

Benedetti now came out actively in support of de Lesseps.[5] He demanded authorization for the canal on the ground that England had withdrawn her opposition and that the Viceroy had complied with the Porte's demand for more information.[6] The Porte found itself in a very embarrassing situation. " Although neither France nor England," wrote the

[1] Égypte, vol. 26, no. 106, Sabatier to Minister, Alexandria, April 9, 1855.

[2] HHSA, rapport politique, no. 14B, Koller to Buol, May 2, 1855, enclosure: account of the conversation of Benedetti with Reshid Pasha on April 9, 1855.

[3] *Ibid.*, no. 14D, réservé, Koller to Buol, Const., May 3, 1855.

[4] *Ibid.*, no. 16A-L, réservé, Koller to Buol, Const., May 10, 1855.

[5] FO 78/1156, no. 283, Stratford to Clarendon, Const., April 2, 1855.

[6] FO 78/1489, Mem. of Corr. etc., no. 374, Stratford, May 21, 1855. Stratford was informed that England had not withdrawn her objections (no. 415, F. O. to Stratford, May 31, 1855).

Internuncio, " have as yet expressed themselves in an official manner, the Ottoman Ministers have learned enough to know that the question cannot be solved without displeasing the one or the other of the two Cabinets." [1]  While the Porte sought by every means to suspend judgment on the question, it was none the less determined to impress upon the Viceroy that nothing could be done without the Sultan's sanction.[2] Meanwhile, it viewed the circumstances as unfavorable for the execution of the project and abstained from giving a definite pronouncement.  Lord Stratford blamed Benedetti's activities for the Porte's embarrassment, and asked for instructions to enable him to counteract them officially.[3]  Again the Foreign Office refused, though it directed Lord Stratford to inform the Porte that in view of the great engineering and financial difficulties involved in the project, de Lesseps must be trying to further political aims detrimental to Turkey.[4]  In the meantime Paris hopefully deluded itself with the rumor that the British Foreign Office was not altogether pleased with Lord Stratford's conduct and would immediately accept his resignation if it were tendered—a rumor the falsity of which is clearly demonstrated by the archives in London.[5]

[1] HHSA, rapport politique, no. 20C, Koller to Buol, Const., June 7, 1855.

[2] *Ibid.*

[3] FO 78/1156, most confidential, no. 398, Stratford to Clarendon, Const., June 2, 1855.

[4] FO 78/1489, vol. 5, Mem. of Corr. etc., F. O. to Stratford, no. 415, May 31, 1855 and FO 78/1156, no. 429, confidential, F. O. to Stratford, June 6, 1855.

[5] HHSA, vol. ix/48, France, no. 89 Litt. E., Baron de Hubner to Count Buol, Paris, Sept. 21, 1855.  In this dispatch Baron de Hubner gives the French version of the affair.  According to this, the British Cabinet upon the demand of the French Government and of the Sultan had decided to recall Stratford.  It was charged that the latter used abusive and violent language to M. Thouvenel, the French Ambassador at the

England now decided to take up the matter with the French Government. Lord Cowley informed Count Walewski that Downing Street entertained " insuperable objections to the canal scheme " and doubted its practicability. He urged the minister not to " risk the harmony " existing between the two governments by supporting it. Count Walewski replied that France considered the canal both " feasible and desirable " but, not wishing to offend England, he proposed that both governments should instruct their representatives at the Porte to abstain from interfering in the question and to leave its decision to the Sultan and the Viceroy. This suggestion was not one England was ready to accept. As Cowley observed, it was not equally applicable to both governments, for " Her Majesty's Government was much more concerned in the final solution of this question than the French Government . . . and had no object in view with reference to Egypt but the rapid transmission of their correspondence to India." [1]

The English attitude toward the canal was set forth in a dispatch from Lord Clarendon, submitted by Lord Cowley to the French Government.[2] There were three main objections which the British Government put forward at this time. The first was that the canal was " physically impossible "

Porte, and that he angered the Sultan by protesting against the ministerial changes which had taken place during his absence in the Crimea. Baron de Hubner believed that the Sultan never would have asserted himself before Lord Stratford, had he not been encouraged by M. Thouvenel. In a dispatch of Sept. 25th, to Count Buol (vol. ix/49, no. H91, France), Baron de Hubner gives the English version which was that the Cabinet would not recall Stratford but would accept his resignation with alacrity if it were tendered; but if Stratford did not wish to resign, he could remain. The incident is not mentioned in the English dispatches and there is nothing to show that Stratford's conduct was not approved by the Foreign Office.

[1] FO 78/1156, no. 665, Cowley to Clarendon, Paris, June 1, 1855.

[2] *Ibid.*, no. 606, F. O. to Cowley, June 18, 1855.

except at a cost which would render it unprofitable as a commercial venture. The second objection was that the canal would require a long time for its execution and this

would interfere with and greatly delay, if not entirely prevent the completion of a railway communication between Cairo and Suez . . . All that the British Government want in Egypt is an easy and rapid road to India for travellers, light goods, and letters and despatches: they want no ascendency, no territorial acquisition. They only want a thoroughfare but a thoroughfare they must have, free and unmolested: and the continuation of the railway would give them that . . .

Finally, it was stated that " Her Majesty's Government cannot disguise from themselves that it is founded upon an antagonistic policy on the part of France in regard to Egypt." Supporters of French policy

consider it an object of great importance to detach Egypt from Turkey in order thereby to cut off the easiest channel of communication between England and British India. It was with such view and in that spirit that extensive fortifications, planned at the war office in Paris, were erected by French Engineers along the Mediterranean coast of Egypt in order to defend Egypt in case of need against any force coming to it from Turkey by sea.

It was with this view that the great dam was constructed on the Nile, which under the pretense of irrigation, for which it is perfectly useless, provides the means of inundating for military defense part of the Delta, and which was also intended to serve as a military defense for Lower Egypt against any force from the South.

It is with this view and in this spirit that this scheme was put forward the effect of which would be to interpose between Syria and Egypt the physical barrier of a wide and deep canal defended by military works, and the political barrier of a strip of land extending from the Mediterranean to the Red Sea granted away and occupied by a company of foreigners, between whose government and the Porte questions of the most embarrassing nature to the Porte might arise under circumstances which it is easy to foresee and which it is unnecessary any more particularly to describe.

Such were the objections which England offered. One strongly suspects that they were not the real reasons for her opposition. The argument that the canal was physically impossible of execution and that it would interfere with the completion of the railway in Egypt, especially since the latter had already been taken care of,[1] was hardly a sufficient cause for her excitement. Nor was the concern expressed for the integrity of the Turkish Empire the main reason for British opposition to the canal. The scheme was objectionable to England because it was promoted by a Frenchman, and because it appeared to be a French undertaking and therefore a menace to her communications with India, the keystone of her empire.

The French Government replied with arguments supplied by de Lesseps.[2] It declared that the Company had no intention of asking assistance of any foreign government. If Britain considered the canal as physically impossible of execution, she need not participate. Like England, France was not seeking an exclusive ascendency or territorial control in Egypt; nor were the French agents inspired by a spirit of antagonism toward England. As to the railroad,

[1] The Viceroy, in the hope of winning English support for the canal, agreed to the extension of the railway from Cairo to Suez. To keep out foreign intervention, he decided to construct the line at his own expense. The contract for the rails was given to an English firm, Briggs & Co. (HHSA, no. 83, Huber to F. O., Alexandria, May 17, 1855). The French Government did not object to the extension of the railway (Égypte, vol. 26, no. 3, F. O. to Sabatier, Paris, Feb. 13, 1855). The railroad was completed in 1858.

[2] Ferd. de Lesseps, *Lettres etc.,* 1st. ser., pp. 211-220.

the canal would in no way interfere, since the Viceroy had already made provision for it. The reply to the third objection was that "if the Government of the Emperor thought that the present canal project was founded on an antagonistic policy, it would repulse it immediately." Finally, it was suggested that de Lesseps upon his arrival at London would, if it was thought necessary, supply further information concerning the attitude of the French Government.

Despite these categorical replies the British Government in no way abated its opposition. Visiting London in June 1855, de Lesseps asked Lord Palmerston for his candid opinion regarding the scheme. The latter repeated word for word the objections set forth in Lord Clarendon's dispatch. "It was evident," said de Lesseps, "that he had dictated them himself, or that they had been edited under his inspiration." Lord Palmerston then advanced other objections:

I do not hesitate to point out to you my apprehensions; they consist first, in the fear of seeing the commercial and maritime relations of Great Britain upset by the opening of a new route which, while giving passage to the navigation of all countries, will take away the advantages we possess at the present time. I will also acknowledge to you that I fear the uncertainty of the future concerning France, the future which every statesman must consider in all its unpleasant eventualities; although our confidence in the sincerity and loyalty of the Emperor's attitude is complete, but after him, this attitude could change.[1]

De Lesseps also had an interview with Lord Clarendon, who informed him that "the objections of Her Majesty's Government were insuperable." England was convinced that once the canal was established, Egypt would be completely separated from Turkey and could then declare her independence at any time. Furthermore, in case of war

[1] *Ibid.*, pp. 222-223.

between Britain and France, the latter would immediately seize the two ends of the canal. " It would in fact," concluded Lord Clarendon, " be a suicidal act on the part of England to assent to the construction of the canal." [1]

Both France and England were particularly anxious to avoid misunderstandings while the war lasted. Though he was personally favorable to the canal project, the Emperor had no thought of pressing his views in opposition to his ally. " He was quite ready . . . to desist from further interference but he desired that this should be done in a way which should not give at Constantinople the idea that the English influence had prevailed over the French." Rather than have the Porte pronounce against the canal, the Emperor wished that the question should be dropped and considered as *non avenue*.[2] This announcement was received with great satisfaction by the British Government. Now that the affair was at an end, all that remained to be done was to put a stop to the activities of de Lesseps. Count Persigny, the French Ambassador at London, agreed with this view and predicted that " the whole affair would soon fall to the ground when it became known that it had no support from the English or French Governments." [3]

Neither government, however, wished to push matters too far, and it was agreed that their representatives at the Porte should be instructed to abstain from interfering for or against the canal.[4] The Austrian Ambassador at Paris reported that Count Walewski considered the resistance of the British Cabinet as invincible and " for the moment insurmountable," and that Palmerston and Clarendon " have

[1] FO 78/1156, F. O. to Cowley, July 18, 1855.

[2] *Ibid.*, confidential, no. 835, Cowley to Clarendon, Paris, June 30, 1855.

[3] *Ibid.*, FO 78/1489, vol. 5, Mem. of Corr. etc., F. O. to Cowley, no. 686, July 2, 1855.

[4] HHSA, no. 30C, Koller to Buol, Const., July 26, 1855.

decided to oppose *à outrance* " any attempt of the Porte to grant the sanction.[1]  Count Walewski was convinced that as long as these ministers remained in the Cabinet, England would never consent to the canal.  The only hope lay in the British capitalists interested in the project who might compel the government to yield or force the resignation of the intractable ministers.[2]  France had no desire to risk the alliance by a change in the British Ministry, and for the time being, the canal question would have to remain in abeyance.

[1] *Ibid.*, no. 99 Litt. E., Hubner to Buol, Paris, Oct. 20, 1855.
[2] *Ibid.*

# CHAPTER XI

## PALMERSTON OPPOSES A "BUBBLE SCHEME"

THE first attempt of de Lesseps to obtain the Sultan's sanction had ended in failure. England's opposition blocked the way and checked him at every turn. But it was only the beginning of his difficulties. In the next few years he was to learn how bitter, how tortuous and how illogical England's opposition could be, alleging any pretexts that could be invented, and finding new ones when these were overcome.

In the meantime, the preparatory work had proceeded under the supervision of the engineers, Linant-Bey and Mougel-Bey. In order to verify their report, de Lesseps appointed an International Scientific Commission composed of prominent engineers from France, Austria, Italy, Germany, Holland, Spain and England. The Commission held preliminary meetings in Paris and a sub-committee of five was selected to proceed to Egypt in order to study at first hand the possibilities of constructing the canal. In their report, submitted to the Viceroy on January 2, 1856, it was stated that a maritime canal was the only one which should be considered, that its execution would be easy and its success assured, and that the expense of construction should not exceed 200 million francs.[1]

The report of the International Scientific Commission refuted the British arguments against the practicability of

[1] Égypte, vol. 26, no. 126, Sabatier to Minister, Alexandria, Jan. 5, 1856, annex 2, copy of report of Int. Commission. The estimate of 200 million francs for the construction of the canal was less than half the actual cost, which came to 432,807,882 francs.

the canal, and it was the belief of de Lesseps and the Viceroy that the opposition must now give way.   Indeed, the
Viceroy even thought of sending his minister for foreign
affairs to Constantinople immediately to secure the Sultan's
sanction, but desisted when he learned that Count Walewski
was opposed to this step.[1]   So far from removing the British objections, however, the report had the opposite result.
Undeterred by the refutation of their primary economic
argument, the British fell back on political reasons.   Thus
Lord Stratford was instructed to point out to the Porte the
" great facilities this canal would afford to any Viceroy of
Egypt who might be disposed to throw off his allegiance to
the Sultan and to declare himself independent." [2]    The
Grand Vizir promised Lord Stratford that he would raise
such obstacles as to render the sanction virtually impossible.[3]

The *Edinburgh Review,* the mouthpiece of Lord Palmerston, in attacking the canal, weakly attempted to shift the
economic arguments to a prophecy which did little credit
to British foresight.[4]   The canal, it argued, could perhaps
be constructed, but its usefulness would be limited to Egypt
and the Turkish Empire, and " would not touch the grand
commerce of the world. . . ."   It admitted that steamers
preferred the Red Sea route and that it was more suitable
for passenger and parcel traffic.   " But it is very questionable whether steamers will ever be able to compete with
sailing vessels for the goods traffic."   English merchants
would find the Cape route " infinitely preferable for commercial purposes, and we may rest assured that the Canal
will never be executed. . . ."

[1] *Ibid.,* no. 126.   *Cf.* Turquie, vol. 342, FO to Thouvenel, Paris, Jan. 5,
1856.

[2] FO 78/1340, vol. 3, no. 78, FO to Redcliffe, Jan 2, 1856.

[3] HHSA, no. 74, Prokesch to Minister, Jan. 10, 1856.

[4] *Edinburgh Review,* no. 209, Jan. 1856.

A few days after he had received the report of the International Scientific Commission, the Viceroy granted a new act of concession which replaced the one of November 30, 1854. The new Concession, dated January 5, 1856, was requested by de Lesseps in order to set forth in detail the basis upon which the proposed company should operate, as well as to take into account the recommendations of the Commission—the first Concession being too general. By the provisions of the new document the Company was to construct " at its own expense, risk and peril," a maritime canal, a fresh-water canal derived from the Nile and connecting with the maritime canal, and two other fresh-water canals directed toward Suez and Peluse.[1] The works were to be completed within six years, save for interruptions due to major circumstances, and four-fifths of the workers should be Egyptian.[2] The maritime canal was to be cut to a depth and width determined by the report of the International Scientific Commission. The Egyptian Government reserved the right of delegating a special commissioner to the administrative office of the Company, who should represent the rights and interests of the Government. For the construction of the canal and its adjuncts, the Egyptian Government agreed to turn over to the Company, free from taxes, all necessary lands not belonging to private owners. The Company was also to receive the use of certain uncultivated lands, not belonging to private owners, which it

[1] Compagnie Universelle du Canal Maritime de Suez, *Notice et Renseignements Généraux* (2ème partie, Paris, 1926), pp. 7-15. *Cf. British and Foreign State Papers,* vol. 55, pp. 976-981. The first of these fresh-water canals was turned over to the Egyptian Government by a convention of March 18, 1863. By the conventions of Jan. 30 and Feb. 22, 1866, the Company gave up the branch of the fresh-water canal going toward Suez but retained the one to Peluse. See ch. xiii, p. 212.

[2] Part concerning workers was abrogated by a convention of February 22, 1866.

should irrigate and cultivate at its own expense, such lands to be tax-free for a period of ten years.[1]  The privilege of exploiting mines and quarries situated on these lands, without payment of taxes, was confirmed.  The canal would be open at all times to all ships of commerce without distinction upon payment of the tolls, which should not exceed ten francs per ton of capacity for vessels and ten francs for each passenger.  In any case, the Company could not accord to a vessel, company or individual special advantages or favors not accorded to all other vessels, companies or individuals.  The duration of the Concession was fixed at ninety-nine years from the date of the opening of the canal, at the end of which period it should revert to the Egyptian Government upon the indemnification of the Company.  But in addition, it was stipulated that should the Concession be renewed for successive ninety-nine year periods, the Egyptian government would receive for the second period 20% of the annual net profits of the Company and 25% for the third period.[2]  For the first ten years after the opening of the canal to navigation, de Lesseps was to preside over the Company.  Finally the Concession repeated the requirement concerning the Sultan's sanction.

The Statutes of the Company, drawn up in connection with the second Concession, provided [3] that the central office should be located in Alexandria and the legal and administrative offices in Paris.  The capital was fixed at 200 million francs, divided into 400,000 shares at 500 francs each.[4]

[1] Abrogated by the convention of Feb. 22, 1866.

[2] This was not to exceed 35 per cent for successive renewals.

[3] Compagnie Universelle du Canal Maritime de Suez, *Notice et Renseignements etc.,* pp. 16-38.  Cf. *British and Foreign State Papers,* vol. 55, pp. 981-995.

[4] By a resolution of the General Assembly of shareholders, June 2, 1924, completed by a decision of the Board of Directors, Sept. 1, 1924, the number of shares was doubled though the capital remains the same.

It was provided that the General Assembly of Shareholders should meet annually and that all shareholders possessing at least twenty-five shares should have a right to vote, but no shareholder was to have more than ten votes.[1] The Assembly was to listen to the reports of the Board of Directors, deliberate upon the propositions submitted to it by the latter, appoint its members and determine its powers. All measures concerning new concessions, fusion with other enterprises, modifications of the Statutes, dissolution of the Company, augmentation of the capital, loans, regulation of annual accounts and determination of the annual dividends, must be approved by the Assembly.

The Company was to be administered by a Board of Directors (Conseil d'Administration) of thirty-two members representing the nations chiefly interested in the enterprise.[2] The members of the Board were to be chosen by the General Assembly of Shareholders for eight years and were to be eligible for reappointment. It was required that each member must be the owner of 100 shares which were to be deposited with the Company. In payment for their services, the Company was to set aside three per cent of the annual net profits.[3] The Board was to choose annually, from among its members, a president and three vice-presi-

---

[1] The Statutes fixed the annual meeting for May 15th but this was modified in Aug., 1864, by a resolution that it should take place in the period from May 1st to Aug. 1st.

[2] The number of Directors was reduced to 21 on Aug. 24, 1871, increased to 24 on June 27, 1876 and reached its original number again on May 2, 1884. The change of June 27, 1876, was made in order to provide representation for the British Government, which had recently purchased the canal shares of the Khedive. The directors are assigned to national groups in proportion to the number of shares held by each.

[3] Reduced to two per cent, Aug. 24, 1871. The distribution of the remainder was 15 per cent for the Egyptian Government, 10 per cent for the Founders, 2 per cent for the workers' relief etc., 71 per cent for the shareholders.

dents who were to be eligible for reëlection. Meetings
should be held at least once a month, and at any other time
upon the call of the president of the Board, seven constituting a quorum, and matters should be decided by a majority
of those present.[1] Wide powers were given to the Board.
It was to submit propositions to the General Assembly of
Shareholders, enact measures for the Executive Committee
(Comité de direction) concerning such matters as the disposition of funds, studies and projects for the execution of
works, the acquisition, sale and exchange of real estate,
purchase of vessels and machinery, and the annual budget.

The Executive Committee was to be made up of the
President and four members of the Board and was to have
direct charge of the Company's business. It was to meet
upon the call of the President at least once a week and would
represent the Company and act in its name in all cases which
did not require the approval of the General Assembly or the
Board of Directors. Its functions were to include the appointment and removal of employees, determination of their
duties and wages; supervision of the bureaux; and regulations for the service and expenditures. The Statutes further provided for a Superior Agent and Chief of Services
who, residing in Egypt, should represent the Company in
all its relations with the Egyptian Government, and should
have the necessary powers for supervising the work on the
canal.

Armed with the new Concession de Lesseps renewed his
efforts to secure the Sultan's sanction. Early in 1856 he
visited England and held a conversation with Lord Clarendon who told him that England's opposition to the canal
was inspired by the fear that it would disturb the relations

[1] Except when only seven members are present, in which case five votes
are needed to pass a measure.

between Turkey and Egypt.[1]  Calling on Lord Palmerston, he found him "always the man of 1840, full of defiance and prejudice in regard to France and Egypt." [2]  De Lesseps informed him of his interview with Lord Clarendon.  When he had finished, Palmerston expressed his opinion of the canal.

He advanced the most contradictory, the most incoherent and I even dare say, the most insane views concerning the Suez Canal that one can imagine.  He believed that France had for a long time pursued a machiavellian policy in Egypt against England, that it was the gold of Louis Philippe or his government that had paid for the fortifications at Alexandria.  He saw in the Suez Canal the consequence of that policy.  On the other hand, he persisted in maintaining that the execution of the canal is physically impossible and that he knew more about this subject than all the engineers in Europe whose opinion cannot shake his own.  Then, without holding to that impossibility so well demonstrated, he made a long tirade on the inconveniences resulting from the Concession of the Viceroy and the realization of the enterprise, for Turkey and for Egypt itself.  Finally, he declared that he would continue to be openly my adversary.  While listening to him I asked myself from time to time if I had before me a maniac or a statesman.  Not one of his arguments could be sustained in a serious discussion.

Hoping to remove some of England's objections, de Lesseps, when the Congress of Paris convened, submitted to Count Buol a draft of clauses for the neutralization of the canal which he desired should be inserted in the treaty. When Count Buol informed Lord Clarendon of the draft, the latter opposed it bitterly.  He believed it was a veiled attempt to promote French designs on Egypt and he even

[1] Ferd. de Lesseps, *Lettres etc.*, 1st ser., pp. 368-378.  Note to Thouvenel, dated April 19, 1856.

[2] *Ibid.*, p. 377, Letter to Barthélemy Saint-Hilaire, April 7, 1856.

went so far as to declare that he would make it a " cabinet question " and resign rather than have it adopted.[1]    The result was that Count Buol did not submit the draft to the Congress.

Meanwhile, the English continued their intrigues against the canal.   In Egypt, Bruce endeavored to get the Viceroy to abandon it on the ground that it would involve an enormous expense.[2]   But the latter remained firm and even decided to go himself to Constantinople to demand the Sultan's sanction.   " It is quite on the cards that he may succeed," wrote Lord Stratford.   " I question whether His Majesty's present ministers would screw their courage to the point of a declared resistance." [3]   The Ambassador was instructed to seek an audience with the Sultan and lay before him the British objections.[4]   Lord Clarendon was convinced

that all that the Pasha and M. de Lesseps want, or at least that with which they will be satisfied, will be to cut a wide, deep and defensible breach across the road which leads from Syria to Egypt, so as to enable the Egyptians or a small French force to prevent an army from marching into Egypt from Syria. This once done, at the expense of the dupes who might be

[1] HHSA, $\frac{\text{no. 1586}}{\text{F 406}}$ Dépêche télégraphique from Count Buol, Paris, April 10, 1856.  De Lesseps claimed that the representatives of France, Russia, Sardinia and Prussia would have supported the neutralization clauses. *Letters etc.*, 1st ser., p. 362.

[2] Égypte, vol. 26, no. 7, Sabatier to Minister, Alex., July 25, 1856. Lord Clarendon tried to arouse the French Government to oppose the canal by directing attention to the Viceroy's extravagance, which would not leave him enough to pay his tribute to the Sultan if he persisted in supporting de Lesseps. England and France had an interest in this tribute since it formed a part of the security which they held for Turkish loans under their guarantee. FO, 78/1340, vol. 3, no. 1532, Clarendon to Cowley, copies to Stratford and Bruce, Dec. 24, 1856.

[3] FO, 78/1340, no. 105, Redcliffe to Clarendon, Therapia, Aug. 25, 1856.

[4] FO, 78/1489, Mem. of Corr., FO to Stratford, Sept. 24, 1856.

persuaded to put their money into the speculation, the Pasha and M. de Lesseps would declare the completion of their work impossible, and proceed to wind up, having attained the political object in view, or at least the most essential part of it.[1]

The Sultan did not give his sanction nor was the project any nearer realization. De Lesseps did not minimize the difficulties. He saw clearly that it was useless to expect success at the Porte so long as England maintained her opposition. But was the Sultan's sanction absolutely indispensable? Notwithstanding the stipulation in the Act of Concession, de Lesseps held that it was not. The very fact that the Porte had raised no serious obstacles to the Egyptian railway established, he believed, a precedent for all transit problems in Egypt.[2] But he had no intention of jeopardizing the scheme by exposing it to the difficulties which might arise from the "exclusive and selfish policy" of England.[3] He concluded, therefore, that success depended upon his ability to overcome the opposition. From his own government he had received no official support nor did he care to ask for it at this time. To the Porte, however, this seemed to indicate that England was much more interested in the question. De Lesseps informed the Emperor of a note written by a member of the Divan which intimated that it was just because France showed herself indifferent that the Porte refused its sanction.[4] Austria was still favorably disposed toward the scheme and the Internuncio was directed to lend his support to any measures taken by the French Ambassador for the sanction, but to avoid friction

---

[1] FO, 78/1340, no. 1042, Clarendon to Redcliffe, Sept. 9, 1856.

[2] *Letters etc.*, 2nd ser., Letter to Minister of Public Works, Turin, dated Mar. 12, 1857.

[3] *Ibid.*

[4] *Ibid.*, p. 35, Communication to the Emperor Napoleon, Mar. 20, 1856.

with Lord Stratford.[1] All other tactics having failed, de Lesseps decided to carry his campaign to England and to educate the public there respecting the advantages of the canal. This might, he thought, cause the opposition to break down.

Arriving in London in April 1857, he found that " the Suez Canal Question had made extraordinary progress." [2] He was provided with letters of introduction to merchants, manufacturers, and shippers of the great commercial cities. " Everything is prepared," he wrote to the Viceroy, " to make this tour decisive. My aim is to gather collective and signed declarations from which it will be established that the enterprise of cutting the Isthmus of Suez will be profitable to English interests, and that no government has the right to oppose it." [3] In a little over a month he addressed twenty-two public meetings in the larger commercial centers of the country.[4] He was gratified by the courtesy extended to him and the interest which was everywhere displayed. He believed his campaign a success.

Upon his return to London he discovered that however great might be the interest displayed by the commercial classes of the country, the British Cabinet remained as stubborn as ever in its opposition. Lord Palmerston told him frankly that he was " very openly opposed " to the project.[5]

The canal question was brought up in the House of Commons on July 7, 1857. Mr. Berkely asked whether the Government would use its influence to support the sanction which the Viceroy had applied for, and if any objections

[1] HHSA, Buol to Prokesch, Vienna, May 12, 1856.

[2] *Letters etc.*, 2nd ser., p. 41.

[3] *Ibid.*

[4] See Ferd. de Lesseps, *Inquiry into the opinions of the Commercial classes of Great Britain on the Suez Canal* (1857).

[5] *Letters etc.*, 2nd ser., p. 87.

were being entertained, to state the grounds for the same. Lord Palmerston replied for the Government:[1]

Sir, Her Majesty's Government certainly cannot undertake to use their influence with the Sultan to induce him to give permission for the construction of the canal, because for the last fifteen years Her Majesty's Government have used all the influence they possess at Constantinople and in Egypt to prevent that scheme from being carried into execution. It is an undertaking which, I believe, in point of commercial character, may be deemed to rank among the many bubble schemes that from time to time have been palmed upon gullible capitalists. I have been informed, on what I believe to be reliable authority, that it is physically impracticable, except at an expense which would be far too great to warrant any expectation of any return. . . . However, that is not the ground upon which the Government have opposed the scheme. Private individuals are left to take care of their own interests, and if they embark in impracticable undertakings they must pay the penalty of so doing. But the scheme is founded in hostility to the interests of this country— opposed to the standing policy of England in regard to the connection of Egypt with Turkey—a policy which has been consecrated by the late war, and issue of that war—the Treaty of Paris. The obvious political tendency is to render more easy the separation of Egypt from Turkey. It is founded also, on remote speculations with regard to easier access to our Indian possessions, which I need not more distinctly shadow forth, because they will be obvious to anybody who pays any attention to the subject. I can only express my surprise that M. Ferdinand de Lesseps should have reckoned so much on the credulity of English capitalists as to think that by his progress through the different commercial towns in this country he should succeed in obtaining English money for the promotion of a scheme which is in every way so adverse and hostile to British interests. . . .

[1] Hansard's *Parliamentary Debates*, 3rd ser., cxlvi, pp. 1043-1044.

De Lesseps, who had returned to Paris, addressed a circular to the members of the House of Commons and the Commercial Associations of England, replying point for point to the arguments advanced by Lord Palmerston against the canal.[1] The Austrian Ambassador at London was of the opinion that "despite the positive declarations of Lord Palmerston in Parliament, the cause of the Suez Canal is far from being lost in England; on the contrary, it gains ground from day to day."[2]

On the 17th the question was again before the House of Commons.[3] Mr. Griffiths desired to know "if it be conducive to the honour or the interests of this country that we should manifest and avow the existence of a jealous hostility on our part" to the canal. Lord Palmerston replied in much the same vein as before, again referring to the canal as a "bubble scheme." He admitted that so far as the engineering difficulties were concerned, "there is nothing which money and skill cannot overcome except to stop the tides and make rivers run up to their sources." Mr. Stephenson also took occasion to offer the House the advantage of his knowledge on the subject. He would not, he declared, go so far as to say that the scheme was absurd, but as an engineer he would pronounce it to be undesirable and that the railway would be "more expeditious, more certain, and more economical."

In a note addressed to the Emperor and Count Walewski, de Lesseps called attention to the statement Lord Palmerston had made that the English Government had used all its influence to prevent the realization of the project. Referring to the agreement that the two Powers should not interfere

---

[1] *Letters etc.*, 2nd ser., pp. 94-97.

[2] HHSA, Affaires Politiques, no. 48 B, Apponyi to Buol, London, July 11, 1857.

[3] Hansard, *op. cit.*, vol. cxlvi, pp. 1704-1707.

in the question, he asked: " In view of such an outspoken confession concerning the inveterate suspicions against France, have we need of Lord Palmerston's permission to demand formally of the Sultan the ratification of the Viceroy's Concession . . . ?" [1]

We are told by the British agent at Alexandria that Lord Palmerston's speech made the Viceroy very uneasy.[2] Indeed, the latter even went so far as to request de Lesseps not to visit Egypt as he had planned, " unless the objections of the British Government to the Canal are removed and the consent of the Porte obtained." [3] This would seem a rather sudden change of heart in one who had so loyally and so courageously supported the scheme. Except for the account of the British agent, however, there is nothing to indicate that the Viceroy deserted his friend de Lesseps.

In an effort to offset the English influence at Constantinople, de Lesseps addressed a circular to the foreign ministers of the principal states, requesting their support.[4] Count Buol, whom de Lesseps called upon personally in Vienna, replied that while he fully recognized the commercial advantages of the enterprise, he did not wish to intervene until the Powers had come to an agreement concerning it.[5] He declared " that so long as the English

[1] *Letters etc.*, 2nd ser., p. 98-99.

[2] FO, 78/1340, vol. 3, no. 29, Green (acting Consul-General) to Clarendon, Alex., Aug. 6, 1857. *Cf.* HHSA, no. 15, Huber to Buol, Aug. 5, 1857.

[3] *Ibid.*, no. 47, Green to Clarendon, Alex., Sept. 27, 1857. The French Consul-General reported that Said was alarmed by Palmerston's speech; that he was convinced England would seize Egypt at the first opportunity. Égypte, vol. 27, no. 25, Sabatier to Walewski, Aug. 24, 1857.

[4] *Letters etc.*, 2nd ser., pp. 132-133; Letter to Count Buol, HHSA, Fach 13, Varia de France, Paris, Oct. 21, 1857.

[5] HHSA, Fach 13, Buol to Prokesch, Vienna, Nov. 14, 1857; to Apponyi at London, Nov. 15th; to Hubner at Paris, Nov. 20th; to Coloredo at Rome, Nov. 21st.

Government has not turned from the serious objections it entertained against the canal, Austria, because of the importance she places in her good relations with England, will not be in a position to give an unconditional support at Constantinople." The Internuncio was directed, however, to make it clear to the Porte that Austria still took a lively interest in the scheme.[1]

Count Apponyi, the Austrian Ambassador at London, in explaining to Lord Clarendon the attitude of his government, declared that it had been adopted out of consideration for England.[2]  Lord Clarendon was highly pleased and discussed very frankly the dangers involved in the scheme.  It was, he said, "essentially a French idea and a political rather than a commercial idea."  Moreover, " M. de Lesseps receives from the Pasha of Egypt £20,000 Sterling a year in order to exploit this idea . . . the greater part of which remains in his pockets. . . ."[3]

Politically, the situation remained much the same, for British influence at the Porte was as strong as ever.  When

[1] *Ibid.*

[2] *Ibid.*, no. 69 B, London, Nov. 25, Apponyi to Buol.

[3] *Ibid.*, Green, the acting Consul-General in Egypt, was directed to get particulars concerning the amounts paid by the Viceroy to de Lesseps for the press campaign in favor of the canal (FO, 78/1421, Mr. Hammond of FO to Green, Private, Jan. 7, 1858).  In his reply, Green said that the reports concerning the subsidies were not founded on mere gossip.  "I was assured on such undoubted authority that the sums paid to M. Lesseps were passed in the Government accounts, that I could not feel the slightest hesitation as to alluding to the subject in my official communication to your Lordship.  I am now assured that thirty-nine thousand francs are paid monthly."  He added that "a perfect hurricane of newspaper articles was kept up" at the Viceroy's expense, in every language and in every journal of Europe, propagating the idea of the canal (*ibid.*, no. 10, Green to Clarendon, Alex., Jan. 23, 1858).  The Viceroy admitted to Mr. Green that he advanced 300,000 francs monthly to de Lesseps for the periodical *L'Isthme de Suez* (*ibid.*, Green to Clarendon, Alex., Feb. 8, 1858).

de Lesseps arrived at Constantinople in December 1857, he found Lord Stratford on the point of leaving. Some months before the canal question had been discussed by Lord Palmerston and Count Walewski at Osborne, where the Emperor and Empress had visited Queen Victoria. Unable to persuade Count Walewski to oppose the project, Palmerston consented to a renewal of the previous agreement whereby the representatives of the two Powers should remain neutral. For appearance's sake, Lord Stratford was given his congé and Bruce was recalled from Egypt.[1] But the departure of Lord Stratford did not signify a change in the British attitude toward the canal, nor did it gives more confidence to the Porte. The latter still adhered to its policy of temporizing, fearful that the construction of the canal would mean the loss of Egypt and Syria, and cause the outbreak of war between the Maritime Powers.[2] According to the Grand Vizir, these fears could only be removed by a treaty with the Powers which would give the canal the same status as the Dardanelles and by permitting Turkish troops to guard it.[3]

More important to the mind of the Turk was the fear of England. Lord Clarendon had instructed Mr. Alison, who temporarily replaced Lord Stratford, to inform the Porte that if it consented to the canal, the Powers would be released from their guarantee of the integrity of the Ottoman Empire.[4] Mr. Alison was assured by the Turkish Minister

---

[1] *Letters etc.*, 2nd ser., p. 148; HHSA, no. 55, A-E, vii/48, 1857, Apponyi to Buol, London, Aug. 12, 1857. The Austrian Ambassador at London reported that the Emperor complained bitterly of Lord Stratford and desired his recall. This probably explains the reason for Stratford's congé.

[2] HHSA, no. 85 C, Prokesch to Buol, Dec. 16, 1857.

[3] *Ibid.*

[4] FO 78/1421, FO to Alison, Jan. 1, 1858.

of Foreign Affairs that the Porte " will not give its consent until Her Majesty's Government sanction that undertaking." [1]

When the Palmerston Government fell from power in February 1858, M. Musurus, Turkish Ambassador at London, was directed to learn the views of the new cabinet concerning the canal question.[2] The request was made orally to Lord Malmesbury, who replied that he was not in position to give an opinion on so important a matter without first consulting his colleagues.[3] Several days later, Lord Malmesbury wrote to M. Musurus, stating that the present government would follow the same course as its predecessor, and would place implicit trust in the assurance given to Mr. Alison that the Porte would not sanction the enterprise without the consent of the British Government.[4] The Turkish Ministers were astonished at the manner adopted by Lord Malmesbury in replying to M. Musurus. Since the request had been made orally, they had assumed that the reply would be given in the same manner. Greatly embarrassed, the Turkish Ministers tried to minimize the importance of the assurance given to Mr. Alison. M. Musurus was instructed to inform Lord Malmesbury that the Porte had no thought of alienating its liberty of action nor of depending on a foreign Power for its decision.[5]

In a conversation with the Austrian Internuncio, the

---

[1] *Ibid.,* no. 12, Allison to Clarendon, Const., Jan. 4, 1858.

[2] *Ibid.,* Mar. 5, 1858, Le Ministre des Affaires Étrangères à l'Ambassadeur de Turquie à Londres.

[3] Turquie, vol. 335, no. 23, Trés Confidentiel, Thouvenel to Walewski, Pera, April 5, 1858.

[4] FO, 78/1421, FO to Musurus, March 11, 1858.

[5] Turquie, vol. 335, no. 23, Trés Confidentiel, Thouvenel to Walewski, Pera, April 5, 1858.

Grand Vizir pointed out the dangers which the canal held for the Turkish Empire.[1]

The project has already cost us the island of Perim and we cannot know to what extent England will go in case we pronounce to you in favor of the concession which the Viceroy demands.

There are still other considerations which are not less important. We have the example of Algiers which France has been able to convert into a French province without being called to task by any other Power; we have, moreover, the example of Tunis which, at the instigation of France, became an independent country. . . . We do not wish that with the aid of a French colony established along the canal, France should be definitely introduced into Egypt where she already exercises a preponderant influence.

I think, therefore, that the moment for us to pronounce on the question of the Suez Canal has not yet arrived. . . . "

Count Buol agreed with the Grand Vizir that the time for sanctioning the enterprise had not yet arrived, and that so long as political difficulties remained, Austria should not press for it.[2] It should be said, however, that his colleagues in the Ministries of the Commerce and Finance did not share his view. Staunch supporters of the canal, they urged Count Buol to support it actively and to announce that the Imperial Government favored its construction.[3]

The attitude of Austria and Turkey made it clear that there could be no hope, for the present, of securing the Sultan's sanction. Fear of displeasing England made both Powers reluctant to express any decided opinion in favor of

[1] HHSA, no. 20 T, Prokesch to Buol, Const., March 19, 1858.

[2] *Ibid.*, FO to Prokesch, Vienna, Mar. 27, 1858.

[3] *Ibid.*, $\frac{\text{no. 1042}}{\text{HM}}$ , Toggenburg, Minister of Commerce, to Buol, Vienna, April 11, 1858, Bruck Minister of Finance, to Buol, Vienna, May 14, 1858.

the project. On June 1, 1858, an important debate on the
canal question took place in the House of Commons.[1]  Mr.
Roebuck introduced a resolution calling on the House to
declare: " That the power and influence of England ought
not to be employed in order to induce the Sultan to withhold his consent from the formation of a canal across the
Isthmus of Suez." It was his opinion " that the honour of
England had been sacrificed, that her great name had been
dragged in the dirt, and that we have behaved in a selfish
and base manner in regard to this affair." He declared that
the House was in no way concerned with the physical difficulties of the undertaking. It was only its political aspects
which should be considered and whether it would not be for
the interest of England.

Mr. Stephenson, whose attitude we have already referred
to, again spoke in opposition. The canal would be nothing
but a "ditch," he declared. It was Lord Palmerston, however who came out most strongly against the canal. He
referred to it as " the greatest bubble that was ever imposed
upon the credulity and simplicity of the people of this
country."

I also say that we have an interest in this matter which cannot
be disregarded. . . . It is not to our interest that there should
be open between the Mediterranean and the Indian Ocean a
water-passage at the command of other Powers, and not at ours.
. . . . The object of the Resolution appears to me to be to
obtain a Parliamentary title for a scheme the shares of which
are not marketable and I trust that the House will not lend
itself to a speculation of that kind and agree to a resolution
which I maintain is at variance with the interests of England.[1]

Lord Palmerston was aware that so long as he main-

[1] Hansard, *op. cit.*, 3rd ser., vol. cl, pp. 1360-1401.
[2] *Ibid.*, pp. 1383-1384.

tained his popularity he could say what he pleased. Despite the fact that his arguments were of doubtful accuracy, his stubborn opposition to the scheme would not fail to make a deep impression. When he addressed Parliament, says a recent writer,[1] " he was not so much concerned with the faces he saw around him as with the greater public which would read his speech in the newspapers next morning." Paying slight attention to the particular objections which were brought up, he was chiefly interested in setting forth some general principles which would be remembered throughout the country. Though he knew little of the technique he employed, he " was probably one of the greatest masters in the art of speaking in elusive general terms, calculated to rouse enthusiasm without appearing dangerous to any but his most violent opponents. These latter served his purpose as objects of ridicule."

Mr. Gladstone replied to the allegations of Lord Palmerston and defined the nature of the question.

It was originally a question not of obstructing the means of communication between Europe and India—not of denying that there was an advantage in bringing them together if you could— but it was a question of a competition between the railway and the canal. The canal was in the main a French, the railway was in the main an English scheme. For the moment there was a competition between these two projects, and naturally enough the English Government—having greater confidence, as it was bound to have, in the engineers of its own country— recommended the railway in preference to the canal. The objections now urged by the noble Viscount, if they are good for anything, are good against the railway as well as against the canal . . . But the noble Viscount is not satisfied with denouncing the scheme in this way. He alleges political reasons, and

[1] B. Kingsley Martin, *The Triumph of Lord Palmerston, A Study of Public Opinion in England before the Crimean War* (London, 1924), pp. 56-58.

has transmitted some of his views to the present Foreign Office on this point. . . . There is not a State in Europe which does not declare the opposition of England to this project . . . as unwarrantable, and as a selfish policy . . . Is it not perfectly plain that all Europe will conclude the real ground of your opposition is because you suppose the canal to be injurious to the British Empire, and that the alleged interest of Turkey is hypocritically thrust in for the mere purpose justifying your policy? [1]

Mr. Gladstone then called attention to the advantages of the canal for England:

Who would have control of the Red Sea?   Who has now got control of that sea at its southern issue?   Who has occupied Aden on one side and Perim on the other?—What is the Power that would really possess this canal if it were opened?   Is it not a canal which would necessarily fall within the control of the first maritime Power in Europe?   It is England and no foreign county, that would obtain the command of it. . . .

Neither the oratorical skill of Mr. Gladstone nor his pointed arguments were sufficient to overcome the opposition.   The resolution was defeated by a vote of 290 to 62— an unmistakable indication that official England was opposed to the canal.   Yet, de Lesseps with his never-failing optimism, considered the vote as a moral victory.   "The general opinion," he said, "is that the progress of the canal cannot be stopped and that the opposition is untenable." [2]

The immediate result of the debate was far from encouraging.   The Porte was now more than ever convinced that the time for the sanction had not arrived.   Moreover, Count Buol seemed to be less favorably disposed than formerly, and while he would have been glad to see the canal in actual

[1] *Ibid.*, pp. 1386-1389.
[2] *Letters etc.*, 2nd ser., p. 262.

existence, he did not think it possible under the circumstances.[1]   To the British representative at Vienna he declared that the whole affair was a "bubble scheme," and that it would not "enlist the sympathies of Europe nor would de Lesseps obtain the capital for its construction."[2] The attitude of France remained unchanged; the Emperor and Count Walewski were personally favorable but hesitated to give official support to de Lesseps.   When informed by M. Thouvenel, the French Ambassador at the Porte, that most of his colleagues were prepared to support any steps France might take in favor of the project, Count Walewski replied that "it is a question whose solution depends less on the action of the governments than the influence of public opinion."[3]   De Lesseps, in an effort to tear away the veil by which England covered her "indirect and selfish resistance" to the canal, addressed a note to Sir Henry Bulwer, the British Ambassador at the Porte, calling on him to state frankly his position.[4]   Sir Henry replied that, not

[1] FO, 78/1421, vol. 4, no. 138, Loftus to Malmesbury, Vienna, June 9, 1858.

[2] *Ibid.*, no. 250, Loftus to Malmesbury, Vienna, July 28, 1858.   The Austrian documents do not explain this sudden change on Count Buol's part, nor do they indicate that he held such opinions of the canal. Assuming, however, that Lord Loftus was correct in his version, Count Buol's attitude at this time might have been due to his suspicions that France was veering toward an alliance with Italy, though the Plombières agreement did not take place until a month later.   On the other hand he may have "adopted" this attitude in order to win the good graces of England.

[3] Turquie, vol. 336, no. 64, FO to Thouvenel, Aug. 13, 1858.   Thouvenel was still under the instructions sent to him the previous November which directed him to take no initiative in the canal affair but to give de Lesseps support if he asked for it either as a Frenchman or as a concessionaire of the Canal Company.   He was not to take any measures which might arouse susceptibilities or provoke the antagonism of Great Britain (Turquie, vol. 333, no. 74, Walewski to Thouvenel, Paris, Nov. 20, 1857).

[4] HHSA, no. 62, Rapport politique, M. Wolf to Buol, Const., Aug. 20, 1858.

knowing the intentions of his government, he must await instructions. De Lesseps thereupon claimed the support of M. Thouvenel and declared that he would invoke the protection of the Emperor.

But realizing how futile it was to expect the Sultan's sanction under the present circumstances, de Lesseps decided upon a bold move. In October 1858 he announced that the Company would be organized and that subscriptions for the shares would be opened to the public from the 5th to the 30th of November.[1]   Interest at five per cent was guaranteed on each share while the canal was under construction.   He believed that by presenting to the Powers a *fait accompli,* he would undermine English opposition.   The Continental Governments would feel called upon to intervene in order to protect the interests of their subjects.

Of the 400,000 shares, over 200,000 were disposed of in France, where patriotic sentiment was a prime factor.[2] From other countries there were few subscribers, while England, Austria, Russia, and the United States did not

---

[1] In a circular to his agents dated Oct. 15, 1858, de Lesseps announced that besides the construction of the maritime and irrigation canals, the Company would place in cultivation 63,000 hectares of land granted by the Viceroy, and that 70,000 hectares were reserved for the maritime canal, *Letters etc.,* 2nd ser., pp. 356-357.

[2] There were 21,229 French subscribers who bought 207,111 shares an average of 12.02 shares each; 188 bought from 100 to 1000 shares; while 20,847 bought less than 100 shares. The subscribers represented all classes of society. *Letters etc.,* 2nd ser., pp. 393-395.   There can be no doubt that patriotic sentiments inspired many of these subscribers. De Lesseps relates how an old soldier approached him and said: "These English. I am glad to be able to avenge myself on them by taking shares in the Suez Canal." Another individual wished to subscribe for the railway on the island of Sweden.   He was told that it was not a railway but a canal, not an island but an isthmus, not Sweden but Suez. "It is all the same to me," he replied, "so long as it is against the English." *Ibid.,* 5th ser., p. 380.

participate.[1]  A large bloc of shares (96,517 in number)
was reserved for the Ottoman Empire, including Egypt.[2]

The organization of the Company and the sale of the
shares were to have important consequences.  Every attempt
to secure the Sultan's sanction having been frustrated by
English opposition, de Lesseps was now determined to force
matters to a conclusion—to throw down the gauntlet.

[1] The subscription by countries was as follows:

| | | | |
|---|---|---|---|
| France | 207,111 | Netherlands | 2,615 |
| Belgium | 324 | Portugal | 5 |
| Denmark | 7 | Prussia | 15 |
| Naples | 97 | Tunis | 1,714 |
| Ottoman Empire (including | | Piedmont | 1,353 |
| Egypt) | 96,517 | Switzerland | 460 |
| Barcelona | 4,046 | Tuscany | 176 |
| Rome | 54 | | |
| | | | 314,494 |

The number set aside for England, Austria, Russia and the United States
was 85,506.  *Letters etc.,* 3rd ser., p. 2.

[2] The Viceroy subscribed for 64,000 shares and in May, 1860, accepted
113,642 additional shares.  See p. 183, note 3.

# CHAPTER XII

## FRANCE INTERVENES

No sooner had the Company been organized and the shares marketed than rumors were circulated to the effect that de Lesseps intended to begin work on the canal at once. In a letter to the Viceroy he declared that it was unnecessary to apply for the Sultan's authorization, since it had been clearly implied in the vizirial letter of March 1, 1855, which had stated that the enterprise was a most useful one; and since the Turkish Ministers had told him on a number of occasions that they were not opposed to the canal so far as the interests of the Ottoman Empire were concerned.[1] But the Viceroy would not permit work to start without the approval of the Sultan.[2] He was greatly offended, according to the Austrian Consul-General, because de Lesseps had proceeded independently with the organization of the Company and had set himself up as the sole promoter of the scheme.[3] In reply to a demand from the Consuls in Egypt as to whether he had sanctioned the proceeding, he replied in the negative and refused to assume any responsibility for it.[4] It would seem that the Viceroy experienced a sudden panic when he realized the full significance of de Lesseps'

[1] Ferd. de Lesseps, *Letters etc.*, 2nd ser., p. 409.

[2] HHSA, $\frac{\text{no. } 23}{2.674}$, Huber to FO, Alex., Nov. 17, 1858.

[3] *Ibid.*, no. 7, Schreiner to Buol, Alex., Feb. 6, 1859.

[4] Égypte, vol. 28, no. 76, Consul at Alexandria to Walewski, Nov. 30, 1858.

procedure and was now trying to exonerate himself from the responsibility. He knew that the opposition of England would now be more uncompromising than ever, and hence more unpleasant to encounter.

Having learned that de Lesseps intended to begin work, the British Consul-General demanded explanations of the Viceroy. He was told that " not a sod shall be turned . . . until the Sultan's sanction shall have been obtained." [1] More than that, continued the Viceroy, he would " throw the canal over in a moment " if it suited his purpose. The Consul-General concluded that the proceedings of de Lesseps had " opened the eyes of Said Pasha to the dangerous character of his ' attached friend '." [2] At the same time he did not put too much faith in the words of one who " is so completely a creature of momentary impulse." [3]

On January 3, 1859, Lord Cowley was instructed to speak to Count Walewski concerning the activities of de Lesseps and to make it clear that the British Government had not altered its opinion of the canal.[4] It was convinced, said Lord Malmesbury, " that M. Lesseps is seeking to induce French subjects to embark their capital in a vain speculation, which will entail ruin on all who may become shareholders whatever may be the amount of pecuniary advantage which M. Lesseps may succeed in realizing for himself." Count Walewski professed ignorance of de Lesseps' activities and Lord Cowley had to content himself with warning him of the opinion held by the British Government.[5]

Lord Malmesbury also gave instructions to the British

[1] FO 78/1421, vol. 4, no. 26, confidential, Green to Bulwer, Alex., Dec. 21, 1858.

[2] *Ibid.,* no. 24, Alex., Dec. 16, 1858.

[3] *Ibid.,* no. 26, Alex., Dec. 21, 1858.

[4] FO 78/1489, vol. 5, no. 11, FO to Cowley, Jan. 3, 1859.

[5] *Ibid.,* Mem. of Corr., Cowley to FO, no. 33, Jan., 1859.

Consul-General in Egypt to use his " best endeavours to persuade the Viceroy . . . to abandon altogether the idea of making the canal in question." [1] The Consul-General, however, believed that the scheme was already on the verge of collapse. He reported that the " projectors . . . are in the position of drowning men; their situation is a desperate one, . . . they will catch at anything to save themselves and it is prudent to keep out of their reach. . . . I am assured that M. Lesseps has written a letter to the Viceroy couched in such objectionable terms, as to have given His Highness great offense; and I have no doubt but this letter is the first step towards the ' querelle d'allemand ' which will wind up the proceedings." [2]    The Viceroy had told him that if England had set out to find a man to injure the cause of the canal she could not have found a better one than de Lesseps.[3]

It was evident that a crisis was at hand. During the first months of 1859 de Lesseps and the Viceroy avoided each other as much as possible.[4]  Several attempts to start work on the canal had been prevented by the Egyptian Government, and de Lesseps went so far as to threaten " to fire on the authorities " if they continued to oppose him.[5]  In view of these circumstances the French Consul-General found his position exceedingly awkward but he was directed to maintain a reserved attitude, and to take no part in the negotia-

---

[1] *Ibid.,* vol. 5, no. 1, FO to Green, Jan. 10, 1859.

[2] *Ibid.,* no. 11, Green to Malmesbury, Alex., Feb. 3, 1859.

[3] *Ibid.,* no. 30, Green to Malmesbury, Alex., Mar. 13, 1859.

[4] Égypte, vol. 28, no. 89, Sabatier to Walewski, Alex., Mar. 22, 1859.

[5] FO 78/1489, no. 34, Green to Malmesbury, Alex., April 1, 1859. The Austrian Consul-General reported that orders had been sent to the Governors of the provinces to prohibit the inhabitants from taking any part in the canal works; and that these orders were later cancelled upon the demand of de Lesseps (HHSA, no. 27/15, Schreiner to FO, Alex., April 2, 1859.

tions between the Company and the Egyptian Government.[1]
On the other hand, he was free to aid the members of the
Company by means of his counsel.

The situation was no less difficult for the Viceroy, who
while determined that no work should be started without the
authorization of the Sultan, had no wish to subject himself
to French criticism by depriving the Company of opportunities to study the ground. Accordingly, he permitted
de Lesseps to employ twenty laborers in order to carry on
preliminary studies. This concession was probably due to
the advice of the French Consul-General, who cautioned him
to " show towards the agents of the Suez Canal Company
more courtesy and attention than he had of late exhibited." [2]

In spite of all difficulties de Lesseps remained undaunted,
ever ready to seize upon any opportunity which would help
to promote his scheme. On April 25, 1859, work on the
canal was formally begun near Port Said. This event,
though heralded by de Lesseps with great optimism, only
added to his troubles. The British Consul-General regarded
it as an attempt to create a favorable impression among the
shareholders, and did not believe that the Viceroy would
take any part in the work. " But he is a man of too weak
a character to be relied upon for prohibiting the proceedings
of M. de Lesseps unless he receives from Constantinople
very clear and peremptory orders or from Her Majesty's
Government a very distinct declaration of its wishes and intentions." [3] This suggestion was adopted by Lord Malmesbury who telegraphed Sir Henry Bulwer that " the Porte
should give positive orders to stop a work which is a political
and private piece of swindling." [4] A few days later Sir

[1] Égypte, vol. 28, no. 3, FO to Sabatier, Paris, Mar. 30, 1859.

[2] FO 78/1489, Mem. of Corr., Acting Consul-General Walne, no. 39,
April 12, 1859.

[3] FO 78/1489, no. 45, Walne to Malmesbury, Alex., May 6, 1859.

[4] Ibid., no. 298, FO to Bulwer, Telegr. May 19, 1859.

Henry replied that the Porte would order the Viceroy to stop work on the canal.[1]

The Viceroy now found himself in a more embarrassing predicament than ever.  He wished neither to sanction the proceedings of de Lesseps nor to disavow them completely.  The British Consul-General seized the occasion to discredit the project and endeavored to persuade the Viceroy to oppose it openly.  He pointed out that what de Lesseps and his associates wanted was not so much the construction of the canal " as the opening of a trench to the Egyptian treasury." [2]  The prevailing opinion in Egypt, continued the Consul-General, was that the sooner some arrangement could be arrived at to liquidate the Company, the better it would be for the country.  He demanded that the Viceroy should publicly disavow the work which had been done as unauthorized, and " make a moderate sacrifice to be rid of the very worst speculation on which he has ever entered." [3]

On June 1st, the Grand Vizir addressed a letter to the Viceroy calling on him to permit no further work without the Sultan's authorization.[4]  De Lesseps was ordered by the Viceroy to cease his operations immediately.  Nevertheless, the work continued and the Egyptian Government took no further measures except to withdraw the native workmen.[5]  But enough Europeans remained to keep going and when the British Consul-General protested against their employment,

[1] *Ibid.*, no. 361, Telegr. from Bulwer to Malmesbury, Const., May 23, 1859.

[2] *Ibid.*, no. 55, Walne to Malmesbury, Alex., May 24, 1859.

[3] *Ibid.*, no. 63, Walne to Malmesbury, Alex., June 10, 1859.

[4] *Ibid.*, enclosure in no. 406, Bulwer to Malmesbury, Const., June 3, 1859.

[5] There were only a few hundred workers employed on the canal at this time (*Letters etc.*, 3rd ser., p. 184).  By Nov. of the following year there were 1700 and by Aug., 1861 over 12,000 (*Letters etc.*, 3rd ser., p. 398, 4th ser., p. 87).

he was told by the Viceroy that it was up to the Consular Corps to see to their withdrawal.[1]  Furthermore, the Viceroy announced that he had no intention of sending his troops to Port Said where a collision might arise with Europeans. In reply to the vizirial letter he merely requested definite instructions as to whether the canal should be constructed or not.  These were trying times.  The Viceroy was incessantly reproached by the British Consul-General for permitting the work to go on.  But he remained loyal to the scheme, and even when he had to make some pretense of putting the clamps on de Lesseps, he secretly gave him help.[2]

Just at this point when the outlook was already most discouraging for the Company, the Austrian Consul-General joined his British colleague in carrying on a systematic attack against the canal.[3]  The reason becomes apparent when we remember that Austria was at the moment engaged in fighting France in the Italian War.  By intrigues, insinuations and broadsides, the two agents neglected nothing which might discredit the scheme.  De Lesseps was charged by the Austrian Consul-General with having abandoned the universal character of the enterprise and with having acted as a recruiting agent in raising volunteers for the French army.[4]

[1] FO 78/1489, no. 17, Walne to Bulwer, Alex., July 6, 1859.

[2] The Viceroy occasionally found it necessary to humor the English agents who were continually pressing him to abandon his support of de Lesseps.  In a conversation with the British Consul-General, he said that " M. de Lesseps had shamefully deceived him.  He had never recognized the Company, but every few days de Lesseps sent him a note or a memorandum.  He took no notice of these communications but left them unanswered. . . . He was worried out of his life by the Canal.  A few days since M. de Lesseps had pursued him to Cairo, and he the Pasha was almost ashamed of the maneuvres to which he had been obliged to resort in order to evade an interview " (*ibid.*).

[3] Égypte, vol. 28, no. 97, Sabatier to Walewski, Alex., July 12, 1859.

[4] HHSA, no. 26, Schreiner to Buol, Alex., May 17, 1859.

These charges he denied indignantly and declared that Austria had become an even more dangerous opponent to the canal than England.[1]　The Internuncio also took a hand in the affair and hinted that de Lesseps was really an agent of the French Government and was bent on bringing about a disruption of the Turkish Empire.[2]　But Austria did not wish to have it appear that she was hostile to the canal itself, and the Consul-General was accordingly directed to abstain from acting for or against it.[3]　As for the British Consul-General, he saw in the Company's disregard of the Sultan's authority an attempt to establish a French colony in the Isthmus.　"A French colony established there might," he said, "in the course of a few years become sufficiently strong to domineer over the weak rulers of Egypt, and, supported from without, prove a permanent menace to our communication with India."[4]

Since the work continued despite the vizirial letter of June 1st, the Porte dispatched another note to the Viceroy on September 19th.[5]　This declared that all work which had been done was illegal and would be regarded as non-existent, and the Viceroy was again requested to put a stop to the operations of the Company.　The bearer of this note, Muchtar Bey, had received private instructions to show the Viceroy "the impolicy as concerned his own interests, as

[1] *Ibid.*

[2] *Ibid.*, no. 43 D, Prokesch to FO, Const., June 5, 1859.

[3] *Ibid.*, FO to Schreiner, Vienna, June 5, 1859.

[4] FO 78/1489, no. 83, Walne to Russell, Alex., July 21, 1859. This suspicion that the Company intended to establish a French colony in the Isthmus was repeated in subsequent dispatches of the English agents. It will be remembered that the Company was given lands to cultivate in Egypt. England, however, was seizing upon any pretext to discredit the scheme.

[5] *Ibid.*, enclosure in no. 164, Bulwer to Russell, Therapia, Sept. 20, 1859.

well as those of the Porte, of encouraging an undertaking which would be likely to make Egypt, in any European War, the theater of conflict, and end eventually not only by separating that country from the Ottoman Empire, but by removing the family of Mehemet Ali from ruling over it." [1] Muchtar Bey's mission was inspired by Sir Henry Bulwer who hoped, no doubt, to frighten the Viceroy into abandoning his interest in the scheme.[2]

On October 4th, Cherif Pasha, the Viceroy's chief minister, read the vizirial letter to the Consular Corps which had been assembled for that purpose, and called on them to take action for the withdrawal of their subjects who might be engaged in the work. The Consular Corps agreed unanimously and set November 1st as the date for the complete evacuation of the Isthmus.[3]

The crisis, long threatening, had at last appeared. " The canal question," said the Austrian Consul-General, " has now entered a phase similar to that of a burial. No one will be surprised, for it was inevitable." [4] De Lesseps was discouraged. He saw his " great scheme " facing extinction and the shareholders ruined. In a letter which appeared in *l'Isthme de Suez* on September 19th, he had declared that

---

[1] *Ibid.*, Mem. of Corr., Colquhoun, no. 12, Oct. 7, 1859.

[2] Égypte, vol. 28, no. 103, Sabatier to Minister, Alex., Oct. 4, 1859. The French Ambassador at the Porte, who opposed the mission of Muchtar Bey, reported that Sir Henry in a conversation with the Grand Vizir and Minister of Foreign Affairs went so far as to say that if Turkey disdained his advice England would probably decide to occupy Egypt rather than see in other hands the highway to India (Turquie, vol. 341, no. 60, Thouvenel to Walewski, Therapia, Aug. 23, 1859).

[3] HHSA, $\frac{\text{no. } 48}{78}$, Schreiner to Rechberg, Alex., Oct. 5, 1859, annex, procès verbaux of Consular Meeting of Oct. 4. *Cf.* Égypte, vol. 28, no. 103, cited above.

[4] HHSA, $\frac{\text{no } 48}{78}$, Oct. 5, 1859.

if the canal were not constructed the Viceroy would be
called upon to reimburse the shareholders.[1]    Greatly offended
at this threat, the Viceroy addressed a reply to the Dutch
Consul-General, who acted as Superior Agent for the Company in Egypt, in which he stated that he had from the
beginning protested against the organization of the Company and the call for funds, and did not now consider
himself responsible for the work which had been done.
Furthermore, he did not wish that his name should be used
" to deceive public opinion and, above all, the shareholders." [2]

Work on the canal was virtually suspended and only a
few Frenchmen remained in the Isthmus.   It was feared by
the British Government that de Lesseps would bring forward excessive demands for compensation, and that the
Viceroy, unable to meet these, would be forced to hand over
the railway between Alexandria and Suez.   The Consul-
General was instructed to oppose any attempt on the part
of the Company to secure the railway.[3]   In carrying out this
instruction, he took the opportunity to show the Viceroy the
slight advantage which would result from the canal and the
great dangers to which it exposed Egyptian finances.[4]   But
he made no impression, for it was evident that the Viceroy
" has recently been worked upon by some of the fawning
parasites who never for a day quit him, to profit by his
weak moments."

De Lesseps realized that the time had now arrived when

---

[1] Égypte, vol. 28, no. 103, cited above.

[2] *Ibid.*

[3] FO 78/1489, no. 4, FO to Colquhoun, Oct. 17, 1859. The Austrian
Consul-General feared that France would take Egypt as indemnification
for the French shareholders, in which case " one of the richest and most
beautiful countries of the world will be doomed or be made tributary
to France " (HHSA, $\frac{\text{no. } 48}{78}$, Oct. 5, 1859).

[4] *Ibid.*, no. 22, Colquhoun to Russell, Alex., Nov. 6, 1859.

he must get active support from his government or take
steps to disband the Company and refund the subscriptions.
Writing to the Emperor on August 6, 1859, he declared that
he could no longer continue his struggle against English
opposition, and requested support in order to protect the
interests of the French shareholders.[1] While the Emperor
approved of this note, he desired to wait until after the conclusion of peace with Austria before taking any decisive
steps. In another note, addressed to Count Walewski on
September 15th, de Lesseps complained bitterly of the unfriendly attitude of the French Consul-General in Egypt.[2]
" I am certain," he said, " that M. Sabatier has made every
effort to discourage the Viceroy and to engage him not to
persevere in his enterprise by trying to persuade him that
the Emperor will not counteract the opposition of England,
and will not support the Canal Company." Later he had a
conversation with the Emperor who asked him why it was
that everyone was opposed to his scheme.[3] " Sire," replied
de Lesseps, " it is because everyone believes that Your
Majesty does not wish to support it." The Emperor thereupon assured him that he could count upon his support and
protection.

This marks the turning point in French policy. Neutrality was at last abandoned. As an indication of its
benevolent attitude toward de Lesseps, the French Government recalled M. Sabatier from Egypt. In notifying the
latter of this decision, Count Walewski expressed displeasure
at the manner in which he had conducted himself in the
affair.[4] The instructions sent to M. Sabatier had made it
clear that while the French Government wished to keep

---

[1] *Letters etc.,* 3rd ser., pp. 198-200.

[2] *Ibid.,* p. 201.

[3] *Ibid.,* p. 235.

[4] Égypte, vol. 28, no. 6, Walewski to Sabatier, Paris, Oct. 26, 1859.

aloof from the political aspects of the question, it was none
the less interested in protecting the rights of the French
shareholders.[1]  The Consul-General, said Count Walewski,
had held too rigidly to instructions which advised him to
exercise reserve, and moreover, he had failed to protest
against the severe measures adopted at the Consular meeting
on October 4th.

The French Ambassador at Constantinople was directed
to support the Company in its effort to obtain the sanction,
but was to avoid as much as possible " engaging himself in
a struggle of influence with the Ambassador of His Britannic Majesty." [2]  No precise limits were prescribed to his
actions but it was suggested that he should associate himself
with the representatives of those Powers desirous of protecting the interests of the Company.  Instructions were also
sent to the French representatives at St. Petersburg and
Berlin directing them to request the governments to which
they were accredited to support the French policy at the
Porte.[3]  A similar request was made of the Austrian Government.[4]

With the conclusion of the Italian War the relations of

[1] Sabatier had received instructions on July 7, 1859 (Égypte, vol. 28,
no. 5) to maintain an attitude of reserve and not to intervene in the
political aspects of the question but to support the financial interests of
French subjects.  In defending his conduct, Sabatier asked where the
financial question ended and where the political question began (*ibid.*, no.
108, Sabatier to Walewski, Alex., Nov. 10, 1859).  It is clear that France
wished to avoid a controversy with England which would have resulted
had she supported the scheme on political grounds.  Hence, the emphasis
she placed on the protection of French capital and her insistence that
the canal was a private, commercial project.  This is brought out in
the instructions to the French agents.

[2] Turquie, vol. 342, no. 70, Walewski to Thouvenel, Paris, Nov. 3,
1859.  *Cf. infra*, p. 174.

[3] *Ibid.*

[4] HHSA, no. 13, Litt. D., Metternich to Rechberg, Paris, Oct. 28, 1859.

France and Austria were once more on a friendly basis. Anxious to come to an understanding with Austria concerning affairs in the Near East, Napoleon on November 16, 1859, held a long conversation with Prince Metternich, the Austrian Ambassador at Paris. After dwelling upon the possibilities of an alliance between France, Russia and Austria to settle Eastern affairs, the Emperor suggested that Austria should take Egypt. " But," he added, " what will England say? One really cannot make this susceptible and egoistic country understand reason. I have given myself all the trouble in the world in order to convince the English of the true, glorious aim which they should follow in civilizing the coasts of the Mediterranean. Oh well! England likes better to see the barbarian in Africa than civilization in front of Gibraltar. I can do nothing with them. Can you not in time see the map of Europe . . . which will place Egypt under Austria?" Metternich replied that Austria was not strong enough to maintain such a distant acquisition, and was, moreover, chiefly interested in the Principalities and the Adriatic coast " which will furnish us a more efficacious aggrandizement." The Emperor insisted, however, that Egypt with the Suez Canal would be the center of commerce between Europe and Asia, and would offer Austria greater advantages and would enable her to increase her mercantile marine and her naval fleet. " The Emperor continued to dwell on the advantages of possessing Egypt to which the rivalry of France and England do not permit them to aspire. His Majesty assured me that he would lend his support " to the plan.[1]

What was the Emperor's motive in offering Egypt to Austria? It seems that he believed he might in this way secure concessions from Austria in Italy. Count Rechberg,

[1] *Ibid.*, Band IX/62, France 1859, no. 16, Litt. A-B, Paris, Nov. 16, Metternich to Rechberg.

to whom the proposal was communicated, regarded it in this light. " It cannot be that the Emperor of-the French," he wrote to Metternich, " can deceive himself in this regard and believe that the desire of an increase towards the Orient is strong enough to lead us to make concessions in Italy. The regulation of affairs in the Peninsula is today our first and principal interest, and it is not some vague hope that can make us sacrifice it." [1]   If France and England, how- ever, should through mutual jealousy agree to sacrifice to Austria the peaceful possession of Egypt, she would not refuse it.   Although the question of the dismemberment of the Ottoman Empire was then in the air, the Austrian Gov- ernment had no desire to hasten that operation.

But while she did not accept the Emperor's proposal con- cerning Egypt, Austria did give her support to the canal project.   Baron Prokesch, the Internuncio at Constantinople, was instructed to support the French negotiations in behalf of the Company, but not to go so far as to oblige the Porte to ratify the Concession, nor to awaken political embarrass- ments.[2]   The Spanish Minister also gave his support, while the representatives of Russia and Prussia awaited instruc- tions.[3]

[1] *Ibid.,* no. 2, Vienna, Nov. 24, 1859.   It is interesting to note that in 1857 the Emperor proposed to the British Government a partition of northern Africa with Morocco falling to France, Tunis to Sardinia and Egypt to England (The Earl of Cromer, *Modern Egypt,* 2 vols. in one, N. Y., 1916, p. 91, citing Émile Ollivier, *L'Empire libérale,* vol. iii, p. 418). Lord Palmerston, writing to Lord Clarendon concerning this proposal, said that England had no desire whatever to secure Egypt (Ashley, *The Life of Henry John Temple, Viscount Palmerston,* vol. ii, p. 126, letter dated Mar. 1, 1857).

[2] *Ibid.,* FO to Prokesch, Vienna, Nov. 3, 1859; to Metternich at Paris, Nov. 4th; to Rome Nov. 6th; to Apponyi at London, Nov. 14th.

[3] Turquie, vol. 342, no. 78, Thouvenel to Walewski, Pera, Nov. 23, 1859. The Prussian Minister was later advised " to remain passive " (FO 78/1489, Mem. of Corr., Lord Bloomfield, no. 471, Dec. 16, 1859).

Having given his promise of support to de Lesseps, Count Walewski now appealed to England to abandon her opposition in view of the interest which the Emperor displayed in the enterprise. He proposed that England should either join the French Government in obtaining the sanction from the Sultan, or at least abstain from offering any further objections to the scheme.[1] France, said Count Walewski, was prepared to enter into any agreement either by conversation or by exchange of notes, in order to remove the British objections. If, however, England persisted in her opposition, the Company would be compelled to wind up its affairs. As a basis for an understanding, he suggested that the two Cabinets should either demand in concert the sanction with guarantees for the security of the canal, or they should equally abstain from any interference and leave the decision to the Sultan.[2]

Count Walewski's overture availed him nothing. He was informed that the British Government had not altered its manner of viewing the project and could not associate itself in the French proposals. The British objections, said Lord Russell, "remain unshaken . . . and there can be no advantage in reviving the discussion . . . as the opposition of Her Majesty's Government will not be relaxed."[3] In his disappointment Count Walewski declared that if England refused to abstain from using her power against the canal,

[1] FO 78/1556, "Substance of Correspondence respecting the 'Suez Canal', moved by Mr. Duff, M.P., Feb. 18, 1860", no. 606, Oct. 19, 1859.

[2] Turquie, vol. 342, no. 69, Oct. 28 and no. 70, Nov. 3, 1859, Walewski to Thouvenel.

[3] FO 78/1489, no. 410, FO to Cowley, Oct. 11, 1859, copies to Bulwer and Colquhoun. Walewski made his appeal to the English Government early in October but for some reason delayed several weeks before informing M. Thouvenel. This explains why the date of the dispatch to Cowley is earlier than those from Walewski to Thouvenel.

there would be a struggle of influence between the two governments, as France could not abandon the interests of the Company.[1]

The French Ambassador at Constantinople, having re-received his new instructions [2] to support the Company, lost no time in seeking out the Grand Vizir. The latter assured him that Turkey was not in principle opposed to the construction of a canal, but insisted that the Sultan's sanction was an absolute necessity and must not be regarded as " a dead letter." [3]  Until France and England had come to an understanding, said the Grand Vizir, the Porte must delay its decision. The Ambassador had to content himself with a promise that until the sanction was granted, every facility would be given to de Lesseps in order to preserve the property of the Company and the works which had already been executed.

It was still the fear of England which haunted the minds of the Turkish Ministers.[4]  But now that France, Austria and Russia [5] were apparently united in supporting the project, was it necessary any longer to give heed to British objections? Upon this question the Turkish Ministers were divided. One group, headed by the Grand Vizir, held to the opinion that the scheme should be considered as any other commercial project.

[1] FO 78/1556, Sub. of Corr. etc., no. 663.

[2] *Cf. supra*, p. 170.

[3] Turquie, vol. 342, no. 76, Thouvenel to Walewski, Therapia, Nov. 9, 1859.

[4] The appearance of several British warships before Alexandria in August, 1859, was looked upon by the Turkish Ministers as a demonstration against the canal and as a threat of what might happen if they ever granted the sanction (Turquie, vol. 341, nos. 59 and 60, Thouvenel to Walewski, Therapia, Aug. 17 and 23, 1859).

[5] The Russian Ambassador supported M. Thouvenel in his demands for the Sultan's sanction although he had received no definite instructions. *Cf. infra*, p. 176.

If we invite Europe to treat this affair as rather of European than Turkish importance, we pass it out of our hands and must eventually receive the law from Europe whatever that law may be, as a matter of course. We also deal with disadvantage with Europe when we deal with it collectively, and we shall, in the present instance bring England into conflict with Powers less friendly to us, but who will have a great majority against her opinion.[1]

He was in favor of keeping the matter in Turkish hands and heeding the wishes of England. The other group, headed by the Minister of Foreign Affairs, maintained that

If the matter is once brought forward by M. Lesseps backed by the French Embassy, the Porte will either have to accept M. Lesseps' conditions, which would be hostile to England, or reject them, which would be hostile to France. By leaving Europe to decide the matter we escape from this, which is our first difficulty, at once and if Europe does not agree, we may yet escape from the second.

While the representatives of Austria and Russia supported the French policy at the Porte, they did so on the basis of general European interests rather than the interests of the French investors.[2] Considering the circumstances, their viewpoint was more judicious than that of France. As Baron Prokesch pointed out to M. Thouvenel, to demand the sanction solely on behalf of French capital would destroy any chance of securing it, since England would never relent so long as the enterprise had a French character.[3] Count Walewski admitted the weight of this argument but nevertheless directed M. Thouvenel to confine his conduct exclu-

[1] FO 78/1489, no. 289, Bulwer to Russell, Dec. 7, 1859.
[2] Turquie, vol. 342, no. 79, Thouvenel to Minister, Nov. 30, 1859.
[3] HHSA, no. 87, A-C, Prokesch to FO, Const., Nov. 23, 1859.

sively to what concerned the French capital.[1] By adopting this policy France would avoid political arguments and rest on apparently less aggressive grounds. The Russian Ambassador supported the French negotiations though he had received no definite instructions in the matter. Gortchakoff, the Russian Chancellor, did not feel such instructions were necessary, since " the French Government places French interests above everything else." [2] Thus the alliance which united the representatives of the three Continental Powers was none too firm and Sir Henry Bulwer spared no efforts in his attempts to destroy it.[3] Between him and the French Ambassador there was an " armed courtesy " and any discussion of the canal question was avoided as much as possible.[4]

The situation was becoming more and more embarrassing for the Turkish Ministers. Pulled one way by Sir Henry Bulwer, and another by M. Thouvenel, they seemed unable to make up their minds as to what should be done. They could not afford to risk the displeasure of England which alone of the Powers could be relied upon to support Turkey in case of a conflict. Little confidence was placed on France, because of her alliance with Russia, nor did the Turkish Ministers count on the support of Austria.[5] England's wishes in the canal question must therefore be respected. Sir Henry Bulwer let it be known that Turkey would be toying with her existence if she dared to grant the sanction without England's consent.[6]

[1] Turquie, vol. 342, no. 78, Walewski to Thouvenel, Paris, Dec. 9, 1859.

[2] HHSA, Rapp. dipl., Const., 1859, Prokesch to Rechberg, Const., Dec. 21, 1859.

[3] Turquie, vol. 342, no. 80, Thouvenel to Walewski, Pera, Dec. 7, 1859.

[4] *Ibid.*

[5] HHSA, Cons. Ber., no. 89, Prokesch to Rechberg, Const., Nov. 30, 1859.

[6] *Ibid.*, no. 91, A-D, Prokesch to Rechberg, Const., Dec. 7, 1859.

It was rumored, however, that a group within the British Cabinet was favorable to the canal and might be strong enough to overcome the opposition. Eager to grasp at any opportunity which might relieve the situation, the Porte instructed its ambassador at London, M. Musurus, to learn the attitude of the English ministers. In case a majority was favorable to the canal, the Porte would come out openly and grant the sanction, whereas if Palmerston really had the support of his colleagues, it would postpone a decision.[1] M. Musurus reported that the British Cabinet was free from dissension and united in opposition to the scheme.[2]

As both M. Thouvenel and Sir Henry Bulwer were determined that the Porte must make a definite pronouncement of its stand on the question, the Turkish Ministers decided that the best way out of the predicament was to dispatch identic notes to London and Paris setting forth the conditions under which they were prepared to sanction the enterprise. Action of some kind was imperative.

The necessity for the Porte to break its silence [wrote Baron Prokesch] is generally understood. The Ottoman Ministers and the two ambassadors equally admit it, but the English Ambassador insists that the note to be addressed by the Porte to its representatives at Paris and London . . . should be so worded as to make it understood that the project of cutting the Isthmus is considered at Constantinople, as contrary to Ottoman interests. The French Ambassador, on the other hand, wishes the note in question to show the Porte as favorable to the project. Finally, the Porte desires to say neither the one or the other, or to offer either Power any basis on which to support their pretensions.[3]

[1] *Ibid.*, no. 86 B, Nov. 18th and no. 89 C, Nov. 30, confidential, Prokesch to Rechberg.

[2] *Ibid.*, Cons. Ber. XII, no. 91 A-D, Prokesch to Rechberg, Const., Dec. 7, 1859.

[3] *Ibid.*, Cons. Ber., no. 89 C, Prokesch to Rechberg, Const., Nov. 30, 1859.

The notes, dated January 4, 1860, stated that the solution of the canal question depended upon three factors: (1) an examination of the plan of execution to see that it held no dangers for the Ottoman Empire in general and Egypt in particular; (2) guarantees concerning the administration of Egypt; (3) guarantees against a conflict among the Powers over the Canal, and security of navigation based on the interests of Europe in general and Turkey in particular.[1]

The British Government refused to give the guarantees requested in the note and brought forth all the old objections: alienation of land to the Company, employment of forced labor, dangers of foreign colonization and fortifications, as well as the physical difficulties involved in constructing the canal.[2] Meanwhile, work on the canal proceeded with the tacit approval of the Egyptian Government, despite the declaration given to the Consular Corps on October 4th.

[1] Turquie, vol. 342, annex to no. 83, Thouvenel to Walewski, Pera, Dec. 27, 1859. *Cf.* FO 78/1556, vol. 6, copy of letter from Min. of Foreign Aff. at the Porte to Turkish Ambass. at London, dated, Jan. 4, 1860; *Parl. Papers, Egypt*, no. 2 (1883), disp. from Porte to the Representatives at London and Paris, Jan. 4, 1860.

[2] The Porte could hardly have expected England to accept the guarantees in question. It seems that the purpose of the identic notes was to give some kind of a pronouncement on the subject and thus to get release from an embarrassing position. Sir Henry Bulwer prevailed upon the Porte to accept as a basis for any negotiations relative to the canal, the stipulation that no sanction would be given until the project was "stripped of its features of colonization and forced labour", that whatever fortresses were constructed in the Isthmus should be kept in Turkish hands, and "that the Guarantee of England which implies her assent should be held as a *sine qua non* to the whole undertaking". Sir Henry Bulwer was secretly pleased with his success, though he thought it better to appear discontented in order to disarm the French. He was determined, nevertheless, to have his way, for, as he said, "to be beaten here in any question about the Canal, would be to be beaten in a question of influence, the effects of which would possibly extend throughout the East . . . even to India as well as Persia, and provoke dangers which are now slumbering, and apparently unconnected with it" (FO 78/1489, no. 312, Bulwer to Russell, Const., Dec. 28, 1859).

The English press was at this time conducting a veritable campaign against the canal. The *Times* on December 16, 1859, declared that it could see no reason why

if the French or any other people are bent upon sinking their money in the sand, we should concern ourselves in doing more than we have done to counteract the delusion. If France, Austria, Prussia, Russia and Sardinia are so decidedly committed to this unpromising enterprise as to concert measures for investing it with the patronage of the Sultan, we need go no farther . . . in our opposition to the scheme. In fact, as we are firmly convinced that the works can scarcely be executed, and can certainly never be maintained, we cannot profess to conceive any apprehension of an impossible result, while as to the money, not much of that will come out of British pockets. . . . If, however, contrary to all probabilities, the project should be actually realized, we can only say that the Canal will be so far a British Canal that it will be traversed by British ships, devoted to British traffic, and maintained by British tolls. . . .

The *Morning Herald* called the canal " one of those magnificent ' ideas ' of which France . . . claims the monopoly." France had just gone to war for an ' idea ' in Italy.

We are naturally suspicious, then, when we see the idea of M. de Lesseps so prominently brought forward as to become a matter of joint remonstrance of France, Prussia, Russia, Austria, and Sardinia, and when Sir Henry Bulwer's name is alone absent from the list of ambassadors who demand from the Sultan the Firman for the Suez Canal. It would be affectation to disguise the fact that a great portion of the pertinacity with which the scheme of M. de Lesseps is clung to abroad, is owing to the very general belief that the opening of the Suez Canal will be a great blow to English interests in the East, and consequently an enormous benefit to the Continent.

The object, no doubt [said the *Daily News*] of bringing forward the Suez scheme at the present moment is to show how

England is capable of taking a mean and selfish ground, unsupported by any other Power. The expected inference is that we are as perverse and retrograde in Italy as we are in Egypt, and that we deserve to be isolated in the same manner. . . . Our policy is simply to sink this Turkish question altogether: at least for the present time, and to suffer M. de Lesseps to sink his shareholders in the Suez Canal.

The *Morning Post,* the personal organ of Lord Palmerston, announced that: " It forms no part of the interest of England to assist in carrying out a scheme, either wholly impracticable, or, of which the practicability would be shown in creating for the especial benefit of France an Egyptian Dardanelles or an Egyptian Gibraltar. . . ." [1]

Such pronouncements only faintly disguised the real motive back of England's opposition, which was to prevent any other Power from controlling the route to India. Her policy might well be labeled " opportunist," in that she seized upon any pretext that at the moment appeared to be the strongest for opposing the scheme. Thus she would point to technical difficulties, to the ruin of Egyptian finances, to the dismemberment of the Ottoman Empire, to the employment of forced labor on the canal, to the establishment of a French colony in the Isthmus and the construction of French fortifications—in fact, any reason at all so long as she could prevent the Porte from granting the sanction. That other countries were favorable only served to arouse her suspicions. A scheme designed to shorten the route to India, promoted by a Frenchman and supported by the French Government, was simply unthinkable in Palmerstonian England. In a conversation with Count Apponyi, the Austrian Ambassador at London, Lord Russell made it clear that he was opposed to the canal because the Conces-

[1] HHSA, Cons. Ber., VIII/54, no. III A-B, Apponyi to Rechberg, London, Dec. 21, 1859, enclosures.

sion made " M. de Lesseps the veritable Pasha of Egypt,"
and because the employment of fellahs was really intended
to establish an armed force against Turkey or to sustain a
French expedition and would end by setting up a French
colony in Egypt. " The Porte," continued Lord Russell,
" has no need of our counsel in order to understand its own
interests; we limit ourselves then to encourage it in its resistance." Furthermore, the canal was merely a pretext for
political *arrière pensées*. " It is not the first time that France
has tried to bring up an *Egyptian Question*." [1]

England's suspicions of France were set forth in a memorandum entitled, " Insuperable Objections of Her Majesty's
Government to the Projected Suez Canal." [2]

The Suez Canal once made, Egypt is completely separated
from Turkey and may declare its independence whenever it
pleases. Fortifications of immense strength have been erected
all around Alexandria and along the coast, in its neighborhood
to defend it against an attack from the Sea, and if Egyptian
troops could not garrison the forts, French troops could easily
be put into them. These works have all been planned in the
War Office at Paris, and have been erected by French Engineers
on the spot; they are large enough for a garrison of 20,000 men.
These works are to defend Egypt against an English attack
from the Mediterranean, the French being able from Algiers
and Toulon to throw an army into Egypt before our Fleet could
be made strong enough to prevent it.

It is perfectly well known that the Great Dam of the Nile
which the French persuaded Mehemet Ali to undertake under
the pretense of watering and fertilizing Lower Egypt, was in
fact a military work intended for the double purpose of arrest-
ing any force which might come from the Red Sea and march
downwards on Alexandria, and of adding to the defences of

[1] *Ibid.*, no. 112 D, Apponyi to Rechberg, London, Dec. 27, 1859.
[2] FO 78/1556, vol. 6, Suez Canal 1860.

Lower Egypt by affording the means of directing inundations at will. This work then was to defend Egypt from the South.

There still remains the Eastern Frontier open to attack, and the proposed Canal would complete the system of defenses— a great cut three hundred feet wide and twenty-eight feet deep, as this ship canal is meant to be, with fortifications on its bank, and war steamers properly placed in it, would effectually stop any army coming from Syria, and from the day when such a Canal was finished, Egypt might be reckoned a dependency of France.

But, if war should unfortunately arise between England and France, France would at once seize hold of the two ends of the Canal, which would thus be open for France and shut for England. A French expedition might start at once and carry by a *coup de main* Aden in time of peace weakly garrisoned and not fortified against an European force, although able to resist the neighboring Arabs. A French squadron driving from the Red Sea might sweep our commerce east of the Cape and probably take the Mauritus, and for a time we should be at their mercy.

With reference to the utility as well as the profits of the intended Canal, it must be borne in mind that to sailing ships the navigation of the Red Sea is dangerous in all its length. . . .

Moreover, the cost of the Canal is put at about seven millions sterling, the working expenses could not be less than 120,000 pounds, probably they would be much more—four percent on seven millions would be 280,000 pounds. Thus 400,000 must be raised by tolls to make the undertaking pay, which, if 4000 ships passed the Canal, would be £100 a ship, but the probability is that the cost of the construction would be nearer double that amount. The scheme is recommended on purely commercial grounds, but the maritime commerce of England is equal to that of all the rest of Europe . . . whereas it is evident that France has no commercial interests connected with India, China, or Australia that can be for a moment compared with the interests of England. If then the English Government .are opposed to the scheme, the French Government cannot press its adoption on any commercial considerations, and it would surely be most inadvisable on their part to infuse jealousy and suspicion into the relations between the two countries without sufficient reason for doing so, if they have no ulterior and unavowed views.

While England maintained her unrelenting opposition, the Viceroy, encouraged by the French Government, gave his support to the Company. He now looked upon the canal as his own scheme which would redound to his honor and which nothing could make him renounce.[1] Yet he was anxious to learn what his legal responsibilities were as regards the Company and he dispatched two of his advisers to Paris in order to consult French legal opinion. The French lawyers held that while he was in no way committed to the Company, he was liable as a shareholder.[2]

At the first general meeting of the shareholders on May 15, 1860, the shares which had not been subscribed for were assigned to the Viceroy.[3] His acceptance of these shares brought forth a storm of protests from the British Consul-General, who tried in vain to persuade him to renounce the added responsibility. Only a few days earlier the Viceroy had complained to the Consul-General that the Company had endeavored to fasten on his shoulders the remaining shares and he had declared that he would never accept them.[4] He now tried to justify his action on the ground that by accepting the shares he had prevented them from being thrown upon the market, which would have resulted in a ruinous

[1] Égypte, vol. 29, no. 2, Béchard to Thouvenel, Alex., May 9, 1860.

[2] FO 78/1556, no. 59, Colquhoun to Russell, Alex., May 17, 1860. *Cf.* Égypte, vol. 29, no. 6, Béchard to Thouvenel, May 14, 1860.

[3] The Viceroy had originally subscribed for 64,000 shares. He agreed to take over such shares as were not sold, which in May, 1860, numbered 113,642. By accepting these shares the Viceroy's total subscription was brought to 177,642 (Ferd. de Lesseps, *Letters etc.*, 3rd ser., pp. 3, 371 and 393). It was agreed that he would not be called upon to make any payment on the additional shares for two years.

[4] FO 78/1556, no. 64, Colquhoun to Russell, Alex., June 2, 1860.

depreciation if not the complete break-down of the scheme.[1] Since he has " thrown off the mask," wrote the Consul-General with some bitterness, no reliance can be placed in the word of one " who had thus dared to deceive Her Majesty's agent." [2] The Consul-General was convinced that the acceptance of the additional shares by the Viceroy "must inevitably hurry him to his complete ruin." [3]

These intrigues did not greatly disturb the Viceroy. To the British Consul-General he declared that " this scheme is a child of my own begetting—a scheme I have looked upon—as the one great act of my life, which is to hand me down to posterity as a worthy son of my father. I cannot but consider the junction of the two seas as an undertaking which will immortalize him under whose auspices it is carried out." [4] Furthermore, he had no intention of compromising himself before the Powers by " fetching chestnuts from the fire for England." [5] If England, he said, was displeased with the work on the canal, she should send her fleet and take the responsibility for so doing.[6]

[1] *Ibid.,* no. 82, Colquhoun to Russell, Alex., July 11, 1860. The Austrian Consul-General reported that the Viceroy was very indignant about the transfer of the shares to his name which he said de Lesseps had done without his authorization. He added that the Viceroy at first refused to accept them but later gave in to prevent them from falling to France, which would have made the enterprise almost wholly French (HHSA, Cons. Ber., Cairo, 1860, vol. $\frac{XXXVIII}{12}$, no. 7, pol., Schreiner to Rechberg, Cairo, June 2, 1860).

[2] FO 78/1556, no. 59, Colquhoun to Russell, Alex., May 17, 1860.

[3] *Ibid.,* no. 66, Colquhoun to Russell, Alex., June 3, 1860.

[4] *Ibid.,* no. 82, Colquhoun to Russell, Alex., July 11, 1860.

[5] HHSA, $\frac{XXXVIII}{12}$ Cons. Ber., Schreiner to Rechberg, Alex., June 29, 1860.

[6] The French Consul-General reported that the Viceroy was very irritated by the English attacks and that the attempt of Colquhoun to wean him from his friendship with France had just the opposite effect, namely,

This attitude of defiance was no doubt encouraged by de Lesseps, who held before the Viceroy prospects of independence from the Sultan.[1] When de Lesseps assured him that he could depend on the Emperor's protection, wrote the Austrian Consul-General, "the conceit of the half-insane Viceroy was enhanced to such an extent that he was foolish enough to declare: '*Je ne suis pas fait pour Gouverneur en Orient*'." He meant by this, continued the Consul-General, that if he had been on the throne of France, he would have been a Napoleon I, but in Egypt he was restricted by the influence of the European powers.[2]

Protests against the acceptance of the additional shares were also made at Constantinople, where the Austrian internuncio voiced the opinion that the Viceroy had now "given himself heart and soul to France."[3] Sir Henry Bulwer was instructed to point out to the Grand Vizir that the Viceroy had no right to appropriate the revenues of Egypt to the canal; and a Turkish official was sent to warn the latter that his action had incurred the displeasure of the Porte.[4] This move was frustrated, however, by the determination of the French and Austrian Consuls-General to oppose any action directed against the scheme.[5]

to decide him "to throw himself into our arms" (Égypte, vol. 29, Béchard to Thouvenel, Sept. 9, 1860).

[1] HHSA, Cons. Ber., $\frac{XXXVIII}{12}$, no. 12, Schreiner to the Imperial Attaché at Const., Count Ludolf, Alex., July 27, 1860. *Cf.* FO 78/1556, no. 66, very confidential, Colquhoun to Russell, Alex., June 3, 1860. Schreiner adds that the Viceroy was completely under the influence of de Lesseps, who did not, however, exploit him for his private advantage.

[2] *Ibid.,* no. 15, Schreiner to Rechberg, Alex., May 8, 1862.

[3] *Ibid.,* vol. 12/67, Rapp. Corr. Dipl., Const., no. 41 B, Prokesch to Const., June 20, 1860.

[4] FO 78/1556, no. 407, Bulwer to Russell, Therapia, July 16, 1860.

[5] HHSA, no. 12, copy of a confidential dispatch of July 24, 1860, submitted to the Imperial Attaché at Const., Count Ludolf, by Schreiner, dated Alex., July 27, 1860.

In the meantime, it was reported in Egypt that Austria had changed her attitude and was no longer favorable to the canal. The Viceroy had been so informed confidentially, while the British Consul-General expressed the same opinion.[1] Moreover, Lord Loftus, the British Ambassador at Vienna, had reported that Count Rechberg was not only opposed to the canal on political grounds but had actually declared it to be " a pure swindling transaction." [2] When Count Rechberg was informed of these reports he denied that any change had occurred in the attitude of the Imperial Government, which still favored the construction of the canal and only desired that political difficulties should be avoided by an agreement between the Porte and the Maritime Powers.[3] Despite Rechberg's denial, it seems quite evident that a change did occur in his attitude toward the canal and that he was at this time leaning towards England. The reason for the change is not so clear. It may be that Rechberg considered that the policy which France pursued of supporting the Company solely in behalf of her investors, was designed to emphasize the French character of the project, whereas Austria regarded it as international. Or again, he might have suspected that de Lesseps was merely utilizing the support of the Powers to promote his own ends.

Though the Viceroy continued to support the activities

---

[1] *Ibid.*, pol., no. 10, Schreiner to Rechberg, Alex., July 3, 1860.

[2] According to Loftus, Count Rechberg had expressed himself on a number of occasions as opposed to the canal. Thus on July 18, 1860, he told Loftus that " it was merely destined to serve as a screw for political objects on the part of France " (FO 78/1556, no. 412, confidential, Loftus to Russell, July 19, 1860). Moreover, Colquhoun reported that Schreiner had told him that Count Rechberg had used the word " swindle " in connection with the scheme (*ibid.*, no. 152, confidential, Colquhoun to Russell, Alex., Nov. 10, 1860).

[3] HHSA, vol. $\frac{XXXVIII}{12}$, Rechberg to Schreiner, Vienna, July 14, 1860.

of the Company, he found his position becoming more and more difficult. He had replied evasively to the vizirial letters requesting him to put a stop to the work. Now he felt that the time had come when he must get greater encouragement from the French Government or take active measures to enforce the orders of the Porte.[1]

So precarious was the situation in 1861 that the British Consul-General believed that the whole affair would soon collapse and bring ruin to Egypt. He declared that " peculation must exist to a large degree," that " discontent " among the European workmen was very prevalent, and that the Viceroy and de Lesseps were on unfriendly terms.[2]

The Isthmus of Suez Company is looked on by all classes of his subjects about the Viceroy with feelings of great antipathy. His most intimate and confidential adherents, not French, do not hesitate to say that they date the beginning of his pecuniary embarrassments from the period when in an evil hour he was led by M. de Lesseps to become so large a shareholder, and they consider the enterprise as a millstone about his neck which cannot fail to complete his ruin.[3]

It was at this time that England launched her attack against the employment of forced labor on the canal. By a decree of the Viceroy, July 20, 1856, the Egyptian Government had guaranteed to supply the Company with as many workers as the engineers deemed necessary.[4] Alarmed, however, by the British opposition, the Viceroy had post-

[1] The Viceroy did not believe that France would support him against both England and the Porte (Égypte, vol. 29, no. 1, Beauval to Thouvenel, Alex., Jan. 7, 1861).

[2] FO 78/1715, no. 51, Colquhoun to Russell, Alex., June 8, 1861.

[3] *Ibid.*, no. 72, confidential, Colquhoun to Russell, Alex., July 17, 1861.

[4] *British and Foreign State Papers*, vol. 56, p. 278. " Regulations as to the Employment of Native Workmen by the Universal Company of the Suez Maritime Canal."

poned month after month the supply of native laborers and
progress on the canal was considerably handicapped. De
Lesseps protested against this situation and demanded to
know what grounds England had for complaint since she
herself had permitted forced labor on the Egyptian railroad.[1]
Replying to a statement made in the House of Commons on
May 16, 1862, that the British Government should employ
all its influence to bring about the abolition of forced labor
in Egypt, he wrote to Mr. Layard, Undersecretary for Foreign Affairs:

> Permit me to represent here a preliminary consideration
> which is not a recrimination but a simple reflection of inter-
> national justice.   In admitting that forced labor is an Egyptian
> custom or institution, has a foreign government the right to
> intervene in the internal affairs of the Egyptian Government?
>
> The principle of slavery is established in America.   Has
> England ever tried to bring pressure to bear on the Government
> at Washington in order to demand the abolition of slavery?
> To-day there are 40 million serfs in Russia.   Has England ever
> attempted to express the least dissatisfaction in Russia because
> she maintains serfdom?[2]

Another difficulty arose at this time.   The Viceroy was
compelled to contract a loan and accepted the offers of
French banks whose rate of interest was so high that the
Austrian Consul-General was led to believe that their object

---

[1] Ferd. de Lesseps, *Letters etc.,* 4th ser., p. 215.

[2] *Ibid.,* pp. 225-227. This protest did not remove English opposition to
forced labor. The French Consul-General had in the meantime inter-
ceded for the Company with the demand that the Viceroy adhere to his
engagements and furnish the number of workers needed on the canal.
This he agreed to do. (Égypte, vol. 29, confidentiel, Béchard to
Thouvenel, May 19, 1861). According to Schreiner, the Viceroy refused
to supply native labor, but agreed that de Lesseps could recruit his own
workers (HHSA, no. 11, Schreiner to Minister, Alex., May 4, 1861).

was to place the Viceroy completely under French influence.[1]
He added that what the Company aimed at was the establishment of a French colony in the Isthmus and his report
induced Count Apponyi to call Lord Russell's attention to
the supposed danger and to urge England to join with Austria to counteract " so fatal an influence." [2] M. Revolta,
the representative of the Company at Trieste, was sent to
Egypt in order to verify the Consul-General's report. In
his letter to Count Rechberg, March 17, 1862, he declared
that the Company was in every respect international in character and had no thought of establishing a foreign colony
in the Isthmus.[3]

In spite of these difficulties, however, the work proceeded.
On February 2, 1862, the fresh-water canal from the Nile
to Lake Timsah was completed and a few months later the
waters of the Mediterranean entered the same lake. Such
progress naturally added more heat to the British opposition.

In November of the same year Sir Henry Bulwer visited
Egypt on the pretext of health.[4] His real object, however,
was to learn if fortifications were being erected in the
Isthmus, and to inquire into the general state of affairs,
particularly as to the Viceroy's intentions concerning independence.[5] After viewing the canal works he declared that
he would maintain " not only a diplomatic silence but a

[1] HHSA, Cons. Ber., $\frac{XXXVIII}{12}$ , no. 19, Schreiner to Rechberg, Aug.
20, 1861. No details concerning this loan are given in the dispatch.

[2] Ibid., VIII/63, England, 1862, no. 43 E, Apponyi to Rechberg, London, June 11, 1862.

[3] Ibid., Cons. Ber., Alex., and Cairo (1860-1870), Letter from M.
Revolta to Count Rechberg, Trieste, Mar. 17, 1862.

[4] Ferd. de Lesseps, Letters etc., 4th ser., p. 257.

[5] HHSA, $\frac{XXXVIII}{12}$, no. 41, Schreiner to Rechberg, Cairo, Nov. 17,
1862.

masonic silence." [1]   But he intimated that he would oppose
any measure which might threaten the integrity of the Ottoman Empire or the political *status quo* of Egypt.

From his report to Lord Russell it is evident that the
work in the Isthmus made a deep impression on him.[2]   Most
of the persons who wrote on the English side of the question, he said, " underrated what had been done and rather
overrated the remaining difficulties."   The canal works
were " being pursued with an energy and an *ensemble* which
is striking."   The only question concerning the project is a
question of money.

At the head of the undertaking is a most active and intelligent
man in constant good humour and indefatigable.   He has surrounded himself by degrees with men able and energetic and
skilled in their professions.   They (or at least the French portion of them) are all stimulated in the strongest degree by their
great national stimulant *amour propre*.   I have seen all this,
and till I saw it, I confess I did not conceive it.

He believed that despite all difficulties the Company would
survive.   " Whatever is possible to art, science and perseverance is possible here."   As to the advantages of the canal
his views were not so favorable.   " I incline to the opinion
that they are overrated.   The time of canals seems to me
pretty well past, when that of railroads commenced. . . .
Thus, I say, the Canal will very probably not greatly, if at
all, benefit commerce. . . ." [3]   But if he saw no advantages,

---

[1] Égypte, vol. 31, no. 89, Beauval to Drouyn de Lhuys, Alex., Jan. 2,
1863.

[2] FO 78/1795, vol. 8, confidential, no. 2, Bulwer to Russell, Alex., Jan.
3, 1863.

[3] This view was also shared by Schreiner, the Austrian Consul-General
who was friendly with Bulwer during the latter's visit to Egypt (HHSA,
Cons. Ber., $\frac{XXXVIII}{12}$, no. 47, Schreiner to Rechberg, Cairo, Dec. 15,

neither did he detect any losses from its construction. "If we have still the upper hand at sea, we should . . . be more likely than other nations to get hold of it." What Sir Henry Bulwer objected to was not the canal as such but the canal under French influence. Port Said, Timsah and Suez would soon become "French towns," the territory under cultivation would soon be "French territory," and the Egyptian Government "will become a cypher as well as the Porte." Furthermore, the native workers would actually come under the French Government and French influence would be extended over the entire country.[1] "Thus, my objections, I repeat, are not to the Canal and its adjuncts, but to the Canal as made by the French Company. . . ." In order to diminish the value of the enterprise, he recommended improvements in the railway communications between Alexandria and Suez. He predicted that a crisis in the canal question was inevitable and that the best solution would be to repay the Company for the sums it had advanced and have it wind up its affairs.[2] "The condition," continued the Ambassador, "should be either the total annihilation of the Company and its scheme . . . or a transfer of that scheme . . . to the local Government and the Porte."

To the Viceroy, Sir Henry repeated all the old objections to the canal and with so much emphasis that he believed he had convinced the former of the errors of his ways. In-

1862). Bulwer had told him that he was convinced the canal would materialize in spite of England's opposition if necessary funds could be secured (*ibid.*, no. 46, Schreiner to Rechberg, Cairo, Dec. 9, 1862).

[1] The same arguments were advanced by Schreiner who warned the Viceroy that colonization of the Isthmus by natives under French control would someday give France a pretext for intervening and taking possession of the country, and that once the French had taken root in Egypt it would be difficult to drive them out (*ibid.*, no. 47, Schreiner to Rechberg, Cairo, Dec. 15, 1862).

[2] FO 78/1795, vol. 8, secret and confidential, Bulwer to Russell, Alex., Jan. 3, 1863.

deed, the Viceroy told him that the French had never done him any good and that he had been wrong in supporting the canal.[1]   "He did not disguise that he thought the whole affair a mess, and that he would be glad to get out of it, but seemed desirous to learn how this could be done." [2] To this Sir Henry replied that he could safely leave that problem to him provided he would promise not to supply any more workers and would not go beyond the original agreement in giving additional funds to the Company.   If the Viceroy would agree then Sir Henry would get him " out of his embarrassments without any peril or loss of honour."   The Viceroy gave his promise and " a great weight seemed to be taken off his mind. . . ."   Though he was highly pleased with his success, Sir Henry was rather anxious that the Viceroy should not forget his advice.[3]   " His two distinctive passions are fear and vanity; both must be worked on simultaneously and without relaxation or his changeable and variable character will not be under any fixed impression." [4]   Sir Henry recommended that the Consul-General should follow this line " strictly and incessantly," and concluded:

[1] FO 78/1795, vol. 7, Bulwer to Russell, Cairo, Dec. 15, 1862.

[2] FO 78/1795, vol. 8, no. 3, confidential, Bulwer to Russell, Alex., Jan. 4, 1863.

[3] Schreiner, who was convinced that Bulwer's victory was "complete at the moment," reported that the Viceroy had dismissed some of his ministers who were supporters of the French policy and favored those who leaned toward England (HHSA, $\frac{XXXVIII}{12}$, no. 47, Schreiner to Rechberg, Cairo, Dec. 15, 1862).

[4] FO 78/1795, no. 3, confidential, Jan. 4, 1863.   It is interesting to note the impressions of Schreiner, who said of the Viceroy that "he is arrogant, cruel, quarrelsome, sensitive, suspicious, extravagant, heartless, destructive, whimsical, vacillating, ambitious, false and cowardly—all in a superlative degree" (HHSA, $\frac{XXXVIII}{12}$, no. 15, pol., Schreiner to Rechberg, Alex., May 8, 1862).

The impression I shall endeavour to leave him [the Viceroy] with is that I am his friend, and shall be willing and ready and able to serve him—if he acts so as to merit it, but that I shall consider his reign as Viceroy inconsistent with the well being of Egypt and the Ottoman Empire, if he pursues a different course and that I shall then have both the will and the power to curb, if not overthrow his authority.

That said Pasha had any intentions of keeping the promise he gave to Sir Henry is doubtful in view of his great loyalty to the scheme. At any rate, he did not live long enough to carry it out, for after a brief illness, he died on January 18, 1863. De Lesseps was considerably shaken. " I am disconsolate," he said, " not because of my enterprise, for which I maintain the most serene faith . . . but for the cruel separation from a faithful friend who, for twenty-five years, gave me so many evidences of affection and confidence." [1]

[1] *Letters etc.,* 4th ser., p. 276.

# CHAPTER XIII

## England Reluctantly Agrees

De Lesseps might well have mourned the passing of his trusted friend, for it was expected that the new Viceroy, Ismail Pasha, would lean more strongly toward England than toward France. Ismail, however, was too prudent to fall into the extremes of his predecessor and had no desire to endanger his position by incurring the displeasure of either Power. He announced himself as favorable to the project and said to the French Consul-General: " I am more canalist than M. de Lesseps but I am also of a positive mind; I believe that no work is so grand, none will be so productive for Egypt, but as to the present, its bases are uncertain and badly defined. I will affirm them and then, surpassing my predecessor, will push the works to their completion." [1] For the present, he would maintain the status quo and write to the Porte for instructions.

In his address to the Consular Corps the Viceroy announced that he would abolish the *corvée*. " The expression ' *corvée* ' was so often repeated," wrote the French Consul-

---

[1] Égypte, vol. 31, no. 93, confidentiel, Beauval to Drouyn de Lhuys, Alex., Jan., 1863. The British Consul-General believed that Ismail was personally hostile to the scheme and would be glad to see it come to an end (FO 78/1795, no. 11, Colquhoun to Russell, Alex., Jan. 24, 1863). Schreiner, on the other hand, reported that Ismail felt that France alone would support him and that he was as friendly to the French and their projects as any of his predecessors had been with the exception of Abbas Pasha (HHSA, Cons. Ber., $\frac{XXXI}{24}$, no. 16, Schreiner to Rechberg, Cairo, Mar. 11, 1863).

General, " it established so vaguely the distinction between public services and those of the Government, in a word, the allusions to the canal works were so strong and so clear that all eyes were turned toward me." [1]

The Porte was somewhat relieved with the passing of Said Pasha, who had pushed his pretensions of sovereignty to the limit. After all, declared the Grand Vizir to the French Ambassador, the office of Viceroy possessed no more power than that " of the most modest of provincial Governors save that it was hereditary." [2]

As for England, the death of Said Pasha offered a favorable opportunity for renewing her opposition to the canal, and Sir Henry Bulwer was not slow to recognize it. He believed that Ismail shared his views concerning the project : that it would " be disastrous to Egypt, and to the Ottoman Empire." [3] Since the Sultan had not granted the sanction, the enterprise was illegal and the the only safe course was for the Egyptian Government to take it over. " It could then shorten the railways and would find them cheaper and better and consequently lay aside the Canal as a useless project." [4] If the Egyptian Government was to be saved it was urgent to set aside the French Company. Having thus found his own solution for the difficulties, Sir Henry devised a scheme for carrying it out. He would have the Porte notify the Viceroy that the project was illegal and the latter would then submit a report showing that it involved great danger for Egypt. Upon receiving this, the Porte

---

[1] *Ibid.*, no. 93, confidentiel, Beauval to Drouyn de Lhuys, Alex., Jan., 1863. Ismail assured him, however, that his reference to the *corvée* was not directed against the canal.

[2] Turquie, vol. 357, no. 28, Pera, Feb. 12, 1863, de Moustier to Drouyn de Lhuys.

[3] FO 78/1795, no. 60, Bulwer to Russell, Const., Feb. 4, 1863.

[4] *Ibid.*

should order all work on the canal to be discontinued immediately.[1] Sir Henry's proposal that the Company should be bought out and the canal turned over to Egypt, which should be placed under European guarantee, did not meet with the favor of his government. Lord Russell replied that the " British Government can in no case guarantee or favor the Suez Canal, which they would see abandoned." [2]

The arrival of Ismail Pasha at Constantinople for his investiture furnished the occasion for further intrigues. He told Sir Henry that the Canal Company was a great misfortune for Egypt but added: " We may often wish to check an evil and yet not be able to do so." [3] He would obey the Sultan's orders, he said, but did not feel strong enough to stand alone against France. Sir Henry warned him that the time had come for decided action, and declared that if England she had so desired, she

might have had Egypt long ago, that even but lately, if we had agreed to the Russian proposals, it would have fallen to our share. We had never taken it, we did not want it. We preferred its remaining independent of any special foreign influence in the hands of the Viceroy and the Porte, but if the Viceroy and the Porte were inadequate to fulfill their duty and maintain their position, if they were merely a cloak for foreign usurpation, the sooner they were swept away the better.[4]

---

[1] HHSA, Diplo. Corr., Const., 1863, no. 96, Feb. 4, 1863, Prokesch to Rechberg. In reporting this plan to his government the Internuncio said that the Porte and the Viceroy had already come to an understanding whereby forced labor was to be abolished in the Isthmus and the lands allotted to the Company by Said Pasha returned to the Egyptian Government to be distributed to the inhabitants.

[2] FO 78/1795, no. 65, FO to Bulwer, Feb. 2, 1863.

[3] *Ibid.*, no. 103, Bulwer to Russell, Const., Mar. 3, 1863.

[4] *Ibid.*, Bulwer tried his best to persuade Ismail to abandon the canal altogether (Turquie, vol. 352, no. 44, confidentiel, de Moustier to Drouyn de Lhuys, Pera, Mar. 5, 1863). He also tried to obtain from

Under the present circumstances, continued the Ambassador, the Porte and the Viceroy must recognize that the Company "would make Egypt a French province," and it was therefore incumbent upon them to get rid of the Company.

To the French Ambassador, Ismail showed a different front. " I am persuaded," he said, " that France alone has a policy entirely sympathetic to Egypt. I will consecrate all my cares to realize the execution of the canal." [1] Apparently the shrewd Viceroy was playing a double game and was endeavoring to pacify both sides at the same time. It was, no doubt, the safer policy in view of the Anglo-French rivalry.

Upon his return to Egypt the Viceroy signed two conventions: one governing the participation of the Egyptian Government in the capital of the Canal Company; the other relating to the construction of the fresh water canal from Cairo to Ouady.[2] No sooner were these conventions announced

the Viceroy a written engagement that he would purchase all the shares of the Company within six months (Égypte, vol. 31, no. 19, Taster to Drouyn de Lhuys, Alex., June 30, 1863). However, Bulwer won the approval of both the Viceroy and the Grand Vizir to his views concerning the demands which should be made of the Company (FO 78/1795, no. 103, Bulwer to Russell, Const., Mar. 3, 1863).

[1] Turquie, vol. 357, no. 39, confidentiel, de Moustier to Drouyn de Lhuys, Pera, Feb. 26, 1863.

[2] The first of these dated, Mar. 20, 1863, was to liquidate the participation of the Egyptian Government in the subscriptions of the Company. Said Pasha had subscribed for 177,642 shares representing a capital of 88,821,000 francs. Of this sum one-fifth had been paid. Deductions were made for the interest at 5% given to all shareholders during the period of construction, and for sums advanced to the Company for preparatory studies and works. By the Convention of March 20, 1863, the Egyptian Government agreed to pay 35,150,977 francs (representing the second and third payments for the shares at 100 francs per share) at the rate of 1,500,000 per month beginning Jan. 1, 1864, until paid. As for the other two-fifths the Egyptian Government reserved the right of making such arrangements with the Company as would be convenient for its Treasury (*British and Foreign State Papers*, vol. 55, p. 1002). By

than the English fury burst forth anew. He " has set the Sovereign authority altogether at defiance. He has evidently been entrapped into engagements which he does not understand," declared Lord Russell.[1] The British Consul-General was the butt of criticism by his government for not having prevented the conclusion of the conventions. " Whilst I have been settling canal business here," [at Constantinople] complained Sir Henry Bulwer to Lord Russell, " Colquhoun has allowed the Viceroy to make new conventions with de Lesseps. It is too bad." [2] Lord Palmerston was particularly angry. " Mr. Colquhoun," he wrote, " ought certainly to be stirred with a long pole to rouse himself to act with energy in support of the Viceroy. I am afraid he is wanting in this respect. . . . When I saw Mr. Colquhoun before he returned to Egypt he spoke favourably of Lesseps saying that he is a perfectly honest and honourable man. Now as Lesseps is, to speak in plain terms, a rogue and a swindler, this opinion expressed by Mr. Colquhoun seems to imply that somehow or other Lesseps has the length of his foot and has trammelled his mind." [3] Lord Russell directed Mr. Colquhoun to warn the Viceroy that de Lesseps was undermining his authority and that he ran the risk of losing his throne.[4] He was also to use all his influence to induce the Viceroy to cancel the conventions.[5]

the other convention, dated March 18, 1863, the Company gave up the part of the fresh-water canal from Cairo to Timsah (derived from the Nile) together with the lands necessary for its construction. This section was completed by the Egyptian Government (Compagnie Universelle du Canal Maritime de Suez, *Notice et Reseignements Généraux* (2ème partie, Paris, 1926), pp. 39-42).

[1] FO 78/1795, vol. 8, no. 18, FO to Colquhoun, April 9, 1863.

[2] FO 78/1796, vol. 9, no. 173, Bulwer to Russell, Const., April 6, 1863.

[3] FO 78/1795, note dated Oct. 31, 1863, attached to no. 103, Bulwer to Russell, Const., Mar. 3, 1863.

[4] FO 78/1796, no. 21, FO to Colquhoun, April 27, 1863.

[5] FO 78/1795, vol. 8, no. 16, FO to Colquhoun, April 7, 1863.

Meanwhile Sir Henry's intrigues had met with complete success. Under his direction the Turkish Minister for Foreign Affairs wrote two notes: one to be addressed to the Ambassadors of the Porte at Paris and London; the other to the Viceroy. The one which was to be sent to the Viceroy protested against the employment of forced labor on the canal and the alienation of so much land to the Company.[1] The joint note to Paris and London stated that the consent of the Porte to the undertaking was contingent upon an agreement concerning the neutrality of the canal, the abolition of forced labor and the abandonment by the Company of the adjoining lands and the fresh-water canal.[2]

These notes were approved by the Sultan. When the French Ambassador was informed of their contents, he protested so vigorously and employed such " violent language " to the Grand Vizir that the latter agreed to submit them to the Council.[3] The Ambassador demanded that the dispatch of the notes be suspended until they were drawn up in a modified form.[4] The British Government, however, warned the Porte that if the notes were modified, the independence of Turkey would " no longer be supported by England." [5] Sir Henry was instructed to act energetically in upholding the authority of the Porte.[6] The result was that the notes were dispatched as originally draw up on April 2nd.

---

[1] FO 78/1796, no. 171, Bulwer, Const., April 6, 1863, enclosure, copy of Grand Vizir's letter to Ismail Pasha dated April 2, 1863.

[2] Egypt, no. 20 (1883), "Despatch from the Porte to the Ottoman Ambassador in London Relative to Suez Canal, April 6, 1863."

[3] FO 78/1796, no. 166, secret and confidential, Bulwer to Russell, Const., April 1, 1863.

[4] HHSA, no. 26 B, Cons. Ber., Const., April 2, 1863, Prokesch to Rechberg.

[5] FO 78/1795, no. 165, FO to Bulwer, April 4, 1863.

[6] *Ibid.*, no. 171, FO to Bulwer, April 9, 1863.

While the situation was in this unsettled state, it was announced that the Sultan would visit Egypt. Considering that such a visit might endanger the success of his maneuvers against the canal, Sir Henry made every effort to persuade the Sultan not to undertake it.[1] Failing in this, he tried to influence the Sultan to adopt an attitude compromising to the French interests in the project.[2]

During his visit to Egypt the Sultan did not see the canal works nor did he express any opinion concerning the scheme. Yet the French Government was not convinced that the visit was devoid of political motives and Drouyn de Lhuys instructed the Consul-General to watch the activities of the Sultan and to see that no decision was arrived at in regard to the canal without the knowledge of France.[3] At the same time the British Consul-General seized the occasion to warn the Viceroy that England was determined to uphold firmly and vigorously the rights of the Porte.[4]

In June 1863 Nubar Pasha, Egyptian Minister of Foreign Affairs, went to Constantinople in order to discuss with the Porte the conditions under which the Company could continue its work. However, his real mission was to bring about a dissolution of the Company and though his instructions were signed by the Viceroy, they were dictated by English agents.[5] Nubar was well qualified for the mission as he was among the " most formidable opponents " of the

---

[1] Turquie, vol. 358, no. 63, de Moustier to Drouyn de Lhuys, Pera, April 1, 1863. *Cf.* HHSA, $\frac{\text{vol. XXI}}{18}$, no. 23, Prokesch to Rechberg, Const., Mar. 23, 1863.

[2] Égypte, vol. 31, Telegr., Minister to Taster, Paris, April 4, 1863.

*Ibid.*

[4] *Ibid.*, no. 4, Taster to Minister, Alex., April 4, 1863.

[5] J. C. T. Roux, *op. cit.*, vol. ii, p. 338. Nubar carried with him a letter from the Viceroy replying to the vizirial letter of April 2nd.

scheme.[1] The note which he submitted to the Grand Vizir provided that the Company should return the lands it had received from Said Pasha, that the dimensions of the canal should be revised by a commission of engineers, and that the number of workers should be reduced to 6,000.[2] The Company was to comply with these conditions within six months or the work would be interrupted by force. On July 1, 1863, the Grand Vizir sent a note to the Viceroy embodying these conditions.[3]

The Porte declared that by the employment of forced labor in the Isthmus 60,000 men were removed from productive enterprises. This figure was based on the fact that while 20,000 (the monthly quota furnished by the Viceroy) were employed on the works, 20,000 were on the way to the Isthmus and 20,000 returning to their homes. Egyptian agriculture, it was said, suffered disastrously as a consequence.

To these charges the Company replied by stating that forced labor had always been the custom in Egypt, and that the native workers employed in the Isthmus received wages, food and medical attention.[4] It was pointed out, moreover, that at the very moment the Peninsular and Oriental Company was employing native workers without wages at Suez for loading and unloading cargoes.

In regard to the question of the land grants, the Company maintained that these were indispensable for the transformation of the desert into a fertile region, and one of the important sources of revenue promised to the shareholders.

[1] FO 78/1796, no. 272, Bulwer to Russell, Const., June 11, 1863.

[2] J. C. T. Roux, *op. cit.*, vol. ii, p. 338.

[3] FO 78/1796, enclosure in no. 340, confidential Bulwer to Russell, Ad. 7954/78, Const., July 22, 1863. *Cf.* Turquie, vol. 359, annex to dispatch no. 141.

[4] Égypte, vol. 31, Note in reply to the Turkish communication submitted by Company to the French Government, no date.

De Lesseps declared to the Viceroy that he would rather throw the affair " on the rocks " than to cede so important a privilege.[1]

The view taken by the British Government was that the Viceroy could not alienate to a foreign company any part of his territory and that the Sultan as sovereign had a perfect right to decree the abolition of forced labor in Egypt, as had been done in other parts of the Empire.[2]   Nubar Pasha was assured by Sir Henry Bulwer that if the Viceroy prohibited forced labor and if France endeavored to compel him to furnish it, England would support the Viceroy.[3]   In the House of Commons, Lord Palmerston declared that the Sultan and the Viceroy would " receive the most energetic and active support of England." [4]

Though the vizirial letter of April 2nd,[5] had directed the Viceroy to abolish forced labor and to suspend all work on the canal pending the definitive solution of the difficulties, he had taken no steps to execute this order and as a consequence, was " tormented " by the British Consul-General.[6] When the latter protested that the supply of native workers remained the same, Ismail replied that he could make no change for the present " without exposing himself to a degree of pressure he was unable to bear." [7]

As neither the Porte nor the Egyptian Government wished

[1] *Ibid.*, no. 11, Taster to Drouyn de Lhuys, Alex., April 30, 1863.

[2] FO 78/1796, FO to Cowley, seen by the Queen and Palmerston, May 20, 1863.

[3] *Ibid.*, no. 292, Bulwer to Russell, Const., June 25, 1863.

[4] Hansard, 3rd ser., vol. 170, May 15, 1863.

[5] *Cf. supra*, p. 199.

[6] Égypte, vol. 31, no. 12, Taster to Drouyn de Lhuys, Alex., May 9, 1863.

[7] FO 78/1796, no. 87, confidential, Colquhoun to Russell, Alex., May 27, 1863.

to be too severe with the Company, they might have reached a more immediate settlement of the difficulties had it not been for the opposition of England. During his visit to Egypt with the Sultan, Fuad Pasha, the Grand Vizir, showed that he was not opposed to forced labor. He admitted to the Austrian Consul-General that it would be very difficult to abolish it and that it might therefore remain; but he insisted on the surrender of the land grants, for to allow them in the possession of a foreign company would be tantamount to European colonization on Turkish soil.[1] His view, as expressed by Sir Henry Bulwer was: " The concession of territory is a danger, the employment of forced labour an inconvenience, it may therefore be well to suffer the inconvenience if we escape the danger." [2] While such was the opinion of the Grand Vizir it is not surprising that the Viceroy hesitated to abolish forced labor, particularly since this would have subjected him to French pressure. But the British Government was uncompromising on this point and insisted that the conditions set forth in the vizirial letter of April 2nd must be carried out.[3]

The questions concerning forced labor and the land grants could be settled only by the Egyptian Government and the Canal Company.[4] In order to find a basis for a settlement, the Viceroy sent Nubar Pasha to Paris, instructing him to communicate with the Board of Directors of the Canal Company. Informed of this, de Lesseps, who had just arrived in

[1] HHSA, Cons. Ber., vol. xxxi, no. 27, Schreiner to Rechberg, Cairo, April 16, 1863. *Cf.* Turquie, vol. 358, no. 69, de Moustier to Drouyn de Lhuys, Pera, April 8, 1863.

[2] FO 78/1796, no. 272, Bulwer to Russell, Const., June 11, 1863.

[3] *Ibid.*

[4] This was the view of the Grand Vizir in his letter to the Viceroy, Aug. 1, 1863. Enclosure in FO 78/1796, no. 340, confidential, Bulwer to Russell, Const., July 22, 1863.

Egypt, telegraphed to the Board not to see or treat with Nubar Pasha.[1] The latter arrived in Paris at the end of August 1863 and published several articles in the press attacking the legality of the Company and falsifying facts concerning the situation. For these articles the Board of Directors brought suit against him in the Civil Tribunal of the Seine.[2] Nubar entered a countercharge on the ground that de Lesseps by giving publicity to the suit before it had come to trial had damaged his reputation.[3] In its decision of February 26, 1864 the Tribunal gave judgment to both parties, holding that Nubar by attacking the legality of the Company had injured its credit, and that de Lesseps had no right to give publicity to the suit before it was brought to trial.[4]

Nubar called at the Quai d'Orsay and endeavored to get the views of Drouyn de Lhuys concerning the canal question but the latter refused to treat with him, maintaining that if the Egyptian Government wished to modify the Concession given to de Lesseps, it must negotiate directly with the Company.[5] The Minister refused to intervene in the affair and would not do so except on demand of the Company and on behalf of French interests.

Nubar's activities in Paris roused the French Government to enter a vigorous protest with the Viceroy. In an inter-

---

[1] Égypte, vol. 32, Taster to Drouyn de Lhuys, no. 32, Alex., Aug. 30, 1863.

[2] *Note pour la Compagnie Universelle du Canal Maritime de Suez contre S. E. Nubar Pasha*, Paris, 1863. *Cf.* Ferd. de Lesseps, *Letters etc.*, 4th ser., p. 370. The Company claimed damages to the extent of 300,000 francs. In attacking the legality of the Company, Nubar cited the opinion of three lawyers, MM. Odilon Barrot, Dufaure and Jules Favre.

[3] *Ibid.*, de Lesseps had published several articles in the press giving publicity to the charges brought by the Company against Nubar.

[4] *Ibid.*

[5] Égypte, vol. 32, no. 20, Drouyn de Lhuys to Taster, Paris, Sept. 18, 1863.

view with the latter at Constantinople, the French Ambassador charged that Nubar was attempting to settle the questions at issue without the knowledge of France.[1] The Viceroy denied that any secret arrangement would be made and promised that the canal would be completed if France would support him against England. To the French Consul-General, he complained that the English had made it appear that he was back of all the opposition and had urged the Porte to stand against the canal—in other words, that he had been the victim of a plot.[2] For having escaped the consequences of the English intrigues, he was congratulated by the Emperor and Drouyn de Lhuys.[3]

As both the Viceroy and de Lesseps were anxious to arrive at a settlement without further delay, they decided to submit their differences to arbitration. A petition was addressed to the Emperor on January 6, 1864 by the Board of Directors requesting him to intercede on behalf of the Company in order to protect French capital engaged in the enterprise. The Emperor agreed to act as arbitrator and in March appointed a commission with Thouvenel as president to examine the litigious questions.

The Commission, on April 15th, drew up a compromise which was signed by de Lesseps for the Canal Company and by Nubar Pasha for the Egyptian Government. This stipulated the questions which the Emperor would be called upon to arbitrate. When Bulwer was informed of the compromise, he protested that it was invalid since it had not been sanctioned by the Porte.[4] He was angry with the Turkish Ambassador, Djemal Pasha, for having allowed Nubar to

---

[1] *Ibid.*, confidentiel, de Moustier to Drouyn de Lhuys, Oct. 11, 1863.

[2] *Ibid.*, no. 52, Taster to Drouyn de Lhuys, Alex., Dec. 19, 1863.

[3] *Ibid.*, no. 25, FO to Taster, Pera, Dec. 28, 1863.

[4] FO 78/1849, vol. 10, confidential no. 89, Bulwer to Russell, Const., May 9, 1864.

sign it. The Turkish Ambassador had been instructed to watch the proceedings of the Commission but not to involve the Porte in the affair and he had construed this to mean that he was to say nothing.[1] " But he, good man," expostulated Bulwer, " with somewhat of oriental pride and nonchalance considered he might wait quietly with his telegram in his pocket, till Nubar Pasha called on him. Nubar Pasha hearing nothing that was positive on the subject, and fancying that he was left alone in the dispute, signed the compromise, and only called on Djemal Pasha to tell him so. . . ."[2]

The Commission finished its labors on June 19th and submitted a report to the Emperor setting forth in detail the issues he was to arbitrate: the amount of indemnity to be paid to the Company for the suppression of the *corvée* and the retrocession of the lands, the extent of territory necessary for the construction of the maritime canal, and whether the fresh-water canal should remain with the Company or be turned over to the Egyptian Government.[3]

The Emperor announced his decision on July 6, 1864.[4] The regulation of July 20, 1856, concerning the employment of native workers, was stated to be a contract containing reciprocal engagements to be executed by the Viceroy and the Company.[5] For the annulment of this regulation, the Em-

---

[1] *Ibid.,* no. 121, Bulwer to Russell, May 25, 1864.

[2] *Ibid.*

[3] Égypte, vol. 33, copy of report.

[4] *British and Foreign State Papers,* vol. 55, p. 1004. *Cf. Livre Jaune, Affaires Étrangères, Documents Diplomatiques,* 1864, vol. v, pp. 121-138.

[5] The Commission had recommended to the Emperor as a basis for a settlement that forced labor should be abolished and that the lands which the Company had received from Said Pasha for cultivation should be returned to the Egyptian Government. His decision, therefore, concerned the amount of indemnity which the latter should pay the Company. By the regulation of July 20, 1856, the Viceroy had agreed to furnish the Company with a minimum of 20,000 workers a month. De Lesseps esti-

peror awarded the Company an indemnity of thirty-eight million francs. The branch of the fresh-water canal from Timsah to Suez was turned over to the Egyptian government but the Company was to have the enjoyment of all fresh-water canals until the completion of the maritime canal.[1] The Company was compelled to give back to the Egyptian Government 60,000 hectares of land in the Isthmus, for which it was also indemnified.[2]  The total indemnity which the Egyptian Government was to pay the Company amounted to eighty-four million francs, payable over a period of fifteen years.  The two demands which England had insisted upon, namely, the abolition of forced labor and the retrocession of the land grants, had been acceded to, and it now remained to be seen what attitude she would adopt.

If the Emperor by his decision had expected to disarm English opposition, he was soon undeceived.  Though the English Government, ever since the visit of Sir Henry Bulwer to Egypt in the last weeks of 1862, had resigned itself to the realization that the canal was inevitable, it did not relax its opposition.[3]  In a conversation he had with the Em-

mated that the reduction of the number of workers from 20,000 to 6,000 as provided in the ultimatum of April 2, 1863, represented a loss to the Company of 40,000,000 francs. This estimate was based on the fact that 20,000 workers were required to keep the works going at all times and to replace 14,000 native workers by the same number of Europeans would have meant a great increase in expenditures (*Letters etc.*, 4th ser., p. 383).

[1] The branch of the fresh-water canal from the Nile to Timsah had already been turned over to the Egyptian Government by the Convention of March 18, 1863. *Cf. supra*, p. 197, note 2.

[2] The Company retained 10,264 hectares for the construction of the maritime canal.

[3] That England realized that the canal was inevitable seems to be indicated by the fact that she began the construction in 1863 of a new port at Malta, equipped with special docks, protected by fortresses of the first order, and designed to meet the demands of the expected increase in

peror on January 9, 1864, Sir Henry Bulwer had made it clear that England did not object to the canal itself but only to the manner in which it was being executed, and that if the *corvée* were abolished and the lands handed back to the Egyptian Government, there would be no further opposition.[1]

But Sir Henry did not fancy the idea of having the Emperor decide the litigious questions. " How can the Emperor," he asked, " alienate any portion of the Ottoman territory with the Viceroy's consent or even at his request? The Ottoman Empire is guaranteed by five Powers. Would they like to see one Sovereign charged with the right of disposing of a portion of territory, and that at so important a point as the one referred to." [2]  When the arbitral sentence was announced, he objected strenuously to the extent of land awarded to the Company for the maritime canal. " I cannot but think," he expostulated, " that the Emperor's intentions must have been somewhat forced in this matter, and that he would never, with the deliberate sagacity for which he is so remarkable, have, as the result of his own judgment, placed himself in so false a position." [3]  He continued his intrigues in order to persuade the Porte to withhold the sanction on the ground that it had never consented to have the Emperor act as arbitrator in any except the pecuniary

traffic through the Mediterranean which would follow the completion of the canal. (Archives Nationales—Marine-Carton, BB 4, 1036, annex to letter of Ministry of Foreign Affairs, dated June 3, 1863, Sevenier to Minister of For. Aff., Malta, May 29, 1863).

[1] FO 78/1849, confidential, Bulwer to Russell, Paris, Jan. 9, 1864. Sir Henry informed Schreiner that he had told the Emperor that England would offer no objections to the canal as such but would be ready to go to war in order to prevent it from falling under French control (HHSA, vol. $\frac{XXXI}{24}$, Cons. Ber., Schreiner to Mensdorff-Ponilly, Cairo, April 24, 1865).

[2] *Ibid.*, no. 121, Bulwer to Russell, May 25, 1864.

[3] *Ibid.*, no. 244, Bulwer to Russell, Const., Aug. 16, 1864.

question.[1]  According to Sir Henry, the Porte was in no way pledged to accept the arbitral sentence, though he admitted that the affair had gone too far for it to back out.[2] England, however, must continue to oppose the canal so long as there remained a possibility that the Company might establish a foreign colony in the Isthmus and convert the warehouses and magazines into " disguised fortresses." [3]  To accept the present situation, would mean a loss of English influence in the Near East.  " The resistance," he continued, " must come from giving France clearly to understand that Great Britain and other States would not submit to it." For the first time in three years the canal question was discussed between the French and British Ambassadors at the Porte.  " Without doubt," Sir Henry said to the French Ambassador, " this canal from the commercial viewpoint will not be what one at first expected to make it, but *in more limited dimensions* it could be very useful for the internal commerce of Egypt." [4]

The British Foreign Office shared the views of its ambassador at the Porte that the land awarded to the Company by the arbitral sentence was " for purposes of colonization " and " in fact for the purpose of wresting Egypt from the Domain of the Sultan," and this must be resisted if the integrity of the Ottoman Empire was to be preserved.[5]  " But it may be hoped," wrote Lord Russell, " that when better informed His Imperial Majesty will withdraw his sanction

[1] The Emperor had refused to arbitrate unless the whole affair was submitted to him.

[2] FO 78/1849, no. 291, secret and confidential, Bulwer to Russell, Const., Sept. 7, 1864.  *Cf. ibid.*, Sept. 30, 1864.

[3] *Ibid.*, Bulwer to Russell, Const., Sept. 30, 1864.

[4] Turquie, vol. 362, no. 87, de Moustier to Drouyn de Lhuys, Therapia, Aug. 3, 1864.

[5] FO 78/1895, no. 67, FO to Stuart, Feb. 28, 1865.

from a document, which if adopted would be injurious to his good ally, and dangerous to the integrity of the Turkish Empire." [1]  Lord Cowley was instructed to inform Drouyn de Lhuys of the British objections, but the latter insisted that the Emperor's award must be executed. [2]

When they accepted the Emperor's arbitration, de Lesseps and the Viceroy hoped that the opposition would be at an end and that the Sultan's approval of the Concession would follow as a natural consequence.  But the delays exasperated the Company and on February 4, 1865, the Board of Directors petitioned the Emperor to urge the Ambassador at Constantinople to demand the Sultan's sanction. [3]  The Ambassador was instructed to lay the matter before the Porte and to emphasize the special interest which the French Government attached to the sanction. [4]  But the Porte, encouraged by the British Chargé d'Affaires to resist the demand of the French Ambassador, replied that the sanction would be granted only when the Viceroy and de Lesseps had drawn up an agreement on the basis of the Emperor's award. [5]  Negotiations thereupon followed to determine the provisions of this agreement and a special commission was appointed to effect a delimitation of the lands awarded to the Company.

While the Company and the Egyptian Government were endeavoring to work out a final settlement, Sir Henry Bulwer paid a visit to Egypt.  " It is easy to see," wrote the French Consul-General, " that the British Ambassador desires to as-

---

[1] *Ibid.*, no. 54, Russell to Stuart, Feb. 21, 1865; seen by the Queen and Palmerston.

[2] *Ibid.*, no. 245, confidential, Cowley to Russell, Paris, Feb. 25, 1865.

[3] Égypte, vol. 35, annex to letter from de Lesseps, Feb. 5, 1865.  Letter to Napoleon III, dated Feb. 4, 1865.

[4] *Livre Jaune, Aff. Étr., Doc. Dipl.*, 1867, vol. viii, Drouyn de Lhuys to de Moustier, Feb. 10, 1865.

[5] FO 78/1895, vol. 12, no. 82, Stuart to Russell, Const., Feb. 21, 1865.

sure himself by a general visit to the works, of the harm
which has been occasioned by the last compaign and the temporary disorganization which followed, and still seeks elements of a new struggle." [1]   Indeed, Sir Henry declared
with some satisfaction that nothing was finished and that the
Powers would intervene as the Emperor's decision was illegal. [2]   He still professed to see in the scheme " a plan less
and less disguised." [3]   To offset French influence in Egypt,
he recommended to his government that a British warship
be stationed at Suez, that British warehouses and hospitals
be established in the Isthmus, and that Englishmen be encouraged to settle there. [4]   Yet in spite of his unfriendly attitude, Sir Henry was convinced that the canal would be
completed.   Responding to a toast in his honor at a banquet
on March 30, 1865, he said that he was certain of the success
of the enterprise which inspired him with a " sense of its
greatness. . . ." [5]

[1] Égypte, vol. 35, no. 114, Taster to Drouyn de Lhuys, Alex., Feb. 28,
1865.

[2] *Ibid.*, no. 118, Taster to Drouyn de Lhuys, Alex., Mar. 31, 1865.

[3] FO 78/1895, no. 25, Bulwer to Russell, Cairo, Mar. 10, 1865.

[4] *Ibid.*

[5] Égypte, vol. 35, annex to no. 119, Taster to Drouyn de Lhuys, Alex.,
April 9, 1865. A few days before the departure of Sir Henry there
arrived in Egypt a delegation representing chambers of commerce of
France, England, Italy, Austria, Russia and the United States. They
had come in response to an invitation addressed by de Lesseps on Jan.
31, 1865. De Lesseps took this means of combating certain reports
which had been circulated in Europe to the effect that the canal works
had not progressed. The delegates were conducted to various points in
the Isthmus, saw what had really been accomplished and came away
convinced that the completion of the canal was only a question of time
and money. Mr. Cyrus Field, who represented the Chamber of Commerce of New York City and who was then engaged in laying the first
Atlantic Cable, was unstinting in his praise. The visit did much to
remove the doubts as to the success of the enterprise and probably
helped the Canal Company diplomatically (Ferd. de Lesseps, *Letters etc.*,
5th ser., pp. 118-123).

The agreement between the Company and the Egyptian Government was finally settled and the terms were set forth in two conventions of January 30 and February 22, 1866.[1] The wishes of the Porte having been complied with, there was no reason for the Sultan to withhold his sanction. On March 19th, therefore, the Porte gave official recognition to the Concession of January 5, 1856, the various agreements arrived at between the Egyptian Government and de Lesseps, and the works which had been constructed in the Isthmus.[2] The preamble of the Sultan's Firman declared that the construction of a canal between the Mediterranean and the Red Sea was one of the most desirable events of the century. Thus ended the tortuous diplomatic struggle de Lesseps had embarked upon so hopefully twelve years before. He had triumphed over the bitter opposition of England, over the vacillation of the Porte; he had matched his determination against the wrathful scorn of Palmerston, the skill of Stratford de Redcliffe and the persistence of Bulwer. He had injected new hope into the drooping spirits of Said Pasha and had held his slippery successor to the bargain and had twice rescued his scheme from disaster. Perhaps he felt the flush of victory as he stood before the General Assembly of the Shareholders on August 1, 1866, and announced that the Sultan had given his sanction and that the success of the project " was no longer a hope but an incontestable fact." [3]

The removal of the political difficulties made it possible for the Company to proceed rapidly with the construction of the canal. Already considerable progress had been made. The excavation of the channel presented no major obstruc-

[1] *British and Foreign Papers*, vol. 56, p. 274, for agreement of Jan. 30th, and p. 277 for agreement of Feb. 22nd. In the main, these repeated the decisions of the Emperor's award.

[2] *Ibid.*, vol. 56, p. 293.

[3] *Letters etc.*, 5th ser., p. 247.

tions since the canal followed a natural depression for almost the entire distance. The first task which was undertaken after preliminary work had been completed, was the building of a harbor on the Mediterranean side and this was begun in April 1859 when the foundations were laid for Port Said. A breakwater was constructed outside of the harbor to give protection to the shipping from the strong currents of the Mediterranean. Considerable dredging was necessary to provide suitable approaches at both ends of the Canal, where the seas were shallow and muddy. From Port Said the works proceeded in general toward the Red Sea. The shallow basin of Lake Manzala was excavated and before the end of 1862 Lake Timsah was connected with the Mediterranean. The political difficulties of 1863 and 1864 checked the progress but it was speeded up in the beginning of the following year. After the withdrawal of forced labor in 1863 the Company relied more and more upon machinery, which, though involving heavy expense, required fewer workers.[1] The problem of furnishing an adequate supply of water to the workers which had caused considerable anxiety in the early years, was overcome with the completion of the fresh-water canal from the Nile to the maritime canal. Moreover, the finances of the Company were somewhat improved by the indemnity paid by the Egyptian Government on the basis of the Emperor's award. Remarkable headway was made during the last four years. Towns sprang up along the course of the canal, buildings were erected, docking facilities, lighthouses, sidings, and a system of signals were installed. When on March 14, 1869 the Bitter Lakes re-

[1] Though he wavered occasionally, Said Pasha furnished the monthly contingent of 20,000 men to the Company with more or less regularity. The number was reduced to 15,000 under Ismail, and in Aug., 1863, to 6,000. The Company then brought in a number of dredgers and other machines.

ceived the waters from the Mediterranean and in the following August those from the Red Sea, the great scheme was
realized and its projector took his place among the famous
engineers of all time.   The channel was over ninety miles
long.   It proceeded from the Mediterranean through a narrow region to Lake Manzala, traversed this shallow lake,
continued its course through a stretch of land to Lake Balla,
five miles in length, then again cut through flat country to
Lake Timsah, four miles in length, and then crossed a plateau
to the Bitter Lakes, which cover a distance of twenty miles.
From these lakes there is a short stretch to Suez, the terminal on the Red Sea.   Lakes accounted for more than one-
third of the total distance.

De Lesseps had prophesied that the canal would be opened
to navigation by the end of 1868.   But unfortunate circumstances such as cholera, labor shortage and so on, had interfered.   On November 17, 1869, the inauguration was cele-
brated with oriental magnificence.   Distinguished guests
from all parts of the world were entertained at the Khedive's
expense.   The Empress Eugénie, who had been one of de
Lessep's strongest supporters, was there together with other
royalty including the Emperor Francis Joseph, Prince Frederick William of Prussia, and Prince Henry of the Netherlands.   The British Government was represented by Sir
Henry G. Elliot, the new Ambassador at Constantinople.
At Port Said, sixty-seven vessels headed by the French royal
yacht, *Aigle,* bearing the Empress and de Lesseps, awaited
the signal to enter the canal.   In single file they moved
slowly southward amid the cheers of the crowds along the
banks, the martial strains of the bands and the thunder of
guns.   " All were united in that celebration to appeal to
the mind, the imagination, the heart.   In that land of Egypt,
one of the cradles of humanity, the modern world revealed
its power in a most striking and durable form.   Science

roused the land of the Pharaohs from its ancient sleep and traced for civilization a pacific and productive route across the sands of the desert." [1]   In the words of his biographers M. de Lesseps

has transformed into a living and fruitful reality an idea which seduced the greatest minds of our century, Napoleon, Thiers, Guizot, Lamartine, Metternich, Cavour, Cobden, Gladstone.

By his energy, his valor, his persistent and victorious struggles against obstacles accumulated in his path by nature, politics, speculation, ill-will or intrigues—Ferdinand de Lesseps has been great.

Ferdinand de Lesseps has enriched the patrimony of France at the same time that he has increased the field of action for humanity. [2]

[1] Bridier, *Une famille français—Les de Lesseps.*  Quoted in J. C. T. Roux, *op. cit.,* vol. ii, p. 388 *et seq.*

[2] A. Bertrand and E. Ferrier, *op. cit.,* preface.

# CHAPTER XIV

## DIFFICULTIES

THE impressive ceremonies which marked the opening of the canal to navigation were a splendid tribute to the courageous efforts of Ferdinand de Lesseps. His great work was finished and the advantages which he and other advocates of the project had promised, were now to follow. The canal was to inaugurate a second commercial revolution, a new era in eastern trade as important as the one which followed the Portuguese voyages of the fifteenth century. Europe was entering a period of rapid expansion. Factories were springing up like mushrooms, the production of coal, iron and steel was increasing enormously, great railway systems were being laid out, ocean liners were becoming larger and faster, population was growing by leaps and bounds. All this was to lead to a feverish search for new sources of raw materials, and for new markets to absorb the surplus of manufactured goods poured out by the busy factories of England, Germany and France. Within a few years of the opening of the canal there began a renewed interest in imperialism, followed by the partition of Africa, the acquisition of distant colonies and naval bases, and the spreading of European civilization to the farthest corners of the globe. Important changes were also taking place in the Far East. Japan was about to be modernized along European lines; China was to become the happy hunting ground for imperialists seeking concessions for railways, mines and ports; Australia and New Zealand were to blossom forth as important industrial nations. As the great artery to the East, the shortest route to India and China, the Suez Canal would play its part in meeting the demands of this tremendous expansion of trade and industry. And England, the most bitter opponent of the canal, the greatest Power in the East, the mistress of the seas, was to be the chief gainer from this new highway! Ferdinand de Lesseps had triumphantly refuted before the world the Palmerstonian dictum that the canal was physically impossible of execution. But the new channel had still to prove its commercial and financial possibilities. Would that other charge of Palmerston's, that the canal would not be a profitable undertaking, be repudiated also?

One of the greatest difficulties which faced the Company during the first four years of operation was financial. The shareholders naturally expected returns on their investment as soon as the canal was opened to navigation. But the cost of construction had been much greater than was expected when the Company was organized in 1858. The International Scientific Commission had estimated the cost at 200,000,000 francs, but had not foreseen the complications which arose over the withdrawal of forced labor or the diplomatic difficulties.[1] Actually the total cost of constructing the canal was 432,807,882 francs, more than double the estimate of the Commission.[2] From the sale of the shares, the Company had received 200,000,000 francs, the Emperor's award brought in 84,000,000 francs from the Egyptian Government and an additional 30,000,000 francs was realized by an agreement between the Khedive and the Company in 1869.[3] Altogether the Company had somewhat over

[1] See ch. xi, p. 137.

[2] J. C. T. Roux, *op. cit.*, vol. ii, p. 4.

[3] Two conventions were signed by Ismail and de Lesseps on April 23, 1869. By the first of these the Company renounced certain privileges it had received by the second Concession of Jan. 5, 1856, such as exemption

300,000,000 francs for building the canal, and 100,000,000 francs more were necessary. To raise this sum, the Company in 1867 had recourse to a loan and offered to the public 333,333 bonds having a par value of 300 francs, payable in fifteen years and carrying an annual interest of twenty-five francs.[1] But the sale was disappointing; by the end of June 1868, only one-third had been purchased. In order to dispose of the remaining bonds, the Company secured permission from the French Government to issue them in the form of *obligations à lots* which added the attractions of a lottery and found a ready market. With the sum realized from this loan, the Company was able to complete the canal.

In the first year of operation the financial prospects were far from encouraging. The capital on hand in January 1870 was only 20,836,000 francs while the expenditures for the year included arrears on the coupons of the shares, payment of amortization and interest, as well as administration charges, all of which would require an outlay estimated at

from customs duties for articles brought into Egypt or from other taxes and dues, the privilege of fishing in the Lakes, exploiting mines and all special rights with regard to the fresh water canal. The Egyptian Government purchased the Company's warehouses and hospitals in the Isthmus. In return for all this it agreed to pay the Company thirty million francs. As Ismail did not have this amount, he turned over to the Company the coupons on his shares for twenty-five years. By this action he lost his votes as a shareholder, since voting depended on full strength shares, but he still retained two important connections with the Company: he could nominate the Director (president) and he received fifteen per cent of the net profits annually. The second convention regulated the sale of 10,414 hectares of land which the Egyptian Government and the Company undertook jointly. Compagnie Universelle Maritime de Suez, *Notice et Renseignements Généraux* (2ème partie), pp. 77-82. The Company used the coupons as collateral for a new bond issue; 120,000 *délégations* were issued of 250 francs each.

[1] *Ibid.*, p. 296. *Cf.* Voisin-Bey, *Le Canal de Suez: historique, administratif, description de travaux* (7 vols. and atlas, Paris, 1902-1907), vol. ii, ch. i.

over thirty million francs.[1]  The Company hoped to cover the deficit of about ten millions from the revenues of the canal.  Unfortunately the revenues for the first year fell far below expectations, as the European shippers were not as yet attracted to the new channel.  From November 17, 1869 to the end of 1870 only 486 vessels with a total tonnage of 436,609 passed through the canal, yielding returns of 4,345,758 francs.[2]

Unable to pay either the dividends or the five per cent interest on the shares, and with its credit declining rapidly, the Company faced bankruptcy.  The shares having a par value of 500 francs were quoted at 272 in 1870 and 208 in the following year.[3]  Payment of the coupons falling due in July and October was postponed while rumors that the canal would be sold caused considerable consternation among the shareholders.[4]

It was evident that drastic measures must be taken to tide the Company over these lean years.  At the general meeting of the shareholders on July 20, 1871, de Lesseps proposed that a loan should be contracted for twenty million francs in order to meet the deficit.  As security for this loan the Khedive[5] allowed the Company to levy a surtax of one franc a ton to be added to the regular tolls of ten francs.

Subscriptions for the new loan were opened on September 9, 1870, and it was hoped that the full amount could be raised in nine days.[6]  The bonds, called *bons trentenaires,*

[1] Voisin-Bey, *op. cit.,* vol. ii, p. 4.  The actual deficit for two years, 1870-1871, was twelve million francs, about six million francs for each year.

[2] For further details see Appendix A.

[3] These are average yearly quotations.  See Appendix B.

[4] Voisin-Bey, *op. cit.,* vol. ii, p. 4.

[5] The new title assumed in 1866.

[6] Voisin-Bey, *op. cit.,* vol. ii, pp. 9-13.  *Cf.* J. C. T. Roux, *op. cit.,* vol. ii, p. 297.

were issued to the number of 200,000 with a par value of 100 francs each, paying eight per cent interest and redeemable at 125 francs in thirty years. But public confidence in the canal was then at a very low ebb and there was little response to the loan. As only five million francs were raised in the nine-day period the Company decided to prolong the sale until February 1, 1872, by which time 120,000 bonds were taken. This was sufficient, however, to relieve the financial situation temporarily and it was possible to pay the first coupon (due July 1870) in April 1873, and the second (due January 1871) in February 1874. The remaining coupons, seven in all, represented a value of thirty-five million francs, or 87.50 francs per share. At the general meeting of the shareholders on June 2, 1874, it was decided to capitalize these coupons, deducting from each 2.50 francs for charges, which made the value 85 francs per share. Bonds were issued, called *bons représentatifs de coupons consolidés,* paying five per cent interest and redeemable at 85 francs in forty years.[1]

The financial difficulties of the Company brought into prominence proposals for the sale of the canal. As early as December 30, 1870 Colonel Stanton, the British Consul-General in Egypt, called Lord Granville's attention to the prospect of acquiring the canal for England. Colonel Stanton had had an interview with the Khedive in which the latter had spoken of the financial difficulties facing the Company and had intimated " that the only way to ensure the Canal being made really serviceable for general navigation was for an English Company to obtain possession of it." [2] He added that he favored the acquisition of the canal by

---

[1] *Ibid.,* p. 15.

[2] *Egypt no. 2 (1876),* appendix: Correspondence Respecting M. de Lesseps' Proposal for the Sale of the Suez Canal, 1871-1872, no. 1, Col. Stanton to Earl Granville, Cairo, Dec. 30, 1870, extract.

such a company and would " do everything in his power to facilitate the transfer into their hands." Colonel Stanton's letter was sent to the Secretary of the Admiralty, the Board of Trade and the India Office, but the Government took no action in the matter.

In the following year de Lesseps in a letter to the Viceroy proposed that the canal should be sold to the European Powers in order to render it international.[1] He stated that he had received the approval of both M. Thiers and M. de Rémusat, the French Minister for Foreign Affairs, and that he intended to request the Italian Government to act as mediator in bringing about an understanding among the Powers. The Khedive opposed the scheme but referred it to the Porte for consideration.

The financial plight of the Company prompted Sir Daniel Lange, one of de Lesseps' strongest supporters in England, to write to Granville in April 1871, urging that the British Government should seize the opportunity of acquiring the canal. This course, in his opinion, was more desirable than a system of joint international control.[2] Some weeks later, he informed Granville that de Lesseps was prepared to sell the canal to the Maritime Powers for £12,000,000 and the payment of the shareholders' dividends, which amounted to £400,000 yearly. Lord Granville replied that it was premature for the British Government to discuss the proposal.[3] The Board of Trade, however, was favorably disposed, and suggested that an arrangement might be concluded whereby the canal would be placed under a European commission for its management and neutralization.[4]

[1] *Egypt no. 5 (1876)*. Précis by Lord Tenterden of the Published Correspondence Relating to the Suez Canal.

[2] *Ibid.*

[3] *Ibid.*

[4] *Egypt no. 2 (1876)*, appendix, no. 31, Mr. Farrer to Mr. Hammond, Board of Trade, Jan. 22, 1872.

The Porte, after considering de Lesseps' proposal, announced through its ambassador at London, on January 10, 1872, that it

could not admit, even in principle, the sale of the Canal or the creation of an International Administration on its own territory. On the other hand, M. de Lesseps, having only the concession of the undertaking, could never have the right of raising questions of such a nature. The Suez Canal Company is an Egyptian Company, and therefore subject to the laws and customs of the Empire.[1]

The opposition of the Porte and the British Government, coupled with the fact that Italy had taken no action in the matter, killed the proposal. A combination which had been formed by the Duke of Sutherland and Mr. Pender for the purchase of the canal, likewise fell through, due " to the volume of cold water poured on it by the Government of the day." [2] In 1874 the Board of Trade again expressed its approval of international control and declared " that complications and difficulties will be endlesss so long as this great highway of nations remains in the hands of a private company." [3] Lord Derby, addressing the House of Lords on June 5, 1874, indicated that he favored the transfer of the canal to an international commission.[4] By 1875, however, the finances of the Company had improved and the question of selling the canal was dropped.

Another great difficulty which the Company had to face concerned the method of levying tolls. The first and second

[1] *Ibid.*, enclosure in no. 32, note from Server Pasha to Musurus Pasha, Jan. 10, 1872, communicated by the latter to Earl Granville, Jan. 22, 1872.

[2] *Quarterly Review*, vol. 142, July-October, 1876, " The Suez Canal an International Highway," p. 436, unsigned.

[3] *Egypt no. 5 (1876)*.

[4] *Hansard*, 3d series, House of Lords, June 5, 1874, vol. 219, p. 1036.

concessions had given it the right to levy tolls on vessels and passengers passing through the canal. Article 17 of the second concession fixed the maximum charge at ten francs per ton for vessels but made no provision for measuring tonnage capacity. How should the Company determine the tonnage? Did Article 17 refer to ton of measurement or ton of displacement? Should the Company accept the tonnage shown on the ship's papers or should it adopt a uniform system for all vessels?

In order to find a solution for this problem the Company in October 1868 appointed a Commission on Navigation which studied the various systems of measurement employed at that time. In its report of November 14th, the Commission recognized that the English official tonnage was the best, but in the absence of any uniform system, it recommended that the Company should accept the tonnage shown on the ship's papers without distinction of flag.[1] This recommendation was adopted and was published in the Navigation Rules of the Company on August 17, 1869. An additional ruling of February 1, 1870, stipulated that the measurement of steamers would be according to the official net tonnage. As this did not take into account the space occupied by machinery, the Company soon realized that there existed a substantial difference between the tonnage as determined by this method and the actual tonnage, which was generally much higher. It therefore took up the question of a uniform system and appointed an international commission to look into the matter. The report of the commission was not altogether satisfactory, for it advised that no attempt to settle on a uniform system should be made until a test case arose, and that the Company in the meantime should be willing to suffer a temporary financial

[1] Voisin-Bey, *op. cit.*, vol. ii, p. 58. *Cf.* J. C. T. Roux, *op. cit.*, vol. ii, p. 11.

loss in order to encourage vessels to employ the canal.[1]
Desiring to arrive at a uniform system as soon as possible,
the Company petitioned the French Government to negotiate with the other Powers. When these negotiations were
interrupted by the Franco-Prussian War, the Company decided to take upon itself the task of finding a satisfactory
method and appointed a commission of engineers and shippers to study the problem. This body recommended the
Moorsom system employed by English vessels, which had
been provided for in the Merchant Shipping Act of 1854
and had subsequently been adopted by several other nations.
According to this system, the contents of the hull and permanent erections were ascertained and the number of cubic
feet thus arrived at divided by 100, giving the gross tonnage. Deductions were then made in the case of steam
vessels for the space occupied by machinery and coal, vary-
ing from twenty-five to fifty per cent, and this resulted in
the net tonnage.[2] Discovering, however, that the Moorsom
system allowed too much space for machinery and coal, the
commission suggested that thirty per cent should be added
to the gross tonnage and from this new figure there should
be deducted twenty-five per cent to get the net tonnage.[3]
As this would involve two distinct calculations which very
nearly offset each other, the Company decided to accept only
the gross tonnage in levying the tolls and on March 18,
1872 issued a ruling to that effect. In practice this would
mean an increase of nearly thirty per cent in the tolls.

No objections were raised when the new ruling was announced and the French and British Governments gave their
approval. Before very long, however, complaints began to
pour in from shippers, especially in England, and the in-

[1] J. C. T. Roux, *op. cit.,* vol. ii, p. 11.

[2] *Ibid.,* p. 10. *Cf. Egypt no. 5 (1876).*

[3] *Ibid.,* p. 12.

creased tolls were paid only with a good deal of protest.[1]
Lord Granville seized the occasion to instruct Sir Henry
Elliot on August 31, 1872, to request the Porte not to
sanction the new system.[2]   A suit was brought against the
Canal Company in the Tribunal of Commerce of the Seine
by the *Compagnie des Messageries Maritimes,* which claimed
that the tolls should be determined by the official tonnage
listed on the ship's papers.[3]   De Lesseps declared that the
court had no jurisdiction in the case as the Canal Company
was Egyptian but this contention was overruled and judgment was awarded to the *Messageries Maritimes.*[4]   The case
was then carried to the Court of Appeals of Paris which
held that the Tribunal of the Seine had jurisdiction, but it
reversed the decision on merits, gave judgment to the Company with costs and ordered the restitution of the fine imposed by the lower court.[5]   This sentence was not carried
out by the French Government but was held in reserve as
an argument in favor of the Company.[6]

De Lesseps, in the meantime, had appealed to the Khedive,
who referred him to the Porte.  The latter addressed a dispatch to its representative at Paris arguing against the
competence of the French Court and declaring that it could
not permit the Company to be withdrawn from the jurisdiction to which it was amenable by the Act of Concession.[7]

[1] *Hansard's Parl. Debates,* 3d ser., vol. 211, p. 1687, vol. 212, p. 101.

[2] *Egypt no. 5 (1876).*

[3] *Ibid.  Cf.* J. C. T. Roux, *op. cit.,* vol. ii, p. 13; Voisin-Bey, *op. cit.,*
vol. ii, p. 87.

[4] Decision rendered Oct. 26, 1872.

[5] Decision rendered March 11, 1873.

[6] *Egypt no. 5 (1876).*

[7] *Documents Diplomatiques.* Affaires du Canal de Suez, vol. 104, de
Rémusat to Minister of Justice, Dec. 19, 1872.  Details concerning the
tonnage controversy will be found in volumes 104, 105 and 106 of the
*Documents Diplomatiques.*  The correspondence on this subject is
voluminous.

At the same time the Porte announced that it would summon an international conference to settle the tonnage question. Accordingly, in January 1873 it addressed a circular to its representatives at the foreign courts inviting the Conference to meet at Constantinople. Delegates from the principal Maritime Powers, with the exception of the United States, assembled there in October. Throughout the sessions the views of the British delegates prevailed.[1] In its report on December 18th the Conference adopted the Moorsom system as the most satisfactory for measuring tonnage and advised that every ship's papers should contain a certificate showing the gross and net tonnage which should be accepted for all tolls levied on the net tonnage.[2] The Company was permitted to levy a temporary surtax of four francs (in some cases only three francs) a ton on the net registered tonnage of vessels. This surtax was fixed on a sliding scale so that when the net tonnage reached 2,600,000 the original ten francs alone would be charged.

The report of the Conference was sent to the Khedive along with a vizirial letter stating that the new arrangement must take effect within three months. De Lesseps replied to it by proposing an alternative plan according to which the Company should accept the new system of measurement and the surtax but the latter should be maintained until the shareholders had received the amount due on their coupons (30,000,000 francs), the improvements on the canal had been carried out and the net revenue on the capital had

[1] *Egypt no. 5 (1876)*. The British delegates were Colonel Stokes and Sir P. Francis. The French and Russian delegates desiring to secure better terms for the Company than the Conference seemed disposed to give, and limited by the instructions to consider only "utilizable tonnage", withdrew, but later returned and signed the report. *Doc. Dipl.,* vol. 104, Minister of Foreign Affairs to French Chargé d'Affaires at Const., Aug. 8, Sept. 10, 1873.

[2] Report of the Conference given in *Egypt no. 5 (1876)*.

reached eight per cent.[1] The Porte, however, refused to accept any alternative and warned him that if he did not comply within the time set, the original tolls of ten francs a ton would be reverted to, without the surtax. This produced a vigorous protest from de Lesseps who declared that he would hold the Porte responsible for all the losses to the shareholders, estimated at 700,000 francs a month, which might arise from the new system.[2] Finding that he made no impression, he threatened to abandon the canal, extinguish the lights and stop all telegraphic communications.[3] The Khedive, ordered by the Porte to execute the decision of the Conference without delay, on April 29, 1874, sent a military force of 10,000 men, commanded by an Englishman, to take possession of the canal, if the Company persisted in its opposition. De Lesseps thereupon gave way and the new regulation went into effect. His stubbornness was probably due to the pressure of the shareholders, since the financial situation of the Company was still unfavorable.[4]

One of the points raised by the tonnage controversy concerned the legal position of the Canal Company. In the case of the *Messageries Maritimes,* de Lesseps pleaded that the Company was Egyptian and was thus amenable only to the authority of the Porte. In another case, however, that of the Khedivian Mail-Packet, in May 1872, he contended that the Company could only be sued in the French Consular Court.[5] He referred to article 17 of the Convention of February 22, 1866, which provided that "disputes in Egypt

---

[1] *Egypt no. 5* (1876), de Lesseps to Khedive, Jan. 31, 1874.

[2] *Ibid.,* de Lesseps to Khedive, March 20, 1874.

[3] *Ibid. Cf.* Voisin-Bey, op. cit., vol. ii, p. 244; *cf. Doc. Dipl.,* vol. 104, Telegram, April 5, 1874, French Chargé at Const. to Minister of Foreign Affairs.

[4] J. C. T. Roux, *op. cit.,* vol. ii, p. 26.

[5] *Egypt no. 5 (1876).*

between the Company and individuals of any nationality whatever, shall be tried by the local tribunals, in accordance with the forms sanctioned by the laws and customs of the country and by treaties." The term " local tribunals," according to de Lesseps, meant consular courts. In a dispatch to the French Ambassador at London, May 5, 1873, M. de Rémusat formally repudiated this claim of the Company to be under French jurisdiction.[1] The Company was Egyptian in accordance with the Act of Concession, and as such was subject to the jurisdiction of the Ottoman Empire. But it was also made clear that it could be sued in French courts.

Not only was the question of the legal position of the Company brought into prominence but the international character of the canal, as well as the British influence, was made apparent.

Hardly had the new method for measuring tonnage been put into effect than the British shippers complained that the Company violated its provisions.[2] The British Ambassador at the Porte made several protests but the violations continued.[3] The high-handed methods pursued by the Company officials provoked the hostility of the English shippers and led to an agitation for a second canal under the control of Great Britain.[4]

[1] *Doc. Dipl.*, vol. 104.
[2] See *Egypt no. 2 (1876)*.
[3] *Egypt no. 5 (1876)*.
[4] On the agitation for the second canal see ch. xvi.

# CHAPTER XV

## DISRAELI'S MASTER STROKE—THE PURCHASE OF THE KHEDIVE'S SHARES

ENGLAND'S policy concerning the Suez Canal went through several phases during the nineteenth century. When the project first came into prominence in the last years of the administration of Mehemet Ali, she expressed her disapproval in unmistakable terms. Controlling the Cape route to India she saw no reason for change so far as commerce was concerned. But a shorter route was desired for travellers and for the transmission of dispatches and she succeeded in winning the consent of Abbas Pasha for a railway across Egypt. From her viewpoint a canal was quite unnecessary and especially a canal not subject to her control. The success of Ferdinand de Lesseps in securing the Concession aroused her fury and at every step she opposed him, making use of any pretext which at the moment seemed most expedient. Imperial considerations lay back of her opposition. The repeated assertions of de Lesseps that the canal was an international undertaking designed to serve the shipping of all nations without discrimination, did not sound convincing in English ears. After all, de Lesseps was a Frenchman, and France from the Emperor down to the man-in-the-street regarded the scheme as predominantly French in character. Could England be expected to favor a highway under French control and hence a menace to India, a highway, moreover, which would be of greater advantage to the commerce of the Mediterranean countries than her own? Would not her supremacy in eastern trade vanish once this canal were opened to navigation? Yet, in spite of her opposition, the " bubble scheme " was completed and she had to face the accomplished fact.  Her fear of losing commercial supremacy was soon shown to be unfounded.  From the first England was the most important patron of the new channel and this fact alone made it necessary for de Lesseps to pay some attention to her wishes.[1]  In the tonnage conference at Constantinople, her influence was uppermost and it was obvious that she was still a factor to be reckoned with.  The officials of the Company, however, adopted a most arrogant attitude and openly violated the regulations concerning tonnage measurement.  Under the circumstances it was quite natural that Englishmen should have considered the possibility of acquiring the canal or of constructing a second channel.  As soon as the canal became " vital " for England's trade with India, it was inevitable that it should pass under her control.  That, at any rate, seemed to be the sequence.  England at first opposed the canal, then accepted it as inevitable, and finally secured control.  A situation now presented itself which gave her an opportunity for increasing her voice in the management of the Company.

The reckless expenditures of the Khedive Ismail Pasha were bringing Egypt to the verge of bankruptcy.  During the reigns of Mehemet Ali and his immediate successors, the country was practically without debt.  Said Pasha set an unfortunate precedent when he contracted a loan in 1862.[2] At his death in the following year the public debt of Egypt amounted to £3,293,000, most of which represented sums he had advanced to the Canal Company.[3]  For a country whose natural resources were still undeveloped, this was a heavy burden, but it was increased many-fold by Ismail.  Imbued with thoughts of independence, he sought to free himself as

---

[1] For the details on British shipping through the Canal see appendix A.

[2] *Cf. supra*, ch. xii, pp. 188-189.

[3] The Earl of Cromer, *Modern Egypt* (two volumes in one, N. Y., 1916), vol. i, p. 11.

much as possible from the jurisdiction of Constantinople by ingratiating himself with the Sultan. In the seven visits he made to the Porte, he secured each time some addition to his prerogatives, but always returned with a lighter purse. His increasing independence only led him to rash expenditures and he sank deeper and deeper into debt. He contracted loans in 1864, 1865, 1867, 1868, all of which were guaranteed by the revenues of Egypt. A Firman of the Sultan, September 25, 1872, gave him the privilege of borrowing without authorization, and other loans followed, including one for 800 million francs in 1873. " There was neither limit nor intelligence in his borrowing. He took money wherever it was to be had, and, with oriental largess of spirit, never haggled about the rate of interest, with the result that harpies robbed him right and left." [1] By 1876 he had increased the public debt to over ninety-eight million pounds, an average of about seven million pounds a year for thirteen years.[2] " For all practical purposes," says Cromer, " it may be said that the whole of the borrowed money except £ 16,000,000 spent on the Suez Canal, was squandered." [3]

In November 1875 Ismail found himself in urgent need of funds to meet obligations coming due in December and the following months. The rumor had reached Europe that he was planning to secure these funds by selling his shares in the Suez Canal, 177,642 in number, to a French combination. On the 15th Lord Derby instructed Major-General Stanton, the British Consul-General in Egypt, to ascertain if this report was correct.[4] On the following day General Stanton

---

[1] Ward and Gooch, *Cambridge History of British Foreign Policy*, vol. iii, p. 155.

[2] Cromer, *op. cit.*, vol. i, p. 11.     [3] *Ibid.*

[4] FO 78/2432, Suez Canal, vol. 38, no. 87, telegram, Derby to Stanton, Nov. 15, 1875. *Cf. Parl. Paper, Egypt no. 1 (1876)*, correspondence respecting the purchase by Her Majesty's Government of the Suez Canal shares belonging to the Egyptian Government, no. 1.

wired back that the report was well-founded, and as the Khedive was pressed for money " there is every reason to believe that he will be forced to accept the offer." [1] In another telegram sent on the same day he stated that the *Société Générale* had made an offer to buy the shares for ninety million francs, while the Anglo-Egyptian Bank had offered to advance eighty million francs on the shares as security.[2] General Stanton succeeded in having the negotiations suspended until the 18th to enable him to communicate with London. On the 17th he received a telegram from Derby stating that " it is of great importance that the interest of the Viceroy of Egypt in the Suez Canal should not fall into the hands of a foreign Company. Press for suspension of negotiations, and intimate that Her Majesty's Government are disposed to purchase if satisfactory terms can be arranged." [3] The Khedive, however, informed General Stanton that he had no intention of selling the shares, but if he changed his mind he would give Great Britain the option of purchase.[4] Meanwhile, he would be obliged to accept the offer of the Anglo-Egyptian Bank to enable him to convert the floating debt on reasonable terms.

Upon receiving Lord Derby's telegram of the 15th, General Stanton had immediately sought out Nubar Pasha and had protested against the secrecy which covered the negotiations with the French banks.

I expressed to His Excellency, my surprise that on the receipt of such a proposal, no intimation of the same should have been made to myself . . . as the Egyptian Government could hardly suppose that Her Majesty's Government would see with indifference the transfer of the Khedive's interest

---

[1] *Ibid., Cairo*, Nov. 16, 1875.

[2] *Ibid.*

[3] *Ibid.*, no. 67, Derby to Stanton, FO, Nov. 17, 1875.

[4] *Ibid.*, telegram from Stanton to Derby, Cairo, Nov. 17, 1875.

in the Suez Canal to any Foreign Company, and I was satisfied His Highness would get better terms from England than from any other country should he wish to dispose of his shares.[1]

That England should have desired a voice in the management of the Company now that the canal had become so important for her commerce was perfectly natural. In 1871, as we have seen, Granville had vetoed the suggestion that England should purchase the canal. The very idea, no doubt, ran counter to the anti-imperialist views of the Liberals. When the Conservatives came into office in 1874, Disraeli is said to have authorized Baron Rothschild to intimate confidentially to de Lesseps that England was prepared to purchase the canal.[2] The proposal was rejected though Rothschild " endeavoured in vain during 1874 and down to the summer of 1875 to purchase the Khedive's shares." [3] In answer to a question in the House of Lords on June 5, 1874, as to whether it would not be advisable for England to purchase the canal in view of the financial predicament of the Company, Lord Derby replied:

No such offer has been put before us. I hope, however, that my noble Friend will not ask me to express an opinion on a

---

[1] *Ibid.*, no. 125, Confidential, Stanton to Derby, Cairo, Nov. 18, 1875.

[2] This is the statement of Mr. Julien Wolff in the *London Times*, Dec. 26, 1875. De Lesseps called on Lord Lyons, British Ambassador at Paris on July 11, 1874 and informed him " that two persons from England had sounded him about the sale of the Canal, one a member of the English branch of the Rothschild family, and the other a Baron Émile d'Erlanger, a well-known banker living in Paris." Nathaniel Rothschild was at that time in Paris. De Lesseps, being asked to name a price for the canal, mentioned £40,000,000, a sum that " startled even a Rothschild." By naming so high a figure, he indicated that the Company had no intention o'f selling the canal. Lord Newton, *Lord Lyons. A Record of British Diplomacy* (2 vols., London, 1913), vol. ii, p. 91.

[3] *Ibid.*, *London Times.*

transaction of that kind; because when a man wants to buy a house, or an estate or anything else, he does not, if he is a man of sense, begin by telling the party who has it to sell that its possession is indispensable to him. If a proposition for the transfer of the Canal to an International Commission were to come before us, framed in such a manner that all Governments would participate in the advantages of the Canal on equal terms, I do not say that might not be a fair proposal to entertain. But it has not been made, and I have no reason to think it will be made.[1]

The idea of purchasing the shares, then, was certainly entertained in England before the rumor that the Khedive was negotiating with the French banks had come to the attention of Lord Derby. In France, however, there were on foot two distinct and mutually conflicting movements with regard to the Khedive's shares. The first was for the purchase of the shares. This was being promoted by the brothers Édouard and André Dervieu, members of the firm of Dervieu, Chenaud and Company, bankers of Paris and Alexandria.[2] Édouard Dervieu was well acquainted with the financial situation of the Egyptian Treasury and was convinced that the Khedive would soon be compelled to part with his canal shares. He confided this idea to his brother early in November 1875, intimating that if the Khedive would agree to sell, he could find a market in Paris, on condition, however, that the Egyptian Government would pay interest for the nineteen years during which the shares carried no dividends.[3] On November 11th, he telegraphed his brother making a definite proposal to find purchasers for the

---

[1] *Hansard's Parl. Debates*, 3rd ser., vol. 219, p. 1036.

[2] For an account of the French negotiations, see Charles Lesage, *L'invasion anglaise en Égypte. L'achat des actions de Suez* (Paris, 1906).

[3] See note 3, p. 217.

shares in Paris and demanding an annual interest of twelve per cent for the alienated coupons to be secured either from the customs of Port Said or from the fifteen per cent net profits which belonged to the Khedive.[1] Upon receiving this communication, M. André Dervieu called on the Egyptian Minister of Finance, who arranged an interview with the Khedive. The latter agreed to sell the shares for ninety-two million francs and to pay eight per cent interest instead of the twelve per cent demanded, to be secured from the customs of Port Said. Not being in a position to accept this offer on the spot, André secured an option until November 16th. This news he telegraphed to his brother, who set out to find the funds. But the latter no sooner entered upon this quest than word came from André that the Anglo-Egyptian Bank was negotiating for the Khedive's shares. This announcement meant trouble for the Dervieu plan.

There were at this time several great French banking houses deeply involved in Egyptian finances. Among these were the *Crédit Foncier* and the *Crédit Agricole,* which were represented in Egypt through the Anglo-Egyptian Bank. The *Crédit Agricole* had purchased claims to Egyptian debts through the Anglo-Egyptian Bank, with money advanced by the *Crédit Foncier.*[2] To guarantee repayment, the *Crédit Agricole* had turned over to the *Crédit Foncier* titles to Egyptian claims amounting to some 170 million francs, from 1873 to 1876. Other French banks holding Egyptian claims were the *Crédit Lyonnais* and the *Société Générale.* The combined claims of the French banks amounted to about a billion francs.[3]

M. Édouard Dervieu first called at the office of the *Société Générale,* where he met with partial success, for the

[1] Lesage, *op. cit.,* p. 37.

[2] *Ibid.,* p. 44.

[3] *Ibid.,* p. 46.

bank was willing to participate in, but not to promote, the scheme. His next call was at the *Crédit Foncier*. Baron de Soubeyran, one of the bank's officers, did not hesitate to express his doubts concerning the proposal and intimated that it was somewhat unreasonable of the Khedive to enter into an important negotiation with a minor firm such as Dervieu's. He then disclosed a plan which had been devised for the consolidation of the Egyptian floating debt. This called for the conversion of the debt from short to long term and to do this guarantees were necessary. It was proposed to include the Khedive's canal shares among these guarantees, which meant of course, that the French banks holding Egyptian claims desired that the Khedive retain his shares. The plan ran directly counter to the one proposed by Dervieu. Moreover, it was supported by the powerful Anglo-Egyptian Bank and Baron de Soubeyran made it appear that it would be impossible to raise the money for the purchase of the shares in either Paris or London.[1]

Frustrated in his efforts to secure funds from the Paris bankers, M. Édouard Dervieu secured an extension of the option for three days, that is, until the 19th. Having received word from his brother [2] that General Stanton was interviewing the Khedive regarding the shares, he knew he had not a moment to lose. He called on one of the leading financiers of Paris and proposed that a syndicate should be formed immediately to secure the funds. But so great was the influence of the *Crédit Foncier* that nothing could be done and on the 18th he wired his brother that he had failed.[3] Before the telegram from Paris arrived, M. André Dervieu had come to an arrangement with the Khedive which called

[1] *Ibid.*, p. 51.

[2] On November 17th.

[3] Lesage, *op. cit.*, p. 55. *Cf. Documents Diplomatiques Français (1871-1914)*, 1re série, vol. ii, no. 18.

for a loan for three months of eighty million francs with interest at eighteen per cent.[1] The loan was to be secured by the canal shares together with the Khedive's fifteen per cent interest in the profits of the Company, and it was agreed that if it were not repaid at the end of three months, the shares and the fifteen per cent interest would become the property of the French syndicate advancing the money. The Khedive, moreover, promised to pay an interest of ten per cent in place of the alienated coupons to be secured by the customs of Port Said. In spite of these highly favorable terms, M. André Dervieu stipulated that the transaction would be valid only after it had been ratified by the Paris syndicate and he was given until the 26th to secure this ratification.

Once more M. Édouard Dervieu set out to find the funds. He received the active support of de Lesseps, who begged the French Minister of Foreign Affairs, the Duc Decazes, to intervene at the Ministry of Finance in order to put an end to the opposition of the *Crédit Foncier*.[2] De Lesseps declared that the Khedive would be unable to repay the loan at the end of three months and thus the shares would become French property. But the Duc Decazes' "resisted the persuasive and really seductive addresses of M. de Lesseps." [3] The Minister of Finance, M. Léon Say, opposed the Dervieu scheme, and supported the program of the *Crédit Foncier* and the Anglo-Egyptian Bank.[4] As the French Government was rather closely associated with these firms, he felt in a measure responsible for their welfare. Thus, there was no hope of breaking the opposition of the *Crédit Foncier*. Moreover, the Duc Decazes, rescued from one war scare by

[1] *Ibid.*, p. 56.

[2] *Ibid.*, pp. 58-59.

[3] G. Hanotaux, *Contemporary France*, vol. iii, p. 389.

[4] Lesage, *op. cit.*, p. 77.

England and Russia,[1] had no desire to take any steps prejudicial to friendly relations with England. Although he
promised that he would sound out the British Government,
he seems in fact to have made no inquiry at London concerning the loan project, but merely instructed M. Gavard,
French Chargé d'Affaires at London, to ask whether Lord
Derby had any objections to the purchase of the Khedive's
shares by a French syndicate—a question to which Lord
Derby of course returned an emphatic affirmative.[2] The
opposition of the French banks, coupled with the unsympa-
thetic attitude of the Government, defeated the efforts of
Dervieu to raise the funds for the loan. The time for the
option passed [3] and Disraeli stepped in and secured the prize.

[1] In the famous War Scare of May, 1875, Bismarck was said to have
threatened war against France but was restrained by England and
Russia. See J. V. Fuller, "The War Scare of 1875," in *Amer. Hist.
Rev.*, vol. xxiv, pp. 196-226 (Jan., 1919) ; also *Documents Diplomatiques
Français (1871-1914)*, 1re série, vol. i, nos. 428, 429.

[2] *Egypt no. 1 (1876)*, no. 4, Lord Derby to Lord Lyons, Nov. 20, 1875 ;
cf. *Hansard's Parl. Debates*, 3rd ser., vol. 227, p. 97, Feb. 8, 1876, speech
of Mr. Disraeli. The dispatch from the Duc Decazes to M. Gavard has
not been found though it is mentioned by M. Gavard in his *Un diplomate
à Londres, Lettres et notes 1871-1875*, p. 275. See *Documents Diplomatiques Français (1871-1914)*, 1re sér., vol. ii, p. 19, note under no. 13. In
a private letter to the Duc Decazes on Nov. 21st, M. Gavard confined
himself to an account of the attitude of Lord Derby (*ibid.*). Why the
Foreign Minister instructed the Chargé to make an inquiry concerning
the purchase of the shares and not the loan, is somewhat of a mystery.
It would seem that the Duc Decazes, likè de Lesseps, was convinced that
the Khedive would never be able to repay the loan within three months
and hence the shares would fall to the French capitalists. On the other
hand, de Lesseps sought his aid for the loan project and at the behest
of M. Dervieu. But as Lesage points out, de Lesseps frankly told the
Duc Decazes that the advance on the shares was only a "blind," and that
it really meant the purchase of the Khedive's shares. This attempt to
give the purchase the appearance of a temporary loan was adopted in
order not to arouse the susceptibilities of England. The Duc Decazes
preferred to ignore the loan feature and made a direct inquiry concerning the purchase of the shares. Lesage, *op. cit.*, p. 59.

[3] M. André Dervieu did not wait until the 26th, the day when the ratifi-

On November 23rd, General Stanton sent the following telegram to Lord Derby:

Cherif Pasha has just called stating he was charged by the Viceroy to inform me that the offers on mortgage of his Canal shares have been withdrawn and offers for their purchase are now alone made.

One hundred millions of francs are offered through Monsieur Lesseps who has telegraphed to His Highness offering to undertake the placing of the shares in Paris and London without a commission or profit. His Highness will sell the shares to Her Majesty's Government for that amount. M. de Lesseps' offer is supposed to be on account of French Government. An answer is required by Thursday next the 25th instant.[1]

fication of the loan project was due, to notify the Khedive of his failure. Lesage, *op. cit.*, p. 58. It is likely that he informed Ismail as early as the 23rd, for we find a telegram from Stanton on that day, stating that the offers for a mortgage on the shares had been withdrawn. *Cf. infra,* p. 239. The French agent at Alexandria wrote to the Duc Decazes saying that it was Stanton's opposition which caused the failure of the Dervieu negotiations and that Stanton demanded that English capitalists should be given the preference. (*Documents Diplomatiques Français (1871-1914)*, 1re sér., vol. ii, no. 14, Alexandria, Nov. 22, 1875). In a dispatch to M. de Laboulaye, French Chargé d'Affaires at St. Petersburg, the Duc Decazes makes the same statement, adding that the Khedive was urged by one of the Consuls-General to learn the attitude of the Powers concerning a sale of the shares to England. Supported by the English and German agents, however, the Khedive replied that "he preferred to take the responsibility of a definitive solution rather than run the risk of entering upon general negotiations which might lead to a European conflict" (*ibid.*, no. 16, Paris, Nov. 27, 1875).

[1] FO 78/2432, Suez Canal, vol. 38, telegram, Stanton to Derby, Cairo, Nov. 23, 1875. In this telegram Stanton refers to an offer made by de Lesseps for the French Government to purchase the shares for 100 million francs. Whether such an offer was really made is questionable. Certainly, the Duc Decazes would not have made it after the positive refusal of Lord Derby to countenance the purchase of the shares by French capitalists. General Stanton was not always correctly informed. In his dispatches he makes no mention of the Dervieus but attributes their offer to purchase the shares to the *Société Générale*, and their offer to make an advance on the shares to the Anglo-Egyptian Bank. FO

On the following day Lord Derby wired an acceptance of the Khedive's offer stating that Messrs. N. de Rothschild and Sons would handle the transaction.[1] One million sterling would be paid on December 1st and the remaining three millions in December and January according to arrangements which would be concluded between the Egyptian Government and the Rothschilds. Though the Khedive agreed to pay five per cent interest until the alienated coupons were free, Lord Derby was prepared to purchase the shares without this security.[2]

Upon receiving Lord Derby's telegram, General Stanton went immediately to the Khedive's Palace. He did not see the Khedive, who was ill, but was informed by the Minister of Finance and Nubar Pasha that the offer was accepted.[3] On the 25th he notified Lord Derby that the agreement for the sale of the shares was signed.[4] It was discovered, however, that the number of shares was not 177,642, but 176,602, as 1040 had been disposed of in Paris some years before. The purchase price was accordingly reduced from £4,000,000 to £3,976,580. Seven large cases containing the shares were turned over to General Stanton on the 26th.

The purchase of the shares had been carried through in ten days. How the rumor that the Khedive was negotiating with the French banks had first reached the British Foreign Office is not entirely clear.[5] According to one explana-

78/2432, Suez Canal, vol. 38, telegram to Derby, Nov. 16, and no. 77 to Derby, Nov. 18, 1875. Lesage, who made a careful study of the purchase question, does not believe such an offer was made (*op. cit.*, pp. 242-245).

[1] FO 78/2432, Suez Canal, vol. 38, no. 75, Derby to Stanton, Nov. 24, 1875.

[2] *Ibid.*, no. 76, Derby to Stanton, Nov. 24, 1875.

[3] *Ibid.*, no. 139, Stanton to Derby, Cairo, Nov. 27, 1875.

[4] *Ibid.*, telegram, Stanton to Derby, Cairo, Nov. 25, 1875.

[5] For a detailed discussion of this point see Lesage, *op. cit.*, pp. 83-98.

tion, Mr. Frederick Greenwood, the editor of the *Pall Mall Gazette,* had conveyed the story to Lord Derby. Mr. Julien Wolff writing in the *London Times* on December 26, 1875, states that Mr. Greenwood had dined with Mr. Henry Oppenheim, the banker, on November 14th, and that the latter had told Greenwood that a French syndicate had offered a loan to the Khedive to be guaranteed by the shares. Mr. Greenwood called on Lord Derby the following day and informed him of what Oppenheim had said. It is probable, however, that Disraeli had heard of the French negotiations about the same time from Baron Lionel de Rothschild, who had reports from Paris or Cairo as to what was going on.[1]

Lord Derby, however, was not enthusiastic over the idea of purchasing the shares. When informed by General Stanton's telegram of the 17th that the Khedive had no intention of selling, he wrote to Lord Lyons: " I sincerely hope we may not be driven to that expedient. The acquisition would be a bad one financially, and the affair might involve us in disagreeable correspondence both with France and the Porte." [2] Holding such opinions, one would hardly expect Lord Derby to act decisively to secure the shares. Nor was Sir Stafford Northcote, the Chancellor of the Exchequer, more eager. He favored a plan to place the canal under an international commission. " I am inclined to seek my leverage in the acceptance of this mortgage by the *Société Générale* rather than in any attempt to get it for ourselves, which I fear may set other countries against us." [3] On the 24th, he wrote to Disraeli: " We are in deep water . . . I am

[1] G. E. Buckle, *The Life of Benjamin Disraeli: Earl of Beaconsfield,* vol. v, p. 440.

[2] Lord Newton, *Lord Lyons. A Record of British Diplomacy, op. cit.,* vol. ii, p. 87, date of letter Nov. 19, 1875.

[3] Andrew Lang, *The Life, Letters and Diaries of Sir Stafford Northcote—First Earl of Iddesleigh* (2 vols., Edinburgh, 1890), vol. ii, p. 85, Northcote to Disraeli, Nov. 23, 1875.

much averse from holding the shares and greatly desirous to bring about an international Commission." [1]

Apparently there were differences of opinion in the British Cabinet as to the feasibility of purchasing the shares and it is all the more remarkable, therefore, that the transaction was carried through with such swiftness. The credit goes to Disraeli, the Prime Minister, whose " imagination discerned at once the high political value of the purchase." [2] At the Cabinet meeting on November 17th, he left no doubt as to his determination that England should acquire the shares.[3] Disraeli furnished the driving power which overcame all opposition. " It is clear . . . ," says Buckle, " that the initiative was his, and that the Cabinet though in the end unanimous, contained influential members who were reluctant to take such a very new departure." [4] Writing to the Queen on November 18th, Disraeli said:

It is vital to your Majesty's authority and power at this critical moment, that the Canal should belong to England, and I was so decided and absolute with Lord Derby on this head, that he ultimately adopted my views and brought the matter before the Cabinet yesterday. The Cabinet was unanimous in their decision, that the interest of the Khedive should, if possible, be obtained, and we telegraphed accordingly.[5]

---

[1] *Ibid.* Northcote was outspoken in his disapproval of the purchase. In a letter to Disraeli on Nov. 26, 1875, he wrote: " Our policy, or our proceedings, with regard to the Canal, has not been such as to gain us much credit for magnanimity. We opposed it in its origin; we refused to help Lesseps in his difficulties; we have used it when it has succeeded; we have fought the battle of our shipowners very stiffly; and now we avail ourselves of our influence with Egypt to get a quiet slice of what promises to be a good thing . . . I don't like it" (*ibid.*).

[2] Buckle, *op. cit.*, v, p. 439.

[3] *Ibid.*, v, p. 442.

[4] *Ibid.*

[5] *Ibid.*, v, p. 443.

On the 20th he informed the Queen, that the Cabinet had given him *carte blanche* to carry through the affair.[1] The Khedive's offer to sell the shares to England, which was relayed by General Stanton on the 23rd, was accepted by the Cabinet on the following day.

It was not only for his success in winning over the Cabinet and in pushing the negotiations to a conclusion, that Disraeli deserves the credit for this master stroke of British diplomacy, but it was he who secured the capital without which the transaction would have fallen through. As Parliament was not at the time in session where was the Cabinet to procure the funds? That question naturally concerned the Chancellor of the Exchequer but on the 22nd he wrote to Disraeli: "I am sure there is no way by which we can raise the money without the consent of the Parliament, and that the utmost we can do would be to enter into a treaty engaging to ask Parliament for the money, and then let the K[hedive] get it in advance from some capitalist who is willing to trust to our power of getting Parliamentary authority."[2] Fortunately, Disraeli knew where he could find such a capitalist. Baron Rothschild was his friend, who had already given him aid in connection with his Egyptian policy. Buckle repeats a story to the effect that Disraeli instructed his private secretary, Corry, to wait just outside the Cabinet room and when the signal was given, he should go immediately to Baron Rothschild and say that the Prime Minister wanted £4,000,000 'Tomorrow'. Corry carried this message to Rothschild, who "picked up a muscatel grape, ate it, threw out the skin, and said deliberately, 'What is your security?' 'The British Government.' 'You shall have it'."[3] It was either on the 17th or the 18th of November

---

[1] *Ibid.*, v, p. 444.

[2] *Ibid.*, v, p. 446.

[3] *Ibid.*, pp. 446-447.

that Disraeli obtained a promise of cooperation from Baron Rothschild. As the arrangements were finally decided upon, the Rothschilds received for their services a commission of two and one-half per cent upon the purchase price and five per cent interest until the date of repayment.

The manner in which the transaction was carried through produced an outburst of criticism in Parliament.[1] Particularly did the Opposition score the Government for the amount of commission the Rothschilds were to receive for advancing the money. Disraeli justified the commission on the ground that the Rothschilds ran a great risk. Addressing the House of Commons on February 8, 1876, he said:

> There is no violation of the law in what has taken place. . . . The Bank of England would have been ready I dare say, if it were legal to advance £4,000,000 to the Government. But the house of Rothschild did not merely advance £4,000,000. We said—" Will you purchase these shares on our engagement that we will ask the House of Commons to take them off your hands?" They did so. That was a great risk, and I believe they would not have undertaken it if they had not felt that it was of great consequence to the country that they should do so.[2]

[1] Lord Granville, writing to Mr. Bright on Dec. 31, 1875, refers to the opposition: " I should expect you to be in favour of the purchase of the ten votes in the Suez Canal, and the ostentatious mission of Cave. But I doubt it.

"Seebohm, Cardwell, and I were together when the news came. We were all dead against it, though Cardwell somewhat relented, Goschen and Halifax were in favour, Forster doubtful, Lowe rather unfavourable, but both are now strongly opposed. Gladstone, as you may suppose, indignant.

" Notwithstanding the chorus of approbation in the press, I find there is a great undercurrent against what has been done.

" I am told that the sensible people in the City are opposed." (Lord Edmund Fitzmaurice, *The Life of Granville George Leveson Gower. Second Earl Granville, K. G., 1815-1891* (2 vols., London, 1905), vol. ii, p. 252.

[2] *Hansard's Parl. Debates*, 3rd ser., vol. 227, pp. 99-100.

In a letter to the Queen on November 24, 1875, Disraeli wrote, " Four millions sterling! and almost immediately. There was only one firm that could do it—Rothschilds. They behaved admirably, advanced the money at a low rate and the entire interest of the Khedive is now yours, Madam." [1]

It would appear from Disraeli's statement to the House of Commons, that the Rothschilds had purchased the shares and had then resold them to the British Government. As the documents reveal,[2] however, the Government had purchased the shares with the money secured from the Rothschilds, knowing well that Parliament would not refuse to sanction the undertaking. Disraeli's motive, no doubt, was to give a constitutional appearance to a transaction which violated one of the most sacred rights of the House, namely, the right of controlling the purse strings.

The motives which inspired England to purchase the shares are not hard to find. She was the first Maritime Power in the world, controlling most of the carrying-trade to India and the Far East, and more than half of the vessels passing through the Suez Canal carried her flag.[3] Thus, for commercial reasons alone, she would naturally desire a voice in the management of the canal. The tonnage controversy[4] had not been forgotten and it was certainly to the interest of British shippers that the tolls should be as low as

[1] Buckle, *op. cit.*, v, pp. 448-449.

[2] The telegram from Lord Derby to Stanton on Nov. 24th, accepting the offer, said: " Her Majesty's Government agree to purchase the one hundred seventy-seven thousand six hundred and forty-two shares of the Viceroy for four million pounds sterling and to recommend to Parliament to sanction the contract." (FO 78/2432, Suez Canal, vol. 38.) There is no doubt whatever that the British Governmment, not the Rothschilds, purchased the shares.

[3] See Appendix A.

[4] See chapter xiv.

possible. Politically, the British Government was strongly opposed to the acquisition of the shares by any other nation, particularly by France.

Already half of the shares were owned by the French. To have secured the other half also, would have made it difficult, if not impossible, for the French Government to have acted in a spirit of impartiality in any international controversy involving the canal.

It would have exercised in the choice of administrators, in the enlistment of the personnel, in the engagement of ordinary expenses, and especially in the execution of the great works, a preponderant influence, sometimes excellent, but often grievous. It would have made the great enterprise founded by de Lesseps a vast bureaucratic organization, which would have possessed all the very real qualities of French Administration, but which, also, would have been deprived of all good industrial and commercial qualities.[1]

Moreover, if the French Government had purchased the shares it would have been obliged to support the Company in controversies with foreign shippers and there would have been no end of dangers.

To prevent France from acquiring the shares was certainly one reason why the British Government made such haste to close the deal. "We purchased them," said Disraeli, "from high political considerations and had it not been for those considerations we should never have entered into those negotiations."[2] Another motive for the purchase was the belief that if Great Britain was an important shareholder there would be less chance of controversies arising between the Company and British shippers.

From the financial viewpoint alone, the purchase was justified. The shares were listed at 685 francs early in No-

[1] Lesage, *op. cit.*, p. 247.

[2] *Hansard's Parl. Debates*, 3rd ser., vol. 231, Aug. 8, 1876, p. 852.

vember 1875 but Great Britain paid only 568 francs per share or about £23. No dividends would be paid for nineteen years, that is, until July 1894, but during this period the British Government would receive interest at five per cent on the entire purchase.[1] By 1881 the price of each share had climbed to £78, a gain to the Government of £4,750,000 in five years.[2] After that date the shares increased enormously in value and in 1905, the investment was worth £33,000,000, upon which the Government received £1,040,000 a year or twenty-six per cent.[3]

The advantages which England expected to derive from the purchase were not immediately fulfilled. The Government had been somewhat too optimistic concerning a voice in the management of the Company. By article 51 of the Statutes, every owner of twenty-five shares was entitled to one vote in the General Assembly of Shareholders but no one was to have more than ten votes. When the Viceroy turned over the coupons on his shares to the Company in 1869, he transferred his ten votes to de Lesseps. Lord Derby was not ignorant of this situation, for on the 19th of November he had been informed of it by Colonel Stokes.[4] The question was whether the British Government as the owner of 176,602 shares from which the coupons had been alienated, had a right to vote at all. Even if this point were conceded, the Government at the most could cast only ten votes.[5]

[1] No dividends would be paid on the shares for nineteen years since Ismail had turned over the coupons to the Canal Company. See note 3, ch. xiv, p. 217.

[2] *Hansard's Parl. Debates*, 3rd ser., vol. 260, Mar. 31, 1881, p. 349.

[3] *Ibid.*, 4th ser., vol. 144, April 10, 1905, p. 1103. The British government received dividends of £682,497 in 1919-1920, £798,566 in 1920-1921 and £1,094,303 in 1921-1922 (*ibid.*, 5th ser., vol. 164, p. 832).

[4] FO 78/2432, Suez Canal, vol. 38, confidential, Stokes to Derby, Chatham, Nov. 19, 1875.

[5] FO 78/2540, Suez Canal, vol. 39, no. 5, Col. Stokes to Derby, Cairo, Dec. 25, 1875.

Colonel Stokes, who was intrusted by Lord Derby to investigate the exact status Great Britain occupied with regard to participation in the affairs of the Company, held to the opinion that the shares, despite the alienation of the coupons, possessed full voting power.

The severance of the coupons has not weakened the shareholders' rights to the property of the Company; their concern in the successful working of it is not only not diminished thereby, but on the contrary increased. . . . Those therefore who contend that the severance of the coupons from the shares debars the shareholders from having any voice in the affairs of the Company for so long as the shares remain without available coupons take a position opposed to the common sense view of the transaction.[1]

Not only did Colonel Stokes contend that Great Britain had the right to vote but he went further and declared that as the shares were the property not of one person but of a nation of the articles of the Statutes which limited the owner of these shares to ten votes, " do not apply to the case of a nation."[2] He recommended, therefore, that the shares should be vested in trustees named by the Government. Great Britain would then be able to send 706 trustees to the General Assembly of the Shareholders armed with 7060 votes and would be in a position to control the affairs of the Company. This suggestion was not adopted, and Colonel Stokes was directed to negotiate with de Lesseps for the participation of Great Britain in the management of the Company. After discussions extending over several weeks there was concluded on February 3, 1876, the Stokes-Lesseps Agreement.[3] De Lesseps turned over to England the ten

[1] *Ibid.*

[2] *Ibid.*, no. 7, secret and confidential, Stokes to Derby, Cairo, Dec. 31, 1875.

[3] For the text of this agreement, see *Egypt no. 9 (1876)*.

votes he had received from the Khedive and arranged that three British Directors should be chosen to the Board of Directors.[1]

The purchase of the Khedive's shares was hailed with enthusiasm in England. Here was a master stroke of diplomacy, effected with consummate skill, with audacity and with speed and secrecy; startling to a world not yet accustomed to transactions involving millions. The Empire would be strengthened, British interests in the Mediterranean would be preserved and the road to India would be kept open.

The Queen greeted the announcement as " a great and important event " which would be most popular in the country. She considered it a ' blow at Bismarck,' and when she received a letter of congratulations from the King of Belgium the Queen " was in 10th heaven." [2] Disraeli was exultant. Writing to Lady Bradford on November 25th, he said:

After a fortnight of the most increasing labour and anxiety, I (for between ourselves, and ourselves only, I may be egotistical in this matter)—I have purchased for England the Khedive of Egypt's interest in the Suez Canal.

We have had all the gamblers, capitalists, financiers of the world organized and platooned in bands of plunderers, arrayed against us, and secret emissaries in every corner, and have baffled them all, and have never been suspected.[3]

The British press was no less enthusiastic.

[1] By a resolution of the General Assembly of Shareholders, June 27, 1876, the number of Directors was reduced from 32 to 24. England thus had one-eighth of the membership. In 1884 the number was increased again to 32. As article 28 of the Company Statutes required that each Director must be the owner of 100 shares, deposited with the Company, the British Government purchased 300 additional shares.

[2] Buckle, *op. cit.*, v, pp. 449, 450.

[3] *Ibid.*, p. 450.

While people are looking towards the East in doubt and apprehension [said the *London Times*] discerning nothing but darkness and trouble, political confusion and financial collapse, while they are wondering what is to be the end and how far England will be perforce concerned in it, the Queen's Government resolves on an act which will at once fix the regards of the world. No waiting for Parliament, no feeling of public opinion, no mysterious hints to prepare the city and the country for something remarkable. The nation wakes this morning to find that it has acquired a heavy stake in the security and well-being of another distant land, and that it will be held by all the world to have entered upon a new phase of Eastern policy.[1]

An editorial in the same journal on November 27th, referred to the advantages of the purchase.

The possible results of this national investment are so large and indefinite that it would be vain to speculate upon them, and yet they present themselves persistently to the imagination. It is plain that we acquire an interest in Egypt and its administration which will compel the constant attention of the Queen's Government. We have purchased nearly half the shares of the Suez Canal. We are the largest proprietors, and it need not be said that the others will look to us for the management of the property, the maintenance of satisfactory relations with the local Government, and with the other Powers of the world. To this country will belong the decision on every question, whether scientific, financial or political; administration and negotiation will be in our hands, and as we have the power, so we shall have the responsibility before the world. . . . We have now an abiding stake in the security and welfare of Egypt.

The same journal on January 7, 1876, made the following comment:

The political right we may claim to have acquired in the purchase of the canal shares is the right to forbid any change in

[1] November 26, 1875.

the relations with the Ottoman Empire and with other Powers; and generally any act which may prejudice our interest in the Canal or in freedom of our passage to India.

Queen Victoria was right when she said that the announcement of the purchase would be popular in England.

For the despondent the purchase was a ray of light; for the speculator Egyptian would be up; for the trader and ship-owner the tolls were to be lowered and freights raised; for the politician it floated the "Vanguard"; for the philanthropist it liberated the fugitive slave; for the patriot it was a peaceful triumph. To everyone the act came home with a feeling of pleasure and hope; pleasure somewhat dampened perhaps by later events, but hope not to be entirely blighted. Everywhere the news was received with welcome. . . . [1]

In France, as might be expected, there was no rejoicing. "France was grieved and bruised. The War, the defeat, and also the alarms which always follow great misfortunes, had heightened her sensibility." [2]

It is impossible to preserve silence on the deep impression produced here by the measure just taken by the English Government [wrote the Paris correspondent of the *London Times* on November 29, 1875] even though it would be difficult to give that general impression a concrete form. What is certain is that it exists, that it permeates—which is a very rare thing—

[1] *Quarterly Review*, vol. 142, 1876, "The Suez Canal an International Highway," p. 430.

[2] Lesage, *op. cit.*, p. 144. In France it was feared that the purchase of the shares was the first step toward the acquisition of Egypt by England. (*Documents Diplomatiques Français (1871-1914)*, 1re sér., vol. ii, p. 26, note). On November 27th, the French Ambassador at London, the Marquis d'Harcourt, informed Lord Derby that France feared that the purchase of the shares would lead to English interference in Egypt. Lord Derby denied this "but he said it with a certain embarrassment which left some doubt in my mind" (*ibid.*, no. 17, d'Harcourt to the Duc Decazes, London, Nov. 27, 1875).

here all classes of society, while assuming various forms according to the circle in which it is manifested. . . .

The Duc Decazes came in for a good deal of criticism. " The minister has, in this circumstance," said the *République Française* on November 29th, " given proofs of a blindness unequalled save in the worst days of Imperial diplomacy." [1]

De Lesseps, however, expressed himself as satisfied with the purchase.

The English nation now accepts that share in the Canal which had been loyally reserved to her from the outset; and if this action is to have any effect, that effect, in my opinion, can only be the abandonment by the British Government of the long-standing attitude of hostility towards the interests of the original shareholders of the Maritime Canal, whose perseverance has been at once so active and so well directed.

I therefore look upon the close community of interest about to be established between French and English capital, for the purely industrial and necessarily peaceful working of the Universal Maritime Canal, as a most fortunate occurrence.[2]

Outside of France the announcement was well received. Leopold II of Belgium declared it " the greatest event of modern politics." [3]    Prince Bismarck congratulated the British Government and said that it had " done the right thing at the right moment in regard to the Suez Canal." [4]    Speak-

[1] Quoted in Hanotaux, *op. cit.*, vol. iii, p. 391.

[2] *Egypt no. 1 (1876)*, enclosure in no. 11, Lord Lyons to Derby, Paris, Nov. 30, 1875, letter from de Lesseps dated Nov. 24, 1875.

[3] Buckle, *op. cit.*, v, p. 450.

[4] *Egypt no. 1 (1876)*, no. 18, Lord Odo Russell to Derby, Berlin, Nov. 29, 1875. M. de Sayve, French Chargé d'Affaires at Berlin, reported that the press of Berlin hailed the purchase of the shares as a new humiliation for France and as a natural consequence of the Battle of Sedan; and that it would strain the relations between France and England. On the

ing for the Italian government, the Chevalier Visconti
Venosta considered the purchase " as highly advantageous
for the commercial interests of all nations," and rejoiced
" at an act which tended to increase the influence of Great
Britain in the Mediterranean." [1] The Italian journal
*Opinione,* justified the purchase but referred to England's
earlier opposition:

Strange contradiction of events! The Suez Canal against
which England manifested so much hostility, becomes an
English canal. As she could not prevent its being opened,
she wished to keep the keys in her own hands. Aden was not
sufficient. It seems to us an act of great political ability
which does great honour to the perspicacity of Mr. Disraeli's
Government.[2]

Count Andrassy, the Austrian Foreign Minister, " was
confident the purchase would prove as advantageous to Austrian as to British commerce," and added " that he was also
happy to feel that there is not one question in the east or in
the west of Europe in which the interests of Austria and
Great Britain are not, in his opinion, identical." [3]

other hand, he stated that Prince Bismarck regarded the transaction as
of commercial rather than political importance. Prince Gortchakoff, who
was visiting Berlin, maintained an attitude identical with that of Bismarck
but M. de Sayve believed that Russia was none the less bitter at the
increasing influence of England in the East. (*Documents Diplomatiques
Français (1871-1914)*, 1re sér., vol. ii, no. 52, M. de Sayve to the Duc
Decazes, Berlin, Dec. 3, 1875).

[1] *Ibid.,* no. 25, Sir A. Paget to Derby, Rome, Dec. 3, 1875.

[2] *Ibid.,* enclosure in no. 12, Sir A. Paget to Derby, Rome, Nov. 29, 1875.

[3] *Ibid.,* no. 40, Sir A. Buchanan to Derby, Vienna, Dec. 16, 1875. The
French Ambassador at Constantinople reported that the Porte was very
angry over the transaction since it had not been consulted beforehand.
(*Documents Diplomatiques Français (1871-1914)*, 1re sér., vol. ii, telegram from Bourgoing to the Duc Decazes, Nov. 29, 1875, p. 27).

## CHAPTER XVI

PROTECTION OF THE CANAL—BRITAIN OCCUPIES EGYPT

THE sale of his canal shares brought only temporary relief to the harassed Khedive. He continued his reckless expenditures and borrowed money at ruinous rates of interest,[1] while the Egyptian Treasury was rapidly approaching a state of collapse. Seeing no way out of his predicament, Ismail requested the British Government for the services of an expert to aid in regulating his disordered finances. For this mission Lord Derby selected Mr. Stephen Cave, who went to Egypt, studied the situation, and reported in March 1876, recommending the consolidation of the Egyptian debt and the establishment of a commission of financial control.[2] These suggestions were adopted and on May 2nd the Khedive issued a decree instituting the *Caisse de la Dette* with commissioners from France, Austria and Italy, and later from Great Britain. Another decree of May 7th, consolidated all existing loans into a general debt amounting to £91,000,000.

But the *Caisse* did not satisfy the French and British bond-

---

[1] An example of Ismail's extravagant borrowing was the loan he contracted in 1873 with the Oppenheim firm. The nominal sum was for £32,000,000 at 7 per cent. It was issued, however, at a discount of 33 per cent and Ismail received only £11,000,000 in cash and £9,000,000 in depreciated scrip, and had to pay £2,560,000 interest annually. M. G. Mulhall, *Contemporary Review*, London, Oct., 1882, cited by Lieut.-Col. P. G. Elgood, *The Transit of Egypt* (London, 1928), p. 57.

[2] On Cave's mission see *Egypt no. 4 (1876)*. His report, dated March 23, 1876, is found in Egypt no. 7 (1876). For further details concerning the financial situation in Egypt see Cromer, *Modern Egypt* (two vols. in one, N. Y., 1916), vol. i, pp. 11-40.

holders and it was replaced by the Dual Control with a British official, Sir Rivers Wilson, to supervise the revenues, and a Frenchman, M. de Blignières, to audit the expenditures. Even this change brought little marked improvement in the Egyptian finances and in March 1878 an Anglo-French commission was directed to make a further inquiry. The commission proposed drastic financial and political reforms. Ismail was to cease being an oriental despot, and was to become a constitutional ruler assisted by a responsible ministry and a Chamber of Notables while France and England agreed to suspend the operation of the Dual Control in return for representation in the new cabinet. Sir Rivers Wilson was given the portfolio of Minister of Finance and M. de Blignières that of Public Works.

Ismail, however, had no intentions of entering wholeheartedly into the new scheme and in April 1879 he dismissed his ministers and attempted to resume his former powers.[1] France and England protested immediately, but as Ismail persisted in his folly, they induced the Sultan to depose him in June.[2] He was succeeded by his son Tewfik, who proved more amenable and who revived the Dual Control with M. de Blignières and Major Baring (later Lord Cromer) as Commissioners.

It was not long before new trouble arose. A nationalist

[1] *Documents Diplomatiques Français (1871-1914)*, 1re sér., vol. ii, no. 405, Godeaux to Waddington, Cairo, April 8, 1879. Ismail announced that he would form a new cabinet composed only of Egyptians.

[2] On April 10, 1879 the Grand Vizir confidentially informed the French Chargé d'Affaires at Constantinople that the Sultan was prepared to use his authority to depose Ismail and he intimated that France might take advantage of the change to secure control of the Egyptian Ministry of Finance (*ibid.*, no. 407, M. de Monthalon to Waddington, Const., April 10, 1879). Waddington refused this suggestion and stated that he wanted no Turkish interference in regulating Egyptian finances (*ibid.*, no. 428, Waddington to Monthalon, Paris, May 28, 1879). For further details concerning the deposition of Ismail see nos. 432, 434-440.

movement appeared as a protest against foreign influence and rallied under the slogan "Egypt for the Egyptians."[1] The grievances were many. Since the beginning of the nineteenth century the number of Europeans in the country had increased rapidly and they enjoyed extraterritorial privileges such as the use of their own courts and exemption from certain taxes. Many of them had received lucrative concessions or important posts in the public service. But it was not only the influence of Europeans which aroused the ire of the Egyptian nationalists. They were equally resentful against the Turks and Circassians who held the highest posts in the army. A riot broke out in Cairo in 1879 when the native force in the army was suddenly reduced and 2500 officers placed on half-pay. Under the leadership of Colonel Arabi Pasha the nationalist movement gathered considerable momentum, attracting not only the discontented army officers but the intellectual classes as well. Indeed, all classes of the native population felt a deep resentment against alien influence. Matters came to a head on September 9, 1881, when Arabi with 5000 troops surrounded the palace and compelled Tewfik to dismiss the Minister of War. In February of the following year Arabi was appointed to that post.

The nationalists were now virtually dictators of Egypt and European bondholders began to fear that Arabi and his followers would repudiate Egyptian debts and abolish the Dual Control. Moreover, England was solicitous about the security of the canal which had by this time become her great highway to India and for which she felt a certain sense of responsibility after the purchase of the Khedive's shares. The Powers, particularly France and England, would hardly remain passive while their interests in Egypt were threatened.

[1] On the nationalist movement in Egypt see M. Travers Symons, *Britain and Egypt: The Rise of Egyptian Nationalism* (London, 1925).

Active intervention did not at first find much favor with Lord Granville and the initiative was taken by Gambetta who came into office on November 10, 1881, with the fall of the Ferry Cabinet. A strong supporter of Anglo-French co-operation in Egypt, Gambetta had not forgotten what Thiers had once told him: "Whatever you do, never let go of Egypt."[1] Convinced now that the time for action had arrived, he suggested in December that France and England should present a united front in Egypt and be prepared to take steps for immediate interference in case of need.[2] Granville agreed that the two Powers should act together but refused to enter into a definite arrangement. On December 24th, Gambetta again referred to the situation in Egypt and this time suggested that the two governments should dispatch a joint note to the Khedive assuring him of their sympathy and support and urging him " to maintain and assert his proper authority."[3] Granville accepted but with the reservation that the British Government was not thereby committing itself to any particular mode of action,[4] and on January 8th, the Joint Note was communicated to Tewfik.

Far from improving matters, the Note had the opposite effect. It was

received without gratitude by the Khedive and with angry surprise by every one else. The Sultan read it as an usurpation of his supreme authority, and as a sign that Egypt would share

[1] P. E. L. Deschanel, *Gambetta* (N. Y., 1920), p. 304.

[2] *Egypt no. 5 (1882)*, no. 24, Lyons to Granville, Paris, Dec. 15, 1881. The documents dealing with the question of intervention are: for England, *Parl. Papers, Egypt no. 1 (1882), Egypt no. 3 (1882), Egypt no. 5 (1882), Egypt no. 7 (1882), Egypt no. 12 (1882), Egypt no. 17 (1882)*; for France, *Documents Diplomatiques, Affaires d'Égypte*, vols. 46 and 47; for Austria, HHSA, Ägyptische Frage, vol. $\frac{xxxi}{24}$.

[3] *Ibid.*, no. 32, Lyons to Granville, Dec. 24, 1881.

[4] *Ibid.*, no. 44, Granville to Lyons, Jan. 6, 1882.

the fate of Tunis; the Chamber of Notables, which had just met, regarded it as an encouragement to the Khedive to resist its advice; the Nationalist Party resented it as a threat of intervention; and the Powers began to murmur.[1]

Foreign intervention, in the words of Lord Cromer, became " an unavoidable necessity." [2] Certainly the Note was a blunder. Early in February the representatives of Russia, Italy, Austria and Germany presented an identic communication to the Porte declaring for the preservation of the *status quo* in Egypt.[3] Realizing that matters had gone beyond what he had expected, Granville had tried to draw back by stating that he had not committed the British Government to any specific measures, but Gambetta had refused to accept this limited view.[4]

Gambetta's Cabinet was overthrown on February 1, 1882, and he was succeeded by Freycinet, who was opposed to a forward policy in Egypt and who believed that the affair should be regulated by the Concert of Europe. The lead was now taken by Granville, who proposed to Freycinet, on February 6th, that France and England should communicate with the other Powers in order to determine the best method for the preservation of order in Egypt. " Her Majesty's Government do not consider that a case for intervention has at present arisen. . . . But should the necessity arise it would be their wish that such intervention should represent the united action and authority of Europe." [5] A few days

[1] G. P. Gooch, *History of Modern Europe 1878-1919* (N. Y., 1922), p. 77. *Cf.* HHSA, Ägyptische Frage, $\frac{xxxi}{24}$, no. 13, Kosjek to Kalnocky, Cairo, Jan. 9, 1882.

[2] Cromer, *op. cit.*, vol. i, p. 235.

[3] *Egypt no. 5* (*1882*), no. 110, Dufferin to Granville.

[4] Cromer, *op. cit.*, vol. i, p. 238.

[5] *Egypt no. 5* (*1882*), no. 124, Granville to Lyons, Feb. 6, 1882.

later France and England addressed an identic note to the principal Powers inviting an exchange of views.

Bismarck had no political interest in Egypt or the Suez Canal but he was anxious to prevent a quarrel between France and England. While admitting that these Powers had acquired a " diplomatic status quo " in Egypt, he desired that intervention, if it should be necessary, should come from the Sultan as the Sovereign of that country.[1] He appreciated the interests which England had acquired in Egypt but regretted that she had so closely associated herself with France and he hoped that Freycinet would be less aggressive than Gambetta and more ' European ' in his views.[2] It was necessary to prevent this ' Schleswig-Holstein ' of the two Powers from kindling quarrels which might affect all Europe.

Yet, as intervention of some sort was necessary, Freycinet proposed that an Anglo-French squadron should be sent to Alexandria for the protection of the foreign population, and that the Porte for the time being should refrain from any interference in Egypt.[3] On May 30th, he went a step further and proposed that a Conference of Ambassadors should assemble at Constantinople to concert measures for suppressing the revolt.

Before the Conference could get under way a riot occurred at Alexandria on June 11th in which more than fifty Europeans were killed. Freycinet demanded that the Conference assemble immediately. The first meeting was held on June 23rd and two days later the Ambassadors signed a Self-

---

[1] *Ibid.*, no. 130, Lord Ampthill to Granville, Berlin, Feb. 15, 1882. For Bismarck's views on Egypt see *Documents Diplomatiques Français* (*1871-1914*), 1re sér., vol. ii, nos. 408 and 440; *Die grosse Politik*, vol. iv, no. 729; *German Diplomatic Documents 1871-1914*, vol. i, pp. 53, 163-165; Kleine, *Deutschland und die agyptische Frage 1875-1890.*

[2] Fitzmaurice, *Life of Granville*, vol. ii, p. 259.

[3] Cromer, *op. cit.*, vol. i, p. 269.

Denying Protocol agreeing that if intervention became necessary, their respective Powers would not seek territorial advantage or an exclusive position in Egypt.[1]  The Sultan was
invited to dispatch troops to Egypt subject to certain limitations concerning their employment, but as he refused to
accept any conditions, the troops were not sent.

In the meantime, Arabi was preparing to resist a foreign
invasion and took steps to fortify Alexandria.  Freycinet
was in favor of coming to terms with him, but Granville
refused, and on July 3rd Admiral Seymour was ordered to
destroy the forts if Arabi continued his preparations.  As
the Egyptians showed no signs of abandoning their work,
Admiral Seymour opened fire on July 11th and demolished
the fortifications.  A riot followed and British troops were
landed to restore order.  The French fleet which had been
sent to cooperate with the British in protecting European
interests, sailed away before the bombardment began.

Though England had thus acted alone she had no desire
to detach herself from the European Concert and on the day
following the destruction of the forts Granville addressed a
circular to the Powers calling attention to the dangers threatening the security of the Suez Canal.[2]  Some time before
this, on June 22nd, Lord Lyons, British Ambassador at
Paris, had proposed to Freycinet that France and England
should take measures for the defence of the canal, but the
French Minister, believing that the canal was in no danger,
had rejected the proposal.[3]  The recent riot had changed
matters, however, and Freycinet was now willing to coop-

[1] *Egypt no. 17 (1882)*, enclosure in no. 28, Dufferin to Granville, June
26, 1882.

[2] *Ibid.*, no. 237, Circular to British Representatives at Paris, Berlin,
Vienna, Rome, St. Petersburg and Constantinople.

[3] *Doc. Dipl., Affaires d'Égypte*, vol. 46, no. 133, Freycinet to Tissot,
Paris, June 22, 1882.

erate on condition that the Conference give a mandate delegating France and England to undertake the work. With such a mandate he would have less difficulty in persuading the Chamber to sanction the credits. Granville agreed but declared that he had no objection to the cooperation of the other Powers. When the Ambassadors of France and England brought the matter before the Conference on July 19th, the delegates refused to confer a mandate but were quite willing to have France and England take action if the need arose.[1] Bismarck was opposed to a mandate, believing that it would give the question " greater proportion " and would convert it " into a war between the Christian Powers of Europe and the Mohammedan countries." [2] On the other hand, he was prepared to give England his moral support.

On the 19th Freycinet went before the Chamber and asked for preliminary credits in order to prepare the French fleet, explaining, however, that no definite action was contemplated. He was supported by Gambetta, who pleaded eloquently for cooperation with England.

I have seen enough to tell you this : never even at the cost of the greatest sacrifices break the English alliance . . . I am certainly a pronounced and sincere friend of the English, but not so much as to sacrifice to them French interests. Moreover, be convinced that the English, good politicians that they are, esteem those allies who know how to earn their respect and who know the worth of their interests . . . What I fear most of all . . . is that you will surrender to England, and for all time, territories, rivers and passages where your right to live and to trade is as good as hers. . . .[3]

---

[1] *Egypt no. 17 (1882)*, no. 432, Dufferin to Granville, Therapia, July 19, 1882. *Cf.* HHSA, Ägyptische Frage $\frac{xxx}{26}$, no. 180, Baron Calice to Min. of For. Aff., Const., July 19, 1882.

[2] *Ibid.*, no. 370, Granville to Sir J. Walsham, July 21, 1882.

[3] Quoted in J. C. T. Roux, *op. cit.*, vol. ii, p. 75.

Freycinet secured the credits and a French squadron was ordered to join the British in patrolling the canal. But it was necessary to provide troops also and on the 29th he asked the Chamber for nine million francs in order to send 4000 men to occupy points along the northern part of the canal. An equal number of British troops would take positions in the south. Freycinet argued that the defense of the canal was entirely different from intervention in Egypt and would lead to no international complications.[1] He appealed to the chivalry of the Chamber not to leave the protection of the canal to England alone and he promised that the credits would be used only in case of actual danger. Clemenceau made a bitter attack on the policy which Freycinet had followed, characterizing it as full of contradictions and half-measures.[2] Since the Powers had refused to confer a mandate, he believed that France should also hold herself aloof and preserve her liberty of action. The credits bill was defeated and on the following day Freycinet submitted his resignation.[3] Public opinion had become decidedly unfavorable to intervention in Egypt as it was believed that Bismarck was trying to drag France into foreign complications.

Freycinet's vacillating policy had cost France her position in Egypt and one French writer has characterized the period of his ministry as " the most painful of our Egyptian

---

[1] Étienne Velay, *Les rivalités franco-anglaises en Égypte (1876-1904)* (Thesis, Montpellier, 1904), p. 90.

[2] *Ibid.*, p. 91.

[3] On the 30th, Freycinet received a visit from Prince Hohenlohe who informed him that Berlin " was ready, if I desired it, to propose a collective protection in the form that I had judged most practicable." (Freycinet, *op. cit.*, p. 312). Similar communications were received from Italy (July 31st) and Russia (Aug. 1st), and Freycinet believed that if these assurances had reached him sooner, he would not have fallen from office. " How different the discussion would have been if I had been furnished with their adhesions! France would still be in Egypt or England would no longer be there " (*ibid.*, p. 313).

policy." [1] Freycinet, indeed, did not seem to have a clear idea of what he wanted. He changed his views almost daily, adopting " successively all the forms of intervention and non-intervention imaginable: Anglo-French, European, Turkish, Anglo-French-Turkish, English interventions, and finally abstention." [2] Guided apparently by no other thought than to maintain himself in office, he had made himself subservient to the Chamber, which in turn, could agree on no settled policy. In fact, the Chamber had come to consider the Ministry as a " sort of a committee charged to execute its sovereign will," and it constantly interfered not only in the administration but in foreign policy as well. [3] England, at least, knew what she wanted, and Parliament on July 22nd by an overwhelming majority voted credits for £2,300,000.

Having failed to secure aid from France, Granville turned to Italy. But while the latter considered that next to England she had the greatest interest in the security of the canal, she refused to cooperate. [4] Granville was not at all disappointed. " I have just received from Membrea the refusal which delights me," he said. " We have done the right thing: we have shown our readiness to admit others and we have not the inconvenience of a partner." [5]

The Porte had taken no part in the conference but now decided to participate and expressed a willingness to send troops to Egypt provided the British force would withdraw.

[1] Jules Cocheris, *Situation internationale de l'Égypte et du Soudan* (Paris, 1903), p. 98.

[2] *Ibid.*, p. 100.

[3] M. Gabriel Charmes in *Revue des deux mondes*, Nov. 1, 1888, tome lx, p. 59.

[4] *Egypt no. 17 (1882)*, no. 515, Sir A. Paget to Granville, Rome, July 31, 1882.

[5] Fitzmaurice, *Life of Granville etc.*, vol. ii, p. 271.

Granville refused to accept this proposal and though negotiations for a military convention with Turkey were started, they never reached a conclusion.[1] The way was cleared for England to intervene alone and on July 31st the Khedive gave permission to the British commander to occupy such points in the Isthmus as might be necessary to secure the free navigation of the canal. A few days later Admiral Hewett occupied Suez on behalf of the Khedive.

On August 2nd the Conference adopted a proposal submitted by the Italian Ambassador, recognizing the "expediency of proper organization, with the concurrence of the Porte, for the safety of free passage of the Suez Canal, coincident with a purely maritime service for the police and supervision of the Canal, in which all the Powers should be invited to take part. . . ."[2] This proposal was accepted by Granville with the reservation that it did not prevent the landing of troops in order to hold certain posts for the security of the canal.[3] Germany, Austria, Russia and Turkey adhered to it but the French Government agreed on condition that it should be free "to evaluate the measures it might be called upon to take by virtue of the arrangement."[4] The Conference held its last meeting on August 14th, after deciding that the naval commanders should be instructed to fix such rules as would be necessary to put the proposal into operation.[5]

Convinced that any further delay would be dangerous to the security of the canal, England took decisive steps to

[1] For an account of these negotiations see Cromer, *op. cit.*, vol. i, pp. 312-320.

[2] *Egypt no. 17 (1882)*, enclosure in no. 544, Dufferin to Granville, Const., Aug. 2, 1882.

[3] *Ibid.*, no. 615, Granville to Sir J. Walsham, Aug. 9, 1882.

[4] *Doc. Dipl., Affaires d'Égypte*, vol. 47, no. 23, Duclerc to Noailles, Aug. 12, 1882.

[5] *Ibid.*, no. 3, Noailles to Duclerc, Aug. 14, 1882.

crush Arabi. General Wolsley with an expeditionary force was ordered to Port Said and on September 13th he defeated the Egyptians at Tel-el-Kebir. British troops entered Cairo a few days later.

The action taken by Great Britain for the defense of the canal was vigorously objected to by de Lesseps. In a telegram to the Superior Agent of the Company in Egypt, he stated: " Any action or demonstration of war is prohibited at the entrance or on the route of the Maritime Canal. The firman of concession proclaims its absolute neutrality which was recognized and practised by all the Powers during the two wars, Franco-German and Russo-Turkish." [1] He declared that Arabi would respect the neutrality of the canal so long as it was " not made use of by any hostile Power for the furtherance of its designs." [2] To this the British Government replied that the Khedive still possessed executive rights over the canal and had empowered the commander of the British naval forces to land troops for its protection.[3] De Lesseps' protest availed him nothing and only aroused ill-feeling in England. " The old rogue is playing us tricks," was Lord Granville's comment. " I trust we shall get the better of him." [4]

It seems that de Lesseps had entered into some sort of an

[1] *Egypt no. 17 (1882)*, no. 530, Brit. Suez Canal Directors to Granville, Paris, July 31, 1882. De Lesseps was opposed to the landing of any troops, French or British (HHSA, Ägyptische Frage, vol. $\frac{xxxi}{26}$ , Consul at Alexandria to FO, July 30, 1882).

[2] *Ibid.*, *cf.* HHSA, Ägyptische Frage, vol. $\frac{xxxi}{26}$ no. 14 B, Count Beust to Count Kalnocky, Paris, March 23, 1882, reporting a conversation with de Lesseps, who held that the Khedive could do nothing better than to abandon himself to the nationalist movement. De Lesseps spoke very highly of Arabi.

[3] *Ibid.*, no. 666, Granville to Brit. Suez Canal Directors, Aug. 14, 1882.

[4] Fitzmaurice, *Life of Granville etc.*, vol. ii, p. 272.

agreement with Arabi whereby the latter promised to respect the freedom of navigation in the canal. Whether this agreement would have prevented danger if England had not interfered, is doubtful. Blunt states that Arabi strenuously opposed the advice of his colleagues who wished to block the northern end of the canal.[1] Arabi is said to have assured de Lesseps that he would scrupuously observe the neutrality of the canal

especially in consideration of its being so remarkable a work, and one in connection with which your Excellency's name will live in history, I have the honour to inform you that the Egyptian Government will not violate that neutrality, except at the last extremity, and only in case of the English having committed some act of hostility at Ismailia, Port Said, or some other point of the Canal.[2]

Blunt, however, relates that secret preparations were made for " blocking the Canal at a certain point between Ismailia and Port Said," but that Arabi refused to give the final order.[3] Later when orders were issued for the " temporary " destruction of the canal, they came too late to be carried out, for General Wolsley had already passed through. " If Arabi had blocked the Canal," said Wolsley, " as he intended to, we should be still at the present moment on the high seas blockading Egypt. Twenty-four hours delay saved us." [4]

Tel-el-Kebir brought with it the complete abdication of France in Egypt and the end of the Dual Control. A few days after the battle M. Duclerc requested that England should explain what she intended to do with regard to

[1] Wilfred Scawen Blunt, *Secret History of the English Occupation of Egypt* (N. Y., 1922), p. 300.

[2] *Ibid.*, p. 301.

[3] *Ibid.*

[4] *Ibid.*

Egypt. France wanted to revive the Dual Control but the Egyptian Government and English public opinion were opposed to this. On October 23rd, the French Government was informed through Lord Lyons that while England recognized the efficiency of the two controllers, she considered that the system presented certain dangers and should therefore be abolished.[1] As a substitute, she recommended the establishment of a European financial commission to be named by the Khedive and to possess only advisory functions. France was offered the presidency of this commission, but refused, declaring that it would be inconsistent with her dignity " to accept as equivalent for the abolition of the Dual Control, a position which was simply that of Cashier." [2] Negotiations were continued for a while and then dropped altogether. France resumed her ' liberty of action in Egypt' and remained more or less hostile to England's policy until 1904.

Having thus rid herself of the inconvenience of a partner in Egypt, England sought to justify her occupation. Lord Cromer maintained that since intervention was necessary, England was best qualified to assume that responsibility. " The special aptitude shown by Englishmen in the government of oriental races pointed to England as the most effective and beneficent instrument for the gradual introduction of European civilization into Egypt." [3] That England's intentions were benevolent and disinterested is the theme of numerous declarations by her leading statesmen. Certainly the Liberal Ministry contemplated no permanent occupation of Egypt and Gladstone's anti-imperialistic views are well-known. But there were other than benevolent reasons which brought England to Egypt. English bondholders

[1] Velay, *op. cit.*, p. 110.
[2] Cromer, *op. cit.*, vol i, p. 340.
[3] *Ibid.*, p. 328.

held about £30,000,000 of Egyptian debts.[1]     The Suez
Canal was the great highway to England's eastern empire
and Liberals and Conservatives alike were determined to
keep it open at all costs.     The British occupation of Egypt,
like the French occupation of Tunis, is one of the shining
examples of modern imperialism which Disraeli had inaugurated only a few years before by acquiring the canal shares
of the Khedive.     British imperialism may have been more
subtle than the French, and more careful in hiding selfish
motives behind the gospel of the " White Man's Burden,"
but the ends were the same.

It is precisely in this falsification of the real import of motives
[said Hobson] that the gravest vice and most signal peril of
Imperialism reside.     When, out of a medley of mixed motives,
the least potent is selected for the public prominence because it
is the most presentable, when issues of a policy which was not
present at all to the minds of those who formed this policy are
treated as chief causes the moral currency of the nation is
debased. . . . Though the reasons openly assigned for the
British occupation of Egypt were military and financial ones
affecting our own interests, it is now commonly maintained that
we went there in order to bestow the benefits which Egyptians
have received from our sway, and that it would be positively
wicked to withdraw in a short term of years from the country.
. . . Even if one supposes that the visible misgovernment of
Egypt, in its bearing on the life of the inhabitants, did impart
some unselfish element to our conduct, no one would suggest
that as an operative force in the direction of our imperial policy
such motive has ever determined our actions.     Not even the
most flamboyant Imperialist contends that England is a knight-
errant everywhere in search of a quest to deliver oppressed
peoples from oppressive governments, regardless of her own
interests and perils.[2]

[1] P. T. Moon, *Imperialism and World Politics* (N. Y., 1926), p. 228.
[2] J. A. Hobson, *Imperialism.   A Study* (London, 1902), pp. 209-210.

It was the canal which had furnished the pretext for intervening in Egypt and it was because of the canal that British troops remained. Egypt was important in British eyes because it is on the highroad to India. The control of Egypt meant nothing less than the control of the Suez Canal.

Bismarck had long urged England to take over Egypt. Late in 1876 when war between Russia and Turkey seemed imminent, he wished to keep England out of the conflict and suggested that she " should seek compensation not by war with Russia, but by acquiring Suez and Alexandria." [1] During the following months he tried to persuade the British Government to agree to a solution of the Eastern Question which would permit Russia to have a free hand in Constantinople while Egypt should fall to England.[2]

He encouraged us [said Lord Salisbury] to take Egypt as our share; failing that he thought it would be useful to European civilization that we should occupy Constantinople. . . . I think he will help us in the Conference to any solution that seems practical. But he does not believe in a solution; and is only occupied with settling what shall be done when the Turkish Empire comes in pieces. Bosnia and Herzegovina for Austria; Egypt for us; Bulgaria possibly for Russia; the Turks in Stamboul with some of the surrounding country like the Eastern Empire in its latest days, and the rest for Greece. That I take to be his new map of Europe . . . [3]

The proposal did not in the least tempt Lord Derby.

It is evidently useless [he said] to say that we don't want

[1] *German Diplomatic Documents 1871-1914.* Selected and translated by E. T. S. Dugdale (4 vols., London, 1928), vol. i, " Bismarck's Relation with England 1871-1890." Extract of a memorandum from Prince Bismarck, Oct. 20, 1876.

[2] *Ibid.*

[3] *The Life of Robert Marquis of Salisbury,* by his daughter Lady Gwendolen Cecil (2 vols., London, 1926), vol. ii, pp. 96-97, Salisbury to Derby, Berlin, Nov. 22, 1876.

Egypt and don't intend to take it: we must leave our friends to be convinced by the event. I have no doubt that everybody out of France would be glad that we should seize the country. Russia would like it, as making us an accomplice in her plans. Germany would like it still more, as ensuring our being on uncomfortable terms with France for some years to come. Italy would see in it a precedent and a justification for seizing Tunis; Spain, the same, in regard to Morocco. But you may be assured that we have no such designs and we are not going to run into adventures of this kind.[1]

He directed Lord Lyons to dispel any suspicions that France might have of English designs on Egypt. "We want nothing and will take nothing from Egypt except what we have already and what other Powers share equally with us."[2]

In April 1877 Bismarck returned to the subject. Nubar Pasha, who was then in exile but was later to return to power in Egypt, expressed a preference for British control if control should become necessary. Bismarck regarded Nubar's suggestion as a "very comprehensible" proposal which it would be in the interest of the peace for England to accept.[3] Though the Egyptian Question was not included in the agenda of the Congress of Berlin, Bismarck, according to Blowitz, asked Lord Beaconsfield why he did not take Egypt. "France would not bear you any ill-will on that account very long. Besides, you could give her a compensation,—Tunis or Syria for instance—and then Europe would at last be free from this question of Turkey, which is constantly bringing her within an ace of a fresh war."[4]

[1] Lord Newton, *Lord Lyons etc.*, pp. 104-105, letter from Derby to Lyons, Dec. 6, 1876. *Cf. Documents Diplomatiques Français (1871-1914)*, 1re sér., vol. ii, nos. 138, 221, 283, 285.

[2] *Ibid.*, p. 121, Dec. 21, 1877.

[3] *German Diplomatic Documents*, vol. i, p. 53.

[4] Blowitz, *Memoirs*, p. 166, quoted in Fitzmaurice, *Life of Granville etc.*, vol. ii, p. 426.

England at this time was in no position to take advantage of Bismarck's generous proposal and repulsed every suggestion toward that end. During the Congress of Berlin, Lord Salisbury assured M. Waddington, the French delegate, that England was harboring no designs on Egypt.

I am telling your Excellency no mean secret when I say that we have been very earnestly pressed, by advisers of no mean authority to occupy Egypt—or at least to take the borders of the Suez Canal. Such an operation might have been very suitable for our interests and would have presented no material difficulties. No policy of this kind, however, was entertained by Her Majesty's Government . . . We have . . . turned a deaf ear to all suggestions of that kind.[1]

Now that England had entered Egypt, Bismarck seemed highly gratified and only desired that the occupation should last, believing that " *a gradual dismemberment* of the Turkish Empire is the only pacific solution to the Oriental Ques-

[1] Lord Newton, *Lord Lyons etc.*, pp. 149-150, Salisbury to Waddington, July 6, 1878. In a dispatch to Waddington, Oct. 10, 1878, the Marquis d'Harcourt noted a change in the attitude of Beaconsfield and Derby regarding Egypt. Beaconsfield had told d'Harcourt that England had often been urged to take Egypt but had refused and would still refuse even if it were to her interest because she desired to keep on good terms with France. Derby had repeated the same assurance. Lately, however, both Beaconsfield and Derby had changed their attitude while it was evident that Salisbury had submitted to Berlin, and there was noticeable at Downing Street a veiled antagonism toward France. Beaconsfield had a thirst for popularity which increased with his age. "Upon his return from Berlin furnished with the acquisition of Cyprus, all his wishes appeared to be gratified; but the English public, though temporarily dazzled by this new addition, was soon disillusioned when it was seen that it [Cyprus] was more brilliant than useful..." The merchants of London and the shipping interests of Liverpool were unanimous in their desire that England should occupy Egypt. It was difficult for Beaconsfield to resist public opinion but he hoped to satisfy it by forcing France out of the administration of Egypt and by filling all the important financial and military positions with Englishmen. (*Documents Diplomatiques Français (1871-1914)*, 1re sér., vol. ii, no. 350, London, Oct. 10, 1878).

tion." [1]    In September 1882 he sent his son, Count Herbert, to England in order to learn what arrangements had been made concerning Egypt.

> The future of Egypt [said Count Herbert to Lord Granville] is from the point of view of the German interests entirely indifferent to my father . . . If England . . . should prefer to annex Egypt, she would not meet with opposition from the side of Germany.  The solid and lasting friendship of the British Empire is much more important for us than the fate of Egypt. . . . The settlement of this question rests of course with the English government and we mean to leave it to them; but my father wants you to know that Germany never will stand in the way of England whatever arrangements she will make in Egypt. [2]

The British Government, however, shrank from the idea of annexation, for Egypt was still nominally a part of the Turkish Empire.  On the other hand, a prolonged occupation was not intended and upon this point Gladstone was most emphatic.  " Undoubtedly of all things in the world," he said in the House of Commons on August 10, 1882, " that is a thing which we are not going to do.  It would be absolutely at variance with all the principles and views of Her Majesty's Government, and the pledges they have given to Europe. . . ." [3]    Though English statesmen were insistent in their declarations that the occupation of Egypt was only temporary, yet year after year went with no attempt to evacuate. [4]    " Personally," said Dicey in 1883, " I utterly

[1] Fitzmaurice, *Life of Granville etc.*, vol. ii, p. 273, Lord Ampthill to Granville, Sept. 9, 1882.

[2] *Die grosse Politik*, vol. vi, no. 729, Count Herbert Bismarck, Sept., 1882.

[3] *Hansard's Parl. Debates*, 3d ser., vol. 273, p. 1390.

[4] Over seventy declarations to this effect were made since 1882. See Mme. Adam (Juliette Lamben), *L'Angleterre en Égypte* (Paris, 1922), pp. 73-79.

disbelieve in the possibility of these declarations being carried out in practice, although they are made in good faith." [1]

But while England did not choose to annex Egypt, she did convert it into a veiled protectorate under her control and she was now in a stronger position than ever to assert her wishes so far as the canal was concerned. If the purchase of the Khedive's shares was a sign that she had at last abandoned her hostility to the new highway, the occupation of Egypt was an unmistakable indication of how greatly she valued it. The stubbornness displayed by de Lesseps in trying to prevent the landing of a British force in the Isthmus had provoked much bitterness in England. No sooner had the troops been installed in Egypt than there began an agitation for a second canal under British control. In a letter to Lord Dufferin, Granville said:

One of the most difficult questions with which we have to deal is the possibility of the Suez Canal being used on some future occasion in the same way as Lesseps tried to use it the other day. It is a matter on which French chauvinism is more likely to be excited than the control.

We have two weapons against the Company, the defect of which is that they are both rather too strong: the legal argument that the Company have given ground to the Khedive to withdraw the Concession; the other, that we may encourage a rival Canal from Alexandria to Suez by Cairo. [2]

The idea of constructing a rival canal had been put forward some years before. On September 24, 1872, Colonel Stanton wrote to Granville that the Khedive was prepared to consider a scheme for constructing a new channel from Alexandria to Suez " and gave me to understand that nego-

[1] Edward Dicey, "Why not purchase the Suez Canal?" in *The Nineteenth Century*, Aug., 1883, vol. xiv, p. 194.

[2] Fitzmaurice, *Life of Granville etc.*, vol. ii, p. 305, date of letter: Nov. 16, 1882.

tiations were actually in progress for the formation of an English Company, with the view to providing the funds necessary for the construction of the canal, and that engineers would shortly be sent here to examine the line proposed to be followed." [1] De Lesseps immediately protested on the ground that he had a monopoly of canal construction in the Isthmus. He declared that a rival channel would be an infringement of his concession, and that he would put in a claim for compensation if it were executed.[2] The proposed company was never formed and nothing further was heard of the project.

But in 1883 the agitation for a second canal assumed great prominence in England and numerous complaints were made against the Company. It was said that the French employees adhered too closely to printed regulations; that pilotage charges were exhorbitant and that vessels were required to use the Company pilots who were generally quite unsatisfactory; that the rules were too arbitrary.[3] The English attitude was set forth in memorandum to Lord Granville by Captain Rice:

There is a strong feeling that the autocratic management of the Company and of the navigation of the Canal (virtually by M. de Lesseps) in Paris is adverse to the commercial interests of those who bring the far larger share of grist to the mill, and that a moral right (the strongest and most endurable of all rights) exists that a far better representation should be accorded both in Paris and amongst the staff of employees actually in Egypt.

But when all is said and done, I cannot disguise from myself the primary cause of the present unsatisfactory state of feeling and fact, viz., that English commerce is controlled by a French Company.

[1] *Parl. Papers, Egypt no. 18 (1883)*.
[2] *Ibid.*, no. 2, Sir H. Elliot to Granville, Therapia, Sept. 24, 1872.
[3] *Egypt no. 3 (1884)*.

The real panacea for all this is competition, and competition means another Canal.[1]

The fact that nearly four-fifths of the traffic passing through the canal was British,[2] gave added weight to the arguments of the shipowners. Numerous petitions and memorials were addressed to Granville urging a second canal which should be under the exclusive control of Great Britain.[3]

De Lesseps again brought forward the claim of a monopoly, pointing to the preamble of the first concession (Nov. 30, 1854) which gave him " exclusive power of constituting and directing a Universal Company for the cutting of the Isthmus of Suez and the exploitation of a canal between the two seas." He maintained that a second canal could not be constructed without the approval of the Company and in this he was upheld by the Egyptian Government.[4] The Law Advisers of the British Crown also recognized his claim and Gladstone and Granville accepted it.[5]

Secure though he seemed to be in his claim to a monopoly, de Lesseps nevertheless realized that some concession must be made to English public opinion. On July 10, 1883, he signed an agreement with representatives of the British Government, providing that the Company was to complete a second canal, if possible, by the end of 1888, and to reduce the tolls, beginning January 1, 1884.[6] Arrangements were

[1] *Ibid.*, Memorandum on Suez Canal, by Ernest Rice, Capt. and Senior Officer in Egyptian Waters, Aug. 28, 1883.

[2] See Appendix A.

[3] See *Egypt no. 15 (1883)*.

[4] F. Yeghen, *Le Canal de Suez et la réglementation internationale des canaux interocéaniques* (Thesis, Montpellier, 1927), p. 52.

[5] *Hansard's Parl. Debates*, 3d ser., vol. 281, July 12, 1883, p. 1232.

[6] *Ibid.*, pp. 1089-1091, for the full text of this agreement; cf. *Egypt no. 12 (1883)*.

also made for increasing the English share in the management of the Company.[1]  On its part, the British Government was to use its influence to aid the Company in obtaining the concession for the new canal and for the necessary lands, and was to lend the Company a sum of not more than £8,000,000 for its construction.

This agreement did not meet with public approval in England, where it was felt that the provisions concerning the tolls and representation in the management of the Company were inadequate.  Moreover, it left undecided a number of points such as whether the new channel would be the property of the Canal Company, whether the Egyptian and French courts would have jurisdiction over it, whether Great Britain would have the right to take measures for its protection.  Parliamentary ratification was necessary before the agreement could be carried out, but when it came up for a vote, it was decisively defeated.

Negotiations were thereupon resumed and in November 1883 de Lesseps, accompanied by his son, Charles, arrived in London.  He had several interviews with Granville, who convinced him " that his own interest lay in a good understanding with Great Britain, and that the days of Arabi were definitely over." [2]  At a meeting on November 30th attended by Charles de Lesseps and representatives of the *Association of Steam Ship Owners engaged in the Eastern Trade,* a voluntary agreement was drawn up.[3]  By its terms,

[1] This provided that one of the three British Directors was always to be a Vice-President of the Company, another was to become a regular member of the Executive Committee (Comité de Direction), while the third should be nominated to the Finance Commission.  It was further provided that an English officer, named by the British Government, should be appointed Inspector of Navigation, and that the Company in the future should employ a fair proportion of English pilots.

[2] Fitzmaurice, *Life of Granville etc.*, vol. ii, p. 312.

[3] The full text is given in *Parl. Papers, Egypt no. 3 (1884).*

the Company was to facilitate transit either by enlarging the present canal or by constructing a second channel. Seven directors, in addition to the three already representing the British Government, were to be chosen by the shipowners and merchants.[1] The Company consented to employ a larger number of English-speaking officials and to reduce the tolls on a sliding scale, depending on the profits, until they reached the minimum of five francs.[2] The agreement took on an official character when Lord Granville gave his approval, January 15, 1884.[3]

Strictly speaking, the agreement was not a contract, but more in the nature of a program setting forth reciprocal obligations. The second channel was not constructed, but instead the Company enlarged and improved the canal in order to facilitate the transit of the increasing number of vessels passing through it.

[1] The number of Directors was increased from 24 to 32 by a resolution of the General Assembly of Shareholders May 29, 1884. England had approximately one-third of the total.

[2] See Appendix B.

[3] Voisin-Bey, *op. cit.*, vol. iii, p. 82.

# CHAPTER XVII

## " NEUTRALIZATION "

THE crisis of 1882, followed by the British occupation of Egypt, raised a new problem in connection with the Suez Canal. Since England had intervened to protect the canal and had landed troops along its banks, it was quite obvious that neither the Concession of 1856 nor the Sultan's Firman of 1866, gave sufficient guarantees for its neutralization. There were no rules of international law which were applicable to the canal and a special agreement would be necessary in order to define its legal status and to guarantee its security against future attacks.[1] In the meantime, England's occupation of Egypt gave her virtual control over the new highway.

Proposals for the neutralization of the canal began to appear many years before its construction. In 1838 Prince Metternich, whose interest in the Suez route has already been alluded to,[2] made such a proposal to Mehemet Ali which was not accepted.[3] Three years later, he again brought up the subject and suggested that the Treaty of London which neutralized the Dardanelles should be used as a model for

[1] See Thomas Erskine Holland, *Studies in International Law* (Oxford, 1898), ch. xiv; T. J. Lawrence, *Essays on Some Disputed Questions in Modern International Law* (2nd ed., Cambridge, 1885), essay ii; Henry Bonfils, *Manuel de droit public (droit des gens)*, (7th ed., Paris, 1914), by Paul Fauchille, section iv, nos. 506-515. Charles Calvo, *Le droit international* (5th ed., Paris, 1896), no. 376.

[2] See chapter vii.

[3] *Revue de droit international et de législation comparée,* vol. vii (1875), p. 682, " La neutralisation du Canal de Suez," by Sir Travers Twiss.

the Suez Canal but the idea was dropped due to England's opposition.[1]

The Concessions of 1854 and 1856 made no direct provision for the neutrality of the canal, though article 14 of the second Concession states that the canal shall always be open as a " neutral passage " without distinction, while the next article prohibits the Company from according " to any vessel, company or individual, any advantages or favors which are not granted to all other vessels, companies or individuals, in the same conditions." These statements, however, did not neutralize the canal, for a status of neutrality can only be conferred by an international agreement.[2]

When the Congress of Paris convened in 1856, de Lesseps submitted a project of neutralization to Count Buol which provided:

1. The signatory Powers guarantee the neutrality of the Maritime Canal for all time.

2. No vessels can be seized in the Canal or within four leagues of the entrance on both seas.

3. No foreign troops can be stationed on the banks of the Canal without the consent of the territorial Government.[3]

As we have already seen,[4] this project was defeated by the opposition of Lord Clarendon. In the same year, Metternich suggested that the Viceroy should propose a conference

[1] *Ibid.*

[2] T. J. Lawrence, *op. cit.*, p. 41. The Concession of 1856 " is a charter granted by a Government to a private company, not a treaty between two or more governments, and a charter of neutrality cannot be imposed upon a locality which does not possess it according to the common law of nations except by treaty . . . that no nation which has not bound itself to do so is obliged to respect an artificial neutrality." (T. S. Holland, *op. cit.*, p. 280.)

[3] Ferd. de Lesseps, *Lettres etc.*, 1st ser., p. 353.

[4] See ch. xi, p. 143.

of the Powers to meet at Constantinople for the purpose of "regulating by a convention the perpetual neutrality of passage in the Suez Canal."[1] He contended, however, that the principle of neutrality was already set forth in article 14 of the second Concession.

Some years later, on March 3, 1864, de Lesseps in a note to Drouyn de Lhuys, French Minister of Foreign Affairs, sketched the bases of a treaty of neutralization which differed somewhat from his earlier proposals. The new project suggested an international agreement which should:

1. Proclaim the complete neutrality of the Canal and freedom of passage for all merchant vessels regardless of nationality in time of war and peace.

2. Prohibit war vessels from passing through the Canal except with special authorization of the local government.

3. Prohibit vessels passing through the Canal from landing troops in the Isthmus.

4. Prohibit the Company from erecting any fortifications whatever.[2]

Though de Lesseps in this note declared that the neutrality of the canal was already provided for in article 14 of the second Concession, it is clear that he did not attach importance to it. Otherwise there would have been no need to make further proposals.[3]

With the opening of the new channel to navigation the question of its security became of greater interest. An international trade conference which had assembled at Cairo in November 1869, declared that it was "desirable that the

[1] HHSA, Fach 13, Suez Canal, Note on Prince Metternich's views, Vienna, July 8, 1856. *Cf.* Ferd. de Lesseps, *Lettres etc.,* 1st ser., p. 402.

[2] Egypte, vol. 33, 1864, Paris, March 3, 1864.

[3] The Viceroy was opposed to the neutralization of the canal, as he believed it would be dangerous to Egypt. (*Ibid.,* no. 78, Taster to Drouyn de Lhuys, Alexandria, June 19, 1864.)

neutrality of the Canal be recognized and guaranteed by all Powers." [1] During the Franco-Prussian War which followed soon after, the Company made no attempt to prevent the free usage of the canal to vessels of the belligerent Powers.[2] However, the presence of French warships at the approaches of the canal gave rise to no little anxiety in England and the Admiralty proposed for Lord Granville's consideration an understanding among the Powers concerning its neutrality.[3]

The first international measure concerning the canal was taken by the Tonnage Conference which met at Constantinople in May, 1873. A declaration was adopted which recognized the right of warships and transports of belligerents to employ the canal and thus admitted in principle that its navigation was under the protection of all Europe.[4]

The outbreak of the Russo-Turkish War in 1877 made the question of protection for the canal of vital concern, since Egypt was a part of the Turkish dominions, and since Russia would have been justified from a legal standpoint in

---

[1] *Revue de droit international et de législation comparée*, vol. ii (1870), p. 516, article by G. Rolin-Jaequemyns. On June 24, 1869, the Marquis de La Valette suggested to Lord Lyons that "the Great Powers should without delay take into consideration the question of the neutrality of the Suez Canal." (FO 78/2170, no. 647, confidential, Lyons to Clarendon, Paris, June 24, 1869.)

[2] During the war the belligerents made no attack on the freedom of navigation in the canal.

[3] FO 78/2170, confidential, Admiralty to Under Secretary for Foreign Affairs, Aug. 1, 1870.

[4] *Revue de droit international et de législation comparée,* vol. xiv (1882), p. 574, "De la securité de la navigation dans la Canal de Suez," by Sir Travers-Twiss. *Cf.* vol. xx (1888), p. 530, "La Convention de Constantinople pour le libre usage du Canal de Suez," by T. M. C. Asser. The declaration, dated Dec. 14, 1873, concerned only warships and transports and did not include the situation which might arise for merchant vessels in case Turkey was at war. Thus it did not declare for complete liberty of navigation.

occupying the Isthmus for military purposes.[1]   De Lesseps hastened to draw up a plan for the neutralization of the canal which he submitted to Lord Derby, but the latter rejected it on the ground that it was "open to too many objections."[2]

The British Government, however, was determined to prevent any interference with the free navigation of the canal and on May 6, 1877, Lord Derby sent warning to Russia.

Should the war now in progress unfortunately spread, interests may be imperilled which they [the British Government] are equally bound and determined to defend, and it is desirable that they should make it clear, so far as at the outset of the war can be done, what the most prominent of those interests are.

Foremost among them is the necessity of keeping open, uninjured and uninterrupted, the communication between Europe and the East by the Suez Canal.   An attempt to blockade or otherwise to interfere with the Canal or its approaches would be regarded by them as a menace to India, and as a grave injury to the commerce of the world.   On both these grounds any such step—which they hope and fully believe there is no intention on the part of either belligerent to take—would be inconsistent with the maintenance by them of an attitude of passive neutrality.[3]

To this warning Prince Gortchakoff replied: "The Imperial Cabinet will neither blockade, nor interrupt, nor in any way menace the navigation of the Suez Canal.   They consider the Canal as an international work, in which the com-

---

[1] Egyptian troops participated in the War on the side of Turkey, and Egyptian vessels carried soldiers and supplies from Egyptian ports to the scene of conflict.   (T. J. Lawrence, *op. cit.*, p. 59.)

[2] *Parl. Papers, Egypt no. 6 (1877).*   Cf. T. S. Holland, *op. cit.*, p. 281.

[3] *Parl. Papers, Russia no. 2 (1877)*, no. 1, Derby to Count Schouvaloff, May 6, 1877.   Cf. *Documents Diplomatiques Français (1871-1914)*, 1re sér., vol. ii, no. 171.

merce of the world is interested, and which should be kept free from any attack." [1]

Though neither belligerent attempted to interfere with the navigation of the canal, the war raised the question once more of an international agreement for its security. At its meeting in Paris in 1878, the Institute of International Law adopted a resolution declaring: " It is to be desired, in the interest of all nations, that the navigation of the Suez Canal be placed by an international act outside of all hostile acts during the war." [2]

Five years later the revolt of Arabi placed the canal in great danger. Egypt was unable and Turkey unwilling,[3] to take any steps to suppress the insurrection; France and Italy had refused to intervene; the Conference of Ambassadors which had met at Constantinople to consider means for restoring order, had failed to reach an agreement; and as a consequence, England had intervened alone.[4] The need for some sort of a collective agreement to secure the protection of the canal had thus been clearly demonstrated. During the crisis de Lesseps had stoutly maintained that the canal was already neutralized. When English troops were landed at Suez, he wrote to Admiral Hoskins: " It is an act of war which constitutes a flagrant violation of the neutrality of the Canal and against which I formally protest." [5] But he was

---

[1] *Ibid.,* no. 2, Prince Gortchakoff to Count Schouvaloff, St. Petersburg, May 18/30, 1877, communicated to Derby, June 7, 1877. *Cf. Documents Diplomatiques Français (1871-1914),* 1re sér., vol. ii, no. 182.

[2] *Revue de droit international et de législation comparée,* vol. x (1878), p. 380. At the session of 1879 the Institute adopted a more detailed resolution which was communicated to Ferd. de Lesseps personally [*ibid.,* vol. xii (1880), pp. 100-101].

[3] Perhaps because of England's attitude.

[4] See chapter xvi.

[5] Compagnie Universelle du Canal Maritime de Suez, *Bulletin Décadaire,* Aug. 12, 1882.

no doubt aware that his contention was invalid though it served " as a convenient controversial missile to throw at Great Britain . . . when she seized the Canal in spite of his protests. . . ." [1]

Hardly a month after Tel-el-Kebir, Lord Granville discussed the question of an agreement concerning the canal with Count Herbert Bismarck.

> We wish to suggest [said Granville] that free passage through the Suez Canal in time of peace and war be secured to all seafaring nations under an international guarantee of the Powers, and that Egypt be recognized by the European Powers as a neutral state " à la guise de la Belgique ". We believe that thus we shall disarm the greed and jealousy of other nations and also be relieved of the burden of keeping troops in Egypt. This would cost us too much, as we should have to provide first-rate fortresses. Egypt, if a neutral state, would only require a very small army which would not be costly to her.[2]

Lord Granville did not propose to neutralize the canal. On this point he said to Count Bismarck, " we can never agree to the Suez Canal being neutralized. No British Minister can agree to this sea passage being closed to us in the event of war. But if Egypt is not declared neutral, we shall have to undertake all alone the protection of that country. . . ." [3] A few days later Granville abandoned the idea of neutralizing Egypt and announced that he would shortly propose an international agreement to secure the free navigation of the canal.[4] While Prince Bismarck was willing

---

[1] T. J. Lawrence, *op. cit.,* p. 41.

[2] *German Diplomatic Documents*, vol. i, pp. 163-164; memorandum by Count Herbert Bismarck, London, Oct. 22, 1882, reporting conversation with Lord Granville.

[3] *Ibid.*

[4] *Ibid.*, p. 165, telegram, Stümm, Chargé d'Affaires in London, to Count Herbert Bismarck, Oct. 31, 1882.

to accept the principle of free navigation of the canal, he would not at this time, guarantee it.[1]

On January 3, 1883, Granville addressed a circular dispatch to the British representatives at Paris, Berlin, Vienna, Rome and St. Petersburg.[2] He proposed:

1. That the Canal should be free for the passage of all ships in any circumstances.

2. That in time of war a limitation of time as to ships of war of a belligerent remaining in the Canal should be fixed, and no troops or munitions of war should be disembarked in the Canal.

3. That no hostilities should take place in the Canal or its approaches, or elsewhere in the territorial waters of Egypt, even in the event of Turkey being one of the belligerents.

4. That neither of the two immediately foregoing conditions shall apply to measures which may be necessary for the defense of Egypt.

5. That any Power whose vessels of war happen to do any damage to the Canal should be bound to bear the cost of the immediate repair.

6. That Egypt should take all measures within its power to enforce the conditions imposed on the transit of belligerent vessels through the Canal in time of war.

7. That no fortifications should be erected on the Canal or in its vicinity.

8. That nothing in the agreement shall be deemed to abridge or affect the territorial rights of the Government of Egypt further than is herein expressly provided.

The Circular brought no immediate response. Two years later, when representatives of the Great Powers met in London to discuss the financial situation in Egypt, M. Waddington, in a letter to Granville, January 17, 1885, proposed that a conference should be called to conclude a definite arrange-

[1] *Ibid.*, Count Herbert Bismarck to Baron Stümm, Nov. 2, 1882.

[2] *Parl. Papers, Egypt no. 10 (1885).*

ment for the free passage of the canal.[1]  He followed this
with another letter on February 9th, suggesting that the conference be held at Cairo.[2]   Granville, however, objected to a
conference as " an useless excrescence " and stated that all
that was necessary was to draw up an agreement in accordance with his circular dispatch.[3]   After an exchange of
views on the subject, it was finally decided that a Committee
of Experts should meet in Paris to draft the agreement on
the basis of the Circular.   A declaration to this effect was
signed by the representatives of the Powers gathered at
London, March 17th.[4]

Hardly had the Conference assembled on March 30th
when differences arose.[5]   The British delegates, Sir Julian
Pauncefote and Sir Charles Rivers Wilson, insisted that
Lord Granville's Circular must be used as the basis for any
agreement and that there must be no departure from its main
provisions.   The French delegates, on the other hand,
brought in a project which provided for an international
commission composed of delegates from those Powers which
had signed the Declaration of London together with one
Turkish and one Egyptian representative, whose duty it
would be to secure the protection of the canal.   The commission was to have authority to take steps for the execution
of the treaty, and to concert measures with the Company for
the observation of the navigation rules.   The French proposal was not in accordance with Granville's Circular, which

---

[1] *Ibid., Egypt no. 16 (1885)*, no. 2, M. Waddington to Granville, London, Jan. 17, 1885.

[2] *Ibid.*, no. 4.

[3] *Ibid.*, no. 5, Granville to Lyons, Feb. 13, 1885.

[4] *Ibid.*, no. 12, Declaration of London.

[5] For an account of the sessions of the Conference, see *Parl. Papers,
Egypt no. 19 (1885)*. Cf. *Doc. Dipl., Affaires d'Égypte*, vols. 104,
105, 106.

contemplated nothing more than a general agreement binding the Powers not to violate the free navigation of the canal. An international commission was therefore wholly unnecessary and the enforcement of the treaty, from the British viewpoint, should be left entirely to the Khedive. With England in occupation of Egypt the canal was virtually under her control and should the Khedive be unable to secure its protection British troops would most likely come to his assistance. Would not the French proposal for an international commission disturb England's anomalous position in Egypt and her control of the canal? Sir Julian Pauncefote endeavored to dismiss the plan for an international commission on the ground that it did not conform to Granville's Circular; but as the Russian and German delegates joined the French in upholding it, the Conference decided to use it concurrently with the Circular as a basis for discussions. It was quite evident, however, that an agreement could not be reached. While many minor points were settled, the fundamental difference concerning the methods for securing the protection of the canal still remained. After drawing up a draft treaty the Conference came to an end on June 13th.[1] In accepting this treaty, Sir Julian Pauncefote added a general reservation that it did not limit the freedom of action of England so long as she was in occupation of Egypt.[2]

It was clear that any collective agreement concerning the security of the canal would have to take into account the British occupation of Egypt. From the first England had insisted that her occupation would be temporary but as it was prolonged year after year, France and Turkey showed signs of impatience. In 1883 Lord Cromer had declared optimistically: " Give me 2000 men and power to settle matters between the English and Egyptian Governments, and I

[1] See *Egypt no. 19* (*1885*).
[2] *Ibid.*

will guarantee that in twelve months there shall not be a British soldier in Egypt. . . ." [1]  All hopes of a speedy evacuation vanished, however, with the destruction of General Hicks' army in the Sudan in November of the same year.

Though it was hardly possible for England to fix a date for the withdrawal of her garrison, she had no objections to entering into discussions concerning the matter. In August 1885, Lord Salisbury dispatched Sir Henry Drummond Wolff on a mission to Constantinople. [2]  On October 24th, Wolff signed a convention with the Turkish Minister for Foreign Affairs which provided that a British and a Turkish High Commissioner should be sent to Egypt in order to assist the Khedive in reorganizing his army and in reforming the general administration. [3]  As soon as the Commissioners were convinced that security had been established in Egypt, they were to report to their governments " who will consult as to the conclusion of a convention regulating the withdrawal of the British troops from Egypt in a convenient period." [4]  The two Commissioners departed for Egypt in order to take up their new duties.

In November the French Government proposed that the negotiations relative to the canal should be resumed. Lord Salisbury endeavored to temporize by saying that the moment was inopportune. [5]  But France was anxious to conclude an agreement as soon as possible in order thereby to remove the principal reason for England's occupation of Egypt. On January 13, 1886, M. Waddington informed

---

[1] Cromer, *op. cit.*, vol. ii, p. 359. He later admitted that his forecast " was unquestionably much too sanguine " (*ibid.*).

[2] See *Parl. Papers, Egypt no. 1 (1886)*, and *Egypt no. 7 (1887)*.

[3] *Egypt no. 1 (1886)*.

[4] *Ibid.*, cf. Cromer, *op. cit.*, vol. ii, p. 373.

[5] *Egypt no. 1 (1888)*, no. 35.

Lord Salisbury that the French Government had consulted the other Powers who had "expressed their readiness to concur in any solution of the questions left in suspense . . . which might be acceptable to both Great Britain and France."[1] Again Lord Salisbury offered the excuse that the moment was unfavorable to renew discussions on the subject. Negotiations between the two Governments continued, however, during 1886 without arriving at any definite conclusion.

In October, Herbette, the French Ambassador at Berlin, endeavored to get German support in order to secure the withdrawal of England from Egypt. He assured Count Herbert Bismarck that if Germany would use her authority to maintain the *status quo* in the Mediterranean, the idea of *revanche* would soon disappear. England's withdrawal from Egypt, declared the Ambassador, was absolutely imperative if France was to maintain her position as a Great Power.[2] Germany, however, declined to take any part in the Egyptian Question, considering that the friendship of England was worth more to her than that of France.

Wolff returned to England late in 1886 to present his report. In January Lord Salisbury sent him on a second mission to Constantinople whose object was to effect an understanding with Turkey concerning the withdrawal of the British troops from Egypt. On May 22nd, a convention was concluded providing that the British garrison should be withdrawn at the end of three years.[3] Great Britain, however, reserved the right of reëntry "if there are reasons to fear an invasion from without, or if order and security in the interior were disturbed." The same privilege was ac-

[1] *Doc. Dipl.*, vol. 106, nos. 1 and 2.

[2] *Die grosse Politik*, vol. vi, pp. 144-152, Conversation with Count Herbert Bismarck, Oct. 18, 1886.

[3] Text in *Egypt no. 2 (1887)*.

corded to Turkey. After the withdrawal of the British troops, Egypt was to enjoy " territorial immunity." The Convention was to be submitted to the Powers for their approval. It was provided that in case of interference with the navigation of the canal, those powers which had ratified the Convention should have the right of sending troops across Egypt for its protection.

No sooner was the Convention announced than it encountered the opposition of France and Russia. The French Ambassador protested against the right of reëntry and held that in any case Great Britain should only take action at the invitation of the Porte.[1] The Russian Ambassador was equally firm in his opposition " and reproached the Grand Vizir with having gratuitously sacrificed the rights of the Sultan to England." [2] Indeed, the Porte was warned that if it ratified the Convention, France and Russia would consider themselves free to occupy Turkish territory and remain until a similar convention had been signed.[3] Alarmed by the opposition, the Turkish Ministers requested an extension of the time set for the ratification. But as they took no steps to ratify the Convention during this time-limit, Wolff left Constantinople in July. Though the Convention was dropped, it strengthened England's position diplomatically, for it revealed her willingness to reach an agreement for the withdrawal of her garrison. France had blundered again. Instead of expelling England from Egypt, her opposition to the Convention made the probability of a withdrawal more remote than ever.

Following the failure of the Wolff Convention, Salisbury adopted a more accommodating attitude in regard to an agreement for the protection of the canal. In a note to

---

[1] *Egypt no. 8 (1887)*, no. 5, Wolff to Salisbury, Const. June 2, 1887.

[2] Cromer, *op. cit.,* vol. ii, p. 378.

[3] *Egypt no. 8 (1887)*, no. 45, Wolff to Salisbury, Const., July 9, 1887.

M. Waddington, August 19th, he accepted the French proposal for a commission composed of the Consular Agents of the Signatory Powers to watch over the execution of the treaty.[1] This paved the way to a final settlement. On October 21st, Salisbury forwarded to the British Embassy at Paris a draft of a convention based on the one drawn up in 1885 but with certain reservations representing the British views.[2] The French Government accepted the draft and it was communicated to the other Powers for their approval on November 15th.[3] It was formally signed at Constantinople, October 29, 1888, by representatives of Great Britain, France, Germany, Austria-Hungary, Italy, Russia, Spain, Turkey and the Netherlands, and was later ratified by the governments of these Powers.

The Convention purposes to establish " a definite system destined to guarantee at all times and for all Powers, the free use of the Suez Maritime Canal." [4] It declares that the canal is to be open in time of war as well as in time of

[1] *Egypt no. 1 (1888)*, no. 32, Salisbury to Waddington.

[2] *Ibid.*, no. 39, Salisbury to Mr. Egerton. *Cf. Doc. Dipl.*, vol. 106, no. 50. The reservations of Lord Salisbury were (1) The general reservation expressed by Mr. Pauncefote at the Paris Conference of 1885 that the Treaty must not limit the freedom of action on the part of Great Britain during her occupation of Egypt. In other words, that the Treaty should remain in abeyance during the British occupation. (2) The inclusion in the Treaty of the "approaches" of the canal, and the territorial waters of Egypt, independent of the canal, as well as the inclusion among acts prohibited in the ports of access, of those which had for their object preparations for war. This was objected to by England. (3) Salisbury objected to a provision prohibiting the embarkation or debarkation of troops, munitions or materials of war in the canal or its ports of access in time of war and peace. In his view, this was too wide in its application and should be confined to times of war only and to actual belligerents and should apply to the canal but not to the ports of access.

[3] Lord Salisbury's visit to Paris at this time did much to settle the differences.

[4] *Commercial no. 2 (1889)*. See Appendix D for full text.

peace, to all vessels, whether merchantmen or warships. The entrances to the canal are not to be blockaded and no acts of hostility are to be committed in the canal or its ports of access, or within a radius of three marine miles therefrom, even in the case where the Ottoman Empire is one of the belligerent Powers. No permanent fortifications are to be erected on the canal and belligerent warships may not embark or disembark troops or munitions of war within it or its ports, or revictual or take in stores except where it is strictly necessary, and the stay of such vessels as well as their prizes shall not exceed twenty-four hours. An interval of twenty-four hours shall elapse between the departure from the canal or its ports of any vessel belonging to one belligerent and that of any vessel belonging to another. The Powers may not station warships inside the canal, but each nonbelligerent Power has the right to station two warships in the ports of access. In case the canal is in danger, the Egyptian Government shall take the necessary measures for carrying out these provisions. Should Egypt, however, not have the necessary means, it may appeal to Turkey or through Turkey to the Signatory Powers. The French proposal for an international commission to have general control over the canal and to secure its protection was not included because of England's refusal to consider it. As a concession to France, however, Salisbury permitted an innocuous arrangement whereby the Consular Agents of the Signatory Powers should meet on the summons of three of their members under the presidency of their Doyen in case the canal was threatened and inform the Egyptian Government of the danger, but in any case, they should convene once a year " to take note of the due execution of the Treaty." [1]

[1] Article VIII, see Appendix D. The Convention applies only to the maritime canal and its ports of access to a radius of three marine miles

The term " neutralization " has very commonly been employed to describe the effect of the Convention of 1888.[1] Legal opinion, however, has been by no means unanimous on this question. On the one hand, for instance, Lawrence holds that the canal is permanently neutralized,[2] while Bonfils, on the other hand, argues that it is not. " This term," he says, " fails to define the international situation. If it were neutralized it would be closed to warships of belligerents." [3] Though the word " neutrality " was used at the Paris Conference of 1885, according to Sir Julian Pauncefote it had " reference only to the neutrality which attaches by international law to the territorial waters of a neutral state, in which a right of innocent passage for belligerent vessels exists, but no right to commit any act of hostility." [4] One writer, in pointing out that the expression " neutralization " varies in use and meaning, says with regard to the Suez Canal:

It is neutralized in the sense that no acts of hostility can be

from those ports, and does not include the fresh-water canal. France had proposed that the fresh-water canal should also be declared immune from acts of war but England had refused. Article II of the Convention merely states that the Powers will not interfere with the fresh-water canal and its branches. At the Paris Conference the Russian delegate had submitted a proposal to neutralize all or part of the Red Sea but this was defeated by the opposition of the British and Italian delegates.

[1] See Holland, *op. cit.*, pp. 270-293; L. Oppenheim, *International Law. A Treatise* (2 vols., London, 1926), vol. ii, pp. 148, 166; C. Piccioni, *Neutralité perpetuelle* (Paris, 1902), p. 176; Cyrus F. Wicker, *Neutralization* (Oxford Univ. Press, 1911), pp. 1-4, 9-10, 37, 40; C. H. Stockton, *Outlines of International Law* (N. Y., 1914), pp. 137-143; Calvo, *op. cit.*, vol. iv, p. 526; J. Westlake, *International Law* (2nd ed., 2 vols., Cambridge, 1910-1913), vol. i, pp. 345-346.

[2] T. J. Lawrence, *The Principles of International Law* (Boston, 1895), pp. 181, 490.

[3] Bonfils, *op. cit.*, p. 338.

[4] Quoted in Cromer, *op. cit.*, vol. ii, p. 384.

committed, without a violation of the treaty, within its limits or those of the terminal waters. But it is not neutralized in another sense, as it can be used in war time for passage through by belligerents for any warlike expedition whose objective is exterior to the canal. It is not even similar to marginal territorial waters of a neutral, as these have no limitations as to time of arrival and departure. Certainly it is not like neutralized land territory, for passing through such territory is denied. It is *sui generis,* common to all vessels, to whom warlike operations are denied while passing through.[1]

To the historian it matters less how statesmen and international lawyers describe the consequences of important events and apply a legal nomenclature to them, than what those events serve in fact to bring about. In regard to the Suez Canal this is notably true. It is of utmost importance to take close heed of the extent of the freedom asserted by any State, notwithstanding everything that has taken place, to use the canal for a military purpose in event of war, to close the canal to an enemy, and generally, to commit acts of hostility within its waters. Obviously, in this connection, the attitude of Great Britain has been and remains an outstanding factor.

[1] Stockton, *op. cit.,* p. 138. "Neutralization", says Wicker, "is the imposition by international agreement of a condition of permanent neutrality upon lands and waterways" (*op. cit.,* p. 1). Hershey believes that it would be best to refer to the canal as "internationalized and partly neutralized" (A. S. Hershey, *The Essentials of International Public Law and Organization* (N. Y., 1927), p. 316, note). In the Wimbledon case of 1923 the World Court referred to the Convention of 1888 and used the term "neutralization" in connection with the canal. The majority opinion held that "when an artificial waterway connecting two open seas has been permanently dedicated to the use of the whole world, such waterway is assimilated to natural straits in the sense that even the passage of a belligerent man-of-war does not compromise the neutrality of the sovereign State under whose jurisdiction the waters in question be." [*Publications of the Permanent Court of International Justice. Collection of Judgments.* (Ser. A), no. 1. The S. S. Wimbeldon. (Leyden, 1923), p. 28].

For sixteen years the Convention was held in abeyance because of the British reservation of 1885.[1] Though it was declared in force in the Anglo-French Agreement of 1904,[2] England did not withdraw her troops from Egypt and so long as her troops remain, perhaps it cannot be said that she has abandoned the right to commit acts of war in the canal zone. Indeed, the position of England with reference to the Suez Canal is in practice similar to that of the United States in regard to the Panama Canal though there is no collective agreement for the protection of the latter. In both cases actual defense remains in the hands of a single Power.

The Suez Canal, it should be observed, is not only an international highway designed to serve the commerce of the world. For England it is also a line of defense, a military communication which is considered by many as " vital " for the preservation of her empire. It is true that no other Power has as much interest in protecting the canal from acts of war, in keeping it open at all times; and it is because of her special interest that England has taken upon herself the task of guarding this channel. The canal has a strategic importance for England which it does not have for other Powers. This being the case, in time of war she can be expected to take most drastic measures in order to keep control of the canal while her enemies might find it to their advantage to destroy it. In other words, the canal under such circumstances will become the actual theater of conflict, as it was during the Great War. International agreements carry little weight when they run counter to strategic considerations. Referring to this subject, Professor Hyde says:

A number of States, such, for example, as those whose territories are traversed or separated by an international river, may

[1] *Cf. infra*, p. 298.
[2] *Cf. infra*, p. 306.

profess concern as to conditions of navigation in time of conflict, and conclude an agreement designed to protect the stream and its establishments should war ensue. Upon its outbreak, if the contracting States are aligned as opposing belligerents, there is likely to be a sharp conflict of interest with respect of the proper uses of the river, and one so vital as to encourage disregard of the compact by that party which would suffer a relative strategic detriment should it observe the restraints imposed. The danger of contempt for the arrangement is shown to be proportional to the opportunity which it leaves open to any contracting belligerent party to utilize the stream for a military end. An agreement imposing a duty to protect merely the works and establishments pertaining to navigation, offers a frail bond of restraint. Nor are provisions devised to localize hostilities by forbidding their commission in a particular stream in close proximity to, or in the very path of belligerent operations likely to prove a real deterrent. So long as a waterway is permitted to remain a means of military communication and transportation serving one belligerent and barred to its foe, the latter must be expected to make extraordinary effort to obstruct passage and stop navigation. Conventions which ignore such probabilities and purport merely to impose minor restraints upon the contracting parties fall far short of those designed to attach to an area a status of permanent neutralization. They reveal no collective design to isolate it from warlike operations, and still less a joint undertaking to guarantee the maintenance of such a condition. If it provides for the impressment of permanent neutralization, forbidding all acts within the area or uses thereof as would be denied a belligerent with respect to neutral territory, and especially if it is buttressed by a common guaranty of interested Powers, there is automatically established a check, which, by reason of its very nature, minimizes the grounds and invalidates the excuses for a possible breach.

The States most concerned in the treatment to be applied to an international waterway or other area may not, however, be disposed to consent to an arrangement of large and permanent design. Such reluctance gives rise to the inquiry whether a legal duty rests upon a State to acquiesce in a plan contemplating permanent neutralization or on one of less magnitude. It must be recognized that normally no State is obliged to agree to abandon the right when a belligerent to commit hostile acts within a zone of land or water belonging to or controlled by its enemy, or to yield to foreign powers the right to attach an artificial condition such as a new status to a portion of its own domain.[1]

During the War the ineffectiveness of the Convention of 1888 to provide adequate protection for the canal was clearly demonstrated. The Egyptian Government lacked the necessary means while Turkey adhered to the Central Powers. Protection of the canal fell to Great Britain, the occupying Power, and it would have been much the same if the Convention had not existed. The peace treaties conferred on Great Britain the rights given to Turkey in the Convention,[2] and, having already assumed the authority assigned to the Egyptian Government in Article IX by virtue of her occupation of Egypt, Great Britain acquired a firm hold on the canal. The whole record of events down to the present time reveals a situation where a powerful maritime state, for political and economic reasons which are strengthened by geographical considerations regards the Suez Canal as an artery in which hostile acts in any season should not be committed except when it is to her interests to commit them. It is unnecessary to go further to declare how the international lawyers should describe the situation in legal terms.[3]

[1] C. C. Hyde, *International Law* (2 vols., Boston, 1922), vol. i, pp. 339-340. *Cf.* Joseph P. Chamberlain, *The Danube*, confidential document, Dept. of State, 1918, 76, 107-108, cited by Hyde.

[2] *Cf. infra*, ch. xx.

[3] Concerning the effect of the World War upon neutralization treaties see the article by Malbone W. Graham, Jr., " Neutrality and the World War " in *The American Journal of International Law*, vol. 17 (1923), pp. 704-723, and also his article " Neutralization as a Movement in International Law " in the same journal, vol. 21 (1927), pp. 79-94.

Due to the reservation made by Sir Julian Pauncefote in 1885 and repeated by Lord Salisbury in 1887, the Convention remained in abeyance for many years. On several occasions the question was raised in Parliament as to whether it was yet in force. Thus, on July 12, 1898, replying to such a question in the House of Commons, Mr. Curzon said on behalf of the Government that the Convention " is certainly in existence, but . . . has not been brought into practical operation. This is owing to the reserves made on behalf of Her Majesty's Government by the British delegates at the Suez Canal Commission in 1885, which were renewed by Lord Salisbury and communicated to the Powers in 1887." [1] Two years before, in June 1896, Mr. A. H. Oaks, Librarian of the Foreign Office, prepared a memorandum dealing with the British reservation. Though this memorandum was not included with the correspondence of that year, the circumstances under which it was prepared are explained in the following dispatch from Lord Salisbury to the British Ambassador at Paris, dated July 15, 1896, which refers to certain conversations said to have taken place at St. Petersburg.[2]

Today, and at previous interviews I have had with the French Ambassador, the question of the Suez Canal has been adverted to in our conversation, and especially allusion has been made to the reserve made by Sir Julian Pauncefote in 1885 by which the right of landing troops at the Canal should remain to England as long as she was in occupation of Egypt. I said that Prince

[1] *Hansard's Parl. Debates,* 4th ser., vol. 61, p. 667. On Feb. 25, 1904 the question was brought up in the House of Commons, and the Under Secretary for Foreign Affairs stated that the Convention was not in force since the other Signatory Powers, in view of the British reservation, had abstained from taking any steps in order to bring it into active operation (*ibid.,* vol. 130, p. 1650).

[2] *British Documents on the Origins of the War 1898-1914,* edited by G. P. Gooch and H. Temperley (vol. i, London, 1927), no. 380, p. 321. Memorandum by Mr. Oaks.

Lobanov had alluded in conversation with Sir N. O'Conor to the importance attached by Russia to the free navigation of the Suez Canal, and that he himself had in general conversation, alluded to this reservation, which had consequently been made the subject of consideration. I said that after communication with Lord Cromer I thought there were some questions of detail which have to be examined before effect could be given to any proposal for the withdrawal of the reserve. But I said that an undue importance had been attached to it by the European Powers, and that it was never originally intended by us, and certainly would not be used, for the purpose of jeopardizing the neutrality of the Canal; and for the sake of removing all misapprehension on that head, I should be glad if the reserve, which apparently was connected with the disturbances at the time of Arabi, and had lost its importance, could be modified or withdrawn. I repeated to him as I had already repeated before, that Her Majesty's Government did not contemplate any circumstances under which they could possibly interfere with the neutrality of the Canal; and if any apprehension existed upon this head by reason of the existence of this reserve, I should be very glad if we could find satisfactory means of putting an end to it.

Despite this apparent willingness of Lord Salisbury to withdraw the British reservation, it was maintained and was not modified until the agreement with France in 1904.[1] It should be said, however, that even though this reservation hindered the Convention from entering into formal effect, and although the occupation of Egypt meant a virtual substitution of British for "Khedival" authority, nevertheless Great Britain observed the principles laid down in the Convention. It is significant that it was England and not Egypt who assumed the responsibility for the protection of the canal. When the United States Government wished to send its fleet through the canal, it communicated not with the

[1] *Cf. infra,* pp. 306-307.

Khedive but with London. On June 25, 1898, Mr. Day, Secretary of State, cabled to the American Ambassador at London instructing him to inform Lord Salisbury that the United States desired to send warships through the canal and to find out if the British Government had any objections.[1] Lord Salisbury replied that no protests would be made.

Great Britain's attitude was tested more severely in 1904 when she stood by while the warships of Russia, with whom she was on very precarious terms, passed through the canal on the way to fight Britain's ally, Japan.[2] One of the Russian vessels even disregarded the Convention of 1888. Permitted to obtain coal at Port Said in order to make the return voyage to Russia, it employed the coal in overhauling neutral ships near the entrance to the canal.[3] By this action it "violated the neutrality of Egypt in a gross and open manner. No proximate acts of war must take place in neutral waters, and they must not be used as a base of operations."[4] In November, Rear Admiral Foelkersham's division passed through the canal and entered the Red Sea after obtaining coal and supplies in Egypt.[5] Italian war

[1] *Foreign Rel.* 1898, 982, cited by John B. Moore, *Digest of International Law* (8 vols., Washington, 1906), vol. iii, p. 266.

[2] See A. S. Hershey, *The International Law and Diplomacy of the Russo-Japanese War* (N. Y., 1906), pp. 189-191. *Cf.* article by H. W. Wilson, "The Voyage of the Baltic Fleet," in *National Review,* Dec. 1904.

[3] Hershey, *op. cit.,* p. 189.

[4] *Ibid.,* quoting T. J. Lawrence. No act of hostility can be committed in the canal or its ports of access within a radius of three marine miles from those ports (Art. IV, of the Convention). *Cf. Brit. and Foreign State Papers,* vol. 102, p. 591, "Egyptian Rules regarding coaling by belligerent warships in the Suez Canal and Rules to be observed by them," Feb. 10, 1904.

[5] *Ibid.,* p. 191.

vessels passed through the canal in 1911 during the war with Turkey.[1]

The whole question of internationalizing the canal hinged upon the British occupation of Egypt. With Britain in Egypt, any convention would in reality rest upon her enforcement. Although England scrupuously respected the principle of free navigation, the situation was galling to France who desired to substitute a more genuine internationalization not resting upon British occupation or reëntry. But England, after the failure of the Wolff convention of 1887 was no longer in a mood to discuss the subject of her withdrawal from Egypt. This was made apparent when Turkey tried to reopen negotiations in 1890.[2]

Since 1887, the Sultan had come to realize that he had given too much heed to French and Russian advice. Hoping that a greater display of willingness on his part might induce England to agree to a settlement of the Egyptian problem, he instructed the Grand Vizir in 1890 to draw up a new convention. This provided that England should evacuate Egypt at the end of one year but should have the right of reëntry. Lord Salisbury, to whom the project was submitted, found it unacceptable, and definitely refused to consider any convention which set a date for the withdrawal of the British troops.[3] France, on the other hand, was now prepared to accept a convention if England would agree to a date for the evacuation.[4] Germany was also favorable to the plan and endeavored to bring about an understanding

---

[1] Yeghen, *op. cit.*, p. 112. *Cf. Documents Diplomatiques Français* (*1871-1914*), 3e sér., vol. i, nos. 89, 97, 350.

[2] *Die grosse Politik*, vol. viii, ch. 53.

[3] *Ibid.*, no. 1786, Hatzfeldt to Caprivi, London, June 29, 1890. *Cf.* no. 1787, Radowitz to Caprivi, Therapia, Aug. 19, 1890.

[4] *Ibid.*, no. 1797, confidential (no. 80), Radowitz to FO, Pera, June 26, 1891.

between Turkey and England, though without success. A draft composed by Count Hatzfeldt, German Ambassador at London and submitted to the British Government, was rejected since Gladstone demanded an independent Egypt, whereas, from the Turkish viewpoint, this would be worse than the existing situation.[1] The unwillingness of the British Government to compromise led Germany to adopt a more reserved attitude, though she still hoped to see a settlement of the vexatious question. During the next few years the Porte repeatedly tried to reopen negotiations, but without success. In 1893 Lord Rosebery thought of submitting the question to the Powers but was dissuaded by the German Government, which believed that it would merely give France an opportunity for intervening in Egyptian affairs.[2]

Though England seemingly had no intention of withdrawing from Egypt, the situation was not altogether to her liking. France, full of resentment for having been squeezed out of Egypt, was pursuing a policy of pinpricks in order to make England's position as uncomfortable as possible. Under the circumstances, England depended on the Triple Alliance, and upon Germany in particular, for support in her Egyptian policy.[3] So long as Bismarck remained at the helm, this support was fairly constant, for he had always regarded England as the logical Power to control Egypt.[4] After his retirement in 1890, however, Germany embarked on a world policy and began to display an increasing interest in Near Eastern affairs. The acquisition by a German syndicate in 1888 of the Haidar Pasha-Ismid Railway in Asi-

---

[1] *Ibid.*, no. 1808 (234), Marschall to Hatzfeldt, Berlin, Oct. 25, 1891.

[2] *Ibid.*, no. 1823, Jan. 30, 1893, and no. 1824, Jan. 31, 1893.

[3] *Life of Granville etc.*, vol. i, p. 453.

[4] *Cf. supra*, ch. xvi, pp. 269-270.

atic Turkey, while it was not immediately followed by an imperialistic policy on the part of the German Government, nevertheless paved the way for German penetration in the Ottoman Empire.[1] Though Germany continued to support British policy in Egypt for some years longer, her support was not always given with that willingness shown by Bismarck. Indeed, British statesmen began to find German support quite as uncomfortable at times as French hostility.[2] As the century drew to a close, the clash of interests, and especially Germany's *Drang nach Osten,* produced much suspicion on both sides. It was clear that if England desired to retain Germany's support, she would have to make some concessions to German interests; whereas the only other alternative was to come to terms with France. Without support her anomalous position in Egypt would be very difficult to maintain. " Egypt was like a noose around the British neck, which any Great Power could tighten when it wanted a diplomatic concession from the Mistress of the Seas. . . ." [3]

But to conciliate Germany proved to be quite impossible. Though Joseph Chamberlain tried his best from 1898 to 1901 to conclude an alliance, he met with no success because of mutual distrust.[4] Nor did the prospects for an understanding with France seem particularly encouraging. With France still smarting under the loss of her position in Egypt, resenting the proprietary attitude which England had

[1] On the subject of Turkish railways, and especially the Bagdad Railway, see E. M. Earle, *Turkey, the Great Powers and the Bagdad Railway* (N. Y., 1924).

[2] Viscount Grey of Fallodon, *Twenty-Five Years 1892-1916* (2 vols., N. Y., 1925), vol. i, pp. 9-11, 44, 50.

[3] S. B. Fay, *The Origins of the World War* (2 vols., N. Y., 1929), vol. i, p. 126.

[4] *Ibid.,* pp. 129-141.

adopted in regard to the canal, a work of French genius, and finding herself checked in her imperialistic enterprises by British diplomacy, the establishment of friendly relations would be a most difficult matter. But after the peaceful settlement of the Fashoda crisis, which nearly brought on war between the two Powers, Delcassé, the French Foreign Minister, was determined to effect a *rapprochement* with England. The British Ministers being in a conciliatory mood, an exchange of notes followed.

For England the important thing was to get a recognition from France of her position in Egypt. Delcassé at first desired to include the Egyptian Question as only one part of the larger African Question. Moreover, he pretended to understand by the " Egyptian Question " only a removal of certain financial restrictions which Great Britain found inconvenient.[1] Lord Lansdowne, the British Foreign Secretary, made it clear that England would not consider any proposals which did not include one for the regularization of her position in Egypt.[2] This was a much more serious matter than Delcassé had contemplated.

France had missed her opportunity in Egypt; we had seized ours; but we had announced that our occupation was not to be permanent. The French nation clung to this idea, and held us in theory to that engagement, although, perhaps, with no very definite expectation that we should fulfill it. Any French Government which proposed to recognize the permanency of our hold upon the country would require an immense amount of nerve.[3]

Delcassé had the " nerve " and requested Lord Lansdowne

[1] *British Documents on the Origins of the War 1898-1914,* vol. ii (London, 1927), no. 364, p. 306, Lansdowne to Monson, Aug. 5, 1903.

[2] *Ibid.*

[3] *Ibid.*

to formulate his requirements concerning Egypt. In a memorandum to the Foreign Office, Cromer suggested what the British demand should be. " The first and essential point is that the French Government should recognize our occupation—in other words, that our pledge to withdraw the British garrison should be cancelled with the explicit, or at all events the implied assent of the French Government." [1] This suggestion was adopted and Lansdowne drafted a formula which he submitted to M. Cambon, the French Ambassador, on October 1, 1903.

His Majesty's Government have no desire to alter the political status quo of Egypt or, so far as Powers other than France are concerned, to raise at this moment questions affecting the international position of Great Britain in that country. They desire, however, that the Government of the French Republic should recognize that the British occupation of Egypt, which was originally intended to be temporary, has, under the force of circumstances, acquired a character of permanency. It would therefore, as between Great Britain and France, be understood that the period of its duration should be left entirely to the discretion of His Majesty's Government. [2]

Delcassé considered the British demand as " very far-reaching " and hinted that France would expect a sufficient equivalent " for the immense concessions " which she would be asked to make in Egypt. England was to obtain immediate advantages in Egypt whereas France would get only a hope in Morocco. [3] Lansdowne, however, reminded M. Cambon that England was already in Egypt and " that there was not the slightest prospect of our withdrawing. We were, in reality, only asking the French Government to recog-

[1] *Ibid.*, no. 365, p. 307, Aug. 7, 1903.

[2] *Ibid.*, no. 369, p. 313, Lansdowne to M. Cambon.

[3] *Ibid.*, no. 370, p. 317, Lansdowne to Monson, Oct. 7, 1903, reporting conversation with French Ambassador, M. Cambon.

nize the facts as they exist." [1]   On October 26, 1903, Del-cassé accepted the British demand concerning Egypt.[2]

Included in the negotiations was the question of putting into operation the Suez Canal Convention of 1888.   England was prepared to abandon her general reservation but insisted, upon Cromer's suggestion, that Article VIII which provided that the Consular Agents of the Signatory Powers in Egypt should watch over the execution of the Treaty, be modified as incompatible with the British occupation of Egypt.[3]   The French Government replied that it would be a mistake to denounce this article since the Convention could only be modified with the concurrence of the other Powers.[4] However, a compromise was finally reached concerning this point.

The Anglo-French Agreement was signed on April 8, 1904.[5]   In regard to Egypt, England declared that she had no intention of altering the political status of that country; while France agreed not to obstruct the action of England in Egypt " by asking that a limit of time be fixed for the British occupation or in any other manner." [6]   The provision which concerned the canal, was as follows:

In order to insure the free passage of the Suez Canal, His Britannic Majesty's Government declare that they adhere to the stipulations of the Treaty of the 29th October 1888, and that they agree to their being put in force.   The free passage of the Canal being thus guaranteed, the execution of the last sen-

[1] *Ibid.*

[2] *Ibid.*, no. 373, p. 320, M. Cambon to Lansdowne.

[3] *Ibid.*, no. 376, p. 326, Lansdowne to Cambon, Nov. 19, 1903. *Cf.* Appendix D for text of article VIII.

[4] *Ibid.*, no. 380, p. 334, Lansdowne to Monson, Dec. 11, 1903.

[5] *Ibid.*, pp. 374-398, for full text; *cf. Parl. Papers, Treaty Series 1911,* no. 24 (cd. 5969).

[6] *Ibid.*, p. 385.

tence of paragraph 1 as well as of paragraph 2 of article VIII of that Treaty will remain in abeyance.[1]

The Agreement was a triumph for British diplomacy. England had at last emerged from her " splendid isolation " and was free to negotiate with the other Powers " without the handicap of the Egyptian noose around our necks." [2] She was no longer dependent on German support for her policy in Egypt and she was relieved of the French policy of pinpricks which had for so many years hampered her actions. It was a tremendous comfort to British statesmen to discover that the " gloomy clouds were gone, the sky was clear, and the sun shone warmly." [3]

It should be remembered that the main reason for England's intervention in Egypt was to protect the Suez Canal and it was largely because of the canal that she remained in that country. Her occupation at first rested on no legal basis. She had not declared Egypt a protectorate although in practice it amounted to one. Only indirectly did other Powers recognize her anomalous position in Egypt. In the first Wolff convention of 1885, Turkey gave this recognition though it was not unassailable in law. According to Wolff that convention

[1] *Ibid.*, p. 390. The last sentence of paragraph 1 of article VIII reads: " Under any circumstances, they shall meet once a year to take note of the execution of the Treaty." This had reference to the Consular Agents of the Signatory Powers in Egypt. The second paragraph of the article is as follows: " The last-mentioned meetings shall take place under the presidency of a Special Commissioner nominated for that purpose by the Imperial Ottoman Government. A Commissioner of the Khedive may also take part in the meetings, and may preside over it in case of the absence of the Ottoman Commissioner." Cromer objected to the presence of an Ottoman Commissioner in Egypt who would probably become " a center of local intrigue." (*Brit. Doc. on the Origins of the War 1898-1914,* vol. ii, no. 379, p. 333, Cromer to Lansdowne, Cairo, Dec. 11, 1903).

[2] Viscount Grey of Fallodon, *op. cit.,* vol. i, p. 50.

[3] *Ibid.*

recognizes and adopts the fact of our occupation with the same publicity, and the Sultan as Sovereign of Egypt and Caliph of his religion thus solemnly calls on his temporal and spiritual subjects to concur in the measures which will be jointly recommended. Both the legitimate sovereignty and the *de facto* occupation are acknowledged, and the forces of both are to be utilized for the purposes of a permanent settlement.[1]

By the declaration of April 8, 1904 France recognized the permanency of the British occupation and a month later Germany entered upon negotiations with England toward the same end.[2] On June 19, 1904 Germany promised not to obstruct Great Britain in Egypt by asking that a time-limit be fixed for her occupation, and agreed to the British stipulations concerning Article VIII of the Suez Canal Convention.[3] Similar declarations were signed by Russia, Italy and Austria-Hungary.[4] Thus England's position in Egypt was to a certain extent at least given a legal basis.

The effect of the Agreement of 1904 on the canal was perhaps not so obvious. Though the Convention of 1888 was now in force except for the reservation concerning Article VIII, actually the situation remained as before. Indeed, so long as England stayed in Egypt, the security of the canal, as well as its control, rested with her. The authority conferred upon the Egyptian Government by Article IX of the Convention of 1888 " to take the necessary measures for ensuring the execution of the said Treaty," was now virtually British authority. By her reservation concerning the last sentence of paragraph 1 of Article VIII, England discontin-

---

[1] *Egypt no. 1 (1886)*, Wolff to Salisbury, Oct. 24, 1885.

[2] For an account of these negotiations see *Brit. Doc. on the Origins of the War*, vol. ii, nos. 18, 22.

[3] *Ibid.*, no. 22, Count Metternich to Lansdowne.

[4] *Egypt no. 1 (1905)*. *Cf.* G. L. Beer, *African Questions at the Paris Peace Conference* (N. Y., 1923), p. 344.

ued the annual meetings of the Consular Agents in Egypt who were to watch over the execution of the Treaty. Such meetings, of course, were hardly necessary while England herself assumed the responsibility for guarding the canal. The only concession which Lord Lansdowne made in the Agreement of 1904 was to recognize the Convention of 1888 as being in operation. In reality the canal was no more internationalized than it was in 1888.

One might wonder how England's insistence upon her own single-handed military control over the canal can be reconciled with her willingness to respect the principle of free navigation. But the explanation is not difficult to find. Britain's imperial policy was to keep open the routes of communication and to safeguard her Indian empire. The canal had become the great highway to the East and it was necessary for England that it should be kept open at all times. Mindful of the experience of 1882 she was determined not to leave this " vital artery " to the protection of the European Concert.

# CHAPTER XVIII

## STRATEGIC IMPORTANCE OF THE CANAL

THE importance of the Suez Canal as a link between Europe and Asia is indisputable. As the shortest route from the British possessions in the East to the mother country, it is, to quote Bismarck, ' like the spinal cord which connects the backbone with the brain.' [1] The canal is a most important factor in shaping British foreign policy and its control accounts in no small measure for England's predominant position in world affairs.

To appreciate the tenacity with which England holds on to the canal, one must realize that the cardinal principle of her foreign policy is the preservation and expansion of her empire. The keystone of the Empire is India and once England had established her supremacy there, her main concern was to safeguard it by all possible means. Utilizing her naval superiority, she proceeded to appropriate all the important strategic posts along the routes of communication connecting the Atlantic with the Indian Ocean. Thus she acquired Cape Colony from the Dutch in 1806, giving her command of the Cape route. Gibraltar, the key to the Mediterranean, was taken in 1704; Malta in 1800 and Cyprus in 1878. By her acquisition of Aden (1839) Perim (1847), Northern Somaliland (1884-1886), Socotra (1886), she turned the Red Sea into a " British lake." Egypt, the only

---

[1] M. Busch, *Bismarck* (London, 1898), vol. ii, p. 321. Cited by G. L. Beer, *African Questions at the Paris Peace Conference* (N. Y., 1923), p. 292.

remaining link in the long chain, was also drawn into the British orbit, thanks, ironically enough, to a French promoter and an Egyptian patriot—to de Lesseps and Colonel Arabi. Over the two great water highways to the East, Suez and the Cape, Great Britain reigned supreme.

Napoleon's expedition of 1798 drew England's attention to the strategic importance of Egypt as an outpost for the defense of India. She therefore adopted a policy of maintaining the Ottoman Empire and of tightening the bonds of vassalage between the Sultan and his vassal, the Viceroy.[1] One reason for this policy was the fear that if Russia gained the upper hand in Turkey, and a foothold on the Mediterranean, she would control the Islamic world and endanger the communications to India. Imperial considerations, likewise, led England to oppose the growing influence of France in Egypt. British statesmen were convinced that the political independence and territorial integrity of the Ottoman Empire were essential for the safety of the British dominions in the East.

While England discouraged the agitation for the Suez route, she was determined that under no circumstances should another Power, and particularly France, appropriate it or secure a preponderant influence in Egypt. Protection of India demanded that all the approaches must be in British hands. When de Lesseps received the Concession for the canal, England placed herself squarely against the scheme and for a dozen years relentlessly opposed it.[2] But despite all her efforts the canal was completed and she was faced

---

[1] There are, of course, exceptions to this general statement. British policy was not inflexibly consistent. For instance, during the administration of Abbas Pasha (1849-1854), when England was promoting her railway project in Egypt, the Foreign Office seemed more interested in loosening the bonds between the Viceroy and the Sultan. *Cf. supra*, ch. ix.

[2] *Cf. supra*, chapters x, xi, xii, xiii.

with what from her viewpoint was an intolerable situation.
Here was a highway, the shortest to her Indian empire,
under foreign control! British imperialists trembled at the
very thought. Her shippers, moreover, found it somewhat
uncomfortable to do business with a French Company, particularly when they furnished most of the traffic. It was
annoying to pay the heavy tolls and to submit to red-tape
regulations; but it was most aggravating to realize that they
were permitted to use the canal only on the sufferance of a
foreign concern. Hence the enthusiasm with which was
hailed the purchase of the Khedive's shares.[1] England, it
was thought, would now have a voice in the management of
the Company. But though she had become the largest pro-
prietor, the canal did not pass under her control. The
Company was still French, and French influence in Egypt
was strong. A few years later, however, seizing the occasion presented by Arabi's revolt, England got the upper hand
in the country and with it the virtual control of the canal.

Supreme in Egypt, England adopted a different attitude
toward the Ottoman Empire. Whereas in the earlier years
she had upheld the Dying Turk, she was now much less insistent on that score, since Turkey was no longer necessary
for the protection of India. Indeed, it was quite obviously
to England's advantage to loosen the bonds of vassalage and
to overshadow the Sultan's authority in Egypt. She had already taken a first step in that direction when she had prevented Turkish assistance in suppressing the revolt of 1882.
The conquest of the Sudan in 1898, followed by the establishment of the Anglo-Egyptian Condominium in January
1899, was another indication that England had supplanted
Turkey in Egypt. Even more striking was the authori-
tative attitude which England assumed in connection with
the Akaba incident of 1906. A Firman which the Sultan

---

[1] Cf. *supra*, ch. xv, pp. 249-250.

had addressed to Abbas II, when the latter became Khedive in 1892, contained a clause rectifying the Sinai frontier in favor of Turkey. Early in 1906 the Sultan demanded that Egypt withdraw her troops from certain places in the Sinai Peninsula and from the island of Tiran, in the Gulf of Akaba.[1] Turkish troops were sent to occupy posts in the Peninsula and it was reported that Turkey intended to construct strategic railways to Suez on the banks of the canal.[2] In England the Turkish plan was regarded as a serious menace to the liberties of Egypt and to the security of the canal.[3] The British Government demanded that Turkey abandon her railway scheme and withdraw her troops from the Sinai Peninsula, and in order to back up this demand a powerful squadron of cruisers and torpedo boats was sent to Egyptian waters. The Sultan gave way but the incident was a reminder that England had become the actual ruler of Egypt.

The strategic importance of Egypt, to quote Captain Mahan, " is a commonplace of the ages." [4] Napoleon had once said that who is master of Egypt is master of India, and his expedition of 1798 was a threat which Britain never forgot.[5] With the completion of the canal, Egypt naturally became of greater importance to England, for it was clearly recognized that the Power in control of that country would also control the canal. Thus, Dicey writing in 1877, said:

It would be mere hypocrisy to contend that the primary

---

[1] Grey, *op. cit.*, vol. i, p. 119.

[2] *Egypt no. 2 (1906)*, Correspondence Respecting the Turco-Egyptian Frontier in the Sinai Peninsula, Cromer to Sir Ed. Grey, Cairo, May 21, 1906. *Cf. British Documents on the Origins of the War, op. cit.*, vol. v, pp. 189-195.

[3] *Ibid.*, cf. Grey, *op. cit.*, vol. i, p. 120.

[4] A. T. Mahan, *The Problem of Asia and its Effect upon International Policies* (London, 1900), p. 72.

[5] *Cf. supra*, ch. iv.

motive with which I, and those who think with me, advocate the
occupation of Egypt is a desire to benefit the condition of the
people.   If this were our motive, it would be our duty to recommend the annexation of Upper as well as Lower Egypt.   The
reason why I advocate the measure is because I regard it as
one demanded by our Imperial interests under the changes now
impending in the East.   Still it is not unimportant to show that,
in thus protecting our route to India, we should at the same
time, as I believe, confer a great boon upon the people of Egypt.

Moreover, if we had once a *locus standi* in Egypt as the
dominant power, we should occupy a commanding position
over the whole region lying between the Red Sea and the
frontier of India.   It is no mere accident that the dominion of
Syria and Arabia has with rare intervals, belonged to the Power
which held the Isthmus.   Given a strong military position in
Egypt, and we could afford to be indifferent to any attack on
India along the Euphrates Valley. . . . The one thing needful
for us is to secure the free passage of the Canal.[1]

That England in view of her position in eastern trade
should have desired to keep the canal free from interference
by other Powers can readily be appreciated; that she should
have wished to dominate it herself is also obvious.   But
nothing short of actual control would have satisfied the
British Imperialist.

No scheme of neutralisation [said Dicey] can meet our wants.
Indeed, neutralisation, in any intelligible sense of the word,

---

[1] Edward Dicey, "Our Route to India" in *The Nineteenth Century,*
June, 1877, vol. i, pp. 682-683.   "Egypt," said another English writer, "is
the fulcrum of our Foreign Policy.   She stands about midway, in Diplomacy and in Naval Strategy, between our Eastern and Western Empires.
She is the nodal point which adjusts our Foreign Relations and balances
our Imperial Possessions.   In Egypt, therefore, the political equilibrium
is the most easily disturbed or restored.   The Colossus that bestrides the
Isthmus of Suez necessarily holds a commanding position."   [A. S. White,
*The Expansion of Egypt under Anglo-Egyptian Condominium* (London,
1899), p. 440.]

would place us in a worse position than that which we at present occupy. International guarantees, whatever their intrinsic value may be, are not securities on which we can afford to stake our free communication with India, or in other words, the security of our Empire. . . . As our route to India, thanks to the Canal, lies across the Isthmus, and as the holder of the Isthmus commands the Canal, we ourselves must, for our own safety's sake, be the holders of the Isthmus. Either we must be prepared to see our highway to India barred or interrupted in the event of war, or we must occupy Egypt. From this dilemma I can see no escape.[1]

As soon as the canal became the great highway to India, it was inevitable that England should have desired to control it. The logic of history made it evident. Upon this point, Dicey was no less emphatic.

But in one way or the other [he wrote in 1883] we are bound to get the Canal into our own hands. This, to use an Americanism, is the bottom fact on which all negotiations in the future must be based. It is England's manifest destiny to become the mistress of the Canal as she has already become the mistress of Egypt; and against manifest destiny gods and men fight in vain, whether in Suez or in Panama.[2]

The question was frequently raised in England as to whether the canal was after all so vital for the preservation of the Empire. In 1877 Gladstone asked what would happen if it were stopped.

A heavy blow will have been inflicted on the commerce, the prosperity, the comfort of the world. We, as the great carriers, and as the first commercial nation of Christendom, shall be the greatest losers. But it is a question of loss and of loss only.

[1] *The Nineteenth Century*, June, 1877, vol. i, *loc. cit.*, p. 684.
[2] " Why not Purchase the Suez Canal?", *The Nineteenth Century*, Aug. 1883, vol. 14, p. 205.

It is a tax and a tax only. What came and went quick and cheaply must come and go slow and dearer; and less will come and go accordingly. We have, however, in full proportion to other countries the ability to bear loss, for we have much to draw upon.

It seems to be forgotten by many that there is a route to India round the Cape of Good Hope, as if that route lay by the North-West Passage.[1]

Sir Charles Dilke was of the opinion that the canal would be unsafe in case of war with a great maritime power.

The Canal considered as a means of communication in time of war, is as delicate as a thread of a spider's web. A ship or two sunk in it; two or three charges of dynamite exploded in the portion nearest to the Gulf of Suez; a few torpedoes laid down in the night—none of these difficult matters to manage, especially, when we remember that we are forbidden to take full military steps for watching the Canal—would close the passage against ships for days or weeks, and would prevent the transport by the Mediterranean of anything except troops without baggage. It would be difficult to keep the Canal open, even if it lay within the limits of the British Empire, and the task of guarding it would lock up a considerable force of troops, and that of watching the approaches to it a portion of our active fleet. But we possess no special rights as regards the Canal, and have no power to prevent a dozen merchant ships from sinking themselves in mid channel.[2]

Another English writer held that the canal had altered the position for the worse, since it permitted other Powers to reach India, whereas before its construction, England had undisputed command of the commerce to the East. " The Suez Canal," he said, " . . . is a cause of strife; and if on

[1] W. E. Gladstone, " Aggression on Egypt and Freedom in the East," *The Nineteenth Century*, Aug. 1877, vol. ii, p. 155.

[2] *Problems of Greater Britain* (London, 1890), pp. 657-658.

the golden front M. de Lesseps shines in dazzling lustre as the genius of Progress, on the silver lining he stands as the God of Discord." The canal " has been made against the wish of England, as it was designed to injure her and it is probably the only effectual revenge for Waterloo which Napoleon III was able to inflict." [1]

Captain Mahan did not agree with those who would abandon the Suez route because it was unsafe in time of war. " For, after all," he said, " nothing, not the sanding-up of the Canal itself, can change the natural conditions which make Egypt the strategic centre of the chief highway between the East and the West." [2]   He believed it would be a grave mistake for England to relinquish her hold on Egypt.

Not only is Great Britain for her own credit bound to hold Egypt but the central position of the latter with reference to the whole Eastern world is such that, even under present drawbacks, it is hard to conceive any conditions in which supplies can fail to pour in from several quarters.   In military situation, Egypt approaches an ideal; for to a local concentration of force, defensive and offensive, operating in two directions towards Gibraltar and towards India, it adds several streams of supply, so diverse in origin that no one navy can take position to intercept them all.   Reduced to the fewest, they flow in by two channels, the Red Sea and the Mediterranean: how shall one fleet close both?   If the Mediterranean be blocked, the Red Sea remains, always the shortest route for India, Australia and the Cape, to aid to the fullest extent of their resources, the sole essential being to provide that their resources be adequate.   In the same case, Great Britain herself has the Cape route.   If this be thought overlong, all the more reason not to abandon that of Suez antecedent to necessity arising. . . . In short, sub-

---

[1] George Hooper, " How the Political and Military Power of England is Affected by the Suez Canal," in *United Service Magazine,* September 1890, pp. 505-506.

[2] Mahan, *op. cit.,* p. 79.

mitted to strict military analysis, it would appear that the proposition to abandon the Mediterranean and the Suez route, in favor of the Cape, is a strategic policy defensive rather than offensive. . . . The truer solution for a state already holding Malta and Gibraltar would seem to grasp Egypt firmly, to consolidate local tenure there, and to establish in India, Australia and the Cape, sources of necessary supply . . .[1]

Whether the canal was vital or not, England intended to hold on to it and to prevent other Powers from endangering her communications to the East. For a long time Russia was regarded as the greatest menace to India. Her encoachments in the Middle East, her efforts to win a warm-water port on the Mediterranean and to open the Straits to her warships, her interference in the Balkans and her ambitions concerning Abyssinia,[2] aroused suspicion and fear in England. During the war of 1877-1878, Lord Derby warned Russia against making any attack on the Suez Canal,[3] a British fleet was sent to Constantinople, and in June 1878, England secured a foothold at Cyprus, the island nearest to the canal, and a base for her operations in the eastern Mediterranean. The question of the Straits was for many years a main factor in Anglo-Russian rivalry.[4] Pro-

---

[1] *Ibid.*, pp. 80-82.

[2] After the opening of the Suez Canal, Russia began to take a lively interest in Abyssinia, which she desired to convert into a Russian protectorate as a challenge to Britain's control of the sea-route to the East and as a strategic base in case of a conflict with England. The establishment of Italy's protectorate over Abyssinia in 1889 checked the Russian plan while it also prevented French expansion in that region. England was not averse to having Italy as a buffer against French and Russian aggressions in East Africa and in 1891 she recognized Abyssinia to be within the Italian zone. The defeat of Italy at Adowa in 1896 by King Menelek removed the danger of any Power establishing itself in Abyssinia. (See *Die grosse Politik,* vol. xi, ch. 68, particularly nos. 2756, 2766, 2767, 2771).

[3] *Cf. supra,* ch. xvii, p. 282.

[4] On the Straits question see *Brit. Doc. on the Origins of the War,* vol.

tection of the canal and the shipping in the Mediterranean led England to oppose every attempt on the part of Russia to reopen the Straits for warships.   When Russia obtained permission from the Sultan in September 1902 for four torpedo boats to pass through the Dardanelles and the Bosphorus to join the Black Sea Fleet, England became alarmed and in the following January, Sir N. O'Conor presented a note to the Porte claiming the same privilege for British warships if the occasion should arise.[1]   After the *entente* with France in April 1904, however, England began to feel a greater security in the Mediterranean and seemed disposed to recognize Russian claims concerning the Straits.   King Edward VII and Sir Charles Hardinge, in a conversation on April 22, 1904, agreed that " there did not appear to be any reason for preventing the passage of the Dardanelles by Russian warships as we have endeavoured to do in the past." [2]   British apprehensions concerning Russia were in some measure diminished by the overwhelming victory of Japan in the war of 1904-1905.   In the subsequent negotiations for an Anglo-Russian *entente* Grey admitted that some concession might be made regarding the Russian desire to reopen the Straits and he would be prepared to discuss the question if Isvolsky should introduce it at an opportune moment.[3]   However, no provision concerning the Straits

iv (London, 1929), section iii, nos. 32-56, and especially the memorandum by Sir Charles Hardinge, of November 16, 1906, pp. 58-60; vol. v (London, 1928), nos. 333, 334, 338, 349, 358, 361, 362, 364, 365, 371, 372, 377, 379, 382, 383, 385, 387, 388, 391; *Die grosse Politik*, vol. xviii, ch. 119, vol. xix, ch. 132, vol. xxvi, pp. 30-32, 147-149, 154-155, 157-159; Grey, *op. cit.*, vol. i, pp. 171-178; Sir Sidney Lee, *King Edward VII* (London, 1927), vol. ii, pp. 639-640; Coleman Phillipson and Noel Buxton, *The Question of the Bosphorus and the Dardanelles* (London, 1917), pp. 167-170.

[1] *Brit. Doc. on the Origins of the War*, iv, p. 41.

[2] Sir Sidney Lee, *King Edward VII*, vol. ii, p. 289.

[3] *Brit. Doc. on the Origins of the War*, vol. iv, p. 414, no. 370.

was made in the Anglo-Russian Agreement of 1907 and when Isvolsky reopened the question during the Bosnian crisis of 1908-1909, Grey considered the moment inopportune.[1]

The *entente* with Russia safeguarded the approaches to India from Persia and Afghanistan; that with France removed the danger to the canal from the Sudan. In the meantime a new source of apprehension appeared to disturb British tranquility. Germany was making great strides towards becoming the foremost industrial nation of the world. The rapid development of her commercial power, the acquisition of colonies, the growth of her navy and the inauguration of *Weltpolitik* under William II, were indications that Germany intended to find her " place in the sun."

The rise of a power so formidable and so determined could hardly fail to arouse anxieties in England. Germany had entered the scramble for colonies late and the possessions which she had acquired were not profitable. They were unsuitable as markets and lacking the raw materials needed for German industries. The Ottoman Empire, on the other hand, offered splendid opportunities for German imperialism. Its strategic location, stretching from the borders of Austria-Hungary to the Persian Gulf, made it a natural highway to India and the Far East; its great natural resources and its agricultural possibilities would serve German needs; its economic and industrial weakness would make it an easy prey for exploitation.[2] Moreover, German supremacy in Turkey would effectually thwart Russia's ambitions for Constantinople and the Straits and would cause considerable discomfiture in France and England.

---

[1] *Ibid.*, nos. 349, 358, 364, 371, and especially Grey's memorandum of Oct. 14, 1908 in no. 377. *Cf.* Grey, *op. cit.*, vol. i, pp. 171-179.

[2] Earle, *op. cit.*, pp. 50-51. *Cf.* Moon, *op. cit.*, p. 248.

In 1888 a German syndicate under the leadership of the *Deutsche Bank* had purchased from the English the railway from Haidar Pasha to Ismid and later, under the name of the Anatolian Railway Company, had constructed a branch to Angora. Within ten years the Germans had constructed nearly a thousand kilometers of railway lines in Asiastic Turkey. In March 1903 the *Deutsche Bank* received a concession from the Sultan to construct a trunk line running from Konia to the Persian Gulf.[1] This was the Bagdad Railway by means of which the German imperialists hoped to further the economic, political and military regeneration of the Ottoman Empire.

The Bagdad Railway challenged England's supremacy in the East. As the most rapid means of transportation from Europe, would it not offer serious competition to the traffic through the Suez Canal.[2] With a terminus on the Persian Gulf would it not threaten British interests in that region?[3] Furthermore, since it would connect with the Syrian and the

---

[1] *Ibid.*, p. 70.

[2] This fear, however, was unfounded since the canal, because of the higher rates by rail, would still continue to receive the larger part of the freight traffic. Chiefly the mails and the passenger traffic would be affected by the building of the Railway. Discussing this point, a German writer said: "The Bagdad Railway taken as a whole is of importance only for the through passenger and postal traffic . . . and occasionally for fast freight. The great bulk of freight traffic, on the other hand, carrying the important export trade of the East, hardly can fall to the Bagdad Railway. . . ." [E. Banse, *Auf den Spuren der Bagdadbahn* (Weimar, 1913), p. 145. Quoted in Earle, *op. cit.,* p. 193.)

[3] In order to prevent the Bagdad Railway Company from securing a terminus on the Persian Gulf, Great Britain in 1899 entered into an agreement with the Sheik of Koweit by which the latter promised to make no international engagements without the consent of the British resident adviser. This effectually forestalled the German scheme to carry the line to the Gulf. (Earle, *op. cit.,* p. 198.)

Hedjaz railways, would it not be a grave menace to England's communications to India through the Suez Canal? [1]

The strategic importance of the Bagdad Railway was clearly recognized by German writers. Dr. Paul Rohrbach, one of its leading exponents, pointed out the dangers to the British Empire.

England can be attacked and mortally wounded by land from Europe only in one place—Egypt. The loss of Egypt would mean not only the end of her dominion over the Suez Canal and of her communications with India and the Far East, but would probably entail also the loss of her possessions in Central and East Africa. The conquest of Egypt by a Mohammedan Power, like Turkey, would also imperil England's hold over her sixty million Mohammedan subjects in India . . . Turkey, however, can never dream of recovering Egypt until she is mistress of a developed railway system in Asia Minor and Syria, and until, through the progress of the Anatolian railway to Bagdad, she is in a position to withstand an attack by England upon Mesopotamia . . . The stronger Turkey becomes, the greater will be the danger for England, if, in a German-English war Turkey should be on the side of Germany . . . [2]

During the early years of the Bagdad scheme England was not greatly aroused over this menace to Egypt and the Suez Canal. Indeed, British bankers and the Foreign Office, in April 1903, were prepared to cooperate in the building of the railway and negotiations for an agreement towards this end were carried on with the *Deutsche Bank*. At the last moment, however, attacks in the press and in Parliament caused the Foreign Office to drop the negotiations. [3]  Only

[1] The Bagdad Railway was to connect with the Syrian lines at Aleppo. The Hedjaz Railway ran from Damascus to Mecca and Medina. *Cf.* Earle, *op. cit.,* p. 27.

[2] *Die Bagdadbahn* (2nd ed., Berlin, 1911), pp. 18-19.

[3] For an account of these negotiations see Earle, *op. cit.,* pp. 180-189. *Cf.* Moon, *op. cit.,* pp. 245-246. *Hansard's Parl. Debates,* 4th ser., vol.

then did the British adopt their attitude of fear and opposition to the Bagdad Railway. The Anglo-German Convention of June 15, 1914, by which England, following the lead already taken by Russia and France, agreed to cooperate in the Bagdad Railway and received a share in its management, promised to remove the sting from that scheme.[1]  Final ratification, however, was prevented by the outbreak of the Great War.

The Turco-German menace to the canal now became a reality and the sensational writers in Germany exultingly predicted the end of the British Empire. Dr. Rohrbach showed that an attack on the canal was not an impossible task. Turkish troops could be sent over the Bagdad, Syrian and Hedjaz railways to Haifa which is only four hundred kilometers to El Cantara on the canal.[2]

Many people say: 'Of course it is impossible to destroy England's power in a single war.' That is not impossible, but is quite feasible. That may be done in Egypt. The construction of the Suez Canal was England's misfortune. English statesmanship foresaw the danger. Hence it opposed its building. . . . When the English troops in Egypt capitulate to the Turks the blow will resound from Gibraltar to Singapore. When the keystone is withdrawn the whole vault of English world-power will tumble down . . .[3]

120, pp. 1369-1375; vol. 121, p. 222; *Brit. Doc. on the Origins of the War,* vol. ii, nos. 202-205, 208, 210, 212, 215, 218-220, 223.

[1] The British attitude towards the Bagdad scheme is set forth in Earle, *op. cit.,* ch. viii; *British Doc. on the Origins of the War, op. cit.,* vol. iii, nos. 418, 425, appendix B; vol. iv, nos. 329, 369, 374, 388, 448; vol. v, nos. 17, 147; B. de Siebert and G. A. Schreiner, *Entente Diplomacy and the World* (N. Y., 1921), bk. iii, pp. 459-465, 474-483, 501-576, 656-665. The provisions of the Convention of June 15, 1914 are given in Earle, *op. cit.,* pp. 262-264.

[2] P. Rohrbach, *German World Policies.* Trans. by Dr. Edmund von Mach (N. Y., 1915), p. 165. *Cf. Der Krieg und die deutsche Politik* (Weimar, 1915), p. 42.

[3] From an article by Dr. Rohrbach in " Das grössere Deutschland,"

The danger of a Turkish attack upon the canal and Egypt from the Sinai Peninsula was pointed out by Lord Cromer in 1906 following the violation of the Palestine-Sinai frontier by the Ottoman Government.[1] The British General Staff gave serious consideration to this possibility and drew up a scheme for the defense of the canal.[2] A successful Turkish attack on the canal would interrupt communications with India, Australia and New Zealand and would prove a serious blow to England.

Sept. 11, 1915, quoted in S. Grumbach, *Germany's Annexationist Aims.* Translated, abbreviated and introduced by J. Ellis Barker (N. Y., 1917), p. 101. *Cf.* A. Dix, " Die Verkehrspolitische Bedeutung des Suezkanals," in *Geographische Zeitschrift,* Feb. 1916, vol. 22, pp. 87-91.

[1] *Egypt no. 2 (1906).*

[2] *War Office Report,* part ii, " Suez Canal Defense," May 1910, cited by Lieut.-Col. P. G. Elgood, *Egypt and the Army* (Oxford University Press, 1924), p. 121.

## CHAPTER XIX

### The Canal During the War

The World War was a supreme test both of the value of the canal in war and of the strength of the rules for its protection. Would the canal, as many had contended, be unsafe and hence necessitate the employment of the longer route by the Cape? Would it prove as vulnerable to a land attack as Rohrbach had predicted? Was it, after all, really so vital to the British Empire?

In considering the part played by the canal during the War it is necessary to bear in mind that it is not in itself a route but only one part, if perhaps the most vital, of the great oriental highway. From European ports to the Far East the distance is from 7,000 to 12,000 miles and involves a voyage of a month or six weeks for large steamers. Leaving Aden, the route diverges to the several eastern terminals: the most northerly leads to Karachi and Bombay on the Indian coast; while farther south other tracks proceed to the East African ports, to Mauritius and to Australia. The main trunk line from Aden goes due east for a distance of 2100 miles to Colombo. Passing Ceylon there are tracks to the Dutch East Indies, China and Japan.[1] A glance at the map will show that much of the route traverses enclosed seas, and at certain points, narrow defiles. While England had important naval and coaling stations and fortified harbors, including Gibraltar, Malta and Cyprus[2] in the Medi-

---

[1] C. Ernest Fayle, *Seaborne Trade* (3 vols., N. Y., 1920-1924), vol. i, p. 115.

[2] Annexed by England after the outbreak of the World War in 1914.

terranean; Aden protecting the entrance to the Red Sea from the south; Bombay, Calcutta, Madras and Rangoon on the coast of India; and Singapore and Hongkong farther east; yet there were many places along the way which furnished good targets for enemy attacks. The effectiveness of the canal would depend to a large extent upon conditions in other parts of the route. A serious menace to shipping in the Mediterranean or in the Red Sea or in the Indian Ocean would necessarily be felt in the canal zone also. If England were to derive the advantages she expected from the canal in the War, she would have to keep the entire route cleared of enemy warships or raiders.

Protection of the canal was provided for in the Convention of 1888, which was in force when the War broke out, subject to the British reservations of 1904.[1] Article IX stated that the Egyptian Government should take the necessary steps for the enforcement of the Convention, and if it lacked the means, should call upon the Ottoman Government. The position of Egypt, however, was anomalous, for while it was juridically a part of the Ottoman Empire, it was actually under military occupation of one of the belligerents. Khedivial authority, therefore, virtually meant British authority. It was further provided by Article IX that intervention by any of the Signatory Powers to protect the canal should wait upon notification from the Ottoman Government. In view of Turkey's sympathies for the Central Powers and her actual participation in the War, the method provided in the Convention for the protection of the canal was obviously unsatisfactory. Furthermore, could the Convention be considered in force if one of the Signatory Powers, Great Britain for example, should begin military operations in the canal zone? In 1887 Lord Salisbury had maintained that if the Convention were broken by

[1] *Cf. supra*, ch. xvii, pp. 306-307.

one of the Signatory Powers, it " would lose its force in all respects, and, consequently, would cease to hinder the territorial Sovereign from availing himself of the assistance of any ally he could obtain." [1]    However, England preferred to regard the Convention as being in force though the War made it impossible to carry out all of its provisions.

The status of Egypt at the outbreak of the War was, as we have suggested, somewhat complicated. The Firman issued by the Sultan on June 1, 1841, had conferred the hereditary Pashalik or Viceroyalty on Mehemet Ali and his successors in return for a yearly tribute of about £360,000. Egypt thus became, from an administrative viewpoint, largely independent of Turkey and this status was indirectly guaranteed by the Powers.[2] Other Firmans issued during the next forty years further defined the position of Egypt. In 1867 and 1873 the Khedive received the right to contract non-political treaties. Yet, Turkish sovereignty was by no means an empty phrase. The Khedive could not legally succeed to office without a Firman of investiture from the Sultan; the Egyptian army was restricted to 18,000 men who, in theory, belonged to the Ottoman forces, and there were many other reminders of Turkey's overlordship.[3]

Theoretically, the British occupation of Egypt did not alter the status of the country, but practically it had important results. While on the surface it appeared that the British Consul-General was merely one of the many foreign diplomatic representatives with no greater authority than his colleagues, in reality he was the power behind the throne. As the agent of the protecting powers he was " the ultimate authority in the country in all those matters . . . which the protecting power chose for the moment to regard

[1] *Egypt no. 1 (1888)*, no. 39, Salisbury to Egerton, Oct. 21, 1887.

[2] Freycinet, *op. cit.*, p. 93.

[3] See Beer, *op. cit.*, pp. 349-355.

as calling for the exercise of its control." [1]　Though the administration was principally in Egyptian hands, there were British advisers [2] in the chief departments and British inspectors, whose opinions could not easily be discarded, attached to the Ministries of Finance and Interior.　In theory Egypt was a constitutional monarchy with a Cabinet, Legislative Council and Assembly; in practice it was a veiled British protectorate.　Moreover, to the restrictions already imposed by Turkish suzerainty and the British occupation, must be added the foreign immunities and jurisdictions within the country, which greatly curtailed Egypt's freedom of action. The Capitulations which gave foreigners exemption from certain taxes and freedom from arrest by local authorities and made them subject to the laws of their own countries; the Debt Commission which until 1904 had extensive powers; and the tariff restrictions—all made Egypt far more dependent on foreign states than upon Turkey. [3]

When the hostilities began, the Khedive, Abbas Hilmi Pasha, was in Constantinople and in his absence the Prime Minister acted as regent.　On August 3rd, the latter proclaimed the neutrality of Egypt, but on the following day he issued a decree announcing that the state of war existing between Great Britain and Germany made it necessary to adopt defensive measures.　These measures recognized the fact that Egypt was a belligerent on the side of Great Britain. [4]

[1] Viscount Milner, *England in Egypt* (London, 1920), p. 30.

[2] The financial adviser was the most important.

[3] Beer, *op. cit.,* pp. 355-370.　*Cf.* Cromer, *op. cit.,* vol. ii, pp. 426-428; Sir Valentine Chirol, *The Egyptian Problem* (London, 1920), pp. 57-64.

[4] As a part of the Ottoman dominions, Egypt had no belligerent or neutral character of its own.　The declaration of war by Great Britain against Germany, however, made Egypt a belligerent against Germany, inasmuch as Great Britain was in military occupation of the country.

For England it was a matter of supreme importance to protect her seaborne trade. A serious attack on that trade would have deprived her industries of raw materials, her people of food, her armies of man-power. Thanks to the superiority of the British navy, most of the enemy shipping was swept from the seas within the first few weeks of the War. There was still danger, of course, from German raiders, submarines and mines, and the greatest vigilance was necessary. The presence in the Mediterranean of the two German cruisers, the *Goeben* and the *Breslau,* caused considerable anxiety until the arrival of these vessels at Constantinople prevented them from interfering with British trade. The cooperation of the French and British fleets in the Mediterranean drove the Austrian and German vessels to shelter and by the middle of August the Mediterranean had become an Allied lake.[1] Not only was the northern approach to the canal thus secured from attacks by enemy warships, but the Allied command of the Red Sea, the Indian Ocean and the Far Eastern waters gave protection from the south.

An immediate danger, however, was the presence of enemy vessels in the canal zone. When hostilities began several German merchant vessels were in Egyptian ports while

(Great Britain, Foreign Office, Peace Handbooks, vol. 23, no. 150, *International Canals,* part iii, p. 77.) Actual conditions determine the state of belligerency or neutrality. "When a place is militarily occupied by an enemy, the fact that it is under his control, and that he consequently can use it for the purpose of his war, outweighs all considerations founded on bare legal ownership of the soil." W. E. Hall, *A Treatise on International Law* (7th ed., Oxford, 1917), no. 174.

[1] Fayle, *op. cit.,* vol. i, p. 65. A convention between France and England on August 6, 1914, provided that the British Mediterranean fleet was to be under the command of the French Admiral, Boué de Lapeyrère, who was charged with the protection of British trade and with keeping the Austrian fleet bottled up in the Adriatic. Sir Julian S. Corbett, *Naval Operations* (4 vols., N. Y., 1920), vol. i, pp. 83-88.

others, including Austrian vessels, sought refuge there later.[1]
The presence of such vessels caused some anxiety to Great
Britain, since they could, by sinking themselves in the channel, render it unnavigable. In order to guard against this
contingency the Egyptian Government, on August 5th,
issued a proclamation providing for the removal of enemy
vessels from the canal zone and giving the British naval
and military forces the right of war in Egyptian ports and
territory.[2] On October 23rd, the British Government made
a further announcement concerning such vessels.

His Majesty's Government have issued a notification in the
following terms to the representatives of foreign maritime
Powers in London, and have asked them to communicate it to
their Governments:

Since the outbreak of war certain ships of enemy countries
have remained in the Suez Canal.

Some of these vessels were detained by the Egyptian Government on account of hostile acts committed in the Canal; some
because there was reason to apprehend that they contemplated
hostile acts; others perfectly free have refused to leave the Canal
in spite of the offer to a free pass, thus disclosing their intention
to use the ports of the Canal merely as ports of refuge, a measure which is not contemplated by the Suez Canal Convention.

His Majesty's Government did not admit the conventional
right of free access to and use of the Canal and its ports of
access for an indefinite time to escape capture, since the obvious
result of permitting any such course must be greatly to incom-

---

[1] The total number of enemy ships detained or seized in the canal zone
was fifteen, having a gross tonnage of 79,018. In addition, 55 German
and Austrian vessels were taken in other ports along the oriental route,
including Aden, the Indian ports, Singapore and the Far Eastern and
Australian ports. Fayle, *op. cit.*, vol. i, p. 128.

[2] See text in *Prize Cases Heard and Decided in the Prize Court during the Great War*, by the Rt. Hon. Sir Samuel Evans, under the general
editorship of A. Wallace Grant (London, 1918), p. 475. Cited as *Prize
Cases.*

mode and even to block the use of the ports of and the Canal by other ships, and they are consequently of opinion that the Egyptian Government are fully justified in the steps which they are taking to remove from the Canal all enemy ships which have been long enough in the Canal ports to show clearly that they have no intention of departing in the ordinary way, and that they are putting the Canal and its ports to a use which is inconsistent with the use of the Canal in the ordinary way by other shipping.[1]

The enemy vessels in the canal zone were immune from capture. Nevertheless, some of them, because they committed breaches of neutrality, were detained by the Egyptian Government. Others were offered a free pass to leave, but since this was not accompanied by a promise of safe conduct, they preferred to remain rather than to risk capture in the Mediterranean. The immunity, however, conferred upon shipping in the canal by the Convention of 1888 did not extend to the use of the canal as a permanent port of refuge. Eventually all the enemy vessels were taken outside the three-mile limit where they were captured by a British cruiser and brought to the Prize Court which the British Government had established at Alexandria on September 30, 1914.

As an additional security the British Government had provided that all enemy vessels should be searched within the three-mile limit to determine if they carried anything on board which might be used to injure the canal. Though this procedure was not in conformity with the Convention, it was approved by Sir Edward Grey, who believed " that the object of the Convention was primarily the protection of the Canal itself." [2]

A number of cases involving German and Austrian vessels

[1] *British and Foreign State Papers*, vol. 108, pt. 2, p. 154.
[2] *International Canals*, p. 83.

were decided by the Prize Court at Alexandria.[1] One German vessel, the *Achaia* of the *Deutsche Levante Linie,* arrived at Alexandria on July 31, 1914 and was given until sunset of August 14th to leave. A pass was offered to Piraeus but since no safe conduct was included, the *Achaia* decided to remain. The Egyptian authorities thereupon seized the vessel and made the captain and crew prisoners of war. The Prize Court held that the *Achaia,* by refusing the pass, had lost the protection afforded by Articles I and II of Convention VI of the second Hague Conference and was thus subject to condemnation as a prize.[2]

Early in August three German merchant vessels arrived at Port Said: the *Barenfels* on the 1st, the *Derflinger* on the 2nd, and the *Gutenfels* on the 5th. On the 14th the *Barenfels* and the *Gutenfels* were offered a pass to sail westward without entering the canal. Refusing this offer since it did not include safe-conduct, they remained at Port Said, and on the 16th were taken outside the three-mile limit and captured by a British warship. A similar capture was made of the *Derflinger.* The Court held that when these vessels arrived at Port Said they were in an enemy port; and " that the Suez Canal Convention, 1888, did not apply to ships which were not seeking a pass through the Canal but only sheltering indefinitely in ports ancillary to it."

The *Concadoro,* an Austrian vessel, arrived at Port Said on August 18th, and on September 22nd was offered safe conduct to Port Sudan and to Basra. As the master of the

---

[1] For details concerning these see *Prize Cases,* pp. 36, 40, 46, 58-59, 64-67, 146-149, 473-476.

[2] Article I of this Convention provides that a merchant vessel belonging to a belligerent Power which is in an enemy port at the beginning of hostilities shall be permitted to leave within a reasonable time and proceed after being furnished with a pass to its port of destination or to any port indicated to it. Article II states that a merchant vessel unable to leave the enemy port within a reasonable period, or not allowed to leave, may not be confiscated. *Cf. Prize Cases,* p. 37.

vessel had not been provided with sufficient funds by the owner to continue the voyage, he refused this offer and announced that he would remain at Port Said until the end of the War. The *Concadoro* was taken outside the territorial waters of Egypt and captured by a British destroyer. The Court, in this case, decided that lack of funds could not be construed as invalidating the acceptance of a pass and condemned the vessel as a prize.

Other German vessels brought before the Prize Court included the *Pindos,* the *Helgoland,* the *Rostock* and the *Südmark.* The first had entered Port Said on August 1st, and as the Captain believed that it was a neutral port, he decided to remain. On October 15th, however, the *Pindos* was captured by the usual procedure. The *Helgoland* passed through the canal and arrived at Port Said on July 30th, before the outbreak of the War. It refused a free pass and was thereupon captured. The *Rostock* arrived at Port Said on July 31st after crossing the canal, and as in the case of the *Pindos,* the captain thought he was in a neutral port and could therefore remain. Like the other vessels, it was captured and brought before the Prize Court. In these cases, the Court was called upon to interpret Article IV of the Convention of 1888.

Whatever questions [said the Court] can be raised as to the parties to and between whom the Suez Canal Convention, 1888, is applicable, and as to the interpretation of its articles, one thing is plain—that the Convention is not applicable to ships which are using Port Said, not for the purposes of passage through the Suez Canal or as one of its ports of access but as a neutral port in which to seclude themselves for an indefinite time in order to defeat belligerents' right of capture after abandoning any intention which there may ever have been to use the port as a port of access in connection with transit through the Canal.[1]

[1] *Ibid.,* p. 149.

The *Südmark* was captured by a British warship 170 miles from Suez on August 15th and taken to Port Said, and later to Alexandria, where it was condemned as a prize. An appeal was taken on the ground that the Prize Court had no jurisdiction since the vessel was captured at sea, and that having been compelled to remain in the canal more than twenty-four hours, this constituted a breach of Article IV of the Convention of 1888. The Court, however, denied this appeal, holding that it had jurisdiction and questioning whether the fact that the *Südmark* had remained in the canal actually constituted a breach of the Convention. The Court maintained that it was not the guardian of the Convention and could not " invent and exact penalties for its non-observance." [1]

The capture of the German and Austrian vessels in the canal zone removed one menace. There was still the possibility of a land attack, though as long as Turkey remained neutral the danger was not immediate. Such precautions as were taken in August 1914 were principally intended to guard against acts of sabotage on the canal. On the 31st the Egyptian Camel Corps was ordered to the canal but was warned not to leave the banks except in the case of a raid.[2] The British force in Egypt at this time numbered only 5000 men and was under the command of Major-General Byng until he was succeeded on September 8th by Sir John Maxwell. Early in September reports reached Egypt of Turkish activities behind the Sinai frontier, and on the 23rd it was announced that armed Bedouins had crossed the frontier near Raffah. The situation became

---

[1] *Ibid.*, p. 477.

[2] Lieut.-General Sir George MacMunn and Captain Cyril Falls, *Military Operations. Egypt and Palestine* (London, 1928), vol. i, p. 13. Cited as *Military Operations. Egypt and Palestine.*

more disquieting during October when it was discovered that the Turks were busy preparing roads in the Sinai Peninsula and that German officers were inspecting frontier posts.[1]

The bombardment of Odessa on October 29th by the *Goeben* and the *Breslau,* the German cruisers which had been purchased some weeks before for the Turkish navy, left no doubt as to Turkey's attitude.[2] Protection of the canal against a land attack now became a matter of immediate necessity. On November 2nd, Sir John Maxwell issued two proclamations. The first declared Egypt to be under martial law; the second announced that the military measures to be taken were intended to supplement the civil administration, not to replace it. A third proclamation on the 6th, stated that " Great Britain takes upon herself the sole burden of the present war without calling upon the Egyptian people for aid therein." [3]

England's declaration of war against Turkey on November 5th rendered the position of the Khedive in relation to the Sultan impossible, and on December 18th, Egypt was proclaimed a British Protectorate.

His Britannic Majesty's Principal Secretary of State for Foreign Affairs gives notice that in view of the state of war arising out of the action of Turkey, Egypt is placed under the protection of His Majesty and will henceforth constitute a British Protectorate.

The suzerainty of Turkey over Egypt is thus terminated, and

---

[1] *Ibid.,* pp. 14-15.

[2] Germany and Turkey had signed an offensive and defensive treaty on August 2, 1914 but this was not known to the Allies. (*Ibid.,* note, p. 16, citing Karl Kautsky, *Die deutschen Dokumente zum Kriegsausbruch,* no. 733).

[3] *The Empire at War,* edited by Sir Charles Lucas (Oxford, University Press, 1926), vol. v, pp. 34-35.

His Majesty's Government will adopt all measures necessary for the defense of Egypt and the protection of its inhabitants and interest.[1]

Another proclamation of the following day announced that the Khedive Abbas Hilmi, who had adhered to the enemy, was deposed in favor of Prince Hussein Kamel Pasha.[2] The new ruler received the title of Sultan of Egypt. The British Consul-General was replaced by a High Commissioner who took over the conduct of Egyptian foreign affairs.

Plans for an attack on the Suez Canal were discussed several months before Turkey officially entered the War. Liman von Sanders, Inspector-General of the Turkish Army, was much opposed to the scheme, for he realized that an invasion of Egypt would involve enormous difficulties.[3]    He gives the following account of a military conference at Constantinople.

In the second half of August when the *Goeben* and *Breslau* had been in port for a while, a military conference took place in Enver's office in which participated the German Ambassador, Admiral Souchon who had come in with the *Goeben*, the military and naval attachés, Enver's chief of staff and other high officers, among them myself.    The question was considered whether action against the Suez Canal would be advisable in case Turkey joined in the War.    The representatives of the navy warmly advocated such a step.    In view of the then existing situation on the German-Austrian front I considered a landing in force of Turkish troops between Odessa and Ackerman

---

[1] *British and Foreign State Papers,* vol. 108, pt. 2, p. 185.

[2] *Ibid.,* p. 186.

[3] General von Sanders was appointed head of the German Military Mission to Turkey in Nov. 1913. For the diplomatic controversy which followed his appointment, see S. B. Fay, *The Origins of the World War* (2 vols., N. Y., 1929), vol. i, pp. 498-524.

more timely as it would take the pressure off the southern wing of the Austrians.

No one shared my views and all were convinced of the great effect produced by a swift descent on Egypt. Neither then nor later could I understand how it could be thought possible to conquer Egypt with the limited means of the Turks and in view of the very poor communications. Having command of the sea the British were able at any time and quickly to ship large forces to Egypt from India, from the colonies or from the mother country. The British positions on the Suez Canal were equipped with every kind of modern arms. Four railway tracks on both sides of the canal and ample rolling stock permitted prompt concentration at threatened points. The effect of the long range guns along the canal, the mighty calibers of the British guns on the war vessels and on the floating batteries on the canal reached far out into the flat desert.

While the British were already in, and based on, Egypt, a Turkish expedition could not reach the canal except by traversing the desert of El Tin requiring at least seven days' marches. For such a march water for men and animals would have to be brought across the desert by camels just as would artillery projectiles. Such an enterprise might come as a surprise and thus be crowned by temporary success, but it never could be of decisive character because any expeditionary force advancing across the desert, unless of great strength, would face destruction. But in the first place how could Turkey with its totally inadequate communications assemble a great force at a base of operation against Egypt and keep supplied there? It seems to me that very hazy ideas must have been entertained at home about the possibility of conquering Egypt. This so called fatal spot of England evidently was the subject of fantastic mischief in Germany and the navy was not without a share in it, though it should be stated in extenuation that the navy was wholly ignorant of the conditions surrounding a land expedition on Turkish soil in Asia.

The highest German authorities immediately received reports of my views, which diverged from those of the leading authorities in that there was but limited chance of success in an Egyptian campaign and that I considered other operations more timely. In consequence the Imperial Chancellor directed me on September 17 through the German Ambassador to put aside my views and on September 17 I received direct telegraphic instructions from the German chief of staff of the field army stating:

' In the common interest an undertaking against Egypt is of great importance. Therefore Your Excellency should subordinate to this idea any doubts you may entertain as to the operations proposed by Turkey.' [1]

This account by the chief German military authority in Turkey is interesting not only for the light it throws on the early discussions of the plan to attack the canal, but also as a presentation of the difficulties opposing its success. Events were to prove that von Sanders was right. The plan, however, appealed strongly to some of the Turkish Ministers, and particularly to Djemal Pasha, the Minister of Marine and Commander of the Second Army. " His vain imagination was fired by the thought of a triumphal entry into Cairo, and he allowed himself to be called ' The Saviour of Egypt.' " [2] In November Djemal was given command of the Fourth Army. Based on Damascus, this army was to attack the canal and at the same time guard the coast of Palestine and Syria. His chief of staff was a middle-aged Bavarian, Oberst Freiherr Kress von Kressenstein, a gallant and courageous fighter and a master of guerilla warfare. A splendid organizer, Kress worked feverishly collecting supplies, purchasing camels and building roads while he made a careful study of the terrain over which the expeditionary force must travel. [3]

[1] Liman von Sanders, *Five Years in Turkey* (U. S. Naval Institute, Annapolis, 1927), pp. 25-27.

[2] Elgood, *Egypt and the Army*, p. 108.

[3] See the article by von Kressenstein, " Überblick über die Ereignisse an

An invasion of Egypt from the East involved enormous difficulties. In the first place, the Turkish railway communications were far from adequate. The Bagdad Railway had not been completed; and there were gaps at the Taurus and Amanus mountain ranges so that no train could get as far as Aleppo; and it was necessary to transfer freight to wagons and trucks when crossing these mountains. From Aleppo the troops were carried over the Syrian and Hedjaz railways to the Palestine border and from there by road to Beersheba, the final point of concentration. There was a noticeable lack of locomotives and rolling stock on the Turkish railways and an insufficient supply of coal.[1] Yet these considerations were overshadowed by the task of negotiating the last stage of the journey, from Beersheba to the canal, a distance of about two hundred miles.

The Sinai Peninsula is a waterless region, almost uninhabitable; mountainous in the south but covered with sand dunes in the north. " Not a cloud is ever seen in the burning sky. With the exception of the dry and stunted scrub in the hollows of the southern mountains, Sinai is dead; cursed by an everlasting thirst; silent with the silence of eternal death." [2] No modern communications were available, the most frequented route being the one along the Mediterranean coast, the " Way of the Philistines," over which Alexander and Napoleon had once brought their armies. But even this was only a camel track. There were two other routes, one to the south through Nekl to Suez;

der Sinaifront von Kriegsbeginn bis zur Besetzung Jerusalems durch die Engländer ende 1927," im *Jahrbuch des Bundes der Asienkämpfer, Zwischen Kaukasus und Sinai* (Berlin, 1921), pp. 11-54.

[1] See Elgood, *op. cit.*, pp. 110-111; *cf.* Hauptman Merkel, " Die deutsche Jildirim-Etappe," in *Jahrbuch des Bundes der Asienkämpfer etc.*, pp. 107-125, gives an account of the difficulties over the Syrian and Palestine lines.

[2] Edmund Dane, *British Campaigns in the Nearer East 1914-1918* (London, 1919), vol. i, p. 42.

and a central route through Hasana to Ismailia. Djemal decided on the last-named since it appeared to have certain advantages for an army. Not only was it safe from attacks on the flanks and, for a considerable distance, from aerial observation, but running for the most part across a broad limestone plateau, it was suitable for cavalry and infantry and for wheel transport as well. There were some sandy places along the way but over these the Turks constructed brushwood tracks. The northern route, on the other hand, was difficult to cross because of the sand, and it was dangerous since it exposed an invading army to the long-range guns of the British fleet stationed in the Mediterranean.[1] The main problem was the water supply but this was solved by Major Fischer, a German officer, who employed 5000 camels to carry the water. Moreover, there were several springs on the way which had been filled by the recent rains and no shortage occurred on the march toward the canal.

The Turkish commander counted upon two elements to achieve victory. First, he would cross the desert unobserved, catch the enemy napping and deliver a surprise attack. In the second place, he expected that his appearance on the banks of the canal would be followed by an uprising of the Egyptian nationalists.[2] As Moslems, they would heed the

---

[1] Kress in his article (p. 15) states that it was this danger which decided Djemal to select the central route. However, Kress himself used the northern passage twice in the following year when he led expeditions into Sinai and without apparent danger. Elgood minimizes the risks of the northern route for an invading army. He points out that the warships opposite the Sinai coast must be well out to sea in order to avoid shallow water. "The effect of their fire, directed from long range and upon minute targets, could have been safely discounted by the Turkish commander or the danger incurred by the troops eliminated by marching them across the exposed stretches after nightfall." He agrees, however, that the choice of the central route was correct in view of the Turkish plan to surprise the enemy. (*Op. cit.,* p. 125.)

[2] Kress, *loc. cit.,* p. 15. *Cf.* Djemal Pasha, *Memories of a Turkish Statesman 1913-1919* (N. Y., 1922), p. 154.

call to a Holy War against the Allies, solemnly proclaimed on November 11, 1914, by the Sheik ul Islam. In both expectations he was to be disappointed. But even if Egypt could not be conquered there still remained one attainable goal. The Turks could force their way over the canal, hold the crossing for a few days, and close it permanently.[1] Once on the other side, moreover, they could capture the fresh-water canals near Ismailia and the British troops, deprived of the water supply, would be compelled to surrender.

In the middle of January 1915 the Turkish expedition of about 20,000 men with nine field batteries and one fifteen-centimeter howitzer, set out from Beersheba in two échelons. The main body was to march toward Ismailia while smaller detachments moved on in the direction of Qantara and Suez. It was hoped that this division of the forces would deceive the enemy as to the main point of attack.[2]

Meanwhile, the British were busy preparing the canal defense. The regular garrison of 5000 men had been replaced in September by a territorial division which was reinforced by troops from India. Later there arrived contingents from Australia and New Zealand, the famous Anzacs, who received their war training in Egypt. By February 1915 there were 70,000 British troops in Egypt but not all were available for the defense of the canal and only the Indian infantry brigades were highly trained.[3] The Canal Defense Force included twenty-four battalions of infantry (Indian), a camel corps, a mountain brigade, twelve mountain guns, a detachment of the Royal Flying Corps and a squadron of French sea-planes.[4] The French sea-planes

---

[1] *Ibid.*, p. 16.  [2] *Ibid.*, p. 12.

[3] *Military Operations. Egypt and Palestine*, vol. i, p. 48.

[4] Elgood, *op. cit.*, p. 118. For the disposition of these units see *Military Operations. Egypt and Palestine*, vol. i, pp. 31-33.

operating from Port Said watched the concentration of the Turkish forces at the frontier towns; while the Royal Flying Corps, operating from Ismailia, observed the march of the enemy in Sinai for a distance of fifty or sixty miles from the canal.[1] In addition to the land forces, the Defense could count upon the assistance of several British and French warships, which entered the canal toward the end of January 1915. The presence of these warships, however, was not without danger, for if one of them was struck by an enemy shell, it would probably sink in the channel and thus block navigation for an indefinite period. Thanks to the failure of the enemy to concentrate his fire on one ship, no mishap occurred.[2] Under the supervision of Major-General A. Wilson, the commander of the Defense Force, the preparations were brought well under way by the end of December.

The line of defense selected was the canal itself. The assistance of the warships made this plan the most feasible, though it was not without defects.[3] The canal had certain advantages for defense. From Port Said to Suez the distance is about one hundred miles, but twenty-two miles are covered by the Bitter Lakes and seven by Lake Timsah, thereby considerably shortening the actual line of defense. The canal zone was divided into three sectors: the northern from Port Said to El Ferdan; the central, from El Ferdan to Deversoir; and the southern, from the Bitter Lakes to Suez.[4] A part of the northern sector was flooded in order further to narrow the line of defense. The fresh-water canal and a lateral railway were at the disposal of the British forces. As soon as the War broke out the Canal Com-

[1] *Ibid.*, p. 120.

[2] *Ibid.*

[3] *Ibid.*, pp. 121-122.

[4] *Military Operations. Egypt and Palestine*, vol. i, p. 23.

pany had organized a watch service and upon the slightest warning, it dragged the channel for enemy mines.[1] As January drew to a close the precautions were increased and the canal was closed each night and reopened in the morning for traffic. The attack was expected at any moment.

The careful preparations of Kress enabled the invaders to cross the desert without much difficulty.[2] In the third week of January small Turkish detachments appeared at various points along the eastern bank of the canal and exchanged fire with the British troops. The latter, occupying trenches on the west bank, awaited the main attack which they knew would be directed against the central sector.[3]

During the night of February 2nd–3rd, in the midst of a heavy sandstorm, the Turkish drive began.[4] The troops advanced toward the canal carrying pontoons and rafts with which they hoped to effect a crossing. The main blow was struck between Tussum and Serapeum while a secondary attack was made in the direction of the Ismailia Ferry Post. The fighting began shortly after three in the morning of the third and continued until the late afternoon. The rapid fire of the defenders compelled the Turks to drop most of their pontoons on the bank of the canal and those which were carried to the water were quickly demolished. Only three of the craft succeeded in crossing to the west bank and these

[1] Georges Douin, *Un épisode de la Guerre Mondiale: l'attaque du Canal de Suez 3 février 1915* (Paris, 1922), p. 30.

[2] The troops marched only at night, partly to avoid the heat, partly to escape detection of British planes; but also because the nights were so cold that it was difficult to sleep without shelter. (Capt. Larcher, " La première offensive contre le Canal de Suez, in *La Revue Maritime*, Oct. 1924, p. 461.)

[3] *Military Operations. Egypt and Palestine*, vol. i, p. 30.

[4] *Ibid.*, pp. 37-46 gives further details of the attack. *Cf.* Kress, *loc. cit.*, Elgood, *op. cit.*, pp. 125-137.

were seized by the British troops. One of the warships, the
*Hardinge,* was disabled, but aside from this, the damage
was slight. The main attack failed completely and the guns
of the warships prevented another offensive. In the other
sectors there was little fighting. During the night of the
3rd, the Turks withdrew from the vicinity of the canal and
began their retreat back through the desert, unpursued by
the British. They had lost 44 officers and 1256 men while
the British casualties totaled only 163.[1] Except for a few
nights and during the day of the third, navigation on the
canal was not interrupted. Smaller engagements directed
by the intrepid Kress took place in the following months
and some attempts were made to plant mines in the canal.[2]

Djemal's plan had miscarried. The expected uprising of
the Egyptians did not materialize nor were the defenders
caught napping. The canal was undamaged and the traffic
went on as before. Indeed, the invasion had accomplished
nothing unless it was to show that a modern army could
cross the Sinai Peninsula. But Djemal refused to be disheartened. He announced to his troops that the invasion
had been intended " solely as a demonstration, partly in
order to make the English realize that we had no idea of
sitting down quietly on the Canal, and partly in accordance
with our design of tying down considerable forces in
Egypt." Otherwise, he declared, no attack would have
been made.[3]

The object of our enterprise had been to carry out an offensive reconnaissance against the Canal with a view to finding out
the resources at the enemy's disposal, and also the resources we

---

[1] The Turkish losses are given in Kress, *loc. cit.,* p. 17, and Djemal
Pasha, *op. cit.,* p. 159; the British casualties in *Military Operations.
Egypt and Palestine,* vol. i, p. 50.

[2] See Kress, *loc cit.,* pp. 18 *et seq.*

[3] Djemal Pasha, *op. cit.,* p. 155.

ourselves should require to effect a crossing of the Canal. As our purpose had been completely attained it was advisable to retire in order to procure better material resources rather than expose ourselves to unnecessary losses.[1]

In December 1915 the British Staff worked out a more elaborate system of defense. Instead of defending the canal upon its banks, the troops were sent into Sinai to prevent a Turkish offensive which was expected to follow the Gallipoli campaign.[2] General Sir Archibald Murray replaced General Sir John Maxwell in command of the forces in Egypt. Fighting took place in the Sinai desert in April and August 1916 but the canal was no longer in actual danger of attack.

Though the Turkish menace to the canal was removed, there now appeared a new danger to British shipping along the oriental route. Events in Gallipoli made the Germans somewhat fearful lest the Allies might break through the Dardanelles and defeat the Turks. For this reason and also because they wished to threaten the British military communications with the East, the Germans began to send their submarines to the Mediterranean. A French cruiser was attacked by a German submarine on May 16, 1915, and about a week later two British warships, the *Triumph* and the *Majestic* were sunk off the entrance to the Dardanelles. Encouraged by these successes, and finding the Mediterranean a favorable place for submarine warfare both on account of the high visibility and the many focal points from which to operate, the Germans in September began to concentrate their efforts in that region.[3] The attacks became more frequent and more disastrous for Allied shipping. During the last three months of the year forty-four British

[1] *Ibid.*, pp. 157-158.

[2] *Military Operations. Egypt and Palestine*, pp. 89-94.

[3] Fayle, *op. cit.*, vol. ii, pp. 108-109. *Cf.* A. Hurd, *The Merchant Navy* (N. Y., 1924), vol. ii, pp. 172-173.

and scores of French and Italian vessels, as well as two
Japanese liners were sunk. By the end of February 1916,
sixty-three British merchantmen, nearly all of them ocean-
going steamers, had been destroyed by submarines in the
Mediterranean.[1]

Such losses aroused grave anxiety in England. Finding
that it would be impossible to afford adequate protection to
merchant vessels in the Mediterranean, the British Admiralty
decided to divert Australian and Far Eastern through-traffic
to the Cape route. On March 7, 1916, instructions were
sent to the War Risks Associations stating that until further
notice no vessel trading between European ports and ports
of 100° E. " should, on a voyage begun on or after March
15th, enter the Mediterranean, unless such vessel should be
sailing in an established service having regular ports of
loading or discharge in the Mediterranean itself." [2] Most
of the traffic through and from Australia and the Far East
was thus diverted to the Cape route. For the time being no
change was made with respect to the Indian trade, which
continued to follow the Suez route not only because the
longer voyage would decrease the carrying power, but also
in view of the inadequate coaling facilities along the Cape
route.[3] Shippers were warned, however, that a further
diversion might follow.

Upon the traffic which still entered the Mediterranean the
submarines continued to take a heavy toll. In April 1916,
nine British ships were destroyed and twenty more during

[1] *Ibid.*, p. 257.

[2] *Ibid.*, p. 258. Under ordinary circumstances, about two-thirds of the
traffic to Australia followed the Cape route, in addition to the shipping to
New Zealand. It was chiefly the mail and passenger traffic which passed
through the canal. Of the traffic from Australia, about 60% used the
Suez route, and this included nearly all the wool and meat trade. (Fayle,
*op. cit.*, vol. i, p. 118. *Cf.* Appendix A.)

[3] *Ibid.*, vol. ii, p. 258.

July and August. By this time, however, most of the vessels employing the Suez route had been equipped with transferable armament.[1] In September the Germans redoubled their submarine activity in the Mediterranean and sunk eighteen British steamers and in the following month forty vessels of all nationalities.[2] The diversion of the Australian and Far Eastern traffic to the Cape route was attended by serious difficulties. The coaling bunkers at Durbar and Cape Town were unable to give adequate service and caused long delays. The shipment of frozen meat from Australia by the long route was not satisfactory.[3] With the inauguration of Germany's unrestricted submarine campaign early in 1917 the Allied shipping losses mounted rapidly. In April fifty-six British and foreign steamers were sunk in the Mediterranean, thirty-six in May and thirty in June. A Through Mediterranean Convoy service was organized in October in order to bring back to the Suez route the Australian and Far Eastern traffic as well as the Indian shipping, a large part of which had been diverted to the Cape route. It was estimated that if the Suez route could be reopened, " the whole priority cargo from India and the Far East could be carried by a fleet of 90 steamers instead of about 130 actually employed, thus setting free 40 liners for work in the North Atlantic or elsewhere." [4]

The first outward convoy sailed from Liverpool on October 3rd with eleven ships but lost two in the Mediterranean. A similar disaster attended the dispatch of the first westbound convoy from Port Said in November, when three of the six vessels were destroyed. However, the convoy system

[1] *Ibid.*, p. 330.
[2] *Ibid.*, pp. 357-358.
[3] *Ibid.*, p. 368.
[4] *Ibid.*, vol. iii, p. 185.

worked more successfully thereafter and the losses were few.[1]

While the German submarine campaign in the Mediterranean did not succeed in stopping the source of supply, yet it did diminish the importance of the Suez route. It was clearly demonstrated that without adequate protection for merchant shipping, the Suez route was unsafe in wartime. But when all is said, its importance to the Allies in the War was very great indeed. Not only did Britain receive much of her raw materials and food supply through the canal but her transports from India, Australia and New Zealand made ample use of it also.[2] On the other hand, the War did much to weaken the argument that the canal is vital to the British Empire. On this point, Sir Frederick Maurice wrote in 1926:

The canal is commonly called in the British press " the vital artery of the British Empire ". That, like most catch phrases, is an exaggeration. The British Empire existed long before the Suez Canal was constructed, and if the canal were to disappear today the British Empire would not therefore collapse. From a military point of view the position of Great Britain as regards the Suez Canal is not unlike her position in regard to the Dardanelles, when there was danger of a Russian fleet issuing through those straits to make a flank attack upon her communications with the East. It would be a matter of vital importance to Great Britain if in time of war a hostile fleet could come through the Suez Canal and the Red Sea to attack her communications across the Indian Ocean, but that again would be pre-

---

[1] That the convoy system in the Mediterranean was a success is indicated by the fact that the 25 outward convoys escorted safely 304 ships of a gross tonnage of 1,868,601 and lost only 6 vessels; the 23 homeward convoys escorted safely 344 ships of a gross tonnage of 2,105,896 and lost only 8 ships. (*Ibid.*, p. 472.)

[2] *Cf.* Hurd, *op. cit.*, vol. ii, pp. 89-96 for the transport of troops through the canal in the first year of the War.

vented more certainly by a British fleet based upon Malta and the British possessions of Perim and Aden at the southern exit of the Red Sea than by a garrison in Egypt. If in war with a Mediterranean naval power the canal were to be closed to both belligerents, either by sabotage or by some other means, the loss to Great Britain would not be great, for with the modern large and fast steamers, troops could be sent to the East by the Cape route more rapidly than they could have been sent by the canal route when de Lesseps had completed his great work. Further, in the event of war against a Mediterranean naval power, the submarine for the employment of which the indented coasts of that Sea are admirably adapted, would almost certainly make traffic between Port Said and Gibraltar so precarious that it would have to be abandoned. For this reason we had during the latter part of the War to rely more and more upon the Cape route.

The Suez Canal is not therefore vital to the British Empire because there is an alternative route to the East which in most circumstances can be more easily secured. The canal is the shortest, cheapest and most convenient route to the East and the Pacific in time of peace, and until conditions in Egypt are more settled than they are today it is advisable to keep a small garrison to protect the canal against sabotage.[1]

[1] "British Policy in the Mediterranean," in *Foreign Affairs* (N. Y., Oct. 1926), vol. v, pp. 111-112.

## CHAPTER XX

### EGYPTIAN INDEPENDENCE AND THE CANAL

THE post-war relations between England and Egypt have been characterized by futile attempts to reconcile conflicting aims. The special position which England claims in Egypt is apparently inconsistent with the complete independence and sovereignty of that country. In all the negotiations which have taken place in recent years England has made it clear that she considers the Suez Canal of such vital importance that its protection must, for the time being, remain in her control. The Egyptians, on the other hand, feel that the defense of that highway should be left to themselves or to the League of Nations.

With the establishment of the British Protectorate on December 18, 1914, Egypt was drawn into the war against Turkey.[1] It was an arrangement to which the Egyptians would not have willingly agreed since they had no particular interest in the European conflict and no great fear of an invasion; and since they were much closer to Turkey in religion and culture than to England, France or Russia. Despite the proclamation of November 6th,[2] which stated that England would take upon herself the sole burden of defense, the Egyptians were soon called upon to contribute their share. The Nationalists, who desired complete independ-

[1] On the Protectorate see the article by Sir M. McIlwraith, "The British Protectorate of Egypt," in *Fortnightly Review*, new series, vol. 107 (N. Y., 1920), pp. 375-383.

[2] *Cf. supra*, ch. xix, p. 335.

ence for Egypt, keenly resented the Protectorate, and the military measures created widespread discontent. Censorship of the press, martial law and restrictions on the Egyptian legislative bodies alienated the intellectuals; while price-fixing of cotton, increase of land rents, requisitions of domestic animals and grains, recruiting for the Egyptian Labor and Camel Transport Corps, and collections for the Red Cross fund made the fellahin restive and resentful.[1] Though such measures were probably necessary at the time, they were not always wisely carried out. Only too frequently the recruiting of native labor and the requisitioning of grains and animals, as well as the collections for the Red Cross fund, were accomplished through indirect pressure. Discontent smoldered beneath the surface but so long as the War lasted the British were able to keep the situation well in hand.

No sooner was the Armistice signed, however, than the Egyptian Nationalists began to agitate for the abolition of the Protectorate and for independence. On November 13, 1918, Zaghlul Pasha, leader of the Nationalists, demanded the right to proceed to London to lay the Egyptian demands before the British Government. At the same time, Rushdi Pasha, the Prime Minister, suggested an official mission to London in order to learn the extent of the Protectorate. The British Foreign Office refused to receive Zaghlul holding that " no useful purpose would be served by allowing Nationalist leaders to come to London," and advised that

---

[1] *Egypt no. 1 (1921)*, Report of the Special Mission to Egypt (cmd. 1131). For further details on the situation in Egypt after the War, see H. J. Carman, " England and the Egyptian Problem," in *Political Science Quarterly*, vol. 36, 1921, pp. 51-78; Sir Valentine Chirol, *The Egyptian Problem* (London, 1920), pp. 120-141, 177-205, 243-259; and by the same author " The Egyptian Question," in *British Inst. of Int. Affairs Journal*, vol. i, pp. 55-71 (London, 1922); H. W. V. Temperley (editor), *A History of the Peace Conference of Paris* (London, 1924), vol. vi, pp. 193-205.

Rushdi's mission should be deferred.[1]  This attitude aggravated an already dangerous situation in Egypt and led to the resignation of Rushdi Pasha.  Early in March 1919, Zaghlul announced his intention of going to Paris to lay the Egyptian demands before the Peace Conference, but he was arrested by the Acting High Commissioner and with three of his colleagues was deported to Malta.  A serious outbreak followed, involving the murder of British officials, arson, looting and open revolt in four of the provinces.  On March 25th, Lord Allenby arrived in Egypt and took immediate steps to remove the sources of unrest.  Zaghlul and his adherents were released from Malta and proceeded to Paris to represent their party at the Peace Conference.[2]

In spite of Lord Allenby's conciliatory measures, disorder continued and in May 1919 the British Government appointed a Special Mission under the chairmanship of Lord Milner which was to proceed to Egypt " to inquire into the causes of the late disorders . . . and to report on existing conditions . . . and the form of the Constitution which, under the Protectorate, will be best calculated to promote its peace and prosperity, the progressive development of self-governing institutions, and the protection of foreign interests."[3]  The Mission delayed its departure until the end of November because of the threatening situation in Egypt and

[1] *Ibid.*  On Dec. 14, 1918, Zaghlul drew up a program of Egyptian aspirations which was approved by the Nationalists.  He demanded complete independence for Egypt with a constitutional form of government and promised that the privileges of foreigners would be scrupulously respected.  Concerning the canal, the program stated that Egypt was " ready to accept any measure which the Powers may regard as useful for safeguarding the neutrality of the Suez Canal."  A translation of the program will be found in F. Vályi, *Spiritual and Political Revolutions in Islam* (London, 1925), pp. 100-101.

[2] The Egyptian delegation received no official hearing at the Peace Conference and its demands were ignored (G. L. Beer, *op. cit.,* p. 402).

[3] *Egypt no. 1 (1921).*

when it arrived at Cairo on December 7th, it was received with open hostility.

In strong contrast with the caution and reserve exhibited by the native official world was the storm of protest and disappointment with which the arrival of the Mission was greeted by the native public and the native press. We had not been many days, or even hours, in Cairo before we had ample evidence of active and organized antagonism. Telegrams poured in announcing the intention of the senders to go on strike as a protest against our presence. . . . The Egyptian vernacular press, with rare exceptions, exhausted the repertory of vituperation and innuendo, proclaiming that any recognition of the Mission would be interpreted as an acceptance of the existing situation and that any Egyptian who had dealings with its members would be guilty of treason to his country.[1]

The Mission returned to England in March 1920 and continued its work. The members were convinced from their study of the Egyptian situation that a settlement should be sought in a treaty of alliance between the two countries according to which Great Britain would protect Egypt against foreign aggression, and in return would retain certain rights, such as maintaining a military force for the safety of the canal, managing Egyptian foreign affairs and exercising a measure of control over Egyptian legislation and administration. The Mission believed " that no settlement would be satisfactory which was simply imposed by Great Britain upon Egypt." [2]

In June Zaghlul and seven of his adherents left Paris and proceeded to London in order to discuss with Lord Milner the possibilities of a settlement. The discussions continued for several weeks and resulted in a memorandum known as the " Milner-Zaghlul Agreement " which was signed on

[1] *Ibid. Cf.* Chirol, *op. cit.,* pp. 260-273.

[2] *Ibid.*

August 18th.  This memorandum stated that the relations
between the two countries must be clearly defined and suggested a treaty by which Egypt would be recognized as independent and would " confer upon Great Britain such rights
as are necessary to safeguard her special interests."  In addition, it contemplated an alliance whereby England would
support Egypt in protecting her territorial integrity, while
Egypt would promise to assist her ally in time of war.[1]  For
the protection of the canal, Zaghlul suggested that a British
force should be stationed in the canal zone, but this was
vetoed by Lord Milner on the ground that it would create
trouble with other Powers.

Moreover, Great Britain's strategic interest in Egypt is not
limited to securing a free passage through the Suez Canal.
' The defense of her Imperial communications ' involves much
more than that.  For Egypt is becoming more and more a
' nodal point ' in the complex of these communications by land
and air as well as by sea.[2]

Lord Milner agreed to recommend the adoption of the
agreement by the British Government while Zaghlul promised to bring it to the attention of his countrymen.  Zaghlul
returned to Paris but four of his colleagues proceeded to
Egypt in order to test the feeling there.  The Egyptian Legislative Assembly was favorably disposed but suggested certain modifications in the agreement.  Negotiations were
thereupon resumed and continued until late in 1921 but without reaching a settlement.  The Egyptians firmly refused to
commit themselves to any treaty so long as the Protectorate
was in existence and they objected to the British claim of
a right to maintain troops in Egypt and to the title of High
Commissioner for the British representative.

[1] *Ibid.*
[2] *Ibid.*

The breakdown of negotiations brought about an *impasse* between the two countries and on November 17, 1921 Lord Allenby warned the British Government that refusal to concede Egyptian independence might lead to the outbreak of a revolution.[1] He urged liberal concessions and declared that no Egyptian would sign a treaty ' which in his view is incompatible with complete independence.'[2] In December the Nationalist agitation became so violent that Lord Allenby arrested Zaghlul and several of his adherents and deported them to Ceylon and later to the Seychelles.[3] Serious outbreaks followed and in January Lord Allenby again suggested to the Foreign Office that the Protectorate be abolished and that Egypt be recognized as an independent State. His suggestion was adopted and on February 28, 1922, the British Government communicated to the Sultan of Egypt the following declaration:

Whereas His Majesty's Government, in accordance with their declared intentions, desire forthwith to recognize Egypt as an independent sovereign State; and

Whereas the relations between His Majesty's Government and Egypt are of vital interest to the British Empire;

The following principles are hereby declared:

1. The British Protectorate over Egypt is terminated, and Egypt is declared to be an independent sovereign State.

2. So soon as the Government of his Highness shall pass an Act of Indemnity with application to all inhabitants of Egypt, martial law as proclaimed on the 2nd November, 1914, shall be withdrawn.

3. The following matters are absolutely reserved to the discretion of His Majesty's Government until such time as it may

---

[1] *Egypt, no. 1 (1922, cmd. 1592)*.

[2] *Ibid.*

[3] Zaghlul was later transferred to Gibraltar, where he remained until his release on April 4, 1923.

be possible by free discussion and friendly accommodation on both sides to conclude agreements in regard thereto between His Majesty's Government and the Government of Egypt:

(a) The security of the communications of the British Empire in Egypt;

(b) The defense of Egypt against all foreign aggression or interference, direct or indirect;

(c) The protection of foreign interests in Egypt and the protection of minorities;

(d) The Soudan.

Pending the conclusion of such agreements, the *status quo* in all these matters shall remain intact.[1]

Though the Protectorate was thus abolished, the independence of Egypt was obviously imperfect in view of the reservations. Independence, moreover, was " not a present fact but a formula which expressed the future intentions " of Great Britain in certain contingencies.[2] It was limited also by the notification which was addressed to the Powers on March 15th. In this the British Government announced that the abolition of the Protectorate " involves no change in the *status quo* as regards the position of other Powers in Egypt ", and that it intended to maintain " as an essential British interest the special relations between itself and Egypt long recognized by other Governments," and would not admit these relations to be questioned by other Powers. Great Britain would " regard as an unfriendly act any interference by another Power in the affairs of Egypt " and would " consider any aggression against the territory of Egypt as an act to be repelled by all means at our command." [3]

---

[1] *Egypt, no. 1* (*1922, cmd. 1592*).

[2] A. J. Toynbee, *Survey of International Affairs 1925*, vol. i, *The Islamic World Since the Peace Settlement* (Oxford Univer. Press, 1927), p. 196.

[3] Text in *Cmd. 1617*. The British Protectorate over Egypt was recognized by Germany in article 147 of the Treaty of Versailles, by

While the Egyptian Government did not officially accept the British Declaration, proclaimed at Cairo on March 15th, it proceeded to act in accordance with its terms.  On the same day Ahmed Fuad Pasha took the title of King, thereby recognizing the independence and sovereignty of his country.[1]  A new constitution was promulgated on April 19, 1923.  In the elections held the following September, the Wafd secured a majority and Zaghlul became the first Prime Minister under the new régime.[2]

The British Declaration was at the most only a half-measure which could hardly satisfy the aspirations of the Egyptian Nationalists for complete independence.  The accession of the Labour Government in January 1924 seemed to indicate that the Foreign Office might follow a more conciliatory policy.  In April Mr. MacDonald invited Zaghlul to visit London and resume the negotiations for a final settlement.  To calm the apprehensions of his colleagues, who

Austria, in article 102 of the Treaty of Saint-Germain, by Hungary in article 86 of the Treaty of Trianon. At the time the Declaration of 1922 was issued, Turkish sovereignty over Egypt still existed juridically since it had not been terminated by any treaty signed by Turkey except in article 101 of the abortive Treaty of Sèvres (Aug. 10, 1920). It was not until 1923 by the Treaty of Lausanne (articles 16, 17, 19) that Turkish sovereignty over Egypt was legally terminated.

[1] Ahmed Fuad was the youngest brother of Hussein, who became Sultan on Dec. 19, 1914 upon the deposition of Abbas Hilmi. When Hussein died in 1917, Ahmed Fuad succeeded him as Sultan. A new dynastic law of April 15, 1922 established succession to the throne by primogeniture, with the provision, however, that in case the King has no male issue, he will be succeeded by his eldest brother. The new law excluded the ex-Khedive Abbas Hilmi from the succession.

[2] Zaghlul was the leader of the Wafd and in a sense its founder. The Wafd or Delegation was organized at the close of the War by the Nationalists in order to present Egypt's case to the Peace Conference. A permanent organization followed, and since it was supplied with ample funds, it soon became the dominant party in the country. (Toynbee, *op. cit.*, pp. 191-192. *Cf.* articles in *The Manchester Guardian*, March 30, 31 and April 1, 6, 1925, by Arthur Ransome).

feared that he might concede too much in order to secure an agreement, Zaghlul declared in the Egyptian Chamber on May 10th that he rejected the Declaration of February 28, 1922, and that he would consider no proposals which did not guarantee the independence of Egypt and the Sudan.[1] After some delays caused by the tension in the Sudan and by an attempt on his life in July, Zaghlul arrived in London on September 23rd and engaged in conversations with Mr. MacDonald. Zaghlul, however, showed an uncompromising attitude and demanded as the price of an agreement: (1) the withdrawal of British troops from Egypt; (2) withdrawal of financial and judicial advisers; (3) no interference by the British Government in Egyptian affairs, particularly in the conduct of foreign relations; (4) renunciation by Great Britain of her claim to protect foreigners and minorities in Egypt; (5) renunciation by Great Britain of her claim to protect the Suez Canal.[2] He suggested that after the withdrawal of the British troops the protection of the canal should be entrusted to the League of Nations.[3] Mr. MacDonald, however, made it clear that British interests in Egypt must be safeguarded.

I raised the question of the Canal straight away because its security is of vital interest to us, both in peace and in war. It is no less true today than in 1922 that the security of the communications of the British Empire in Egypt remains a vital British interest and that absolute certainty that the Suez Canal will remain open in peace as well as in war for the free passage of British ships is the foundation on which the entire defense strategy of the British Empire rests. The 1888 Convention for the free navigation of the Canal was an instrument devised to secure that object. Its ineffectiveness for this purpose was

[1] *Ibid.*, p. 207.

[2] *Cmd. 2269.*

[3] London *Times*, Oct. 21, 1924.

demonstrated in 1914, when Great Britain herself had to take steps to ensure that the Canal would remain open. No British Government in the light of that experience can divest itself wholly, even in favour of an ally, of its interest in guarding such a vital link in British communications. Such a security must be a feature of any agreement come to between our two Governments, and I see no reason why accommodation is impossible given good will.[1]

Zaghlul's unwillingness to recognize England's special interests in Egypt brought an end to the conversations. In November the MacDonald Government was succeeded by the Conservatives under Stanley Baldwin. On the 24th, Sir Austen Chamberlain, the Foreign Secretary, addressed a note to the Secretary-General of the League of Nations in which he called attention to the special position of Great Britain in Egypt as set forth in the Declaration of February 28, 1922, and the situation which might arise if Egypt were to sign the Geneva Protocol for the Pacific Settlement of International Disputes. "In these circumstances," wrote the Foreign Secretary, "His Majesty's Government are unable to admit that the Protocol, if signed by Egypt, will enable the Egyptian Government to invoke the intervention of the League of Nations in settlement of matters absolutely reserved by that declaration to the discretion of His Majesty's Government."[2]

That Egyptian independence was little more than a diplomatic fiction was illustrated more than once after 1922. The assassination at Cairo in November 1924 of Sir Lee Stack, Sirdar of the Egyptian Army and Governor-General

[1] *Cmd. 2269. Cf. Brit. and For. State Papers*, vol. 119, pp. 186 *et seq.* This statement of MacDonald's was made on Oct. 3rd after the question of the canal had been discussed by the Committee of the Imperial Defense on the 2nd. (Toynbee, *op. cit.*, p. 208).

[2] Toynbee, *óp. cit.*, p. 212.

of the Sudan, led Great Britain to adopt measures which certainly could never have been directed against a sovereign independent State. On the 22nd Lord Allenby presented two communications to the Egyptian Government containing severe terms which it was stated must be accepted by the following day. The British Government demanded an indemnity of £500,000 and ordered troops to occupy the customs offices at Alexandria until all the terms had been complied with.[1] Again, in May 1927, Great Britain showed how lightly she held Egyptian independence. The War Committee of the Egyptian Parliament submitted a proposal on May 23rd recommending the cancellation of the usual credits for the Sirdar and the removal of the army control from the latter, who was a British officer, to the Egyptian Minister of War. Sir Austen Chamberlain sent a note to the Egyptian Government on the 30th demanding that the Sirdar's contract be renewed and insisting that the *status quo* be maintained in accordance with the Declaration of February 28, 1922 and until a final settlement could be arrived at. Three British warships were ordered to Egyptian waters. Before such a display of authority the Egyptian Government gave way and on June 21st voted the credits for the Sirdar.[2] Another incident occurred in the following year which served as a reminder to the Egyptians that they were not masters of their own fate. A bill had been drawn up by the Egyptian Parliament on November 22, 1927 regulating public meetings. Considering that this bill would not give adequate protection to foreigners in Egypt, the British Government addressed an ultimatum on April 29, 1928 demanding that the Egyptian Government withdraw the obnoxious bill, and on the next day, ordered five

[1] *Ibid.*, pp. 212-217.

[2] A. J. Toynbee, *Survey of International Affairs 1928* (Oxford Univ. Press, 1929), pp. 238-242.

warships to Alexandria. Once more the Egyptian Government had to surrender to British force.[1]

Meanwhile, the relations between the two countries continued to be governed by the unilateral Declaration of February 28, 1922. Since the failure of the Zaghlul-MacDonald negotiations in 1924 no progress had been made toward a final settlement. In the summer of 1927, King Fuad and his Prime Minister, Sarwat Pasha, visited London where the latter had several conversations with Sir Austen Chamberlain and Lord Lloyd, who had succeeded Lord Allenby as British High Commissioner in May 1925. Both sides seemed disposed to make concessions. But neither Sarwat Pasha nor Sir Austen Chamberlain were free agents, since the former would have to win the approval of the Egyptian Chamber to a settlement and the latter of his colleagues in the British Cabinet. In view of this circumstance, no formal negotiations were contemplated but merely an exchange of opinions. After a series of interviews, however, the two statesmen drew up draft treaties which were in agreement on a number of points.[2]

On August 8th, Sarwat sent his draft to Zaghlul in order to learn if it was acceptable to the Wafd. Unfortunately, Zaghlul was very ill when the draft arrived. His death, on the 23rd was a severe blow to the negotiators, for he was the only Egyptian leader whose approval would have assured a majority in the Chamber.[3] As it was, the attention of his followers was turned away from an Anglo-Egyptian settlement to the internal politics of electing a successor. In September Sarwat returned to Egypt and discussed the proposed treaty with Nahas Pasha, the new leader of the Wafd.

[1] *Ibid.*, pp. 270-275.

[2] Text of Egyptian draft of July 18th and British counter-draft of July 28th in *Egypt np. 1 (1928, Cmd. 3050)*.

[3] Toynbee, *op. cit.*, p. 250.

Leaving Egypt again on October 9th, he arrived in London on the 30th and resumed his conversations with Sir Austen Chamberlain. Early in November they agreed upon the text of a draft treaty which represented the limit each party was willing to go in conceding the wishes of the other. It was sent to Lord Lloyd on the 24th together with a note explaining that it had been accepted by Great Britain after communications with the Dominions and India, and authorized him to sign it on behalf of His Majesty as soon as Sarwat was in a position to sign for the Egyptian Government.[1]

The draft treaty provided for an offensive and defensive alliance. Egypt was not to adopt in foreign countries an attitude which was incompatible with the alliance or liable to create difficulties for Great Britain; and was not " to oppose in foreign countries the policy followed by His Britannic Majesty and not to conclude with a foreign Power any agreement which might be prejudicial to British interests." Great Britain was to use all her influence to secure a modification of the Capitulations and her good offices for the admission of Egypt into the League of Nations. The British representative in Egypt was to be an Ambassador with precedence over all other foreign representatives.

The most important provision of the treaty had to do with the maintenance of a British army in Egypt. Article 7 provided that:

In order to facilitate and secure to His Britannic Majesty the protection of the lines of communication of the British Empire, and pending the conclusion at some future date of an agreement by which His Britannic Majesty entrusts His Majesty the King of Egypt with the task of ensuring this protection, His Majesty the King of Egypt authorizes His Britannic Majesty to maintain upon Egyptian territory such armed forces as His Britannic Majesty's Government consider necessary for

[1] *Egypt no. 1* (*1928, Cmd. 3050*).

this purpose. The presence of these forces shall not constitute in any manner an occupation and will in no way prejudice the sovereign rights of Egypt.

It was agreed that after a period of ten years from the coming into force of the treaty, the two countries would consider the localities where the troops should be stationed and that if no agreement was reached on this point, the matter could be submitted to the Council of the League of Nations. In case the decision of the League was adverse to the claims of the Egyptian Government, the question could be " reinvestigated at intervals of five years from the date of the League's decision."

In an annex attached to the treaty it was stipulated that unless an agreement was made to the contrary, the Egyptian Government would prohibit the passage of aircraft over the territory situated on either side of the Suez Canal, and within twenty kilometers of it, but this prohibition was not to apply to the forces of the contracting parties.[1]

Article 7 proved to be the stumbling block, for Egypt could be convinced of the necessity of maintaining a British force in the country only if it could be shown that the advantages of the treaty were such as to outweigh this disadvantage.[2] Nahas Pasha, the Wafd leader, rejected the treaty on the ground that it " clearly failed to provide for the complete evacuation of Egyptian territory by the British army." [3] On March 4, 1928, Lord Lloyd informed Sir Austen Chamberlain that the Egyptian Cabinet refused to accept the treaty since it " is incompatible with the independence and sovereignty of Egypt and, moreover, that it legalizes occupation of the country by British forces." [4] Sarwat Pasha resigned

[1] *Ibid.*

[2] *Ibid. Cf.* Major E. W. Polson Newman, *Great Britain in Egypt* (London, 1928), pp. 277-278.

[3] *Ibid.*          [4] *Ibid.*, no. 13, telegram, March 4, 1928.

on the same day and was succeeded by Nahas, who announced his intention of maintaining the rights and dignities of Egypt. Difficulties, however, soon appeared within the ranks of the Wafd and on June 25th, Nahas was dismissed, and the King appointed Muhammed Pasha Mahmud to carry on the Government. A Royal Decree of July 19th, dissolved Parliament for three years and Egypt reverted to the former autocratic régime.

To reconcile the British claim to maintain an army in Egypt with the Egyptian desire for complete independence was proving a most difficult task. Protection of the canal was considered of such vital importance to Great Britain that she was unwilling under any circumstances to intrust this to the Egyptian Government alone.[1] British apprehension on this point was clearly seen in the note of Sir Austen Chamberlain, May 19, 1928, replying to Mr. Kellogg's peace proposal. This note declared that there were

certain regions of the world the welfare and integrity of which constitute a special and vital interest for our peace and safety. His Majesty's Government have been at pains to make it clear in the past that interference with these regions cannot be suffered. Their protection against attack is to the British Empire a measure of self-defense. It must be clearly understood that His Majesty's Government in Great Britain accept the new treaty upon the distinct understanding that it does not prejudice their freedom of action in this respect.[2]

[1] *Egypt no. 1 (1928, Cmd. 3050)*, no. 6, Sir Austen Chamberlain to Lord Lloyd, Nov. 24, 1927.

[2] Toynbee, *op. cit.*, p. 20. This reservation which has been called the "British Monroe Doctrine" was understood to apply to Egypt though the note did not specify what regions were included. See J. T. Shotwell, *War as an Instrument of National Policy, and Its Renunciation in the Pact of Paris* (N. Y., 1929), pp. 200-208. It was repeated by the British Government in accepting the definitive Treaty on July 18th, and on Aug. 4th the Secretary-General of the League of Nations was requested to communicate it to the other Member States. (Toynbee, *op. cit.*, p. 21.)

Another attempt to reach a settlement with Egypt was made by the Labour Government which came into office in June 1929. Lord Lloyd, who had been opposed to a conciliatory policy, and who had advocated measures quite at variance with the views of Sir Austen Chamberlain when the latter was Foreign Secretary,[1] was replaced by Sir Percy Lorraine. In the summer of 1929 Mahmud Pasha visited London for a discussion of the reserved points and a series of proposals were agreed to on August 3rd.[2] These provided for an offensive and defensive alliance for twenty-five years, and for England's promise to support the admission of Egypt into the League of Nations and in negotiating with other nations for the abolition of the Capitulations. Great Britain agreed to terminate the military occupation of Egypt but was to be permitted to station troops in the vicinity of the canal to the east of longitude 32° E. The prohibition of the passage of aircraft belonging to other Powers over the territories on either side of the canal and within twenty kilometers of it, was repeated; and the Egyptian Government agreed to give all necessary facilities to British military aircraft in Egypt.

The proposals were in general well received in Egypt but the Wafd refused to support them. With the reestablishment of the parliamentary régime, the Wafd returned to power with Nahas Pasha as Prime Minister. In his speech at the opening of the Egyptian Parliament on January 11, 1930, King Fuad referred to the 1929 proposals and announced that negotiations would be resumed.

His Britannic Majesty's Principal Secretary of State for

---

[1] London *Times,* July 27, 1929.

[2] Text in *Egypt no. 1 (1929, Cmd. 3376). Cf.* Thomas Greenwood, "Britain and Egypt at the Cross-roads," in *Empire Review,* vol. 50, Oct. 1929, pp. 271-282; M. S. Amos, "England and Egypt," in *Nineteenth Century,* vol. 105, 1929, pp. 306-316.

Foreign Affairs has presented to the Egyptian Government proposals which are inspired by a spirit of friendship and conciliation. Our Government will be happy to submit these proposals to you and to undertake negotiations with the British Government in a spirit of conciliation and friendship with a view to a firm and honourable agreement between the two countries.[1]

In March 1930 an Egyptian delegation headed by Nahas Pasha reached London and entered upon negotiations with Mr. Arthur Henderson, the British Foreign Secretary, the Secretary for the Dominions and Colonies, the Secretary for War and the Secretary for Air. The meetings were also attended by Sir Percy Lorraine, British High Commissioner at Cairo, and representatives from Australia, New Zealand and India.[2] A lengthy discussion took place in regard to the defense of the Suez Canal. The Egyptian delegation suggested that the British forces should be concentrated on the east bank of the canal at either Port Fuad or Kantara. These places being considered inadequate by the British negotiators, it was finally agreed that the troops should be stationed on the west bank in the vicinity of Ismailia. A British draft treaty was drawn up on April 17th and submitted to the Egyptian delegation. Nahas refused to accept the treaty without first consulting his colleagues in Cairo and sent a messenger to Egypt with a copy. Upon the latter's return to London, Nahas presented a modified draft to Mr. Henderson on May 5th, and during the night of May 7/8 a new draft was prepared to which both sides agreed. The main point of difference was over the status of the Sudan.[3] Negotiations were terminated on the 11th when the Egyptian delegation announced that they could not accept a treaty unless the British Government modified its position.

[1] *Egypt no. 1 (1930, Cmd. 5735).*

[2] *Ibid.*, for an account of the negotiations.

[3] In article XI of the British draft of April 17th, it was stated that the

The draft of May 7/8 incorporated the provisions which were acceptable to both the Egyptian delegation and the British negotiators. Article XI concerning the Sudan was omitted since no agreement could be reached on this point. In general, this draft was similar to the one of November 1927. Great Britain was permitted to station troops in the neighborhood of Ismailia to cooperate with the Egyptian forces for the defense of the canal; and it was provided that the Royal Air Force depot would be transferred from Abukir to Port Said.[1]

The failure of the London conference of 1930 leaves for the future the settlement of the four reserved points in the British Declaration of February 28, 1922. Agreement having been established on all questions except the Sudan, it is quite likely that a treaty will be concluded before long, especially when one considers the mutual good-will which characterized the recent negotiations in contrast with the mutual suspicion and hostility of earlier years. The present Prime Minister of Egypt, Sidky Pasha, who succeeded Nahas on June 20, 1930, has recently announced among the planks in his platform the complete independence of Egypt, maintenance of sovereignty over the Sudan, and an agreement with England.[2]

But whatever arrangements are concluded with Egypt, it is evident from statements made in the House of Commons that neither the War nor the difficulties which followed have diminished British interest in the canal and determination

*status quo* should be maintained in the Sudan in accordance with the Conventions of 1899, whereas in the Egyptian counter-draft of May 5th, the question of the Sudan was to be reserved for future negotiations. On this question see the article by Pierre Crabites, " The Problem of the Nile," in *Current History,* July 1930, pp. 737-742.

[1] Article VIII.

[2] *Current History,* Jan. 1931, p. 631.

to control this highway to the East.  A few typical utter-
ances may be quoted:

I have the firm conviction that British influence and British
control must be maintained in Egypt not merely in our Imperial
interests—they are obvious, the Suez Canal being truly the neck
of the British Empire and the foreign policy of Egypt being one
that is absolutely essential that we should control—but in the
interests of Egypt herself.[1]

Let me, therefore, say very shortly that in our view the question of Egypt, the question of the Sudan, and the question of the
Canal, form an organic and indissoluble whole and that neither
in Egypt nor in the Sudan, nor in connection with Egypt, is
England going to give up her responsibilities.  British supremacy
exists, British supremacy is going to be maintained, and let
nobody either in Egypt or out of Egypt make any mistake upon
that cardinal principle of His Majesty's Government.[2]

Communication through the Suez Canal, communication
through Egypt is a *sine qua non* having regard to the way in
which communications have developed the cohesion and strength
of the British Empire.[3]

It does not seem to me that there could be any interests more
vital to the British Empire than the preservation of our communications through the Suez Canal.[4]

The recent negotiations have shown that the Labour
Party in England is quite as zealous in safeguarding vital
imperial interests as are the Conservatives.  When Zaghlul Pasha went to London in 1924 he no doubt expected that
Mr. MacDonald would be less imperialistic in his aims and
would more openly support the movement for Egyptian in-

[1] *Hansard's Parl. Debates*, 5th ser., vol. 113, p. 2350, Capt. Ormsby-
Gore, March 20, 1919.

[2] *Ibid.*, vol. 121, p. 771, Mr. Balfour, Nov. 17, 1919.

[3] *Ibid.*, vol. 151, p. 2065, Mr. A. Chamberlain, March 14, 1922.

[4] *Ibid.*, vol. 151, p. 2101, Mr. F. C. Thomson, March 14, 1922.

dependence, but he soon discovered that there was no real change.[1] Mr. MacDonald refused pointblank to adopt Zaghlul's proposal to refer the question of the canal to the League of Nations.[2] In the second Labour Government, Mr. Henderson, the Foreign Secretary, endorsed the Egyptian policy of the Conservatives and announced that " there has been no change ".[3] The British Labour Party, as was said in the House of Commons on May 10, 1928, advocates the internationalization of the Suez Canal.[4] Yet, when Mr. Henderson was asked as to whether the Labour Government was prepared to propose that the Canal should be placed under the League of Nations, he replied: " Free navigation of the Suez Canal is already provided for by the Convention of 1888. His Majesty's Government see no reason to propose the modification of this arrangement." [5] Evidently, the Labourites follow in practice the same principles as the Conservatives where the canal is concerned.[6] The Independent Labour Party, on the other hand, in its Empire programme of February 19, 1926, demanded: " The recognition of the independence of Egypt by the withdrawal of British troops, accompanied by the submission of the issues of the Suez Canal and the Sudan to the League of Nations." [7]

[1] London *Times,* June 30, 1924.

[2] *Cf. supra,* pp. 358-359.

[3] The London *Times,* July 27, 1929. *Cf. Labour Monthly,* vol. ii, no. 10, Oct. 1929, pp. 619-625, "Labour Imperialism in Egypt," J. M. B.

[4] *Hansard's Parl. Debates,* 5th ser., vol. 217, p. 483.

[5] *Ibid.,* vol. 230, p. 403, July 17, 1929.

[6] See *Labour Monthly,* vol. ii, no. 10, Oct. 1929, *loc. cit.; cf. Communist Review,* vol. ii, Feb. 1930, pp. 66-70, "Egypt and the Record of two Labour Governments."

[7] *The New Leader,* Feb. 19, 1926. *Cf. Labour Monthly,* vol. ii, no. 10, Oct. 1929, *loc. cit.,* for further details of the Independent Labour Party's attitude.

The Convention of 1888 which theoretically internationalized the Suez Canal is still in force, as Sir Austen Chamberlain announced in the House of Commons on March 28
1928, subject to " the modifications made when His Maj-
ety's Government adhered to its stipulations in 1904 and
those which result from the termination of Turkish suzerainty over Egypt." [1]    By article 152 of the Treaty of Versailles, " Germany consents in so far as she is concerned, to
the transfer to His Britannic Majesty's Government of the
powers conferred on His Imperial Majesty the Sultan by
the Convention . . ."    Similar declarations were signed by
Austria (Article 107, Treaty of St. Germain), by Hungary
(Article 91, Treaty of Trianon) and by Turkey (Article
109, Treaty of Sèvres and Article 99, Treaty of Lausanne).
The effect of these declarations was to modify articles IX
and X of the Convention.    The first of these articles provides that in case the Egyptian Government should not have
sufficient means to ensure the execution of the Convention
" it shall call upon the Imperial Ottoman Government, which
shall take the necessary measures to respond to such appeal."
By article X the Sultan and the Khedive were permitted to
take certain measures " for securing by their own forces the
defense of Egypt and the maintenance of public order."
This substitution of British for Ottoman authority merely
recognizes a situation which had long existed.    Ever since
the beginning of her occupation of Egypt Great Britain overshadowed Turkish sovereignty in the country and forced the
Sultan more and more into the background.[2]    It was England
and not Turkey, or Egypt, or the Powers, who became the
actual guardian of the Suez Canal.    Though she consented
in 1904 to have the Convention declared in force this did not

[1] *Hansard's Parl. Debates,* 5th ser., vol. 215, p. 1147.
[2] *Cf. supra,* ch. xviii, pp. 312-313.

in practice alter the situation. During the War British control of the canal was illustrated in a most striking manner. The recent negotiations for an Anglo-Egyptian treaty have made it clear that England is unwilling to intrust the defense of this " vital artery " to Egypt or to the League of Nations. The Egyptians are not opposed to permitting British troops in the vicinity of the canal so long as this will not lead to a military occupation of the country.

That England will withdraw her forces altogether from Egypt seems unthinkable. The position of Egypt is of such importance that without its control England can hardly expect to maintain her hold on India. Moreover, " Egypt is the center from which British imperialism can dominate the Sudan, Hedjaz and Arabia, Palestine and Mesopotamia, and from which, too, it can exercise an effective surveillance over the operation of French and Italian imperialism in northern and eastern Africa, to say nothing of the French Syrian Mandate." [1] Great Britain will remain in Egypt, declares Major Newman, " as long as the Suez Canal maintains its political, strategical and commercial significance in the well being of the British Empire." [2] In his view there is no other alternative.

Egypt cannot have her independence and we have no right to call her present status by that name. Owing to the geographic position of their country, the Egyptians are among the peoples of the world who have to bow to circumstances and sacrifice some of the advantages possessed by other nations. As they cannot change the configuration of the earth nor hope to modify the conditions governing British Imperial policy they must accept the unalterable facts of their position. [3]

[1] *Labour Monthly*, vol. iv, no. 5, May 1923, p. 286, " Egyptian Nationalism and the Class Struggle," by G. A. Hutt.

[2] Major E. W. Polson Newman, *The Mediterranean and its Problems* (London, 1927), p. 276.

[3] *Ibid.*, p. 277.

When the War ended, Britain's position in the eastern Mediterranean was stronger than ever before. German influence had disappeared from the Near East; Russia under the Bolsheviks had renounced the imperialist aims of the Tsarist régime; England had a Protectorate over Egypt, mandates over Mesopotamia and Palestine and a sphere of influence in the Arab Kingdom of Hedjaz. The island of Cyprus, annexed on November 5, 1914, was formally ceded to England in the Treaty of Lausanne (Article 20.) Thus the northern approach to the canal was firmly secured while British dominance in the Sudan and the Red Sea afforded ample protection from the south. The internationalization of the Straits and the purchase of a controlling interest in the Bagdad Railway, May 1923, further strengthened the British position in the Near East.[1]

But though England now controlled every approach to India, she was still apprehensive and not without reason. The nationalist ferment in Egypt, Palestine, Arabia and India; the French and Italian aspirations in the Mediterranean; the revival of Anglo-French rivalry in the Near East; made Britain realize that her security was more apparent than real. She learned during the War that the Mediterranean is a long death-trap, unsafe for shipping in view of submarines; while there remains the possibility that in the next conflict aerial attacks might completely demolish the canal and cause the greatest havoc to other parts of her trade routes.

Today England is the first Mediterranean Power. Gibraltar, Malta, Cyprus and Suez as well as Haifa in Palestine command the entire length of that sea. But France holding Corsica, Bizerta, Oran and Algiers and having a mandate over Syria, strategically near the canal, is by no means

---

[1] Earle, *op. cit.*, pp. 334-335.

a negligible factor.[1] Italy, who came out of the War with less than she expected, finds her position in the Mediterranean uncomfortable. As one Italian writer pointed out recently:

Only half of the coasts of France and Spain border on the Mediterranean. If that sea were to be blocked some day, if England were to close Gibraltar and Suez to trade, France and Spain would not perish, for they could still reach the sea, could still seek freedom of action and movement on their Atlantic shores.

But unlike any other great Mediterranean Power, Italy is stretched like a bridge in the very centre of that sea, its waters bathe all her coasts. Not only her liberty but her very life depends on the good will of those who hold the keys of Gibraltar and Suez, of those who have installed themselves, for imperial, not national needs in Malta and Cyprus. More than forty-one millions of Italians could be starved in a few weeks if those who hold the gateways of the Mediterranean were suddenly to decide on hostilities and close those gates to the imports of grain, coal, fuel oils, and iron, of all the raw materials, in short, essential to the life of a modern civilized nation.

In view of her geographical position, which makes her a prisoner in her own sea, her almost complete lack of raw materials, and her ever-expanding population, Italy is today the gravest problem of the Mediterranean.[2]

A future struggle in the Mediterranean would not be an

[1] See article by Major E. W. Polson Newman, " The International Situation. Palestine, Syria and Transjordan. Their Political and Strategical Significance," in *United Service Inst. Journal,* vol. 72, Feb.–Nov. 1927, pp. 851 *et seq.*

[2] Count Antonio Cippico, *Italy, the Central Problem of the Mediterranean* (New Haven, 1926), pp. 31-32. *Cf.* article by Francesco Coppola, " Italy in the Mediterranean," in *Foreign Affairs* (N. Y., June 1923), and by Charles Petrie, " The Balance of Power in the Mediterranean," in *Fighting Forces — a quarterly for the Royal Navy, Army and Air Force,* vol. 3, pp. 376 *et seq.*

improbable event but one can be quite sure that England will hold on to her communications to the bitter end. " The Mediterranean," said Sir Arthur Willert in 1928, " is the strategic center of the Empire. If we lose our freedom of communications through the Straits of Gibraltar and the Suez Canal, the backbone of our imperial policy is severed." [1]

So long as Britain holds India, the canal must remain an important factor in her foreign policy. It seems, indeed, a strange irony of history that the great work of de Lesseps should have come under the control of the very nation whose opposition caused him so many difficulties. Yet, it was in strict accord with England's imperial policy, one might say, with England's manifest destiny. Today she has at her command not only the two great sea-routes of the Cape and Suez, but the London-India air service and a motor transport route from Damascus to Bagdad. This last makes it possible to travel from London to Bombay in sixteen days: by direct train service from London to Constantinople and over the Bagdad and Syrian lines from Haidar Pasha to Damascus; by motor convoy from Damascus to Bagdad and then by rail to Basra, and thence by ship to Bombay. [2] Moreover, there is the proposed railway from Haifa on the Mediterranean, across the Syrian desert to Bagdad, with a possibility that it might someday be carried to India. [3] These new routes will probably cut into the mail and passenger traffic of the canal though they should not seriously affect the freight traffic. But such competition will cause no anxiety in England since she controls all of these approaches to India.

[1] Sir Arthur Willert, *Aspects of British Foreign Policy* (New Haven, 1928), p. 22.

[2] See article by H. E. Crocker, " A new Link in the Chain to India," in *Fighting Forces etc.*, vol. v, April 1928–Jan. 1929, pp. 541-547.

[3] See article by Clair Price, " The Bagdad-Haifa Rail Plan," in *New York Times*, Dec. 14, 1930.

For Egypt, the canal has not been what de Lesseps had predicted and there are many Egyptians who no doubt wish that it had never been constructed.

The gigantic work of the Suez Canal [writes the ex-Khedive, Abbas Hilmi II] worthy of the land which witnessed the colossal undertakings of the mightiest Pharaohs of long-past ages, never fails to strike the imagination; but it should ever be borne in mind that a terrible toll of Egyptian lives was taken in the course of its successful execution . . . Ah! it is true that the Canal has proved highly remunerative to the company which exploits it; but Egypt has never obtained the smallest advantage; on the contrary, the Canal has been the principal cause of Egypt's miseries.[1]

On the other hand, the British imperialist takes a different view and feels that the Egyptians show little gratitude for England's beneficent work. If the Egyptians would only stop to consider, says Major Newman, " what the Canal has done to tie Great Britain to Egypt, without which the country would never have prospered as she has done, they would see that in reality the Suez Canal has been and is an untold blessing to Egypt." [2]

The Suez Canal, a work attempted centuries ago by ancient Egyptians, by Persians and Greeks and Romans and Arabs; advocated by some of the greatest minds of history; and finally executed under the genius of Ferdinand de Lesseps, has not been altogether a blessing. While serving the needs of mankind, promoting civilization and progress and bringing closer the East to the West, it has also been the cause of discord, of international rivalries, of economic imperialism and of war.

[1] Abbas Hilmi II, *A few words on the Anglo-Egyptian Settlement* (London, 1930), p. 33.

[2] *The Mediterranean and Its Problems*, p. 255.

# APPENDIX A

## Shipping Through the Suez Canal

### THE EFFECT OF THE OPENING OF THE SUEZ CANAL ON EASTERN TRADE

The opening of the Suez Canal in November 1869, did not, as some of its ardent champions had predicted, bring about an immediate revolution in commerce. Sailing vessels, then more numerous than steamers, preferred the Cape route where the favorable westerlies of the southern ocean gave them a great advantage. Moreover, the canal was at first merely a long narrow ditch not suitable for all types of vessels and available only in daylight hours. The heavy dues also deterred many vessels from employing the Suez route.

Yet, even from the start there were certain obvious advantages for the canal. It shortened the voyage from Europe to India by 4000 to 5000 miles, or about two weeks' steaming for the fastest vessels of the time. The gain, of course, was greater for the Mediterranean countries than for northern Europe. The trade of France, Italy and Austria with the Indian ports increased very rapidly after 1870. Many steamers of the time were not fitted for long voyages and since they required considerable space for coal, there was less room for cargo. The Suez route offered more coaling stations at shorter intervals, more points of call and better weather conditions than the Cape.[1] With the improvement in shipbuilding during the seventies and particularly the adoption of the compound marine engine, the canal came to be employed more and more regularly and as time went on it was widened and deepened in order to facilitate

[1] For a general discussion of the Suez route and shipping see A. J. Sargent, *Seaways of the Empire* (London, 1918), pp. 26-31.

the passage of larger steamers. The opening of the canal led to a rapid substitution of steam for sail in the British mercantile marine and it caused the scrapping of a large number of vessels and the construction of new ones more suitable for transit through the narrow channel.

> Not only were they [the shippers] compelled to scrap large portions of their fleets, in which enormous sums of money were invested, but at the same moment they had to contend with hosts of new competitors. The Canal ended all that was left of the exclusiveness of the East and the retirement of much of the costly equipment of the older and more successful companies made possible mercantile competition on a new basis.[1]

The canal stimulated the export of Indian goods to Europe and especially to the Mediterranean ports. From 1870 to 1880 the direct trade of France, Italy and Austria with India increased very rapidly while during the same period there was a relative decline in the Indian trade with Great Britain.[2] The export of rice and wheat from India more than doubled in the same period and there was a very noticeable increase in the export of cotton, silk, jute and oil seeds.

Not only was the Indian trade stimulated and a new lease of life given to the shipping of the Mediterranean ports, but the canal also attracted Australian trade. This was especially true of the return voyage from Australia, since rapid shipments were necessary in wool and meat for the London market. Mail and passenger traffic to Australia was also diverted from the Cape. On the other hand, much of the outbound traffic from Europe to Australia continued to employ the Cape route which was about 1000 miles longer than by Suez. This was due primarily to the heavy tolls in the canal, offsetting the advantage of the shorter distance, and also to the construction of larger steamers requiring a smaller proportion of available space for coal than the earlier vessels.

[1] Hoskins, *op. cit.*, p. 419.
[2] Sargent, *op. cit.*, pp. 52-54.

TRAFFIC THROUGH THE CANAL

Traffic through the canal has fluctuated a good deal from the date of its opening, November 17, 1869, to the present. The first two years were rather lean but in 1872 there was an increase of over 100% in the number of transits and in net tonnage. In general, so far as transits were concerned, growth continued after 1872 and through the eighties; there was a stagnation in the nineties, a rather slow growth from 1900 to 1910, a rapid increase from 1911 to 1913, followed by a decline during the War and a rapid rise again after 1918. In tonnage there was a rapid increase in the seventies and eighties, a slower tempo in the nineties when the decennial increase was 40% as compared with 120% for the eighties; a fairly rapid increase from 1900 to 1910, amounting to 70%, and a continued growth to 1912. In 1913 there was a slight falling off from the preceding year and during the War a rapid decline, reaching its lowest point in 1917. A speedy recovery set in after the War and from 1919 to 1929 the increase was 100%, the figure for 1929 being 65% greater than the highest pre-war level. The development of the traffic through the canal for the first twelve years is set forth in the following table: [1]

| *Year* | *Number of Transits* | *Net Tonnage* |
|---|---|---|
| 1870 | 486 | 435,911 |
| 1871 | 765 | 761,467 |
| 1872 | 1,082 | 1,439,169 |
| 1873 | 1,173 | 2,085,072 |
| 1874 | 1,264 | 2,423,672 |
| 1875 | 1,494 | 2,940,708 |
| 1876 | 1,457 | 3,072,107 |
| 1877 | 1,663 | 3,418,949 |
| 1878 | 1,593 | 3,291,535 |
| 1879 | 1,477 | 3,236,942 |
| 1880 | 2,026 | 4,344,519 |
| 1881 | 2,727 | 5,794,401 |

By 1890 the numbers of transits had increased to 3389 and the net tonnage to 6,890,000. By 1900, although the number of

[1] *Bulletin Décadaire,* June 15, 1927.

transits was only 52 more than in 1890, the net tonnage had increased to 9,738,000 or about 40%. The reason for this growth in the tonnage was the increasing size of the vessels using the canal. Again, in 1910, the number of transits was 4538, an increase of about 30% since 1890, while the net tonnage jumped to 16,585,000, a gain of 70%. Since 1912 the traffic through the canal has been as follows: [1]

| Year | Number of Transits | Net Tonnage |
|---|---|---|
| 1912 | 5,373 | 20,275,120 |
| 1913 | 5,085 | 20,035,000 |
| 1914 | 4,802 | 19,409,495 |
| 1915 | 3,708 | 15,266,155 |
| 1916 | 3,110 | 12,325,347 |
| 1917 | 2,353 | 8,368,918 |
| 1918 | 2,522 | 9,251,601 |
| 1919 | 3,986 | 16,013,802 |
| 1920 | 4,009 | 17,574,657 |
| 1921 | 3,975 | 18,118,999 |
| 1922 | 4,345 | 20,743,245 |
| 1923 | 4,621 | 22,730,162 |
| 1924 | 5,122 | 25,109,882 |
| 1925 | 5,337 | 26,761,935 |
| 1926 | 4,980 | 26,060,377 |
| 1927 | 5,545 | 28,962,048 |
| 1928 | 6,084 | 31,905,902 |
| 1929 | 6,274 | 33,466,014 |
| 1930 | 5,761 | 31,700,000 |

### TRAFFIC BY NATIONS: GREAT BRITAIN

As was expected, British shipping through the canal secured first place at the very beginning and has held it ever since. The proportion of British traffic to the total has varied from 60 to 80%. During the first two and one-half years, from November 1869 to June 1872, some 1237 British vessels with a tonnage of 1,294,928 passed through the canal, representing 71% of the total.[2] Ten years later, British shipping accounted for 80% of the total and the proportion averaged about 70% during

[1] Memorandum of the Suez Canal Company, furnished to the author.

[2] Voisin-Bey, *op. cit.*, p. 79.

most of the pre-war period. In 1913 British tonnage through
the canal was nearly four times that of Germany, which had
second place, while in 1920 it was seven times as great as that
of Japan, the latter having won second place.[1] The following
table gives British tonnage through the canal for the nine-year
period from 1912 to 1920:[2]

| Year | British Net Tonnage Through the Canal | Percentage of Total |
|---|---|---|
| 1912 | 12,848,000 | 63 |
| 1913 | 12,052,000 | 60 |
| 1914 | 12,910,000 | 66 |
| 1915 | 11,656,000 | 76 |
| 1916 | 9,788,000 | 71 |
| 1917 | 6,164,000 | 73 |
| 1918 | 7,356,000 | 79 |
| 1919 | 11,355,000 | 71 |
| 1920 | 10,839,000 | 61 |

It will be noticed that while British shipping through the
canal in 1917 was only half that of 1914 it accounted for 73%
of the total. This was due to the disappearance of German and
Austrian ships from the canal. The decrease from 71% of
the total in 1919 to 61% in 1920 is partly explained by the fact
that fewer British transports passed through the canal in the
latter year. In 1927 the number of British vessels using the
canal was 3,085, with a net tonnage of 16,534,455 or 57% of
the total; and in 1928 the number of British vessels increased
to 3,393, the net tonnage to 18,124,074, representing somewhat
over 56% of the total.

The principal British lines employing the canal are the
Ellerman Lines, the Peninsular and Oriental Steam Navigation
Company and the Alfred Holt Company.

A large part of the British traffic passing through the canal
represents Indian trade. The great saving in time by the Suez
route as compared with the Cape explains why the former is
used almost exclusively in this trade.

[1] *Bulletin Décadaire*, March 15, 1921.

[2] *Ibid.*, May 15, 1921.

### THE NETHERLANDS

Dutch shipping through the canal progressed steadily in the years before the War and in 1913 ranked third with 6.4% of the total tonnage.  During the War the Dutch flag almost disappeared from the canal, due to the menace of German submarines, the requisitions of the home Government, and the measures adopted by the Allies.[1]  From December 3, 1917 to December 22, 1918, no Dutch vessel passed through the canal.  By 1920, however, the pre-war level was passed and the Dutch again ranked third with 8% of the total.  Since then the increase has been rapid and in 1927 the Dutch were second with 575 vessels and a net tonnage of 3,024,848.  The following table gives the Dutch net tonnage through the canal for the period from 1911 to 1920:[2]

| Year | Net Tonnage | Year | Net Tonnage |
|------|-------------|------|-------------|
| 1911 | 971,000 | 1916 | 643,000 |
| 1912 | 1,240,000 | 1917 | 126,000 |
| 1913 | 1,287,000 | 1918 | 3,000 |
| 1914 | 1,389,000 | 1919 | 755,000 |
| 1915 | 1,334,000 | 1920 | 1,426,000 |

### FRANCE

French traffic through the canal reached its high point in 1913 when it ranked fourth with 4.7% of the total.  In 1928 France was still fourth with 359 vessels and a net tonnage of 1,926,969.  In the period from 1903 to 1912 French imports from the Orient via Suez increased 80%, from 829,000,000 francs to 1,505,-000,000; while her exports to the Orient *via* Suez during the same period increased 40%, from 217,000,000 francs to 299,-000,000.[3]  The *Cie. des Messageries Maritimes* is the most important of the French lines operating through the canal.  The French net tonnage through the canal from 1911 to 1920 is given below:[4]

[1] *Bulletin Décadaire*, April 15, 1921.

[2] *Ibid.*

[3] "Tableau du commerce de la France", cited in *Bulletin Décadaire*, Aug. 2/3, 1914.

[4] *Ibid.*, March 25, 1921.

| Year | Net Tonnage | Year | Net Tonnage |
|------|-------------|------|-------------|
| 1911 ................. | 820,000 | 1916 ................. | 774,000 |
| 1912 ................. | 799,000 | 1917 ................. | 579,000 |
| 1913 ................. | 928,000 | 1918 ................. | 380,000 |
| 1914 ................. | 800,000 | 1919 ................. | 475,000 |
| 1915 ................. | 666,000 | 1920 ................. | 775,000 |

GERMANY

When the canal was first opened to navigation German traffic amounted to hardly more than 1% of the total.[1]  Indeed, direct trade between Germany and the Orient was almost negligible until the eighties.  In 1876 there was only one German line, the *Deutsche Dampfschiff Reederei,* plying between Hamburg and Shanghai with a fleet of eight vessels, which employed the Suez route.[2]  Six years later, however, the Hansa Company established a service to India *via* Suez largely for the importation of jute; the *Sloman Linie* serving Australia was organized about the same time and had a total of 176,000 net tons in the Suez traffic.  In 1882 German vessels accounted for only 3% of the total traffic through the canal; but with the development of German colonial enterprises there was a noticeable increase.  The *Norddeutsche Lloyd* inaugurated a postal service to Eastern Asia and Australia in 1886 and two years later the *Hamburg-Calcutta Linie* was established, which was later absorbed by the *Hamburg-Amerika Linie.*  Other lines made their appearance in the years immediately following, such as the *Deutsche Ost-Afrika Linie* and the *Deutsche-Australische Gesellschaft,* serving East Africa and Australia respectively.  The *Norddeutsche Lloyd* was at first the most important of these lines operating through the canal, but it was soon surpassed by the *Hansa.*  From 1891 to 1895 German traffic in the canal increased to 7.5% of the total, and this proportion was more than doubled from 1895 to 1913, when it reached 16.7% of the total.  Of Germany's eastern imports before the War, the greater part came from British India, with Australia second, and the Dutch

[1] *Ibid.,* July 2, 1914.
[2] *Ibid.*

Indies third. In exports, however, Japan was first, British India was second and Australia third. From 1907 to 1912 Germany's trade with the East increased 30% but with the exception of her trade with Japan, she imported far more than she sold.[1] During the War no German vessels appeared in the canal, except for a few which arrived at Port Said or Suez at the beginning of hostilities.[2] It was not until 1920 that German shipping employed the canal and since that year its growth has been extraordinarily rapid, as may be seen from the following table:[3]

| Year | Transits | Net Tonnage | Percentage of Total |
|------|----------|-------------|---------------------|
| 1913 ................ | 778 | 3,352,287 | 16.7 |
| 1920 ................ | 3 | 14,777 | 0.8 |
| 1921 ................ | 35 | 170,520 | 0.9 |
| 1922 ................ | 149 | 735,129 | 3.6 |
| 1923 ................ | 247 | 1,213,691 | 5.4 |
| 1924 ................ | 350 | 1,646,872 | 6.6 |
| 1925 ................ | 359 | 1,791,228 | 6.7 |
| 1926 ................ | 424 | 2,153,873 | 8.3 |
| 1927 ................ | 529 | 2,763,783 | 9.6 |
| 1928 ................ | 611 | 3,300,018 | 10.3 |

In 1922 Germany ranked sixth among the nations using the canal; fourth in 1923; third from 1924 to 1928 when her traffic was only slightly less than that of the Dutch.

### JAPAN

The development of Japanese traffic through the canal has been quite astonishing. From 1913 to 1920 this traffic increased nearly 500%. In the former year Japan ranked sixth, with 1.7% of the total tonnage, but by 1919 she had climbed to second, with 9% of the total.[4] While the traffic of Austria[5]

[1] *Ibid.*, based on a German report for 1912.

[2] *Cf. supra*, ch. xix, p. 329.

[3] *Bulletin Décadaire*, July 15, 1928.

[4] *Ibid.*, Jan. 25, 1921.

[5] During the pre-war period Austria ranked fifth among the nations

and Germany showed a decrease of 4,183,000 tons from 1913 to 1920, that of Japan increased 1,258,000 tons. Japan did not continue to make the same progress; in 1928 she ranked sixth with 940,000 net tons. Before the War the *Nippon Yusen Kaisha* line carried most of the Japanese traffic through the canal. Today, a second line, the *Osaka Shosen Kaisha* is rather active, and the two lines combined account for three quarters of the Japanese shipping through the canal.

The reason for the phenomenal increase in Japanese traffic during the War is partly explained by the temporary decline of European shipping *via* Suez due to the exigencies of warfare and particularly to the German submarine campaign in the Mediterranean.[1] Japanese vessels were less exposed to the danger of submarine warfare. While much of the British traffic with Australia and the Far East and even with India was diverted to the Cape, Japan was able to carry goods from these countries *via* Suez. In the Mediterranean, moreover, the Japanese fleet, cooperating with the British and the French fleets, was able to offer protection to Japanese merchant vessels. In other words, the dislocation of British shipping in the last year of the War, and especially the concentration in the Atlantic, redounded to the advantage of Japan. British exports to India were one-third less in 1913 than in 1918; while those from Japan had increased six times in that period.[2] With the return to normalcy, the Japanese were no longer able to compete with British shipping. The following table shows the development of Japanese traffic through the canal from 1910 to 1920:[3]

using the canal. In 1913, 246 Austrian vessels with a net tonnage of 845,830 passed through the canal, while in 1914 the number of vessels was 176 and the net tonnage 631,730. (*Bulletin Décadaire*, July 12, 1914 and June 18, 1915).

[1] *Cf. supra,* ch. xix, pp. 345-348.

[2] Fayle, *op. cit.,* vol. iii, p. 45.

[3] *Bulletin Décadaire*, June 25, 1921.

| Year | Net Tonnage | Year | Net Tonnage |
|------|-------------|------|-------------|
| 1910 ................. | 350,000 | 1916 ................. | 70,000 |
| 1911 ................. | 362,000 | 1917 ................. | 155,000 |
| 1912 ................. | 319,000 | 1918 ................. | 502,000 |
| 1913 ................. | 344,000 | 1919 ................. | 1,449,000 |
| 1914 ................. | 354,000 | 1920 ................. | 1,602,000 |
| 1915 ................. | 566,000 | | |

### THE UNITED STATES

Before the War, few American vessels passed through the Suez Canal. Beginning in 1916 there was the first noticeable increase. The greatest progress, however, came after the organization of the U. S. Shipping Board in 1919. In that year American traffic through the canal was 1% of the total, 4% in 1920, but in 1928 it had fallen to 2%. More than half of the American traffic through the canal was furnished by the Dollar Line and the U. S. Steel Products Company. The following table indicates the net tonnage of American vessels using the canal from 1913 to 1928: [1]

| Year | Net Tonnage | Year | Net Tonnage |
|------|-------------|------|-------------|
| 1913 ................. | 7,400 | 1921 ................. | 672,000 |
| 1914 ................. | 2,500 | 1922 ................. | 668,000 |
| 1915 ................. | 3,400 | 1923 ................. | 613,000 |
| 1916 ................. | 34,700 | 1924 ................. | 795,000 |
| 1917 ................. | 27,600 | 1925 ................. | 811,000 |
| 1918 ................. | 7,600 | 1926 ................. | 710,000 |
| 1919 ................. | 168,000 | 1927 ................. | 682,214 |
| 1920 ................. | 725,000 | 1928 ................. | 729,352 |

### ITALY

In contrast with other countries, Italy made her greatest gains in the canal traffic during the War, in 1917. From 1.5% of the total in 1913, Italian shipping climbed to 9.4% in 1917 and then declined to 3.5% in 1920. The great increase in 1917 is partly explained by the fact that Italy borrowed about 60,000 tons of shipping from Allies in that year. In 1913 most of the Italian

[1] *Ibid.*, Feb. 15, 1921, July 25, 1927 and June 5, 1929.

vessels passing through the canal were employed in the postal service, chiefly to India, but in 1920 the merchant vessels carried 193,000 tons and the postal service 189,000, while Government ships accounted for 162,000.[1]  Italy held fifth place in 1928, with 363 vessels and a net tonnage of 1,649,792.  The table below gives the Italian tonnage through the canal from 1911 to 1920:[2]

| Year | Net Tonnage | Year | Net Tonnage |
|------|-------------|------|-------------|
| 1911 | 202,000 | 1916 | 439,000 |
| 1912 | 368,000 | 1917 | 778,000 |
| 1913 | 291,000 | 1918 | 477,000 |
| 1914 | 369,000 | 1919 | 317,000 |
| 1915 | 363,000 | 1920 | 607,000 |

### RUSSIA

In the pre-war period Russia furnished annually a very stable tonnage which in 1913 amounted to 340,000 tons representing 110 transits and 1.6% of the total.  This traffic was largely from Odessa to Bassorah and Vladivostok.  During the War, Russia's participation declined considerably and has not yet regained the pre-war level.  The following table gives some idea of Russian traffic through the canal in the years immediately following the War:[3]

| Year | Net Tonnage | Year | Net Tonnage |
|------|-------------|------|-------------|
| 1919 | 55,000 | 1921 | 11,000 |
| 1920 | 46,000 | 1922 | 64,000 |

[1] *Ibid.*, Feb. 25, 1921.

[2] *Ibid.*

[3] *Ibid.*, Jan. 15, 1924.  Of the net tonnage for 1922 (64,000) almost two-thirds, or 41,000, represented 12 transits by two Russian vessels.

## PASSENGER TRAFFIC [1]

| Year | Number of Passengers | Year | Number of Passengers |
|------|------|------|------|
| 1870 | 26,758 | 1900 | 282,511 |
| 1871 | 48,422 | 1901 | 270,221 |
| 1872 | 67,640 | 1902 | 223,513 |
| 1873 | 68,030 | 1903 | 196,024 |
| 1874 | 73,597 | 1904 | 210,980 |
| 1875 | 84,446 | 1905 | 252,691 |
| 1876 | 71,843 | 1906 | 353,881 |
| 1877 | 72,822 | 1907 | 243,826 |
| 1878 | 99,209 | 1908 | 218,967 |
| 1879 | 84,512 | 1909 | 213,122 |
| 1880 | 101,551 | 1910 | 234,320 |
| 1881 | 90,524 | 1911 | 275,259 |
| 1882 | 131,068 | 1912 | 266,403 |
| 1883 | 119,177 | 1913 | 282,235 |
| 1884 | 151,916 | 1914 | 391,772 |
| 1885 | 205,951 | 1915 | 210,530 |
| 1886 | 171,411 | 1916 | 283,030 |
| 1887 | 182,997 | 1917 | 142,313 |
| 1888 | 183,895 | 1918 | 105,914 |
| 1889 | 180,594 | 1919 | 527,502 |
| 1890 | 161,353 | 1920 | 500,147 |
| 1891 | 194,467 | 1921 | 295,199 |
| 1892 | 189,809 | 1922 | 275,031 |
| 1893 | 186,495 | 1923 | 246,331 |
| 1894 | 165,980 | 1924 | 263,869 |
| 1895 | 216,938 | 1925 | 269,522 |
| 1896 | 308,243 | 1926 | 286,432 |
| 1897 | 191,215 | 1927 | 340,318 |
| 1898 | 219,554 | 1928 | 317,718 |
| 1899 | 221,332 | 1929 | 325,855 |

### SUEZ AND THE CAPE

For a comparison of the Suez route with the Cape route there are no accurate figures available. As has already been said, the opening of the canal diverted a large part of the Indian trade and some of the Australian and Far Eastern trade as well. In the first years, however, before the rapid substitution of steam for sail had set in and before the improvement in shipbuilding

[1] Statistics furnished by courtesy of the Suez Canal Company.

had made itself felt, the Cape route drew more traffic than the canal. A report of the Board of Trade for December 1882 gives the following figures for 1880, showing the proportion of British imports from India and China by the canal and by the Cape: [1]

|  | By the Canal £ | By the Cape £ |
|---|---|---|
| Jute .......................... |  | 3,967,000 |
| Rice .......................... |  | 3,485,000 |
| Cotton ..................... | 3,270,000 | 1,090,000 |
| Coffee ........... . ......... | 680,000 |  |
| Tea ........................ | 3,060,000 |  |
|  | 7,010,000 | 8,542,000 |

The British traffic with India and China passing through the canal that year was barely 10% of the total British imports and exports. The canal by opening up a direct trade between the Mediterranean countries and the East, caused a loss to the British entrepôt trade. The reexports of oriental products from England to the Continent, especially in raw silk and raw cotton, diminished considerably. The Board of Trade report gives the following conclusion:

> It would seem, also that the effect of the Canal in increasing facilities of communication may not have been on the whole beneficial to the shipowning interests of the United Kingdom, and to some capitalist interests. The shortening of the voyages between Europe and the East is, *pro tanto*, a diminution of the demand for shipping; it is also a diminution of the demand for capital to hold the cargoes in transit between Europe and the East, which would be larger than it now is if the voyages were longer. . . . Probably, if there had been no Canal, there would have been more sailing vessels, involving an equivalent employment of English capital, and labour, which has been wanting in consequence of the Canal.[2]

[1] *Parl. Paper*, Board of Trade, Dec. 1882, Mr. T. H. Farrer. Return "showing what Proportion of the Trade of the United Kingdom with the East goes through the Suez Canal, and what proportion round the Cape; the Proportion of such Trade through the Canal to the whole Foreign Trade of the United Kingdom," etc.

[2] *Ibid.*, p. 8.

Yet, while the canal undoubtedly facilitated the direct trade between the Mediterranean countries and the East, the loss for England was temporary.  From 1875 to 1905 British shipping increased 50% more than the increase of all other flags put together.[1]  The great saving in time and distance by Suez to India naturally diverted all of the Indian trade to this route.

So far as Australia and New Zealand are concerned, there is a choice of routes.  From London to Melbourne the distance is about 1000 miles less by the canal than by the Cape.[2]  The advantage of this saving, however, tends to disappear in view of toll charges through the canal.  In general, something like 75% of the outbound shipping to Australia goes by the Cape while more than half of the return shipping passes through the canal.[3]  This contrast is partly due to the necessity of delivering the wool and meat from Australia as rapidly as possible to the London market; and partly to the desire of the shippers to participate in the mail and passenger traffic of the Mediterranean.  Before the War most of the outbound shipping to Australia *via* the canal was postal—about 50% of the total; but since 1919 this has dropped to 10%.[4]  From 1908 to 1913 the Australian traffic in the canal (including New Zealand, Tasmania and New Caledonia) increased 64% and in the last year amounted to 9.4% of the total traffic through the canal.  The following table shows the development for pre-war and post-war years to 1924.[5]  During the War most of the Australian and Far Eastern traffic was diverted to the Cape route because of the German submarine campaign in the Mediterranean.[6]

[1] Sargent, *op. cit.*, p. 55.

[2] *Ibid.*, pp. 9-31.  L. Hutchinson, *The Panama Canal and International Trade Competition* (N. Y., 1915), ch. ii gives a general discussion of routes and the advantages of each.

[3] *Ibid.*, p. 31.

[4] *Bulletin Décadaire*, Sept. 15, 1921.

[5] *Ibid.*, April 25, 1925.

[6] *Cf. supra*, ch. xix, pp. 345-348.

| Year | Europe to Australia | Australia to Europe |
|------|--------------------:|--------------------:|
| 1908 | 394,000 | 814,000 |
| 1909 | 507,000 | 989,000 |
| 1910 | 544,000 | 1,193,000 |
| 1911 | 574,000 | 1,273,000 |
| 1912 | 604,000 | 1,319,000 |
| 1913 | 621,000 | 1,367,000 |
| 1919 | 1,276,000 | 1,320,000 |
| 1920 | 590,000 | 770,000 |
| 1921 | 739,000 | 1,358,000 |
| 1922 | 735,000 | 1,671,000 |
| 1923 | 742,000 | 1,735,000 |
| 1924 | 870,000 | 1,659,000 |

It will be seen from this table that the shipping *via* Suez from Europe to Australia is inferior to that from Australia to Europe. In 1919, however, the outbound and return shipping was very nearly equal. This was unusual and was probably occasioned by the situation immediately following the War.

To sum up, one can say that the canal is practically the only route to consider so far as trade with India from Europe is concerned, but that a larger part of the outbound shipping to Australia and New Zealand follows the Cape route, while in the return shipping the canal has the advantage. The canal dealt a serious blow to the British entrepôt trade and had an unfortunate effect on some of the British Crown Colonies. No longer situated along the most frequented route to India, Mauritius and St. Helena lost much of their former prosperity, while the latter became of less strategic importance than in the heyday of the Cape route. In 1907 the British garrison was removed and the colony " was reduced to the experiment of finding the revenues of civil government in the sale of postage stamps and a livelihood for its population in the proceeds of eleemosynary bazaars from the sale of needlework." [1]   On the other hand, Ceylon, the Straits Settlements and Hongkong profited greatly by the opening of the canal.

[1] Sir Charles Bruce, *The Broad Stone of Empire. Problems of Crown-Colony Administration. With Records of Personal Experience* (2 vols., London, 1910), vol. ii, p. 404.

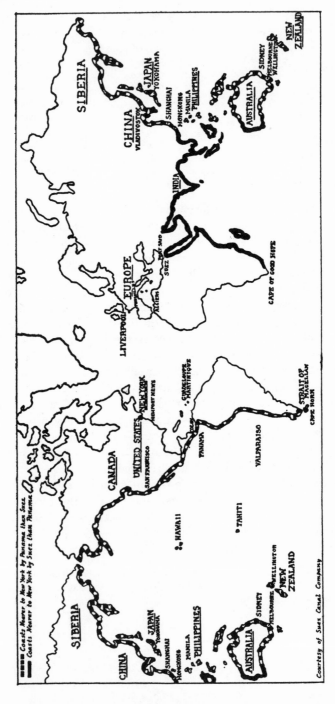

Courtesy of Suez Canal Company

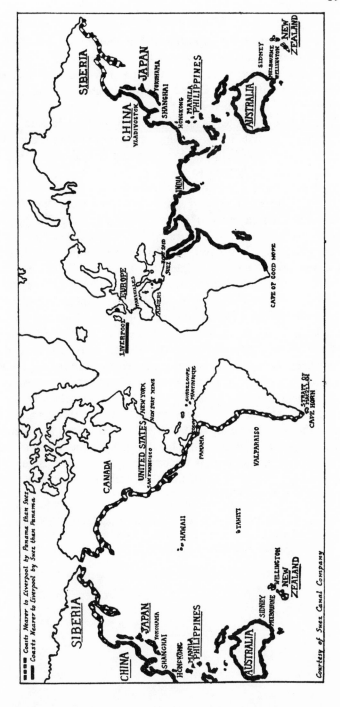

Courtesy of Suez Canal Company

### SUEZ AND PANAMA

Having discussed the importance of the Suez route as a factor in the Eastern trade, we now turn to the effects of the Panama Canal as a competing route. Has the new channel diverted much of the traffic from Suez? To what extent can these two routes be said to compete?

The choice of routes is determined by various factors such as distance, availability of coaling stations and cargo, and the weather. To take distance alone, we can roughly state that it is nearer from Liverpool to the Far East, including Australia, the Philippines and Japan but not New Zealand, by the Suez Canal than by Panama; and that it is nearer from New York to the Far East as far as Hongkong, including the Philippines and the eastern half of Australia, by Panama than by Suez. Thus, we can say in general, that European shipping to the Far East will prefer the Suez Canal to Panama, but will use the latter in trade with Asiatic Russia and the western coasts of North and South America; that American shipping will employ the Panama Canal for all points in the Far East as far as Hongkong and western Australia, and the Suez route for points west of Hongkong, including south China, Indo-China, the Malay Peninsula, India, and the east coast of Africa. However, this does not mean that vessels will necessarily employ a certain route because it is shorter and particularly when the saving in distance is not very great. Where the distance is nearly the same by either route, other considerations may determine the choice. On the other hand, it is none the less true that distance is a very important factor in shipping. The following table shows the saving in distance by each of the routes from London and New York:[1]

---

[1] Sir Charles McLeod and A. W. Kirkaldy, *The Trade, Commerce and Shipping of the Empire* (N. Y., 1924), appendix B, p. 208. (Volume vii of *The British Empire. A survey in 12 volumes,* edited by Hugh Gunn).

|  | Saving via Suez over Panama | Saving via Panama over Suez |
|---|---|---|
|  | (in marine miles) | (in marine miles) |
| London to Freemantle | 5,210 |  |
| New York to Freemantle | 593 |  |
| London to Melbourne | 1,803 |  |
| New York to Melbourne |  | 2,294 |
| London to Sidney | 28 |  |
| New York to Sidney |  | 2,460 |
| London to Wellington |  | 1,077 |
| New York to Wellington |  | 4,597 |
| London to Calcutta | 9,310 |  |
| New York to Calcutta | 4,790 |  |
| London to Singapore | 7,339 |  |
| New York to Singapore | 2,819 |  |
| London to Manila | 4,700 |  |
| New York to Manila | 180 |  |
| London to Hongkong | 4,729 |  |
| New York to Hongkong | 219 |  |
| London to Shanghai | 4,989 |  |
| New York to Shanghai |  | 1,081 |
| London to Yokohama | 1,748 |  |
| New York to Yokohama |  | 2,772 |
| London to Coronel |  | 837 |
| New York to Coronel |  | 3,118 |
| London to Valparaiso |  | 1,417 |
| New York to Valparaiso |  | 3,732 |
| London to San Francisco |  | 5,538 |
| New York to San Francisco |  | 7,853 |

The dividing line in the East between the two routes would seem to be somewhere from Hongkong to Manila. For European trade with eastern Asia, including Australia but not New Zealand, the Panama Canal offers no competition to Suez. The only points where the Panama Canal can compete with Suez are north-eastern Asia, eastern Australia, New Zealand and the west coasts of North and South America.

The Panama Canal was opened to traffic on August 15, 1914. It was closed again for a brief period from the middle of September 1915 to April 1916. The following table shows the net tonnage at Panama and at Suez from 1914 to 1930: [1]

[1] For this table as well as for those which follow and for the discussion

| Year | Panama | Suez |
|------|--------|------|
| | (net tonnage) | (net tonnage) |
| 1914 .......... ................ | 1,302,278 | 19,409,495 |
| 1915 ...... ................ | 3,968,356 | 15,266,155 |
| 1916 ...... ................ .... | 3,933,869 | 12,325,347 |
| 1917 .................. ......... | 6,217,054 | 8,368,918 |
| 1918 ................. .... | 6,408,886 | 9,251,601 |
| 1919 ...... ................. | 6,932,984 | 16,013,802 |
| 1920 ...... ................. | 10,378,265 | 17,574,657 |
| 1921 ............... .... .... | 11,435,811 | 18,118,999 |
| 1922 .......... ............ | 12,992,573 | 20,743,245 |
| 1923 .......... .... ......... | 24,737,437 | 22,730,162 |
| 1924 ................. ........ | 24,411,760 | 25,109,882 |
| 1925 ................ .... | 22,958,158 | 26,761,935 |
| 1926 .......... ........... .. | 25,836,241 | 26,060,377 |
| 1927 .................... ... | 28,610,984 | 28,962,048 |
| 1928 .................. ... | 28,943,437 | 31,905,907 |
| 1929 (6 mos.) ............. | 15,105,283 | 16,853,998 |

It will be noticed that the tonnage at Panama surpassed that at Suez only in 1923 and since that year the Panama traffic has averaged about 10% less than that of Suez. The phenomenal increase from 1922 to 1924 was due to the great traffic in petroleum from California in those years. In the latter year oil tankers accounted for 10,212,000 net tons or 39.1% of the total tonnage. After 1924, however, the importance of this type of traffic diminished and in 1928 accounted for only 6,244,000 tons or 21% of the total. Analyzing the Panama traffic according to its origin and destination, we find the following results for the years 1920 and 1928:

of the effect of the Panama Canal on the Suez Canal, the writer is indebted to the Suez Canal Company for a memorandum entitled *Trafic comparé du Canal de Suez et du Canal de Panama*. For further details on this subject see Hutchinson, *op. cit.*, especially chapter ix and the appendix; and E. W. Zimmerman, *Ocean Shipping* (N. Y., 1922), ch. iii.

| | 1920 | | 1928 | |
|---|---|---|---|---|
| | (tons) | (%) | (tons) | (%) |
| North America: west coast to east coast | 1,064,000 | 10.2 | 10,267,000 | 35.4 |
| Europe to west coast of North America | 909,000 | 8.7 | 6,204,000 | 21.4 |
| Europe to west coast of South America | 1,280,000 | 12.3 | 2,940,000 | 10.2 |
| East coast of North America to west coast of South America .......... | 2,044,000 | 19.6 | 2,815,000 | 9.7 |
| East coast of North America to Far East ........................... | 1,331,000 | 12.8 | 1,810,000 | 6.2 |
| Europe to Australasia .............. | 868,000 | 8.3 | 1,504,000 | 5.2 |
| East coast of North America to Australasia ........................ | 581,000 | 5.5 | 933,000 | 3.2 |
| Total ...................... | 8,077,000 | 77.4 | 26,473,000 | 91.3 |
| Other routes ................ | 2,301,000 | 22.6 | 2,470,000 | 8.7 |
| Total transit via Panama ..... | 10,378,000 | 100. | 28,943,000 | 100. |

From 1920 to 1928, the traffic between the east coast of North America and the Far East *via* Panama increased from 1,331,000 tons to 1,810,000, while the same traffic *via* Suez increased from 665,000 tons to 1,002,000 tons in that period. For the Europe-Australasian traffic in the period 1920 to 1928, the increase at Panama was from 868,000 tons to 1,504,000 tons and at Suez from 1,359,000 tons to 3,401,000 tons. In this route, the Suez Canal obviously has the advantage.

So far as the transit of merchandise is concerned the following table for 1928 will give some idea of the relative importance of the two canals:

| | *Panama* (tons) | *Suez* (tons) |
|---|---|---|
| Mineral oils ................. | 4,728,000 | 3,342,000 |
| Minerals and metals .......... | 2,301,000 | 1,988,000 |
| Wheat ...................... | 2,820,000 | 983,000 |

On the other hand there are some products which figure almost exclusively in the traffic of only one of the canals, as for example, at Panama: timber (3,549,000 tons), nitrate (2,-449,000 tons); at Suez: rice (1,441,000 tons), jute (875,000 tons) and caoutchouc (595,000 tons).

There is a difference in the relative importance of the traffic of the various nations in the two canals as the following table for 1928 shows:

| *Suez* | *Net Tonnage* | *Panama* | *Net Tonnage* |
|---|---|---|---|
| Great Britain ........ | 18,124,074 | United States ........ | 13,752,957 |
| Netherlands ......... | 3,329,628 | Great Britain ........ | 8,976,960 |
| Germany ............ | 3,300,018 | Norway ............. | 1,181,189 |
| France ............. | 1,926,969 | Germany ............ | 995,629 |
| Italy ............... | 1,649,792 | Japan ............... | 909,232 |
| Japan ............... | 940,070 | Netherlands ......... | 644,390 |
| United States ........ | 729,353 | France ............. | 580,769 |
|  |  | Italy ............... | 580,721 |

It is too early to arrive at an accurate determination of the effects of Panama on Suez so far as European trade is concerned, though there are indications that the results will not be altogether favorable to European countries. Before the War, the United States purchased 48% of its imports in Europe and only 16% in Asia. In 1924, however, it purchased 29% of its imports in Europe and 31% in Asia.[1] China, Japan and Australia have purchased more and more in North America since the opening of the Panama Canal and less and less in Europe. Before the War 23% of the total exports of Japan went to Europe but in 1924 this percentage dropped to 6%. It must be borne in mind, however, that the opening of the Panama Canal was only one of the factors, perhaps one of the lesser factors, in this commercial trend.

While the traffic through the Suez Canal has not yet been seriously affected by the Panama Canal, one cannot predict for the future. As one writer has said:

> The United States have expected great results from the saving of distance resulting from the new route. They hope that by using the Panama Canal, and the comparatively cheap coal supplied along that route, American ships will have considerable advantage over European. It must be remembered, however, that there are other considerations which affect the situation. So far as tolls are concerned, this is a matter which can be and has been made satisfactory

[1] *Ibid.*; *cf.* Memorandum of the League of Nations for 1927.

by the American Government, but freights are affected by a number of circumstances, not the least of which is the possibility of continuous freight earning and keeping ships at sea with full cargoes. The Suez route hitherto has presented many solid advantages in this respect. The future will show whether these advantages can be maintained. Then again, the Suez route during its long and successful history has been furnished with a remarkably complete equipment of fuel and repair stations. What the effects of dear coal and the substitution of oil for coal, and the further changes taking place in the type of marine engine will be, remains to be seen. Moreover, whilst there exists any physical condition affecting the certainty of the Panama route, insurance rates may have some influence as to which route shall be selected. The commercial conditions and considerations also come in; and we are only just beginning to realize what previously was known only to experts, that the rates of exchange may have a very great deal to do in deciding which way trade shall flow. In pre-war days there was the difficulty of exchange between gold and silver countries. The position has been complicated by the post-war situation, where some exchanges are backed by neither gold nor silver. Here again it will be necessary to wait and see what the world currency of the future is to be. Moreover, there is the human factor to take into account, human energy, capability, and determination have a curious way of upsetting calculations based on theory. Thus, from many points of view, it is obvious we shall have to wait some decades before we can say for certain whether the great anticipations as to the effect of this new route have been fulfilled.[1]

[1] Sir Charles McLeod and A. W. Kirkaldy, *op. cit.*, vol. vii, pp. 90-91.

# APPENDIX B

## Receipts, Tolls and Shares

The returns of the Company from the operation of the canal have increased enormously since 1869.[1] The receipts for 1870 totaled 5,159,327 francs, but they were 40% more in the following year and nearly 100% larger in 1872 than in 1871. For the first twelve years the returns were as follows:[2]

| Year | Francs | Year | Francs |
|------|--------|------|--------|
| 1870 | 5,159,327 | 1876 | 29,974,998 |
| 1871 | 8,993,732 | 1877 | 32,774,344 |
| 1872 | 16,407,591 | 1878 | 31,098,229 |
| 1873 | 22,897,319 | 1879 | 29,686,060 |
| 1874 | 24,859,383 | 1880 | 39,840,487 |
| 1875 | 28,886,302 | 1881 | 51,274,352 |

After 1881 there was a steady increase, reaching the total of 82 million francs in 1898 and nearly 133 millions in 1912. During the War, there was a decline but a rapid recovery set in after 1919 and in 1927 the receipts totaled 203,966,098 francs. In 1928 the returns given in paper francs, not in gold francs, amounted to 1,057,521,779.[3]

[1] From 1870 to 1927 the receipts increased about 1100%.

[2] Memorandum by courtesy of the Suez Canal Company.

[3] From 1914 to 1928 the receipts have been as follows:

| | | | |
|------|--------|------|--------|
| 1914 | 117,306,612 (francs) | 1921 | 144,492,802 (francs) |
| 1915 | 90,281,441 | 1922 | 162,613,850 |
| 1916 | 76,119,851 | 1923 | 171,961,613 |
| 1917 | 61,076,418 | 1924 | 182,571,582 |
| 1918 | 79,339,542 | 1925 | 189,420,151 |
| 1919 | 136,969,915 | 1926 | 183,866,969 |
| 1920 | 144,593,953 | 1927 | 203,966,098 |
| | | 1928 | 1,057,521,779 (paper fr.) |

### TOLLS

The original toll charge was ten francs per ton on vessels and ten francs for each passenger. In 1873 the Constantinople Tonnage Conference authorized the Company to levy a surtax of three francs per ton on all vessels except warships, transports and vessels in ballast.[1] This surtax was to be reduced by fifty centimes for each increase of 100,000 tons in traffic, so that when the net tonnage reached the figure of 2,000,000 the surtax would be extinguished. In point of fact, the surtax was removed in January 1884.

Moreover, even the normal tolls of ten francs were gradually reduced. By an agreement of November 30, 1883 between the Canal Company and the British Ship Owners, it was provided that beginning on January 1, 1885, the tolls would be reduced on a sliding scale, depending on the revenues, until a minimum of five francs per ton on vessels was reached.[2] Since 1885 the tolls have been as follows:[3]

|  | *Dues* |
|---|---|
| Jan. 1, 1885 to Dec. 31, 1892 | 9 fr. 50 |
| Jan. 1, 1893 to Dec. 31, 1902 | 9 fr. |
| Jan. 1, 1903 to Dec. 31, 1905 | 8 fr. 50 |
| Jan. 1, 1906 to Dec. 31, 1910 | 7 fr. 75 |
| Jan. 1, 1911 to Dec. 31, 1911 | 7 fr. 25 |
| Jan. 1, 1912 to Dec. 31, 1912 | 6 fr. 75 |
| Jan. 1, 1913 to Mar. 31, 1916 | 6 fr. 25 |
| April 1, 1916 to Oct. 4, 1916 | 6 fr. 75 |
| Oct. 5, 1916 to Dec. 31, 1916 | 7 fr. 25 |
| Jan. 1, 1917 to June 30, 1917 | 7 fr. 75 |
| July 1, 1917 to Sept. 30, 1920 | 8 fr. 50 |
| Oct. 1, 1920 to Sept. 30, 1921 | 8 fr. 25 |
| Oct. 1, 1921 to Feb. 28, 1923 | 8 fr. |
| Mar. 1, 1923 to Dec. 31, 1923 | 7 fr. 75 |
| Jan. 1, 1924 to Mar. 31, 1925 | 7 fr. 50 |
| April 1, 1925 to Mar. 31, 1928 | 7 fr. 25 |
| April 1, 1928 to Dec. 31, 1928 | 7 fr. |

[1] *Cf. supra,* ch. xiv, p. 11.

[2] *Cf. supra,* ch. xvi, pp. 22-23 for further details concerning this agreement.

[3] Memorandum by courtesy of the Suez Canal Company.

It will be noticed that the reductions continued until October 1916, when the tolls were increased. The reason for the increase was the abnormal condition caused by the World War. The high figure, eight francs fifty centimes, was maintained until September 1920 and then reduced gradually, twenty-five centimes at a time, until by April 1928 it was seven francs. In January 1929 a further reduction took place of ten centimes, that is, to six francs ninety centimes.[1]

## SHARES

The total number of shares placed on sale in November 1858 was 400,000 at 500 francs each. During the first two years the Company experienced considerable financial difficulty and the shares declined rapidly.[2] In 1872 there began a gradual upward climb and three years later, the shares had passed the par value. From 1870 to 1918, before the depreciation of the franc set in, the increase was about 1800 per cent. The following table gives the average yearly quotation of the shares:[3]

[1] At a meeting of the Board of Directors of the Canal Company, held in Paris on April 13, 1931, a discussion took place concerning a further reduction of the tolls in view of the sharp decline in traffic. During 1930 there was a decrease of about 8% in the number of transits and about 6% in the net tonnage while the receipts fell off about 8%. From January 1 to April 10, 1931, the receipts totaled $15,121,200, a decrease of more than $1,100,000 as compared with the same period in 1930. At the meeting of the Board, some of the members held that by reducing the tolls, vessels using other routes would be attracted to the canal. Others, however, believing that the decline in traffic through the canal is due to the world-wide depression and that it will recover after the end of the depression, opposed a reduction of the tolls on the ground that the canal would not be able to operate at a profit. (Report in the *New York Times*, April 14, 1931).

[2] *Cf. supra*, ch. xiv, pp. 217-220.

[3] Courtesy of the Suez Canal Company.

| Year | 500 franc shares: Price in francs | Year | 500 franc shares: Price in francs |
|------|-----------------------------------|------|-----------------------------------|
| 1870 | 272.86 | 1897 | 3,233.97 |
| 1871 | 208.13 | 1898 | 3,583.37 |
| 1872 | 355.13 | 1899 | 3,620.95 |
| 1873 | 434.93 | 1900 | 3,508.32 |
| 1874 | 422.19 | 1901 | 3,713.67 |
| 1875 | 674.05 | 1902 | 3,923.57 |
| 1876 | 701.63 | 1903 | 3,904.70 |
| 1877 | 677.87 | 1904 | 4,209.50 |
| 1878 | 751.73 | 1905 | 4,461.14 |
| 1879 | 724.40 | 1906 | 4,471.30 |
| 1880 | 1,075.88 | 1907 | 4,552.31 |
| 1881 | 1,975.95 | 1908 | 4,445.94 |
| 1882 | 2,537.24 | 1909 | 4,748.28 |
| 1883 | 2,372.01 | 1910 | 5,330.90 |
| 1884 | 1,967.70 | 1911 | 5,545.56 |
| 1885 | 2,035.39 | 1912 | 6,107.— |
| 1886 | 2,094.43 | 1913 | 5,414.57 |
| 1887 | 2,011.04 | 1914 | 4,866.72 |
| 1888 | 2,168.10 | 1915 | 4,179.50 |
| 1889 | 2,296.09 | 1916 | 4,338.12 |
| 1890 | 2,348.48 | 1917 | 4,444.40 |
| 1891 | 2,660.64 | 1918 | 4,987.26 |
| 1892 | 2,712.88 | 1919 | 5,779.41 * |
| 1893 | 2,674.01 | 1920 | 6,951.01 * |
| 1894 | 2,861.82 | 1921 | 5,981.87 * |
| 1895 | 3,249.10 | 1922 | 6,395.30 * |
| 1896 | 3,347.48 | 1923 | 8,636.84 * |

* Depreciated francs.

A resolution of the General Assembly of Shareholders of June 2, 1924, approved by the Board of Directors on September 1, 1924, doubled the number of shares (from 400,000 to 800,000). Since the capital remained the same, that is, 200,-000,000 francs, the par value of each share was reduced to 250 francs.[1] The increase in the value of these shares is set forth in the following table:

[1] Since two shares were issued for one, the British Government is to-day the owner of 353,204 shares. It has only ten votes in the General Assembly of Shareholders but names three representatives to the Board

| Year | 250 franc shares | |
|------|------------------|---|
| 1924 ............ | 7,857.33 | ⎫ |
| 1925 ............ | 10,425.82 | ⎬ depreciated francs |
| 1926 ............ | 14,015.48 | ⎪ |
| 1927 ............ | 14,250.32 | ⎭ |
| 1928 ............ | 20,225.48 | ⎱ stabilized francs |
| 1929 ............ | 23,605.14 | ⎰ (1 gold franc = 4.92 paper francs) |

of Directors, one of whom is a member of the Directing Committee (Comité de Direction). The British ship-owners choose seven directors, making the British representation ten out of the total of thirty-two directors.

# APPENDIX C

## Question of Renewing the Concession

In 1909 the Canal Company applied to the Egyptian Government for an extension of the Concession for forty years, that is until 2008. The reason for this application, nearly sixty years before the expiration of the old Concession, was that it had been found necessary to enlarge and deepen the canal in order to facilitate the transit of large vessels. For this work the Company would be compelled to contract heavy loans and it was felt that if such loans could be amortized in ninety-nine years instead of fifty-nine, the profits of the shareholders would not be materially reduced and the Company, moreover, would have a share in the profits for another forty years. An agreement was drawn up between the Company and Mr. H. P. Harvey, one of the financial advisers to the Egyptian Government, providing for the renewal of the Concession from November 17, 1968 to December 31, 2008. It was agreed that in the period from January 1, 1969 to December 31, 2008, the profits from the canal were to be shared equally by the Company and the Egyptian Government. In exchange for a renewal of the Concession, the Company promised to pay the Egyptian Government £4,000,000 in four installments, and to turn over to the latter a share of the annual receipts from 1922 to 1968 as follows:

| | |
|---|---|
| 4% from 1922 to 1930 | 10% from 1950 to 1960 |
| 6% from 1931 to 1940 | 12% from 1961 to 1968 |
| 8% from 1941 to 1950 | |

The Egyptian Government was also to have seats on the Board of Directors.[1]

[1] For the full text of this agreement see Ministère des Finances (Égypte), *Recueil des documents concernant le projet de convention avec la Compagnie du Canal de Suez* (Cairo, 1911).

The financial advisers were favorable to the agreement as were the Egyptian Ministers, and there was no reason for submitting the matter to any other authority. However, public interest had been aroused over the negotiations and a section of the Egyptian press began to denounce the Ministers as being too subservient to Great Britain. Under the circumstances, Sir Eldon Gorst, Lord Cromer's successor, decided to submit the matter to the Egyptian Assembly. A commission appointed by the Assembly on February 10, 1910 to study the agreement, rejected it unanimously and on April 9th it was vetoed by the Assembly with only one member voting in favor. "Their vote was intended to be a plain indication of Egyptian hostility towards British domination." [1] The rejection of the agreement aroused a storm of criticism in England, where it was declared that the Egyptians were incapable of self-government.[2] No further attempt was made to secure a renewal of the Concession.[3]

[1] Lieut.-Col. P. G. Elgood, *Egypt and the Army* (Oxford Univ. Press, 1924), p. 30.

[2] See *Hansard's Parl. Debates*, 5th ser., vol. xviii, July 21, 1910.

[3] The ex-Khedive, Abbas Hilmi, is absolutely opposed to a renewal of the Concession and believes that Egypt should make an agreement with England whereby the canal will become Anglo-Egyptian at the expiration of the present Concession (*A few words on the Anglo-Egyptian Settlement*, London, 1930, p. 36).

# APPENDIX D

Convention Between Great Britain, Germany, Austria-Hungary, Spain, France, Italy, The Netherlands, Russia and Turkey, Respecting the Free Navigation of the Suez Maritime Canal. Signed at Constantinople, October 29, 1888 [1]

(Preamble)

### ARTICLE I

The Suez Maritime Canal shall always be free and open, in time of war as in time of peace, to every vessel of commerce or of war, without distinction of flag.

Consequently, the High Contracting Parties agree not in any way to interfere with the free use of the Canal, in time of war as in time of peace.

The Canal shall never be subjected to the exercise of the right of blockade.

### ARTICLE II

The High Contracting Parties, recognizing that the Fresh-Water Canal is indispensable to the Maritime Canal, take note of the engagements of His Highness the Khedive towards the Universal Suez Canal Company as regards the Fresh-Water Canal; which engagements are stipulated in a Convention bearing the date of 18th March, 1863, containing an *exposé* and four Articles.

They undertake not to interfere in any way with the security of that Canal and its branches, the working of which shall not be exposed to any attempt at obstruction.

[1] *Commercial no. 2 (1889, C. 5623).*

### ARTICLE III

The High Contracting Parties likewise undertake to respect the plant, establishments, buildings, and works of the Maritime Canal and of the Fresh-Water Canal.

### ARTICLE IV

The Maritime Canal remaining open in time of war as a free passage, even to ships of war of belligerents, according to the terms of Article I of the present Treaty, the High Contracting Parties agree that no right of war, no act of hostility, nor any act having for its object to obstruct the free navigation of the Canal, shall be committed in the Canal and its ports of access, as well as within a radius of 3 marine miles from those ports, even though the Ottoman Empire should be one of the belligerent Powers.

Vessels of war of belligerents shall not revictual or take in stores in the Canal and its ports of access, except in so far as may be strictly necessary. The transit of the aforesaid vessels through the Canal shall be effected with the least possible delay, in accordance with the Regulations in force, and without any other intermission than that resulting from the necessities of the service.

Their stay at Port Said and in the roadstead of Suez shall not exceed twenty-four hours, except in case of distress. In such case they shall be bound to leave as soon as possible. An interval of twenty-four hours shall always elapse between the sailing of a belligerent ship from one of the ports of access and the departure of a ship belonging to the hostile Power.

### ARTICLE V

In time of war belligerent Powers shall not disembark nor embark within the Canal and its ports of access either troops, munitions, or materials of war. But in case of an accidental hindrance in the Canal, men may be embarked or disembarked at the ports of access by detachments not exceeding 1,000 men, with a corresponding amount of war material.

### ARTICLE VI

Prizes shall be subjected, in all respects, to the same rules as the vessels of war of belligerents.

### ARTICLE VII

The Powers shall not keep any vessel of war in the waters of the Canal (including Lake Timsah and the Bitter Lakes).

Nevertheless, they may station vessels of war in the ports of access of Port Said and Suez, the number of which shall not exceed two for each Power.

This right shall not be exercised by belligerents.

### ARTICLE VIII

The Agents in Egypt of the Signatory Powers of the present Treaty shall be charged to watch over its execution. In case of any event threatening the security or the free passage of the Canal, they shall meet on the summons of three of their number under the presidency of their Doyen, in order to proceed to the necessary verifications. They shall inform the Khedivial Government of the danger which they may have perceived, in order that that Government may take proper steps to insure the protection and the free use of the Canal. Under any circumstances, they shall meet once a year to take note of the due execution of the Treaty.

The last-mentioned meetings shall take place under the presidency of a Special Commissioner nominated for that purpose by the Imperial Ottoman Government. A Commissioner of the Khedive may also take part in the meeting, and may preside over it in case of the absence of the Ottoman Commissioner.

They shall especially demand the suppression of any work or the dispersion of any assemblage on either bank of the Canal, the object or effect of which might be to interfere with the liberty and the entire security of the navigation.

### ARTICLE IX

The Egyptian Government shall, within the limits of its powers resulting from the Firmans, and under the conditions provided for in the present Treaty, take the necessary measures for insuring the execution of the said Treaty.

In case the Egyptian Government should not have sufficient means at its disposal, it shall call upon the Imperial Ottoman Government, which shall take the necessary measures to respond to such appeal; shall give notice thereof to the Signatory Powers of the Declaration of London of the 17th March, 1885; and shall, if necessary, concert with them on the subject.

The provisions of Articles IV, V, VII, and VIII shall not interfere with the measures which shall be taken in virtue of the present Article.

### ARTICLE X

Similarly, the provisions of Articles IV, V, VII, and VIII, shall not interfere with the measures which His Majesty the Sultan and His Highness the Khedive, in the name of His Imperial Majesty, and within the limits of the Firmans granted, might find it necessary to take for securing by their own forces the defense of Egypt and the maintenance of public order.

In case His Imperial Majesty the Sultan, or His Highness the Khedive, should find it necessary to avail themselves of the exceptions for which this Article provides, the Signatory Powers of the Declaration of London shall be notified thereof by the Imperial Ottoman Government.

It is likewise understood that the provisions of the four Articles aforesaid shall in no case occasion any obstacle to the measures which the Imperial Ottoman Government may think it necessary to take in order to insure by its own forces the defense of its other possessions situated on the eastern coast of the Red Sea.

### ARTICLE XI

The measures which shall be taken in the cases provided for by Articles IX and X of the present Treaty shall not interfere with the free use of the Canal. In the same cases, the erection of permanent fortifications contrary to the provisions of Article VIII is prohibited.

### ARTICLE XII

The High Contracting Parties, by application of the principle of equality as regards the free use of the Canal, a principle which forms one of the bases of the present Treaty, agree that none of them shall endeavour to obtain with respect to the Canal territorial or commercial advantages or privileges in any international arrangements which may be concluded. Moreover, the rights of Turkey as the territorial Power are reserved.

### ARTICLE XIII

With the exception of the obligations expressly provided by the clauses of the present Treaty, the sovereign rights of His Imperial Majesty the Sultan and the rights and immunities of His Highness the Khedive, resulting from the Firmans, are in no way affected.

### ARTICLE XIV

The High Contracting Parties agree that the engagements resulting from the present Treaty shall not be limited by the duration of the Acts of Concession of the Universal Suez Canal Company.

### ARTICLE XV

The stipulations of the present Treaty shall not interfere with the sanitary measures in force in Egypt.

### ARTICLE XVI

The High Contracting Parties undertake to bring the present Treaty to the knowledge of the States which have not signed it, inviting them to accede to it.

### ARTICLE XVII

The present Treaty shall be ratified, and the ratifications shall be exchanged at Constantinople, within the space of one month, or sooner, if possible.

In faith of which the respective Plenipotentiaries have signed the present Treaty, and have affixed to it the seal of their arms.

Done at Constantinople, the 29th day of the month of October, in the year 1888.

# APPENDIX E

Section I—Bibliography for the Period to 1870

UNPUBLISHED MATERIAL

Archives Affaires Étrangères. Paris.
  Correspondance Consulaire, le Caire, volumes 24, 25, 26.
  Correspondance Consulaire, Alexandrie, cartons 1812-1817; 1818-1820.
  Turquie: Mémoires et Documents, volumes 7, 8, 145, 170, 172.
  Égypte: Dépêches Politiques, volumes 18-36 (1846-1866).
  Correspondance Politique Turquie, volumes 305-366 (1851-1866).
Archives Nationales. Paris. Marine: cartons B7, 51; BB4, 1036.
Public Record Office. London.
  State Papers, Turkey, volumes 52, 53, 55.
  F. O. Turkey, volume 3.
  F. O. Egypt, volume 1.
  Volumes on the Suez Canal:
      FO 97/411, Suez Canal, 1833-1851, vol. 1.
      FO 78/1156, Suez Canal, 1854-1855, vol. 2.
      FO 78/1340, Suez Canal, 1856-1857, vol. 3.
      FO 78/1421, Suez Canal, 1858, vol. 4.
      FO 78/1489, Suez Canal, 1859, vol. 5. This includes a "Memorandum of Correspondence respecting the Suez Canal projected by M. Lesseps. Confidential. Printed for the use of the Foreign Office. Dec. 28, 1859."
      FO 78/1556, Suez Canal, 1860, vol. 6. Included in this volume is the "Substance of Correspondence respecting the 'Suez Canal,' moved by Mr. Duff, M.P., Feb. 18, 1860."
      FO 78/1715, Suez Canal, 1861-1862, vol. 7.
      FO 78/1795, Suez Canal, Jan.-April, 1863, vol. 8.
      FO 78/1796, Suez Canal, April-Dec., 1863, vol. 9.
      FO 78/1849, Suez Canal, Jan.-Sept., 1864, vol. 10.
      FO 78/1895, Suez Canal, Jan.-Mar., 1865, vol. 12.
Haus, Hof und Staatsarchiv. Vienna.
  For the period from 1854 to 1870 and from 1842 to 1854 the documents include consular reports from Alexandria and Cairo, and diplomatic reports from London, Paris and Constantinople. There are also dispatches from the Minister of Foreign Affairs at Vienna and from the Ministers of Finance and Commerce. The consular reports from Alexandria and Cairo are listed as: Admin. Registraeur, Fach. 13, Suez Canal, 1842-1869.

The diplomatic reports from London, Paris and Constantinople are listed with the place and year, as for example: London, 1857. The abbreviation used in citing documents from the Haus, Hof und Staatsarchiv in the text is: HHSA.

## PRINTED DOCUMENTS

*Parliamentary Papers.* Egypt no. 20 (cmd. 3734, 1883).

*Livre Jaune. Affaires Étrangères. Documents Diplomatiques,* vol. 5 (1864) ; vol. 8 (1867).

*British and Foreign State Papers,* volumes 55, 56.

Hertslet's *Commercial Treaties,* volume ii.

Baron I. de Testa, *Recueil des Traités de la Porte Ottomane avec les Puissances étrangères depuis le premier traité conclu en 1536 . . . jusqu'à nos jours* (6 vols., Paris, 1864), vol. i.

Compagnie Universelle du Canal Maritime de Suez, *Notice et Renseignements Généraux* (2ème partie, Paris, 1926). This contains concessions, statutes and various conventions of the Canal Company.

## PARLIAMENTARY DEBATES

*Hansard's Parliamentary Debates,* 3rd ser., vols. cxlvi, cl, House of Commons.

## SECONDARY SOURCES

### Books

Anderson, Arthur, *Communications with India, China, etc. . . . Observations on the Practicability and Utility of opening a Communication Between the Red Sea and the Mediterranean by a Ship Canal through the Isthmus of Suez* (London, 1843).

Aristotle, *Meteorologica,* Eng. trans. by E. W. Webster (Oxford, 1923).

Ashley, E., *The Life of Henry John Temple Viscount Palmerston, 1846-1865* (2 vols., London, 1878), vol. ii.

Avenel, le Viscomte G.d', *Richelieu et la monarchie absolue* (2nd ed., 4 vols., Paris, 1895), vol. iii.

Baldwin, George, *View of the advantages and the possibility of pursuing, by the navigation of the Red Sea to Suez, a commerce between India and Egypt* (London, March 22, 1776, Brit. Mus., Add. Mss 29210 Fos. 422-424).

——, *Political Recollections relative to Egypt; Containing Observations on its Government under the Mamelukes; its Geographic Position; its intrinsic and extrinsic Resources;—Its relative Importance to England and France; also its Dangers to England in the Possession of France; with a Narrative of the Ever-Memorable British Campaign in the Spring of 1801* (London, 1801).

Bertrand, A., and Ferrier, E., *Ferdinand de Lesseps, Sa Vie, Son Oeuvre* (Paris, 1887).

Borde, P., *L'Isthme de Suez* (Paris, 1870).

Bourdon, Claude, *Anciens canaux, anciens sites et ports de Suez. Ouvrage publié sous les auspices de Sa Majesté, Fouad I, Roi d'Égypte.* Société Royale de Géographie d'Égypte (Cairo, 1925). Mémoires de la Société Royale de Géographie d'Égypte, tome vii.

Breasted, J. H., *A History of Egypt* (N. Y., 1916).

——, *Ancient Records of Egypt* (Chicago, 1906), vols. ii, iii, iv.

Bridier, L., *Une famille française—les de Lesseps* (Paris, 1900).

Brugsch-Bey, H., *Egypt under the Pharaohs* (new ed., London, 1891).

Butler, A. J., *The Arab Conquest of Egypt and the Last Thirty Years of the Roman Dominion* (Oxford, 1902).

*Cambridge Ancient History,* vol. ii, ch. vii; vol. iv, chs. i, iv.

*Cambridge Modern History,* vol. viii, ch. xix.

Capper, James, *Observations on the Passage to India Through Egypt. Also by Vienna Through Constantinople to Aleppo, and from thence by Bagdad and directly across the Great Desert to Bassora* (London, 1785).

Cecil, A., *British Foreign Secretaries, 1807-1916* (London, 1927).

Charlesworth, M. P., *Trade-routes and Commerce of the Roman Empire* (Cambridge, 1924).

Charrière, E., *Négociations de la France dans le Levant* (4 vols., Paris, 1860), vol. iv.

Chesney, Lieut.-Col. F. R., *The Expedition for the Survey of the Rivers Euphrates and Tigris . . . carried on by orders of the British Government in the years 1835, 1836 and 1837* (4 vols., London, 1852).

——, *Narrative of the Euphrates Expedition* (London, 1858).

Cromer, the Earl of, *Modern Egypt* (two vols. in one, N. Y., 1916).

De Lesseps, Ferdinand, *Lettres Journal et Documents pour servir à l'histoire du Canal de Suez* (5 vols., Paris, 1875-1881). Cited by series, each volume one series: i (1854, 1855, 1856); ii (1857, 1858); iii (1859, 1860); iv (1861, 1862, 1863, 1864); v (1864-1865, 1866, 1867, 1868, 1869).

——, *Mémoire présenté au Conseil d'État . . . Exposé des faits relatif à la Mission* (Paris, May, 1849).

——, *Percement de l'Isthme de Suez . . . Exposé et documents officiels* (Paris, 1855).

——, *British opinions on the Isthmus of Suez Canal. Inquiry into the opinion of the Commercial Classes of Great Britain on the Suez Canal* (London, 1857).

——, *Recollections of forty years.* Trans. by C. B. Pitman (two vols. in one, N. Y., 1888).

*Description de l'Égypte, ou receuil des observations et des recherches qui ont été faites en Égypte, pendant l'expédition de l'armée française; publié par les ordres de Napoléon le Grand* (10 vols., Paris, 1809-1822), vol. i: État moderne, pp. 21-185, " Mémoire sur la communication de la mer des Indes à la Méditerranée par la Mer Rouge et l'Isthme de Soueys" by J. M. Le Père.

Dubois, M., and Terrier, A., *Un siècle d'expansion coloniale, 1800-1900* (Paris, 1902).

Fitzgerald, P., *The Great Canal at Suez, its political, engineering and financial history* (2 vols., London, 1876).

Fortescue, J. W., *A History of the British Army* (London, 1906), vol. iv: 1789-1801.

Freycinet, C. de, *La Question d'Égypte* (2nd ed., Paris, 1905).

Georgi, Dr. and Dufour-Feronce, A., *Urkunden zur Geschichte des Suezkanals* (Leipzig, 1913).

Great Britain. Foreign Office. Historical Section. *Peace Handbooks,* vol. xi, no. 66: " France and the Levant" (London, 1921).

Hasenclever, A., *Geschichte Aegyptens im 19 Jahrhundert, 1798-1914* (Halle, 1917).

Herodotus, *History.* Editor C. Hude (2nd ed., Oxford, 1913-1914).

——, *The Egypt of Herodotus,* second book entitled *Euterpe* (London, 1924, New Aldine Lib., no. 4).

——, *The History of Herodotus.* Trans. by G. Rawlinson (London, 1858), ii.

Hoskins, H. L., *British Trade Routes to India* (New York, 1928).

Husny, H., *Le Canal de Suez et la politique Égyptienne* (Thesis, University of Montpellier, 1923).

Jonquière, Marquis de la, *L'Expédition d'Égypte, 1798-1801* (5 vols., Paris, 1899-1907), iii.

James, W., *The Naval History of Great Britain* (6 vols., London, 1902), ii.

Köster, A., *Schiffahrt und Handelsverkehr des alten Orient* (Leipzig, 1924).

——, *Das antike Seewesen* (Berlin, 1923).

Lane-Poole, S., *The Life of the Right Honourable Stratford Canning— Viscount Stratford de Redcliffe. . . From his Memoirs and Private and Official Papers* (2 vols., London, 1888), ii.

Lee, A. L., *Lord Stratford de Redcliffe—A Sketch* (1897, no place given).

Leibnitz, *Oeuvres de Leibniz . . . publiés pour la première fois d'après les manuscripts originaux, avec notes et introduction,* par A. Foucher de Careil, vol. v: *Project d'expédition d'Égypte . . . présenté à Louis XIV* (Paris, 1864).

*Lettres, Introductions et Mémoires de Colbert. Publiés d'après les ordres de l'Empéreur,* par Pierre Clément (nine vols. in seven, Paris, 1861-1870), ii.

Martin, B. Kingsley, *The Triumph of Lord Palmerston . . . A Study of Public Opinion in England before the Crimean War* (London, 1924).

Mascrier, Abbé le, *Description de l'Égypte. Contenant plusieurs rémarques sur la géographie ancienne et moderne de ce Païs, sur les monumens anciens, sur les moeurs, les coutumes, et la religion des Habitans, sur le gouvernement, et le commerce, etc., etc. Composé sur les mémoires de M. de Maillet, ancien Consul de France au Caire*, par M. l'Abbé le Mascrier (Paris, 1735).

Maunier, R., *Bibliographie économique, juridique et sociale de l'Égypte moderne, 1798-1916* (Cairo, 1918). An excellent bibliography on the Suez Canal.

Micard, E., *Le Canal de Suez et le génie Français* (Paris, 1922).

*Napoléon Inconnu: — Papiers inédits (1786-1793)*. Edited by Frederick Masson and Guido Biagi (2 vols., Paris, 1895), II.

Naville, E., *The Store-City of Pithom and the Route of the Exodus* (London, 1888).

Nourse, J. E., *The Maritime Canal of Suez* (Washington, 1884).

Pémeant, G., *L'Expédition et la politique française* (Paris, 1909).

Pingaud, L., *Choiseul-Gouffier: la France en Orient sous Louis XVI* (Paris, 1887).

Pliny, *The Natural History of Pliny*. Eng. trans. by J. Bostock and H. T. Riley (London, 1855), ii.

Plutarch, *Plutarch's Lives*. Englished by Sir Thomas North (London, 1898-1899), ix.

Puyjalon, J. de, *L'Influence des Saint-Simoniens sur la réalisation de l'Isthme de Suez et des chemins de fer* (Paris, 1926).

Raimondi, J., *Le désert orientale Égyptien—du Nile à la Mer Rouge* (Mémoires de la Société Royale de Géographie d'Égypte, tome iv, Cairo, 1923).

Rapson, E. J., (editor), *The Cambridge History of India* (6 vols., Cambridge), vol. i: *Ancient India* (1922).

Rawlinson, H. G., *Intercourse Between India and the Western World from the Earliest Times to the Fall of Rome* (Cambridge, 1916).

Ritt, O., *Histoire l'Isthme de Suez* (2nd ed., Paris, 1869).

Rostovtzeff, M., *The Social and Economic History of the Roman Empire* (Oxford, 1926).

——, *History of the Ancient World* (2 vols., Oxford, 1926), i.

Roux, J. C. T., *L'Isthme et le Canal de Suez: Historique état actuel* (2 vols., Paris, 1901).

Roux, F. Charles-, *Les origines de l'expédition d'Égypte* (2nd ed., Paris, 1910).

——, *L'Angleterre, l'Isthme de Suez, et l'Égypte au XVIIIe siècle . . . Autour d'une route* (Paris, 1922).

——, *L'Angleterre et l'expédition française en Égypte* (Ouvrage publié sous les auspices de Sa Majesté, Fouad I, Roi d'Égypte. Société Royale de Géographie d'Égypte, 2 vols., Cairo, 1925).

Saint-Simon, *Oeuvres de Saint-Simon et d'Enfantin,* vol. ix: *Notices historiques* (Paris, 1866).

Savary des Bruslons, Jacques, *Le parfait négociant ou instruction générale pour ce qui régarde le commerce* . . . (2nd ed., Paris, 1679).

Silvestre, H., *L'Isthme de Suez, 1854-1869* (Paris, 1869).

Smith, G. Barnett, *The Life and Enterprises of Ferdinand de Lesseps* (2nd ed., London, 1895).

Sorel, Albert, *L'Europe et la Révolution française,* vol. vi: 1800-1805 (Paris, 1903).

Strabo, *Strabo's Geography.* Trans. by H. C. Hamilton and W. Falconer (London, 1854-1857).

Tott, Baron de, *Mémoires du Baron de Tott sur les Turcs et les Tartares* (4 vols., Amsterdam, 1784), iv.

Vandal, A., *L'Odyssée d'un ambassadeur: les voyages du Marquis de Nointel, 1670-1680,* (2nd ed., Paris, 1900).

Volney, C. F., *Voyage en Syrie et en Égypte* . . . *pendant les années 1783, 1784 et 1785* (2 vols., Paris, 1787), i.

——, *Considérations sur la guerre actuel de Turcs* (Londres, 1788).

Waghorn, Lieut. Thomas, *Egypt as it is in 1837* (London, 1837).

——, *Egypt as it is in 1838* (London, 1838).

——, *Particulars of an overland Journey from London to Bombay by way of the Continent, Egypt and the Red Sea* (London, 1831).

Ward, Sir A. W. and Gooch, G. P., *The Cambridge History of British Foreign Policy, 1783-1919* (3 vols., N. Y., vol. iii: 1866-1919 (1923).

Warmington, E. H., *The Commerce between the Roman Empire and India* (Cambridge, 1928).

### Articles

*Académie des inscription et belles lettres* (Paris, 1913, pp. 454-463), " Carte topographique et archéologique de l'Isthme de Suez," by J. C. Barthoux.

*Académie des sciences morales et politiques* (vols. 130 and 131, Paris, 1888, 1889), "Louis XIV et l'Égypte," by A. Vandal.

*Bulletin de l'Institut français d'archéologie orientale* (vols. 16, 17, 21, 22, 23, Cairo, 1919-1921), "Notes sur l'Isthme de Suez," by Jean Clédat.

Daremberg, C. and Saglio, E., *Dictionnaire de antiquités grecques et romans d'après les textes et les monuments,* vol. ii, pp. 1331 *et seq.,* article "fossa" by de la Blanchère.

*Edinburgh Review,* vol. 209, Jan., 1856, article on the Suez Canal.

*Journal British Archeological Association,* vol. 33, 1877, "Suez canals from the most ancient times to the present," by J. W. Grover.

Pauly-Wissowa, W. O., *Realenzyklopedie*, vol. viii, p. 1660.
*Religion Saint-Simonienne. Politique industrielle* (Paris, 1832), "Système de la Méditerranée," by M. Chevalier.
*Revue d'Égypte*, an iii, pp. 205-224 (Cairo, 1896), " Mémoire sur l'Égypte, 9 fév. 1798," by Charles Magallon.
*Revue des Deux Mondes*, July 15, 1841, pp. 215-235, " L'Isthme de Suez. Le canal des deux mers sous les Grecs, les Romains et les Arabes," by J. A. Letronne.
——, Jan. 1, 1844, " Projets de percement de l'Isthme de Panama et l'Isthme de Suez," by M. Chevalier.
——, vol. x, May 1, 1855, pp. 480-536, " Le canal des deux mers d'Alexandrie à Suez, moyens d'exécution," by Paulin Talabot.
*Revue de l'histoire des colonies françaises*, vol. xvii, 1924, 11ème trim., " L'Isthme de Suez et les rivalités Européens au XVI siècle," by François Charles-Roux.
——, vol. xvii, 1925, 3ème trim., " Le projet française de commerce avec l'Inde par Suez sous le règne de Louis XVI," by the same author.

SECTION II—BIBLIOGRAPHY FOR THE PERIOD FROM 1870

UNPUBLISHED MATERIAL

Public Record Office. London.
FO 78/2170, Suez Canal, 1869-1870.
FO 78/2432, Suez Canal, Aug.-Dec., 1875, vol. 38.
FO 78/2540, Suez Canal, Dec., 1875-July, 1876, vol. 39.
Haus, Hof und Staatsarchiv. Vienna.

Ägyptische Frage, fasc. $\dfrac{XXXI}{24}$, $\dfrac{XXXI}{26}$. Cited as HHSA, Ägyptische Frage, vol.

PUBLISHED SOURCES

Board of Trade, *Annual Statement of the Navigation and Shipping of the United Kingdom*.
*British and Foreign State Papers*, vol. 108.
*British Documents on the Origins of the War, 1898-1914*. Edited by G. P. Gooch and Harold Temperley (London, 1927-1929), vols. i, ii, iii, iv, v.
Compagnie Universelle du Canal Maritime de Suez, *Bulletin Décadaire*. Cited as *Bulletin Décadaire*. Serial.
*Die grosse Politik der europäischen Kabinette, 1871-1914. Sammlung der diplomatischen Akten des Auswärtigen Amtes*, vols. iv, viii, xi, xiv, xvii, xviii, xix, xxv. Cited as *Die grosse Politik*.
France. Ministère des Affaires Étrangères, *Documents Diplomatiques. Affaires d'Égypte*, vols. 46, 47, 104.

——, Commission de publication des documents relatifs aux origines de la guerre de 1914, *Documents Diplomatiques Français (1871-1914),* 1re sér., vols. i, ii (Paris, 1930) ; 3e sér., vol. i (Paris, 1929).

*German Diplomatic Documents, 1871-1914.* Selected and translated by E. T. S. Dugdale (4 vols., London), vol. i (London, 1928) ; Bismarck's Relations with England, 1871-1890.

*Hansard's Parliamentary Debates,* 3rd ser., vols. 211, 219, 227, 231, 260, 273, 281 ; 4th ser., vols. 61, 120, 121, 130 ; 5th ser., vols. 18, 113, 121, 151, 179, 215, 217, 230, 242.

Ministère des Finances (Égypte), *Recueil des documents concernant le projet de convention avec la Compagnie du Canal de Suez* (Cairo, 1911).

*Parliamentary Papers,* various numbers.

*Statistical Abstract for the United Kingdom, 1900-1914* (London, 1925), 62nd number.

SECONDARY SOURCES

### Books

Adam, Mme. J. L., *L'Angleterre en Égypte* (Paris, 1922).

Abbas Hilmi II, *A few words on the Anglo-Egyptian Settlement* (London, 1930).

Arthur, Sir George, *Life of Lord Kitchener* (2 vols., London, 1920), vol. iii.

Beer, G. L., *African Questions at the Peace Conference* (N. Y., 1923).

Blunt, W. S., *Secret History of the English Occupation of Egypt* (N. Y., 1922).

Bonfils, H., *Manuel de droit international public* (7th ed., Paris, 1914), by Paul Fauchille.

Bruce, Sir Charles, *The Broad Stone of Empire. Problems of Crown-Colony Administration. With Records of Personal Experience* (2 vols., London, 1910), vol. ii.

Buckle, G. E., *The Life of Benjamin Disraeli: Earl of Beaconsfield* (5 vols., London, 1920), vol. v.

Calvo, C., *Le droit international théorique et pratique* (5th ed., 6 vols., Paris, 1896), vol. i.

Camand, M. L., *Étude sur le régime juridique du Canal de Suez* (Grenoble, 1899).

Cecil, Lady Gwendolen, *The Life of Robert Marquis of Salisbury* (2 vols., London, 1926), vol. ii.

Chirol, Sir V., *The Egyptian Problem* (London, 1920).

Cippico, Count Antonio, *Italy, the Central Problem of the Mediterranean* (New Haven, 1926).

Cocheris, J., *Situation internationale de l'Égypte et du Soudan* (Paris, 1903).

Corbett, Sir Julian S., *History of the Great War. Based on Official Documents. By direction of the Historical Section of the Committee of Imperial Defense. Naval Operations* (4 vols., N. Y., 1920), vol. i. Cited as *Naval Operations.*

Cromer, the Earl of, *Modern Egypt* (two vols. in one, N. Y., 1916).

Dane, Edmund, *British Campaigns in the nearer East, 1914-1918*, vol. i (London, 1919).

Das, T., *India in World Politics* (N. Y., 1923).

Deschanel, P. E. L., *Gambetta* (N. Y., 1920).

Dilke, Sir Charles, *Problems of Greater Britain* (London, 1890).

Douin, Georges, *Un épisode de la guerre mondiale. L'Attaque du Canal de Suez, 3 février, 1915* (Paris, 1922).

Driault, Édouard, *La question d'orient depuis ses origines jusqu'à nos jours* (6th ed., Paris, 1913).

Earle, E. M., *Turkey, the Great Powers and the Bagdad Railway* (N. Y., 1924).

Elgood, Lieut.-Col. P. G., *Egypt and the Army* (Oxford, 1924).

——, *The Transit of Egypt* (London, 1928).

Evans, Sir Samuel, *Prize Cases heard and decided in the Prize Court during the Great War.* Under the general editorship of A. Wallace Grant (London, 1918). Cited as *Prize Cases.*

Fay, S. B., *The Origins of the World War* (2 vols., N. Y., 1929).

Fayle, C. E., *The War and the Shipping Industry* (3 vols., London, 1920-1924).

Fitzmaurice, Lord Edmund, *The Life of Granville George Leveson Gower, Second Earl Granville, K. G., 1815-1891* (2 vols., London, 1905), vol. ii.

Freycinet, C. de, *La question d'Égypte* (2nd ed., Paris, 1905).

Gooch, G. P., *History of Modern Europe, 1878-1919* (N. Y., 1922).

Grey, Viscount Grey of Fallodon, *Twenty-five Years, 1892-1916* (2 vols., N. Y., 1925).

Grigg, Sir Edward, *The Greatest Experiment in History* (New Haven, 1924).

Hall, W. E., *A Treatise on International Law* (7th ed., Oxford, 1917).

Hanotaux, G., *Contemporary France* (4 vols., N. Y., 1903-1909), vol. ii.

Harris, M., *Egypt under the Egyptians* (London, 1925).

Hershey, A. S., *The International Law and Diplomacy of the Russo-Japanese War* (N. Y., 1906).

——, *The Essentials of International Public Law and Organization* (N. Y., 1927).

Hobson, J. A., *Imperialism. A Study* (London, 1902).

Holland, T. E., *Studies in International Law* (Oxford, 1898).

Hoskins, H. L., *British Trade Routes to India* (N. Y., 1928).

Hough, B. Olney, *Ocean Traffic and Trade* (London, 1914).

Hurd, A., *The New Empire Partnership. Defense* (London, 1915).

——, *Britain Prepared* (London, 1916).

——, *Sea Power* (London, 1916).

——, *The Defenses of the Empire* (London, 1917).

——, *The Sea Traders* (London, 1921).

——, *The Merchant Navy* (2 vols., London, 1921).

Hutchinson, L., *The Panama Canal and International Trade Competition* (N. Y., 1915).

Hyde, C. C., *International Law* (2 vols., Boston, 1922), vol. i.

Jemal Pasha, Ahmed (Djemal Pasha), *Memories of a Turkish Statesman, 1913-1919* (N. Y., 1922).

Kleine, M., *Deutschland und die ägyptische Frage, 1875-1890* (Dresden, 1927).

Lambelin, R., *L'Égypte, et l'Angleterre* (Paris, 1922).

Lang, A., *Life, Letters and Diaries of Sir Stafford Northcote, First Earl of Iddesleigh* (2 vols., Edinburgh, 1890).

Lawrence, T. J., *Essays on some disputed Questions in Modern International Law* (2nd ed., Cambridge, 1885).

——, *The Principles of International Law* (Boston, 1895).

Lee, Sir Sidney, *King Edward VII*, vol. ii (London, 1927).

Lesage, Charles, *L'Invasion Anglaise en Égypte. L'achat des actions de Suez* (Paris, 1906).

Lewin, P. Evans, *The German Road to the East* (N. Y., 1917).

Lucas, Sir Charles, *The Empire at War*, vol. i (Oxford, 1926).

MacMunn, Lieut.-Gen. G. and Falls, Capt. C., *History of the Great War. Based on Official Documents. By direction of the Historical Section of the Committee of Imperial Defense. Military Operations. Egypt and Palestine. From the outbreak of the War with Germany to June, 1917* (London, 1928). Cited as *Military Operations. Egypt and Palestine.*

Mahan, A. T., *The Problem of Asia and its Effect upon International Policies* (London, 1900).

Martin, E., *L'Angleterre et le Canal de Suez: La question d'Égypte* (Paris, 1892).

Maurice, Sir Frederick, *British Strategy* (London, 1929).

Mcleod, Sir Charles and Kirkaldy, A. W., *The Trade, Commerce and Shipping of the Empire* (N. Y., 1925), vol. vii of *The British Empire. A Survey in 12 volumes.* Edited by Hugh Gunn.

Milner, Viscount, *England in Egypt* (London, 1920).

Moon, P. T., *Imperialism and World Politics* (N. Y., 1926).

Moore, J. B., *Digest of International Law* (8 vols., Washington, 1906), vol. iii.

Morley, J., *The Life of William Ewart Gladstone* (3 vols., London, 1903).

Mou-Cho, Lui, *De la condition internationale de l'Égypte depuis la declaration anglaise de 1922* (Paris, 1925).

Newbolt, H., *History of the Great War. Based on Official Documents. By direction of the Historical Section of the Committee of Imperial Defense. Naval Operations*, vol. iv (London, 1928). Cited as *Naval Operations*, vol. iv.

Newman, Major E. W. Polson, *The Mediterranean and its Problems* (London, 1927).

——, *Great Britain in Egypt* (London, 1928).

Newton, Lord, *Lord Lyons. A Record of British Diplomacy* (2 vols., London, 1913), vol. ii.

Noradounghian, G. E., *Recueil d'actes internationaux de l'Empire Ottoman* (4 vols., Paris, 1897-1903).

Novion, F., *L'Angleterre et sa politique étrangère* (Thesis, Paris, 1924).

Ogilvie, P. M., *International Waterways* (N. Y., 1920).

Oppenheim, L., *International Law. A Treatise* (2 vols., London, 1926), vol. ii.

Owen, Sir Douglas, *Ocean Trade and Shipping* (Cambridge, 1914).

Parmalee, M., *Blockade and Sea-Power* (N. Y., 1924).

Phillipson, Coleman, *International Law and the Great War* (London, 1915).

Phillipson, C. and Buxton, N., *The Question of the Bosphorus and the Dardanelles* (London, 1917).

Piccioni, C., *Neutralité perpetuelle* (Paris, 1902).

Reinsch, P. S., *World Politics at the end of the Nineteenth Century* (London, 1909).

Rohrbach, P., *Die Bagdadbahn* (Berlin, 1911).

——, *Der Krieg und die deutsche Politik* (Dresden, 1914).

——, *German World Policies*. Trans. by Dr. Edmund von Mach (N. Y., 1915).

Rossignol, L. M., *Le Canal de Suez—Étude historique, juridique et politique* (Thesis, Paris, 1898).

Roux, J. C. T., *L'Isthme et le Canal de Suez: Historique état actuel* (2 vols., Paris, 1901), vol. ii.

Sabry, M., *L'Empire Égyptien sous Mohamed-Ali et la question d'Orient, 1811-1849* (Paris, 1930).

Salter, J. A., *Allied Shipping Control* (Oxford, 1921).

Sanders, Liman von, *Five Years in Turkey* (U. S. Naval Institute, Annapolis, 1927).

Sargent, A. J., *Seaways of the Empire* (London, 1918).

Shotwell, J. T., *War as an Instrument of National Policy and Its Renunciation in the Pact of Paris* (N. Y., 1929).

Siebert, B. de and Schreiner, G. A., *Entente Diplomacy and the World* (N. Y., 1921).

Stockton, C. H., *Outlines of International Law* (N. Y., 1914).

Symons, M. Travers, *Britain and Egypt: The Rise of Egyptian Nationalism* (London, 1925).

Toynbee, A. J., *Survey of International Affairs 1925*, vol. i (Oxford, 1927).

——, *Survey of International Affairs 1928* (Oxford, 1929).

Vályi, F., *Spiritual and Political Revolutions in Islam* (London, 1925).

Velay, E., *Les rivalités Franco-Anglaise en Égypte, 1867-1904* (Thesis, Montpellier, 1904).

Verzijl, J. H. W., *Le droit des prises de la grande guerre* (Leyden, 1924).

Visscher, Charles de, *Le droit international des communications* (Paris, 1924).

Voisin-Bey, *Le Canal de Suez: historique, administratif, description des travaux* (7 vols. and atlas, Paris, 1902-1907), vols. ii, iii.

Wakely, A. V. T., *Some Aspects of Imperial Communications* (London, 1925).

Ward, Sir A. W. and Gooch, G. P., *The Cambridge History of British Foreign Policy, 1783-1919*, vol. iii, 1866-1919 (N. Y., 1923).

Westlake, J., *International Law* (2nd ed., 2 vols., Cambridge, 1910-1913), vol. i.

White, A. S., *The Expansion of Egypt under Anglo-Egyptian Condominium* (London, 1899).

Wicker, Cyrus F., *Neutralization* (Oxford Univ. Press, 1911).

Willert, Sir Arthur, *Aspects of British Foreign Policy* (New Haven, 1928).

Yeghen, F., *Le Canal de Suez et la réglementation internationale des canaux interocéaniques* (Thesis, Montpellier, 1927).

### Articles

*American Journal of International Law*, vol. iv (1910), pp. 314-358, "The real status of the Panama Canal as regards neutralization," by Harry S. Knapp.

——, vol. 17 (1923), pp. 704-723, "Neutrality and the World War," by Malbone W. Graham, Jr.

——, vol. 21 (1927), pp. 79-94, "Neutralization as a movement in International Law," by the same author.

*Army Quarterly*, vol. 8, pp. 86-99, London, 1924, "Imperial Communications", by E. M. S. Charles.

*British Inst. of Int. Affairs Journal*, vol. i, pp. 55-71, London, 1922, "The Egyptian Question," by V. Chirol.

*Communist Review*, vol. ii, pp. 66-70, Feb., 1930, "Egypt and the record of two Labour Governments."

*Contemporary Review*, vol. 127, pp. 24-31, London, 1925, "The Egyptian Situation," by E. Gleichen.

——, vol. 131, Jan.-June 1927, pp. 152-157, "The Occupation of Egypt," by Josiah C. Wedgwood.

——, vol. 132, 1927, pp. 15-23, "The Political Situation in Egypt," by A. H. Beaman.

——, vol. 134, 1928, pp. 282-287, "Egypt Today," by Arthur Ponsonby.

*Current History*, July, 1930, "The Problem of the Nile, by Pierre Crabites.

*Edinburgh Review*, vol. 240, July-Oct. 1924, pp. 32-50, "The Egyptian Factor in European Diplomacy, 1798-1898," by J. A. R. Marriott.

*Empire Review*, vol. xi, 1906, pp. 322-338, "Our Position in Egypt," by E. Dicey.

——, vol. 50, Oct. 1929, pp. 271-282, "Britain and Egypt at the Cross-roads," by Thomas Greenwood.

*Foreign Affairs*, N. Y., vol. v, Oct. 1926, pp. 103-113, "British Policy in the Mediterranean," by Sir Frederick Maurice.

——, June 1923, "Italy in the Mediterranean," by Francesco Coppola.

*Fortnightly Review*, N. Y., 1920, new series, vol. 107, pp. 375-383, "The British Protectorate of Egypt," by Sir M. McIlwraith.

*Geographische Zeitschrift*, vol. 22, no. 2, pp. 87-91, Feb. 1916, "Die Verkehrspolitische Bedeutung des Suezkanals," by A. Dix.

*Jahrbuch des Bundes der Asienkämpfer*, vol. i, Berlin, 1921, pp. 11-54 (Zwischen Kaukasus und Sinai), "Uberblick über die Ereignisse an der Sinaifront von Kriegsbeginn bis zur Besetzung Jerusalems durch die Engländer ende 1917," by Oberst Freiherr Kress von Kressenstein.

——, article v, pp. 107-125, "Die deutsche Jildirim-Etappe," by Hauptmann Merkel, Szt. Chef des Stabes der Deutschen Etappeninspektion in Damaskus.

*Journal of the Royal United Service Institution*, vol. 70, Feb.-Nov. 1925, London, 1925, pp. 31-49, "Trade Defense in War," by Vice-Admiral Sir Richard Webb.

*Labour Monthly*, vol 4, no. 5, pp. 286 *et seq.*, May 1923, "Egyptian Nationalism and the Class Struggle," by G. A. Hutt.

——, Oct. 1929, pp. 619-626, "Labour Imperialism in Egypt," by J. M. B.

*London Times*, June 30, Oct. 21, 1924 and July 27, 1929.

*Naval Annual*, London, 1919, Earl Brassey, editor.

*New Leader*, vol. 13, p. 9, Feb. 19, 1926. Journal of the Independent Labour Party.

*New York Times*, Dec. 14, 1930, "The Bagdad-Haifa Rail Plan," by Clair Price.

*Nineteenth Century*, vol. 2, Aug. 1877, "The Future of Egypt," by E. Dicey.

——, vol. 14, Aug. 1883, " Why not purchase the Suez Canal," by the same author.

——, vol. 2, Aug. 1877, " Aggression on Egypt and Freedom in the East," by W. E. Gladstone.

——, vol. 97, 1925, pp. 252-259, " Our difficulties with Egypt," by P. G. Elgood.

——, vol. 105, 1929, pp. 306-316, " England and Egypt," by M. S. Amos.

*Nineteenth Century and After*, Oct. 1926, pp. 582 *et seq.*, " Ferdinand de Lesseps and the Suez Canal," by Pierre Crabites.

*Political Science Quarterly*, vol. 36, 1921, pp. 51-78, " England and the Egyptian Problem," by H. J. Carman.

*Quarterly Review*, London, 1922, vol. 237, pp. 415-429, " The Egyptian Problem," by J. A. Spender.

*Revue des Deux Mondes*, vol. 60, Nov. 1, 1888, article by M. Gabriel Charmes.

——, 1925-1926, période 7, tome 30, pp. 867-893; période 7, tome 31, pp. 146-179, 391-418, " L'Attaque et la défense du Canal de Suez, Février 1915," by Paul Chack.

*Revue de droit international*, vols. 1, 1870; 7, 1875; 10, 1878.

*Revue Maritime*, Oct. 1924, " La première offensive contre le Canal de Suez," by Capitaine Larcher.

*The Field*, Jan. 15, 1916, pp. 118-119, " The Cape Route v. The Suez Canal."

*The Fighting Forces—a quarterly for the Royal Navy, Army and Royal Air Force*, edited by Lieut.-Col. F. E. Whitton, vol. 3, pp. 376 *et seq.*, " The Balance of Power in the Mediterranean," by Charles Petrie.

——, vol. 4, pp. 583 *et seq.*, "Aircraft an Imperial Necessity," by Captain C. F. Webb.

——, vol. 5, pp. 541-549, " A new link in the Chain to India," by Lieut.-Col. H. E. Crocker.

*United Service Inst. Journal*, vol. 72, Feb.-Nov. 1927, pp. 851 *et seq.*, " The International Situation. Palestine, Syria and Transjordan. Their Political and Strategical Significance," by Major E. W. Polson Newman.

*United Service Magazine*, Sept. 1890, pp. 505-512, " How the Political and Military Power of England is affected by the Suez Canal," by George Hooper.

*Zwischen Krieg und Frieden*, no. 34, Leipzig, 1916, " Um den Suezkanal," by R. Forster.

# INDEX

427